Latin American Mystery Writers

LATIN AMERICAN MYSTERY WRITERS

An A-to-Z Guide

EDITED BY DARRELL B. LOCKHART

GREENWOOD PRESS

Westport, Connecticut • London

Library of Congress Cataloging-in-Publication Data

Latin American mystery writers : an A-to-Z guide / edited by Darrell B. Lockhart.
    p. cm.
  Includes bibliographical references and index.
  ISBN 0-313-30554-4 (alk. paper)
  1. Detective and mystery stories, Latin American—History and criticism—Dictionaries.
  2. Detective and mystery stories, Latin American—Bio-bibliography—Dictionaries.
  3. Authors, Latin American—Biography—Dictionaries. I. Lockhart, Darrell B.
  PQ7082.N7L352 2004
  863'.08720998'03—dc22   2003058415

British Library Cataloguing in Publication Data is available.

Library of Congress Catalog Card Number: 2003058415
ISBN: 0-313-30554-4

First published in 2004

Greenwood Press, 88 Post Road West, Westport, CT 06881
An imprint of Greenwood Publishing Group, Inc.
www.greenwood.com

Printed in the United States of America

The paper used in this book complies with the
Permanent Paper Standard issued by the National
Information Standards Organization (Z39.48-1984).

10 9 8 7 6 5 4 3 2 1

Contents

Contents

Preface

This volume represents an attempt to provide a comprehensive inventory of Latin American mystery writing, from the classic detective fiction model to contemporary hard-boiled literature. My interest in such a project stems from at least two primary motivating factors: first, a personal fondness for a genre that has provided me with a great source of entertainment over the years; second, the desire to engage in the more intellectual enterprise of literary history and interpretation in relation to the detective fiction of Latin America. The principal goal of the sourcebook is likewise twofold. On the one hand, it is meant to underscore the vastness and diversity of this body of writing, present a profile of its development over the course of approximately the last one hundred years, and serve as a point of departure for future research. This leads to the second goal, which has to do with how detective fiction historically has been perceived in the literary environment. In Latin America, perhaps more so than elsewhere, detective fiction has long been considered to be a form of so-called lowbrow art given its initial arrival(s) as a European and North American import, and its popular (mass-media) distribution throughout the continent. This, in spite of the fact that Latin American writers have been extremely successful at adapting the genre to their own realities, beginning with the early puzzle- or enigma-narratives up through their own versions of the hard-boiled novel, at which they have been particularly adept. Therefore, this volume seeks to position detective fiction as a major presence in Latin American literature, an authentic and unique cultural discourse worthy of greater academic attention and analytical interpretation.

The organization of *Latin American Mystery Writers: An A-to-Z Guide* is intended, as stated above, to provide an overview of the genre. The introduction, written by Argentine author and specialist in the genre, Mempo Giardinelli, focuses on hard-boiled detective literature, the most recent manifestation in the development of the genre. He traces the origins of the hard-boiled detective novel, its influence on Latin American writers, and its unique capacity to examine and reflect Latin American reality in the late twentieth century. The sourcebook itself, then, is organized on an author-by-author basis. Entries on the individual practitioners of detective fiction are arranged alphabetically by the author's actual surname, or the pseudonym by which he/she is known. The country listed in each heading is not necessarily the author's country of birth, but rather the country with which he/she is associated as a writer. The volume contains entries on 54 writers, prepared by the collective efforts of 24 contributors. The majority of the authors included are from Argentina and Mexico. Every effort was made to assure that the volume is as all-inclusive as possible. Nevertheless, any project such as this is fraught with a number of difficulties from the outset. It is simply logistically impossible to include every author worthy of inclusion, and I will avoid attempting to list authors who for whatever reason did not make it into the final manuscript. Suffice to say that there are at least as many authors excluded as there are included here. The one consolation is the hope that this will further stimulate academic activity to fill these voids. That women authors seem to be underrepresented reflects the fact that there are very few women writers of detective fiction in Latin America. It is still, clearly, a genre dominated by men. Finally, the volume concludes with a bibliography of literary anthologies and criticism divided geographically by country.

One of the major obstacles facing the project was locating enough scholars who share a common interest and concern for Latin American detective fiction and who were willing and able to contribute to this effort. From the beginning, this was meant to be a collaborative project among colleagues who are spread out from North to South America and Europe. Therefore, contributors were asked to suggest authors who should be added to (or removed from) the original list of names that went out with the call for contributions. The result was a flood of suggestions that stimulated an ongoing dialogue about the nature and parameters of the detective genre in Latin America. Again, far more names were proposed than could be realistically accommodated. The often problematical designation "Latin America" is not invoked here as a totalizing term. I am aware, of course, of the dangers of "lumping together" the diverse regions, realities, identities, and so on that comprise that nebulous territory we call, for lack of a better name, Latin America. In general terms, any author from a Spanish- or Portuguese-speaking country of the Americas was eligible for inclusion. The decision was made to not include Hispanic/Latino/Chicano authors from the United States, more for practical reasons than politically motivated ones. Contributors were given rather lax guidelines to follow in the preparation of the entries with regard to content and approach. However, each was asked to organize the entry by first providing a brief biographical sketch on the author whenever possible, followed by a summary of the author's literary contribution and impact pertaining to the genre, and ending with a bibliography of primary and secondary sources (in some cases, there are no secondary critical sources). The authors included in the volume range from the canonical to the virtually unknown, from those who adhere closely to the conventions of detective fiction (in its varying forms) to those who incorporate only certain elements in the creation of their texts. This is meant to showcase both the wide-arching magnitude of Latin American detective fiction as well as its influence on other, more mainstream literary discourses. By virtue of the nature of the genre, practically all the texts discussed are forms of narrative (either short story or novel).

This endeavor is part of a broader undertaking to examine popular genre literature in Latin America. This book, together with its companion volume, *Latin American Science Fiction Writers: An A-to-Z Guide*, seeks to broaden the scope of Latin American literary and cultural studies. Detective fiction and science fiction, both forms of so-called popular literature (often not taken as "serious" forms of writing), are uniquely equipped to offer critical appraisals of society. The parameters of each genre allow for the creation of ingenious parodies and allegories of all the social, political, and economic components of contemporary life. In Latin American countries, where life is often affected by political unrest, social upheaval, and economic crisis, these two genres have found fertile narrative ground.

I would like to acknowledge all the individuals who made this volume possible, first and foremost the contributors who embraced this project with enthusiasm and without whom it would not have become a reality. I am especially grateful to everyone involved for their patience, as this book as taken several years to come to fruition. I would also like to thank my research assistants; Eric Rojas for his invaluable help in the preparation of this volume, particularly for translating many of the essays into English, and Roberto Ortiz for his help in revising the final manuscript. Pedro Gómez and Carolyn Russum also provided much-needed assistance with translations. Finally, I'm grateful to Robert Kowkabany for his careful editing of the volume.

Introduction
The Hard-boiled Detective Novel in Latin America

MEMPO GIARDINELLI

Let us begin with the questions that motivate this introductory essay: Is there really a hard-boiled detective literature in Latin America? What are the origins of the terms *literatura policial* (detective fiction) and *novela negra* (hard-boiled novel), and how do they surface in Latin America? What are the sources of this literature and to what does it owe its enormous popularity? How has it evolved, what is its stature, and what are the most salient features that define it?

Is There Really a Hard-boiled Detective Literature in Latin America?

Latin American detective fiction indeed exists. It is comprised of a rich and varied body of works written by dozens of authors from various countries. It has a constancy that other genres in Spanish do not share and it must be understood in the sense that was understood in the 1950s by Marcel Duhamel in France, when he created the famous detective fiction *Serie Noir* for the Parisian publishing house Gallimard. According to the definition provided by Javier Coma, "it is a narrative, with origins in the United States during the 1920s and with a typical, primordial North American development, tied to a realist, sociopolitical focus on the contemporary topic of crime, slowly developed as an identifiable genre and practiced mainly by specialists" (Coma 15).

Detective fiction (the North American, French, and now the Latin American versions) has produced a spectacular change in the treatment of crime, especially because it refers to reasons, motives, and causes linked to the reality in which the readers themselves live. The detective genre ties crime to the society in which it occurs, given that all societies (and all literature) has crime as one of its protagonists. Crime is not, in reality, a mathematical problem, a crossword puzzle, or a clever challenge. There is no gratuitous crime and there is no absence of causes (individual or social), in the same way that there is no perfect crime.[1] Every crime is the product of relationships (bad relationships) between human beings. There is not—as the medicolegal sciences have demonstrated—a human model of the criminal as Cesare Lombroso imagined at the end of the nineteenth century. What exist are circumstances that lead a person to commit a crime—any person, from the reader of this text to the one who wrote it.

The principal values on which the detective genre is based are first and foremost power and money. By association one can identify, uncontrolled ambition, personal heroics, hypocrisy, machismo, sexual conquest, an ominous cruelty that humiliates and subdues, and infinite ephemeral forms of the illusion of glory. Having stated this, it should be clear that we are simply speaking of human nature. Like the Hamlet–Faulknerian sound and fury, it is human weakness that leads to crime. Behind every crime there is always a manifestation of power, even if it is the power to end someone else's life. For this reason, the Argentine critic María Rosa del Coto maintains that "the ostentatious scenes of violence in detective fiction are in response to structural necessity" (Coto 4).

Crime, power, and money are like fear and guilt: one cannot live without them. Add to this the physical strength and the acute intelligence of the ambitious character, the opportunist, or the desperate man, and you have a fairly complete list of the values that "humanized" detective fiction. Dashiell Hammett (1894–1961), who at the age of 34 wrote the novel *Red Harvest* (1929)—where these characteristics first appear—must be considered the starting point of the modern detective genre.

Individual courage—tied to audacity, fearlessness, and daring—is a common motif in all detective novels, and especially in the North American model where the philosophical concept of the macho-individualist type is clearly identifiable. In true North American spirit, individual determination and valor enable one to overcome obstacles when faced with difficult situations. Detectives, policemen, prosecutors, lawyers—in sum, "the Law"—triumph not only because of their deductive reasoning and investigations, but also due to their bravery. This comes through in different shades and is evident in all modern detective novels. Such characteristics are not reserved solely for the detectives, but also are found in the criminals and the victims. That is to say that a man's valor, courage, and temerity—his guts—are concomitant with this literature.

Beginning with the unnamed detective of the Continental Agency in *Red Harvest*, this is a successful and defining element in this narrative. This does not seem to be mere coincidence, since Hammett is presumably aware of it. It is hard to imagine his not realizing that his literature formed part of the nineteenth-century North American epic. Surely Hammett wasn't thinking of a renovation, modernization, or much less a recasting of the Western into an urban context, but that is precisely what he was doing. Undoubtedly, he was helped along the way by other traditions such as local color narratives[2] (Mark Twain [1835–1910] and Charles Dickens [1812–1870]) or the Civil War epic, whose mentor was not Margaret Mitchell (1900–1949) in the twentieth-century but much earlier with Stephen

Crane (1871–1900), whom Hammett evidently had read thoroughly.[3] If it is inevitable, then, to consider Crane as a predecessor of the modern detective novel, Hammett cannot have been exempt from such an influence even though ideologically he was at the opposite pole. Therefore, we can conclude that the genre he initiated with *Red Harvest* was, in fact, a contemporary urban epic in which both the cult of machismo and individual daring are as important as the criminal mind.

This literature, which goes beyond the purely enigmatic nature of the locked-room mystery, has entered the realm of the postmodern (understood as the modernity of modernity)[4] for the simple reason that the crisis unleashed beginning on Black Tuesday 1929, has a correlative in the current crisis of capitalism following the demise of the communist paradigm. We have here, in plain view, the brutal injustices of hypercapitalism: unemployment, begging, urban crime, and the problem of the homeless; the unstoppable flow of immigrants and renewed strains of xenophobia; the ever-more subtle forms of repression and brutality; and corruption and political maneuvering.

Since Hammett, North American detective fiction writers of the 1920s and 1930s—as well as the current generation—have not needed to invent reality on any level. They simply described and interpreted it. For this reason, it is impossible for the genre to not have a certain relationship with Naturalism and *Costumbrismo*. These characteristics, by definition, circumscribe the detective novel. It may seem ironic, but the detective genre in our societies *is costumbrista*.

In the case of the hard-boiled Latin American novel, this is becoming increasingly evident. The genre denounces social contradictions, exploitation and violence, and corruption and hypocrisy. Clearly, this is what the practitioners of social realism were doing, but now we see more than just descriptions of injustice, and even fewer instances of lofty revolutionary ideologies being propounded. Nowadays, parody and existentialism are the key components, which in my opinion are typical elements of postmodernism. More importantly, the most polished writers today are conscious of and concerned with exercising complete control over a topic, and no longer allow the topic to control them.

Violence is not an invention of literature. Literary violence is not fine-tuned, exaggerated, or false. We live in the same world described by Malcolm Lowry (1909–1957) in *Under the Volcano* (1947). Incest and corruption are common currency in modern industrial society. The daily sordid dealings and struggles in labor unions and politics are the raw materials of rampant capitalism in the 1990s. Crime is simply the other side of the mirror, the dark half that shame or fear sometimes (and cynicism always) attempts to hide. Crime, it can be said, is an unavoidable part of modern life. Today, anyone can go up on a rooftop and open fire on the neighborhood below; a disgruntled individual can enter a McDonald's restaurant and gun down the customers; any adolescent can enter his school and commit mass murder among his classmates. Why should literature, then, be any different? Why expect "light" literature when in countries like Mexico it is known that 70,000 rapes are reported each year, and in the United States a rape is reported every six minutes. Moreover, in the United States, many more citizens are murdered than soldiers killed in all the wars in which the bellicose country has participated, having participated in practically every war during the twentieth and twenty-first centuries. No, there can be no doubt that literary violence pales in comparison.

Half a century ago, Raymond Chandler (1888–1959) said that the authors of this genre write "of a world in which gangsters can rule nations and almost rule cities . . . a world where a judge with a cellar full of bootleg liquor can send a man to jail for having a pint in his pocket." And he added that "it is not a fragrant world, but it is the world you live in" (Chandler "The Simple Art of Murder," 508). Let us examine the reality of contemporary Latin America, where there have been governments run by drug traffickers such as that of Luis García Meza in Bolivia, and constant accusations involving a president of Mexico or Colombia, and even Argentina, where several prominent members of the last government have strong ties to drug trafficking, yet the courts put away a kid for posssessing a joint of marijuana.

Certainly, one can respond by saying that the world was always like this and that crises and injustice have been around forever. And it's true, it was always like this, but I doubt that any previous crisis in the history of humanity has been on this scale. In 1999, the population of the planet reached the impressive six billion mark, and all human miseries (hunger, violence, stupidity, cynicism) have attained new heights. Man's worst enemy has always been man, but it is likely that man has never been such an enemy as at this turn of the century. This is especially noticeable now with the capability—at once marvelous and terrifying—of seeing all the horrors that go on in the world as they happen, thanks to that Borgesian Aleph each of us has in our television sets. Of course, what is truly amazing is not that these things happen, but that the majority of people really enjoy watching them unfold.

It is not easy to explain why North American practitioners of this genre had—and continue to have—such a wide following throughout the world, and above all in Spain and Latin America. One hypothesis may be that from an ideological standpoint almost all of them can be defined as liberals—understanding that U.S. liberalism is one of the best characteristics of the country, at least one that bolstered and guaranteed the development of the now-proverbial North American creative spirit.

Considered solely as a subliterature aimed at mass consumption, there is no doubt that its popularity and especially the enormous industry of commercial production for the genre (first marketed in the pulp magazines of the 1920s and later in film and television) contributed to deflating its literary prestige. But it would be truly unfair to reduce all detective fiction to the category of subliterature.

The fact is that the structure of the detective story has been used to produce literature that Coma considers to be of wide-reaching literary, sociological, and critical breadth (*La novela negra*). In this sense, almost all authors agree that while there is a lot out there that is truly of poor quality, there is also an outstanding number of authors and hard-boiled texts that can be counted among the best literary works of the twentieth century. Frank MacShane, is his wonderful biography of Raymond Chandler, states that the author of *The Long Goodbye* (1953) always set out to "write real fiction while using the detective-story form" (MacShane 50–51). He recalls an insightful quotation from Chandler: "I look on mysteries as writing, demand the same standards as from any novel, and the extreme difficulty of the form to be met as well" (51). He joins the ranks of Ernest Hemingway (1899–1961), Theodore Dreiser (1871–1945), Ring Lardner (1885–1933), Sherwood Anderson (1876–1941), and even Walt Whitman (1819–1892). In addition, Chandler shared the observation of Gilbert K. Chesterton (1874–1936)—creator of the ineffable priest-detective Brown—that in a sense "the essential value of the detective story lies in this, that it is the earliest and only form of popular literature in which is expressed some sense of the poetry of modern life" (MacShane 47).

Chandler studied nineteenth- and early twentieth-century North American literature in depth and was an avid reader of the detective genre, as his essays and letters clearly demonstrate. He was one of the first to outline the different tendencies of the genre, and while it was never included within social realism, he sustained that critical realism is what made detective fiction so perspicacious in nature. His admiration for Hammett was based on the fact that he "took murder out of the Venetian vase and dropped it into the alley, which is where it happens" (Chandler 2001, 41). He said that Hammett grabbed hold of crime "and returned murder back to the kind of people who do it for a reason, not just to provide a corpse. . . . He put these people down on paper as they are, and he made them talk and think in the language they customariuly used for these purposes" (Chandler 2001, 41–42).

It is fitting to evoke Chandler by way of introduction because his ideas contributed in a foundational and definitive way to how Latin American readers identify with detective fiction. With the changes wrought in the genre by Chandler and Hammett, the readers also changed. Now they were not merely more inclined to play detective in an attempt to anticipate the solving of a crime, but were determined to think of the literature as a source of knowledge and critical reflection of reality that at the same time was entertaining. Literature is, after all, an entertainment—as Cervantes wished to show us. Luis Cernuda, in his prologue to the 1961 Spanish edition of *Red Harvest*, confirms: "the work of Dashiell Hammett always possesses the ability to powerfully entertain the reader. . . . Times change and so do human diversions; the only thing that doesn't change is the everlasting human need for entertainment. Cervantes knew it well (Cernuda 16).

What Are the Origins of "Detective Fiction" and the "Hard-boiled Novel," and How Do They Surface in Latin America?

Forty years ago, Donald A. Yates maintained that "detective fiction is a luxury destined in all likelihood to appeal to a relatively sophisticated reading public. It is essentially a type of literature that avoids direct contact with reality" (Yates 6).

Today this idea—that for years was shared by many critics and authors—has been discounted precisely by reality itself. In fact, all the authors who worked and work in this genre do nothing more than frequent, connect with, and revisit reality time and again. If there is one thing that defines Latin American detective fiction today it is, precisely, its determined realism.

But what Yates in fact hit upon was the definition of the everyday reality of Spanish American society. For him, it is one in which "the authority of the police force and the power of justice are admired and accepted less than in Anglo-Saxon countries (and that) tends to discourage native writers, pushing them away from a serious dedication to the formal composition of stories of crime and punishment" (Yates 6).

It is a well-worn question, and within the body of criticism on the genre there are some works that are true curiosities, like Antonio Gramsci's *Sul romanzo poliziesco* (On the detective novel, 1966), and the great Russian cineaste Sergei Eisenstein's essay "¿Por qué gusta el género policiaco?" (Why is the detective genre appealing?, 1968) published in the Moscow journal *Voprosy Literaty*. Both texts were published in the volume *La novela criminal* (The crime novel, 1982) edited by Román Gubern, which also includes texts by renown authors such as Edgar Allan Poe (1809–1849) (his famous introduction to "The Murders in the Rue Morgue," 1841), G. K. Chesterton's famous lecture "On Detective Novels," and the outstanding *Le roman policier* (The detective novel; 1964) by the contemporary French novelist and theorist Thomas Narcejac.

It is interesting to consider Gubern's work because his effort as compiler demonstrates his willingness to present different tendencies, while his own intention was to underscore the concept that places the origins of the genre in the development of the contemporary "philosophy of insecurity" with the rise of large urban concentrations, the first secret police, and the birth of the sensationalist press. In our day and time insecurity is, more and more, a matter of immense popularity. It is unfortunately so, but numerous surveys (and elections) in many countries illustrate that it is one of the principal preoccupations of end-of-the-millennium postindustrial society. Today, it is evident that insecurity goes hand-in-hand with massive layoffs and unemployment, and with economic greed and the unbalanced distribution of wealth, which in Latin America reaches grotesque levels and is an affront to common decency. The many ways in which private property is made sacrosanct, plus the natural greed that a good part of the species harbors, added to the increasingly abundant crop of litigious lawyers, the decline of ethical values, and the ever more sophisticated rhetoric of hypocrisy, all contribute to the social landscape of our time. If these circumstances want for a literature, it can be no other than hard-boiled fiction.

Herein lies the justification for invoking the texts of Gramsci and Eisenstein. The first relies on a classist perspective based on the disbelief that detective fiction truly constitutes a literary genre, although he only analyzes classic British literature of the 1930s, which he dismisses as bourgeois literature. More interesting is the case of Eisenstein, who adopts the same ideological perspective but admits

that it is a genre and sustains that "it is the genre in which means of communication are brought to the fore" (Eisenstein 29). His idea that detective fiction is a
"literature of property" is indeed a fascinating one, which was true for the nineteenth century. Although for the twentieth century, and beginning with Hammett, it is better explained as a "literature of the destruction of property," and in
Latin America as one of social protest.

With regard to Narcejac—whose work is among the best on the hard-boiled
novel—it must be said that he is one of the critics who knew very well how to
defend the genre against the kind of "racial segregation" to which it was condemned. He declares that the genre, by nature, "is 'a black man' and literature is a
elegant neighborhood to where he has no right to move" (Narcejac 51). Narcejac's
work first appeared in 1958 in volume 3 of *Historia de las literaturas* (History of
literatures) published by Gallimard under the direction of Raymond Queneau. It
is important to note the date because it allows one to recognize the author's acute
perception and better appreciate his perspective. For Narcejac, the origin of the
genre is to be found in the fusion of two essential elements: a mystery, and the
reasoning that explains it. He indicates that it is the "direct descendent of the popular horror novel from the eighteenth century, in its nature it carries the seeds
that will become the 'thriller'" (Narcejac 51–52). This is how, he says, the first
detective novel appeared: "visceral and cerebral at the same time, it didn't have
time to speak to the heart, to show real characters" (Narcejac 53). In other words,
mystery and emotion on the one hand, reasoning on the other. Concerning Poe
and the classic locked-room tale, he states, "it is the problem par excellence" but
that "it is also obvious trickery, fake scenery" (Narcejac 55).

Narcejac's most interesting contribution is, perhaps, the way he manages to
link the gothic novel to Balzac, and Poe to Dickens, and these with the novels
of chivalry. Narcejac does not discount the decisive importance of the novel of
the Far West to contemporary detective fiction. He hints at this tie, although he
doesn't development it.[5] He did, however, analyze the novel's progressive development over time, from the "marvelous candid" (gothic novel) to the "marvelous
logical" (the classic detective formula, rational and positive), that then transforms
the adventure novel into the detective novel. In fact, Narcejac in some way was
anticipating (in 1958) the subsequently famous theorization of the "marvelous
real": "the world around us is but a mere image and the solution to the mystery
does not depend exclusively upon human logic" (Narcejac 75). For this reason,
the modern hard-boiled novel assumes "at once a logical explanation and a met-
alogical explanation: or, in other words, it offers a rational dimension and
another fantastic dimension" (Narcejac 75). Here, he is frankly revolutionary and
anticipatory, because before authors such as Carlos Fuentes (b. 1928), Gabriel
García Márquez (b. 1928) or Julio Cortázar (1914–1984) were to admit the influence of North American literature in general, and detective fiction in particular,
he had already observed that the detective genre, since Hammett, "is situated
between the real (naturalist novel) and the purely imagined (science fiction)"
(Narcejac 80).

All this serves, in passing, to reassert once again that the influence of the detective novel in *all* contemporary Latin American narrative is undeniable. The Latin American detective genre at the turn of the millennium (I'm thinking of authors who published from the 1970s on) is defined more and more as the new hard-boiled genre because its authors:

a. do not consider detective fiction to be a luxury for a sophisticated public;

b. do not believe that it is a type of literature that avoids direct contact with reality, but that, much to the contrary, it fully incorporates it;

c. not only do they admire and accept to a lesser degree the police force and the power of the justice system, but rather they fear, question, and detest them; and

d. they are not discouraged by this, and, in fact, they attack it head-on with works ranging from the poorly crafted to the perfect. Stated another way: detective fiction writers in Latin American countries have no choice but to be hard-boiled. They can no longer write classic fiction. For that very reason, hard-boiled literature has been revolutionary for postboom Latin American letters.

It is no coincidence that in Argentina, Chile, Cuba, Uruguay, or Mexico there are increasingly more authors who—stemming from their admiration for Hammett and Chandler—write literature that incorporates William Faulkner (1897–1962), Hemingway, or Erskine Caldwell (1903–1987) in search of a unique form of expression in which detective fiction in general and hard-boiled in particular, adapted to their circumstances, is indisputably present.

The lack of admiration and acceptance of police power and a generalized detachment from the law are the norm in Latin America. I refer to the concept of the "law" as a code of conduct that North Americans have internalized: the idea that one lives either "within the law" or "outside the law." The early detective characters created by writers such as Borges and Bioy Casares (Isidro Parodi), Antonio Helú ([1900–1972] the very Mexican Máximo Roldán), and the Chilean Alberto Edwards ([1873–1932] Román Calvo) were figures who in certain ways were inhibited from engaging in social criticism. That's why those detectives, although attractive, were false; they were purely literary. On this matter Yates was absolutely right.

But if the modern hard-boiled genre is defined precisely by the opposite (by entering reality through literature and making it the main component of texts), then the genre is particularly suited for Latin Americans and is even an obvious natural fit. In Latin America, there is not only distrust of the police but hatred and anger. A policeman, by definition, is custodian of the established order whose mission is essentially one of preservation. Through the defense of property (individual or collective, since in communist countries there is also a police force) any social mutation not prescribed under the law is quickly squelched. The role of the police, then, is to preserve the established status quo. In and of itself this is not a bad thing. However, in the case of Latin America—and this has almost always been so—the order to maintain the status quo via police force is plainly an unjust one. It is a mandate given by the oligarchy that controls the power and it is by nature unjust.

With the return of democracy in the mid-1980s, there was a period of law-enforcement reorganization (in which these institutions began to respect human rights, and in some cases were purged of bad elements and were even self-critical), but already by the 1990s many of the worst characteristics started to reappear. People were reporting torture, abuse of power, rape, and rampant disregard for procedure. What's worse, reports of misdeeds began to surface, which as in Argentina, led people to begin referring to law-enforcement agencies as "la maldita policía" (the damned police): the terrorist attacks on the Jewish community, the Cabezas case, the Ingeniero Budge killings, the Miguel Bru case, and many more.

All this explains why—after the classic texts by great masters of the genre—detective fiction removed from reality lost its appeal. In fact, Latin American publishers warned that the genre had lost prestige and had begun its decline. They said that there was no interest in it, no audience, that it was out of style, there were not enough writers, and that it was nothing more than pulp fiction for mass consumption that had run its course—that is, until the new generation of writers influenced by Hammett, Chandler, José Giovanni (b. 1923) and others became aware of the hard-boiled novel's potential to question authority. On the one hand, the genre offers other perspectives: the point of view of the victim or the victimizer, especially that of the criminal himself. This is what contemporary detective fiction in Latin American countries embraces as a generalized form of expression. On the other hand, the view of the classics as worn-out seems only natural. Although some remain valid, like Borges's incomparable "La muerte y la brújula" ("Death and the Compass") or some of the stories by Helú with his rogue Máximo Roldán (anagram of "ladrón" [thief], as Yates points out). But what relevance can be found in the tales of Father Brown, the repetitive Mrs. Christie, or the convoluted stories of Ellery Queen (joint byline of Frederick Dannay [1905–1982] and Manfred B. Lee [1905–1971])?

And if Scotland Yard was—even still is—a source of pride for the English (writers or readers) and the FBI and the North American abstract concept of the "law" remain the basis for public conduct in the United States, that has no equivalent within the Latin American world. The fact is that the vast majority of law-enforcement agencies in Latin America are not only fallacious sources for detective fiction, but they are considered to be highly suspect institutions by the social body of each nation.

Why, then, must detective fiction in Latin America be hard-boiled? Because the reality of the genre allows for no other options. The modern hard-boiled genre has given us innovative perspectives like narration in first- and third-person that no longer follows the detective with his likable characteristics, his quirks, likes, and dislikes, but instead corresponds to the voice of the persecuted or the

persecutor, the one who will kill or be killed. It's as simple as that, the same simplicity of Borges's character Daniel Simón Azevedo for whom "medio siglo de
violencia le había enseñado que lo más fácil y seguro es matar" (half a century of
violence had taught him that the easiest and safest thing to do is kill). Of course,
the motivations continue to be the same as for the classics of the genre: money,
power, women. What has changed is the outlook: the genre is no longer approached from the viewpoint of a dubious "justice" system or in defense of the
equally suspect established order. Current Latin American hard-boiled literature
questions everything: the boundaries of the "law" are neither so rigid nor so
clearly defined. For the contemporary reader, and also for the writer of course, the
mysteries of Latin American reality are absolutely more present and more skeptical. They are revolutionaries, in the sense that they revolutionize—by questioning, transgressing, and subverting—an unjust system.

I understand, then, the hard-boiled genre to be detective fiction that firmly
planted its feet on the ground beginning in the 1920s in the United States. Its primary predecessor is the action and adventure literature of the nineteenth century,
and particularly that of the settlement of the West (remember that it also is a
genre that was scorned for having entertained millions of readers—that grave literary sin). At the same time, legions of minor writers were spawned that cheap-
ened its reputation. But it is also a genre that enlightened some of the greatest
North American writers.

What Are the Sources and How Does One Explain Its Enormous Popularity?

The Western is the first antecedent of the hard-boiled novel. Although the
consensus is virtually unanimous that the hard-boiled genre was initiated with
Hammett's famous *Red Harvest*, since the early 1980s I have maintained that
another highly important antecedent of the hard-boiled novel is the North
American literature of the West. The adventure novel in general, and in particular the narrative of the so-called Far West, contain all the elements that later on
will define the peculiar characteristics of the hard-boiled thriller. A narrative style
that fascinates millions of readers around the world and that competes—in a
kind of heated, mute struggle—with the well-traveled locked-room mysteries
whose paradigm was and continues to be the novels of Agatha Christie (1890–
1976) as well as Georges Simenon (1903–1989), John Le Carré (b. 1931) and Eric
Ambler (b. 1909) and others who developed their own unique traits. The aforementioned neither denies nor ignores, in any way, that among the antecedents of
the genre one must count foundational writers of the nineteenth century such as
Edgar Allan Poe, Nathaniel Hawthorne (1804–1864), and Arthur Conan Doyle
(1859–1930).

In twentieth-century North American literature it is possible to identify two
decisive factors: one discards light romanticism, the other adopts brutality and
violence as realist forms of expression. This idea, brilliantly put forth by Jorge
Luis Borges in his prologue to the stories of Bret Harte, helps to explain the

hypothesis of the decisive influence the novel of the American West had on the modern hard-boiled genre. Moreover, that influence is part of a true continuum; there could not have been hard-boiled literature without the antecedent of romantic action/adventure literature of the nineteenth-century Far West writers.

Without a doubt, the writer who stands out as the most capable and who left the most profound mark was Francis Brett Harte (1836–1902), who was born in Albany, New York in 1830 and died in London in 1902. Curiously, although he arrived in California at the age of 17, lived there only a short time and worked as a miner, postman, journalist, and printer, Harte is considered to be the best chronicler of the West, the one who wrote the most extraordinary pages about that world of adventure. It was not by chance that he was the first writer to place California on the map of world literature, as Ned E. Hoopes points out in his introduction to *Harte of the West* (1966).

The literary godfather of Mark Twain, admired by Dickens, Kipling, and Borges, Bret Harte (as author, he eliminated his first name and suppressed a "t" from his second) unmistakably left an indelible mark on the hard-boiled genre. He figured among the best in the North American literary tradition and created unforgettable characters who later were transferred—often in ominous or carica-ture-like fashion—to the big screen and television. Borges points out that Harte was the motivation behind the rupture in North American literature of the twen-tieth century: "The purpose of not being overly sentimental and of being, God willing, brutal, had two consequences: the climax of the hard-boiled writers (Hemingway, Caldwell, Farrel, Steinbeck, James Cain); and the depreciation of many mediocre and some good writers such as Longfellow, Dean Howell, and Bret Harte (Borges 6).

This depreciation, which had mostly to do with the Western, later extended to the hard-boiled genre, perhaps due to the sin of its popularity. Notwithstanding, its models (Harte, but also Crane, Ambrose Bierce [1842–1914], Zane Grey [1872–1939]], and William S. Porter [1862–1910], more commonly known by his pseudonym O. Henry) made an impact through the use of action and the rather brutal behavior that define their characters. Harte's unforgettable creations (like the fascinating John Oakhurst, gambler; stage-driver Yuba Bill; the attorney and colonel Starbottle; and delicate and valiant women like Miss Mary, Betsy Barker, or the enchanting Miggles) survived, more as influences, as a thread of continu-ity than anything else. Today, one can see the image of Oakhurst in Hammett's Madvigs or Beaumont, in Chandler's Vic Malloy, and in James M. Cain's (1892–1977) or David Goodis's (1917–1967) characters, for example, and even in Hem-ingway's character Jack Browning from "The Killers," who was played by the mediocre actor Ronald Reagan in the film version.

Zane Grey is another writer who no doubt played a pivotal role in shaping the narrative style of North American detective fiction; characterized by constant action, crude dialogue, suspense, and individualism. He and Margaret Mitchell, author of *Gone with the Wind* (1936), were the two most-read North American authors of the time. Like Harte, Zane Grey, a dentist by profession, lived only briefly in the West. He accompanied a military caravan for a few years, during which time he gathered enough material to write the most important series of Western novels ever produced. His approximately 30 novels sold 20 million copies between 1912 and 1930, were translated into 15 languages, and turned the genre into a classic of our time. The conquest of territory, battles with Indians, cattle rustling, self-sacrificing pioneers, and the founding of cities were the themes that allowed him to create an entire gallery of characters. Later, these were carried to the silver screen in the burgeoning Western-film industry, whose plots always included action, violence, intrigue, and individual heroism in the struggle for power, glory, and money.

In *West of the Pecos* (1937), one of the most moving novels about the settlement of the West after the Civil War, Grey narrates the story of a Southern family that enters Comanche territory to settle the inhospitable land and begin raising cattle. The novel is impeccably crafted, with a singular descriptive richness underscored by short, crisp dialogues, a sense of humor and irony, and some memorable action and violent passages. *Riders of the Purple Sage* (1912) is another of Grey's most remarkable texts, along with *The Lone Star Ranger* (1952), *Nevada* (1928), *To the Last Man* (1922), and *The Light of the Western Stars* (1917). In his novels, Grey was far from describing and narrating a caricature of the cowboy as Hollywood later did. His realist, local-color sketches portray men and women of flesh and blood that live and speak with authenticity, a style of narrative that obviously influenced Hammett, Chandler, Hemingway, and many others. It is remarkable how this man, imbued with Southern ideology, racism, and a plethora of mythologies, managed to maintain his own critical, non-Manichean vision. In Grey's works, the "bad guys" aren't always the Indians or Mexicans. Furthermore, while there are instances in which he presents misguided versions of history—like his explanation of the Mexican-American War of 1845–48, specifically the Battle of the Alamo—his *bandidos* also include blond Texans of European-Protestant origins.

If one accepts the traditional separation between the classic "whodunit" or puzzle-novel and the hard-boiled novel, it seems clear that the Western was a major influence on the latter type. The North American hard-boiled novel simply would not have existed without that body of preceding works that fall somewhere between epic and puerile, pompous, and ingenuous. In my opinion, the blood transfusion seems to have been direct and is evident in the rhythm, action, and individual heroism as primary components. In addition to humor are certain questionable values like excessive ambition for money and personal glory as well as a penchant for aspiring to political power. In the Western, one also finds the primordial element of hard-boiled fiction: crime. It could even be said that the not-yet-fully appreciated richness of the adventure novel with its Indians, outlaws, and lone cowboys even today seems inexhaustible in spite of the stereotypes fabricated by Hollywood in film and television. And also, the innumerable comic strips—largely of poor quality and implausible—even if they did garner commercial success deformed and devalued this epic literary genre.

Underlying elements present today in the best hard-boiled novel (such as power, corruption, and social criticism) already existed in that previous genre in which authors described the brutal war waged by the white man against the Indians, who were effectively exterminated for the sake of a dubious civilization. In the pages of the Western, the railroad, the founding of cities, the long wagon trains, the fight to tame the land, gambling, and alcoholism formed the picturesque but necessary backdrop to set the ideological advance of capitalism on its course. The philosophical and moral foundations that the novel of the West bequeathed to the hard-boiled genre and to the whole of twentieth-century North American literature are present in its pages as well: individualism, nationalism, religious Puritanism, romanticism, trust in the law and that Manichean vision that people in the United States possess of the struggle between good and evil.

The mere mention of such characteristics demonstrates the profound mark left by that narrative tradition on the creators of the hard-boiled genre like Hammett and Chandler and in the best subsequent authors of the genre, including almost all Latin American writers. The ties between the detective novel and adventure novel, and indirectly with the Western, can also be found in Conan Doyle himself, who was familiar with and had an appreciation for the work of Harte and whose influence together with that of Stevenson has been outlined by the Mexican writer and critic María Elvira Bermúdez in her prologue to the Spanish translation of Conan Doyle's works. The first part of *A Study in Scarlet* (1888), set in the North American West, makes that clear. Of course, that influence is apparent in many of the authors already mentioned in addition to many others who approached crime through money, corruption, machismo, harsh circumstance, and power—authors such as F. Scott Fitzgerald (1896–1940), John Steinbeck (1902–1968), Erskine Caldwell, Horace McCoy (1897–1955), Truman Capote (1924–1984) and even a few women like Carson McCullers (1917–1967).

The conquest of the North American West was a fabulous and contradictory epic story, referred to popularly as "How the West Was Won." It was violent and merciless, unjust and barbaric, although it was done in the name of civilization and progress. And like all conquests, it also consisted of genocide.[6] Juan Tébar, in his prologue to *Historias del Viejo Oeste* (Stories of the old West, 1972), provides a useful analysis on the concept of the West, or Far West, and the ideological, political, and geographic evolution of the term. The literature of that conquest seems to be a logical consequence of the novels of chivalry and in good measure of Greek tragedy (Tébar). At the same time, if the literature of the Far West is eminently rural—given that its settings are usually the Great Plains, the mountains, or the deserts, and occasionally small human settlements—then hard-boiled detective fiction can be seen as its urban counterpart. In fact, the large cities and suburbs where hard-boiled texts take place are nothing more than the same sites, converted decades later into the paved streets of cities in which concrete, glass, and corruption sketch different scenes for the same, eternal human miseries.

These borders are not capricious. At least in literary terms, that gigantic expanse of territory gave way to an eminently epic literature of hope and conquest.

Thus, it is charged with moral intention, given that it was responding to the expansion of a nation about which today one could say many things, but not that its people lacked a vocation for greatness and determination.

Toward the end of the nineteenth century the popular taste that gave rise to the Western genre—a dozen or so authors sold millions of copies—helped create a mythology of remarkable strength and persistence. Although not the first among the authors of Westerns, James Fenimore Cooper (1789–1851) left a work that is one of the earliest predecessors of the hard-boiled genre: his *The Last of the Mohicans* (1826), the novel of a Native American who defends to his last breath his lands against the encroaching "civilization." From it surely sprang other Western classics like those of Harte, Bierce, Grey, and even Twain. All of them are the literary forebears of the writers who decades later invented hard-boiled detective fiction. Without exception, they all helped to elevate the stature of a new type of literary hero: the loner over the superman, the downtrodden and ever-critical over the frivolous genteel, who is out of touch with the social environment—in other words, primitive forms of Sam Spade, Phillip Marlowe, Lew Archer, and other characters who followed.

The story of that conquest is the same as the story of the introduction of capitalism in America. Is not the triumph of rampant capitalism a sure sign of the degree of alienation at which a market-driven, individualistic, society can arrive? One in which personal heroism is the only trait that enables one to withstand the tremendous crime rate? The reasons behind this impressive framework are in the very makeup of capitalism in the United States—that huge country without a name that was formed on the foundation of Anglo-Saxon Puritanism. But it also depended on the extermination of the indigenous population and the devastating conquest of its land, not only in the original 13 British colonies but also with the territory conquered during the war with Mexico. A certain type of personality and action could not help but spring forth from this process, which literature naturally assimilated and transferred, decades later, to the hard-boiled genre. The prolific Georges Simenon once observed something to the effect that the criminal, and especially murder, is an extreme act of human behavior. It would seem that we are condemned to live on the edge, barely holding at bay our extreme acts. In hard-boiled literature the people at the edge are the police, the detectives, and the vague, omnipotent, and abstract concept of the "law" that in the West was embodied by the legendary figure of the sheriff.

The relationship between both literary genres (each habitually considered lowbrow) can be observed also in turns of phrases and expressions in characters and situations from either. I have gone into greater detail concerning these similarities in my *El género negro* (The hard-boiled genre; 1996, 33–42). Evidently, such a relationship implies that there is a "national character" to be found in the transformation from Westerns to the hard-boiled genre. We may refer to this characteristic as "North-Americanness." Clearly, this is present in the entire body of twentieth-century literature, which is why it is important to distinguish the hard-boiled novel from traditional detective fiction or the English puzzle-novel.

The delimitation of the Far West literary boundaries likewise implies the definition of its common themes: the vision of social reality, a certain naturalism, local color descriptions, constant action, individual heroism, machismo, money, power, corruption, irony, and so on. One may also identify a unique style: dry, hard, flat prose. Given its inclusion in the vein of literary realism, it is evident that all this also influenced modern Latin American literature. Theme and style are common to both genres (the Western and hard-boiled fiction) because both are inscribed within critical realism and both correspond to the same society that, although it underwent many changes in less than a century (approximately 1850–1920) still maintained its essence and that continuity is recognizable in the literature. As Juan Martini aptly observed some years ago in his prologue to the Spanish translation of McCoy's *Kiss Tomorrow Goodbye* (1948): "The world of the detective novel is no longer an enclosed space, identifiable, isolated within the wide space of reality. The world of the detective novel is not another world, but the same, the only, world that we know and in which we live" (Martini 5–6). Many of the characteristics that define North American society were repeated in that social environment of almost a hundred years of literature. Martini goes on to state that "violence is something inseparable from the system that is not expressed only in obvious, resounding, bloody ways. Human reactions are, in and of themselves, a form of violence, an expression of power and of submission. All power is a form of violence. Any fate not chosen is a form of violence" (Martini 6).

The link between Harte and his contemporary Western writers and the authors of the magazine *Black Mask* should be fairly evident. They all imbibed, at the very least, the literature of Harte, Grey, and O. Henry. It's no coincidence that California also became the nearly exclusive setting for the hard-boiled novel. Many of the authors who today are known for being the founders of the hard-boiled genre were also, previously or simultaneously, writers of westerns. Among them are Frank Gruber (1904–1969); William Riley Burnett (1899–1982), the celebrated author of two novels that were made into legendary noir films, *The Little Caesar* (1929) and *High Sierra* (1940) both responsible for establishing the fame of Humphrey Bogart; and the already-mentioned Horace McCoy, famous for his novel *They Kill Horses, Don't They?* (1935) as well as for the script of *Texas*, the classic film by George Marshall (1891–1975), starring William Holden and Glenn Ford.

There is yet one more element that can be added to tie the two genres together. This being the way in which both first appeared and became popular. The original, and principal, vehicle were the "pulps," as the action-story magazines were called. The name derives from the cheap pulp paper on which they were printed. Pulps were distributed in the United States on an astounding scale, and in them the hard-boiled story found an ideal space for attaining popularity. Javier Coma states that "normally, each pulp included a variety of stories and was home to a fixed character, just as it was dedicated to a concrete topic, from pseudoscientific fantasy to "sword and sorcery," by way of the Western, aviation, and adventures in exotic locales" (Coma 20). This is also where the first hard-boiled texts appeared.

The bond between literature and society found perfect expression in the North America of the 1920s. Coma declares that the hard-boiled novel enters into "the social and political evolution of the United States in the 1920s. One cannot analyze this tendency properly without following the same path taken by North American history during the century; the stages of one and the other reveal an intimate correspondence during decades and decades" (Coma 15). Clearly, that correspondence also links, from the past, Western and hard-boiled novels. Furthermore, the common thread that unites these with the Latin American detective novel is the same. There is no rupture, but rather an identifiable continuity.

How Has It Evolved, What Is Its Stature, and What Are the Most Salient Features that Define It?

Although the mutual ties and reciprocal influence between the narrative of the United States and that of Latin America has yet to be sufficiently examined, one can state that the evolution of Latin American detective fiction has historically marched in close step with North American literature.[7] Like all great literature, that of twentieth-century North America has common characteristics in all its forms of narrative expression, no matter what the genre. In this sense—just as Miguel de Cervantes Saavedra inaugurated the modern novel in 1600, and the Russians and French wrote the great novels of the nineteenth century—the North American novel of the first half of the twentieth century changed the course of literary history. Similarly, the major literary innovations in the last 40 years have originated in Latin America.

Many of the novels written in the United States during the 1920s and 1930s produced a revolution in the history of narrative, and even film and later television adopted its language. Like Poe, Harte, and O. Henry had done previously, and also Jack London (1876–1916) and John Dos Passos (1896–1970), the writers from this period invented a new way of treating reality, of discussing the world, and of observing daily life. In short stories and novels, they narrated the most miserable aspects of human nature, denounced abuses of political power and the smallness of certain lives, and in general pondered the nature of individualism, racism, violence, and desperation. They exercised an impressive influence on the world through their masterful works that resulted in displays of a formal search of expression. Thanks to excellent translations, they were read and appreciated by several generations of Latin American readers and writers.

As we have seen, the origins of the detective novel hark back to the pamphlets of the nineteenth century where stories of crime and mystery appeared that featured occasional policemen and delinquents. The idea that "crime is popular" is one accepted at least since the time of Thomas de Quincey (1785–1859), since it was widely treated in the sensationalist periodicals of mass distribution.[8] Arthur Conan Doyle established two of the most notable characteristics of detective fiction. First, that the very popularity of this literature and its lack of pretension condemned it to a lesser category. Second, its moral character—chiefly, the struggle between good and evil—would never cease to be a special feature of the genre.

The contribution of the North American "tough writers" was to add violence, humanity, and above all credibility, inasmuch as they were concerned with crime as part of the real world. They attempted what Martini calls "an approach and response to the problem of violence" (Martini 1981, 6). Reality, previously, was outside the realm of fiction, and that is precisely what the hard-boiled genre strives to incorporate. The jungle is found by simply stepping onto the street and confronting its dangers, entering the urban scene, the misery and racism of the individualistic and violent everyday reality of North American life. This is the material that the hard-boiled genre works with as seen in the writing of Nathanael West (1904–1990), James Baldwin (1924–1987), Richard Wright (1908–1960), the already-mentioned Faulkner, Caldwell, McCullers, Hemingway, Fitzgerald, Steinbeck, and Capote, and more recently, J. D. Salinger (b. 1919), J. P. Donleavy (b. 1926), Patricia Highsmith (1921–1995), Raymond Carver (1938–1988), Eudora Welty (b. 1909), John Irving (b. 1942), Donald Barthelme (1931–1989), and many more.

There is increasingly more textual evidence that demonstrates how the detective novel has exerted an extraordinary influence on modern Latin American narrative. As we have seen, that influence comes primarily from the hard-boiled North American novel. In spite of a strong influence also from the French hard-boiled novel, there is that element of "North-Americanness" at the heart of the majority of texts written by Latin American authors of what has come to be called the "Postboom era."[9] This literature is characterized by graphic realism, the crudeness and authenticity of the dialogue, and even the possibility of dramatic representation as seen in North American narrative. In fact, it is the single major source of themes and plots for the film and television industries.[10]

Of course, violence and hardness do not pertain exclusively to the domain of the hard-boiled genre. They are better understood as emblematic of almost all North American literature since the end of the nineteenth century, as if it were all an ongoing heated discussion on racism and violence, but at the same time harboring an intrinsic trust in the corrective potential of the system. Racism and violence, like money and power, and corruption and crime, were the primary ingredients of this narrative style and of the plot structure that shaped the hard-boiled genre. But those ingredients were also present in prior "hard" authors like London, Dos Passos, and many others who traditionally are not considered to belong to the detective genre and who left profound marks on Latin American literature.[11]

The academic world in the United States is obviously flooded with dissertations on North American literature. Likewise, Hispanists have exhausted themes and authors in the Latin American literary world. Yet, what seems to have gone unstudied are the ties between both literatures, and even less so the hard-boiled genre as a point of departure. This violent, merciless view of reality arrived in Latin America in the form of popular collections with massive distribution. These penny dreadful pocket books, which appeared in translations of varying quality (some of them quite bad, some very good), were disdained within academic circles and the intellectual community as lowbrow literature. Such cheap paperback editions circulated in the 1940s and 1950s, but many of them are sought out today by collectors who peruse used-book shops in search of lost treasures. They were the equivalent of the pulp magazines, which naturally inundated kiosks and newspaper stands throughout Latin America. Some of the collections included "Cobalto" (Cobalt), "Débora," "Pandora," and "Linterna" (Lantern) published by Editorial Malinca in Buenos Aires; "Rastros" (Tracks) and "Teseo," by Editorial Acme, also in Buenos Aires; "Policiaca y de misterio" (Detective and mystery) published by Editorial Novaro in Mexico; "Jaguar" and "Caimán also in Mexico, by Editorial Diana; additionally, there were the "Serie Naranja" (Orange Series) by Hachette in Buenos Aires and the extraordinary "El Séptimo Círculo" (The seventh circle) created in 1945 by Jorge Luis Borges (1899–1986) and Adolfo Bioy Casares (1914–1999) for Emecé Editores in Buenos Aires. The "El Séptimo Círculo" series played a key role because it included all the variants of the genre and "discovered" for Spanish-language readers almost all the major detective fiction writers.

With affordable prices, an avid market, and a never-ending offering of titles, the genre arrived in force on the American continent decades ago. Perhaps due to that very popularity—and to the prejudices that the popular always awakens—it met with much resistance and struggled to be considered as anything other than "invasive." With printings of well over 15,000 copies (that today would make Latin American publishers green with envy) and very low prices, these little books cornered the Latin American markets and introduced not only the founders of the genre but also first-rate authors such as McCoy, Gruber, Goodis, Charles Williams (1886–1945), and Gil Brewer (1922–1983), and even second-rate writers like Brett Halliday (1904–1977), Ed McBain (b. 1926), Talmage Powell (b. 1920), and Richard Prather (b. 1921). They even consecrated extremely popular writers like Mickey Spillane (b. 1918), creator of the fascist detective Mike Hammer, who met with greater fortune on post–McCarthyism television than in literature (much to the benefit of literature).

The North American influence—and not only the hard-boiled portion—has been acknowledged by many Spanish American authors. It is safe to say that there is almost no contemporary Latin American author who at one time has not been a fan or habitué of this literature. For the majority of authors from the Boom on, it is undeniable that a good part of their literary formation stems from the North American hard-boiled novel. This influence is present in many writers. It is apparent if Rodolfo J. Walsh (1927–1977), Osvaldo Soriano (1943–1997), Ricardo Piglia (b. 1940), and the much-cited Juan Martini (b. 1944) in Argentina;[12] in the Chileans Poli Délano (b. 1936), Luis Sepúlveda (b. 1949), and Ramón Díaz Eterovic (b. 1956); the Cubans Ricardo Pérez Valero (b. 1947) and Luis Rogelio Nogueras (1945–1985); in Mexico the incomparable Rafael Bernal (1915–1972), and more recently, Paco Ignacio Taibo II (b. 1949), Rafael Ramírez Heredia (b. 1942), and many more. All have adapted the style, the narrative strategies, and a way of looking more critically at their society, each in his own way.

The Chilean writer and critic Jaime Valdivieso holds that if the boundary is the Río Bravo/Grande, to the north there is Puritanism and enterprise while to the south there is Catholicism and feudalism. He states that "the factors that weed us out, the Latin Americans from the North Americans, and by extension, our narrative are: characters driven, from within, by a Biblical moral conscience and a demonic will to act, on the one hand; society, nature, and the State, on the other; in our narrative, more than men acting on deeds, these act on them" (Valdivieso 55). Carlos Fuentes has referred to these differences when he speaks of the preponderant role that the devouring, impenetrable force of nature has played in Latin America (*La nueva novela*, 1969).

Many of the characteristics of the North American novel have been reflected—and are still reflected—in Latin American counterparts. There is virtually no Latin American detective novel that does not approach, even if only tangentially, the same form of racism, violence, and desperation. One cannot state that they do so "owing to" North American influence, but the North American treatment of those elements has indeed influenced the Latin American narrative of the past for at least 50 years.

Make no mistake, our treatment of the topic has its own particular flavor. Money and corruption, for example, have merited a different approach. In the literature of the United States, money has always played a central role, as if it were the true God of the North Americans. Among Latin Americans, it can be said that it is present in all the authors of the hard-boiled genre as an essential motivation (the genre is defined by the presence of crime, and money functions as the catalyst of crime), but the obsession with money is not a determinant. In Latin American hard-boiled literature, money is not the character's primary motivation. Because it deals with societies that are so different from one another, the influence of the hard-boiled novel from the United States is more remarkable for its methods of narration than for the motives of its characters. If for North American writers the core of the plot tends to be money, for Latin Americans the core resides in the social differences that produce the possession, or paucity, of money. North American writers describe the struggles to possess and accumulate money. In contrast, in Latin American literature, more important than money itself are the effects of its unequal distribution—above all, because Latin America is experiencing during the 1980s, 1990s, and 2000s its own Great Depression: economic and political crisis, social marginalization stemming from unemployment, a dismal abyss that separates social classes, individual and family degradation, and the threat of repression make up the social landscape.

In addition to the acquisition of money, North American writers almost invariably treat the topic of corruption. Whether it be police, political, economic, or moral corruption, it is always present in the hard-boiled novel. Theoretically, the commonality lies in the political–ideological footing that considers corruption as a corrosive and morally deleterious element. This is a common denominator for the genre in both literatures. But in the case of North American corruption, there is almost always a way out, and so it is in literature also. Corruption makes a bad example. It is an enemy that must be defeated, and there is almost always hope of a way to overcome it. On the contrary, in what José Martí (1853–1895) called "Nuestra América" (Our America, 1891) corruption is still an incurable disease and in literature it is approached from multiple angles, but most assuredly not from a position of hope.

The relationship that North Americans have with money aids in the comprehension of their relationship with power, which is also different Latin Americans'. Overwhelming loneliness is a concern for the average North American—a product of excessive individualism. In hard-boiled novels, the characters are always presented with a "last hope" (for example, pull-off the job that will lift them out of poverty; be saved from being found guilty of crime; cross the border and flee into Mexico). That life on the edge condemns them to a sense of loneliness and isolation that tends to unleash violent extremes that can end up annihilating them. Latin Americans, by contrast, don't seem to be so isolated. By living in societies that are less individualistic, in which a common destiny—albeit an unfortunate one—is shared, there is a greater sense that destiny is more collective than individual. The Latin American hard-boiled protagonist's solitude is less tragic, at times even humorous because it is so ironic, and thus he is endowed with a dose of hope that the author doesn't always intend to show in plain view, perhaps out of modesty.

The individualism inherent in North American society is also evident in its literary tradition where the young, adventurous, triumphant hero is a classic figure. The creation of the antihero in hard-boiled novels was one reason they were considered, in a sense, to be contestatory. In his introduction to *Luces de Hollywood* (Spanish translation of *I Should Have Stayed Home*), Juan Martini states: "the figures chosen by McCoy as protagonists of his novels live on the margins of the law, which they confront, voluntarily or not. They fight alone, helpless and without hope, against a power that is infinitely superior and capable of absorbing and tolerating rebellion as long as rebellion is not able to substantially alter the imposed order" (Martini 6).

A North American's relationship with power is very different from that of a Latin American's. They both resist, but the first is convinced that he can "do something" to change things, although keeping in line with the system, because deep down he trusts in the virtues of that system. The North American is educated with the conviction that the system is flexible and broad; it is changeable and adapts to modern times. If you give your best effort and work hard, in the end you'll manage to change things. According to Valdivieso, "the United States has created it own system of values, its own philosophy: the pragmatism that incites one to action, to fight the system, the spirit of enterprise, from which has arisen a society and institutions that instill trust, although they may have defects; it is believed that from them the seeds of betterment will sprout" (Valdivieso 76). Surely this is why from Fenimore Cooper, Ralph Waldo Emerson (1803–1882), Henry David Thoreau (1817–1862), Edgar Allan Poe, Emily Dickinson (1830–1886), Nathaniel Hawthorne, Walt Whitman, and Howard Phillip Lovecraft (1890–1937) up to the authors of the present time, works have expressed trust in their society and their belief system. The ideals of personal courage, audacity, and individualism are, as we have seen, the cornerstones of the detective novel, which are undoubtedly alluring to Latin American authors and readers.

Due to that essential trust in the political–social system and its corrective capability, they hold the conviction that the possibilities are endless and anything can be achieved with an honest effort and personal courage. This is why audacity and individualism are so valued. Valdivieso astutely points out that "for them the huge gap between the present political–social reality and the possible one doesn't exist" (Valdivieso 76). That is why their rebellion is individual and can be a heroic and beautiful adventure, but always individual. The North American, when it comes down to it, always submits to power and accepts it because he was educated this way. The "law," in abstract terms, is a code of conduct. Almost all North American authors, even the most critical ones, in their hearts have always trusted in the profound virtues of the system and its regenerative capacity; perhaps the only exceptions are McCoy, Jim Thompson (1906–1977), and Chester Himes (1909–1984).[13]

In Latin America, however, it is very difficult to find a writer who trusts in his country's system. Practically no one can trust in the established power structure. Indeed, one lives in constant revolt against the system, and for as much as one would like to modify it, the end result is a loss of faith. Latin Americans are also full of good intentions and noble sentiments, clearly, but for many life is a constant battle. We live in eternal dissidence and must also take enormous strides to maintain our strength, ideals, and fighting spirit. In fact, making culture in Latin America means resisting, constantly resisting. Of course, many Latin American intellectuals have given up the fight; some have surrendered to the seduction and comfort of power; and many others are convinced that our predicament is irreversible. This produces, then, the major skepticism, the enormous cynicism, and the sense of frustration of which Valdivieso speaks.

In Latin America, sociopolitical reality always produces unstable ruptures, and at the same time, the common history of Latin American countries teaches that little or no good comes from individual efforts and personal courage. Its history has shown that the task of improving living conditions, of overcoming the inefficiency of institutions, and corruption, repression, and social injustice is not an individual one. That need for a collective effort, for an organized social drive, is reflected in its literary demeanor. Writing in Latin America is not just an aesthetic problem but an ethical one as well. This is why the Latin American writer tends to become involved in extraliterary matters that are of concern to his or her society.

North American hard-boiled writers seem to hold the conviction that violence and corruption are irremediable natural "evils," and the social context that produces them is not always apparent. In order to refute those who think that social conscience was already present in the creators of the genre it is helpful to quote Raymond Chandler, who in a letter of January 1945 to his friend Dale Warren wrote:

> I wrote melodramas because when I looked around me it was the only kind of
> writing that was relatively honest and yet was not trying to put over somebody's
> party line. So now there are guys talking about prose and other guys telling me
> I have a social conscience. P. Marlowe has as much social conscience as a horse.
> He has a personal conscience, which is an entirely different matter. (Chandler
> 2001, 50–51)

In an interview with Ross Macdonald (1915–1983), Osvaldo Soriano described the ideology of the then most famous author of the genre; "In reality it was easy to see in Macdonald the North American liberal. Audacious, but to a point; unprejudiced, but not by much; tolerant of radical ideas, if they are distant. He told me: 'I fight so the United States will not be a country of second-rate ideas.' 'What would be some of those second-rate ideas?' I asked him. 'The nazis and the fascists had second-rate ideas,' he answered" (Soriano).

It goes without saying that the problems of conscience, religious fanaticism, and even racism (very Faulknerian topics, one must say) are also present in Latin American authors, but adapted to its own tragedy, which is more Greek than Shakespearian. There is practically no Latin American detective novel that doesn't approach directly or indirectly its own forms of racism, dogma (not so much religious as political or ideological), and above all the forms of social violence that are uniquely Latin American. But at the same time, what contemporary Latin American writer could avoid mentioning *Tobacco Road* or *The Sound and the Fury* (1929) in the inventory of influences that he or she has received?

Guillermo de Torre, citing Morton Dauwen Zabel's *Historia de la literatura norteamericana* (History of North American literature), states:

> One of the defining traits of literature in the United States consists of being a
> derivation of European literature, and at the same time, in its resistance to that
> tradition, it is moved by the desire to find its own character. The child's affection
> and the sibling's opposition; in this tension, in this dialectical struggle in the
> Hispanic case also lies the key to Spanish American literature. However, there is
> a profound difference: in Anglican America the conflict has been resolved by
> recognizing and "digesting" it; eliminating all the harmful toxins. (de Torre 31)

De Torre affirms that North American literature has no prehistory; or better said, it turns its history into prehistory. And after declaring "the abscence of an 'American past,'" he concludes that "the United States of the seventeenth century was not built on that past, but on a European foundation" (de Torre 32).

This concept helps to locate the differences between the two literatures, but also their points of contact. Surely, that lack of adherence to a prehistory, that void, has allowed North Americans to shape a more free literature, one that is unfettered by a prehistory to which it must remain loyal, as in the case of the Latin Americans. If we look at Jorge Icaza's (1906–1978) *Huasipungo* (1934) and Caldwell's *Tobacco Road*, we can perceive that different relationship to the past. Both works denounce injustice, social imbalances, and the violence wielded by the powerful. However, it is evident that Icaza has deeper political, ethnic, and cultural roots, while Caldwell works with greater freedom, without being subjected to History. The old man Jeeter doesn't descend from generations of exploited forebears, his spirit is not anchored in the earth. He lacks four centuries of domination. To clarify, he is a twentieth-century North American, well-nourished, and whose only problem is that he is angry and discouraged because he can't achieve the "American dream."

The characters in North American hard-boiled fiction belong to a well-defined world: the world of capitalist development and individual triumph, of industrialism and alienation in a consumer society at the height of its expression, the struggle to acquire money as the fundamental method of social ascension, the nationalist sentiment for a powerful and egalitarian society that is, however, profoundly racist. In this literature, it is as if neither a history nor prehistory of society exist. There is no evaluative interpretation of the political, economic, and social antecedents that have led the United States to become what it is. In the hard-boiled genre, the idea that the United States is the whole world—so common among North Americans—is a strong presence. By contrast, in Latin American detective fiction one finds all types of political and social cues. And, unavoidably, through the examination of our identity the historical marks of literature and reality appear. The themes of *mestizaje* and our political systems are present in our literature, as well as violence, which almost always refers to dictatorial or falsely democratic authority in the best of cases. An essential part of the Latin American thriller is the interpretation of, or suggestive inferences about, political circumstances. Our literature is also populated with our own complexes and misfortunes as underdeveloped peoples, as unpleasant it may sound to admit. But there is always social and political criticism and varying forms of repression as we see in Walsh, Soriano, Sinay, Bernal, and Taibo.

It may be true that—for their lack of complexes—North Americans have been able to create a literature that is more loose, free, and less subject to social conditions. Therefore it is centered solely on forms of individual violence or that of small groups. Also indicative of this is the individual heroism and personal conscience that North Americans are so fond of. The North American detective is a hero-figure, while in Latin America what matters most is the situation, not the merit of the individual, who many times may even be ridiculed or lampooned.

The role nature plays, as one of the archetypes of Spanish American narrative, must be mentioned in this context as well. As Carlos Fuentes indicates, "next to the voracious force of nature, the Spanish American novel creates a second archetype: the dictator on a national or regional scale. The third could only be the exploited masses, that suffer the rigors of both the unforgiving natural world and the bloodthirsty chieftain" (Fuentes 11). And there is yet a fourth factor, adds Fuentes, that we may assert is present in a very specific way in the Latin American detective novel: "The writer, who invariably takes the side of civilization over barbarism, who is the spokesman for those who cannot make themselves heard, who feels that his function consists of denouncing injustice, defending the exploited, and documenting the reality of his country (Fuentes 11–12). This declaration is qualified by Fuentes himself who recognizes that "at the same time the Latin American writer, by virtue of being one in a semifeudal, colonial, and uneducated community, belongs to an elite class. His work is defined in large part by a feeling—mixture of gratitude and shame—that he should pay for the privilege of being a writer and living among the elite" (Fuentes 12). Fuentes doesn't stop there. He also maintains that Latin American writers have the suspicion, which also defines their work, that "in spite of everything, they speak from the liberal wing of the elite and they are heard from the conservative wing, and that the conservatives only listen to their declarations with supreme indifference (Fuentes 12). This tends to lead to the decision to abandon literature or at least share it with militant political movements. Fuentes reasons:

> The Latin American novel emerged as the immediate chronicle of the proof that, without it (political militancy), it would not reach the public conscience. In countries subjected to the swinging pendulum of dictatorship and anarchy, in which the only constant has been exploitation . . . the individual novelist felt himself compelled, simultaneously, to be legislator and reporter, revolutionary and thinker. (Fuentes 12)

Obviously, if today it is possible to speak of Latin American hard-boiled literature, it is because it evolved, like any other, from universal sources. But as we have traced here, its fundamental sources are in the North American hard-boiled novel that abandoned the classic model based on the well-known "whodunit" or puzzle-story in which an investigator looked for clues in order to incriminate the guilty party. Although hard-boiled literature has preserved the element of mystery (no narrative exists without it), its presence is not what characterizes the text. Rather, the description of the setting, the element of causality, the motives of the characters, and above all the use of a language that is violent, hardened, machista, and completely merciless are what defines a text as "hard-boiled."

One cannot deny that Faulkner, Hemingway, Hammett, and Chandler are necessarily present in Latin American modernity. Masters, all of them, at creating interior monologue as a way of presenting the character's thoughts, at the art of describing action that takes the place of explanation, and at the difficult task of being witness–narrator–protagonist. It seems to me that that influence is implicit already in writers such as Ernesto Sabato (b. 1911), for example, whose novel *El túnel* (*The Tunnel*, 1948) deserves recognition for being one of the first attempts at the hard-boiled novel in the Southern Cone. It can be found later in the works of numerous authors like Silvina Ocampo (1903–1993), María Angélica Bosco (b. 1917), Augusto Roa Bastos (b. 1917), Marco Denevi (1922–1998), Elvira Orphée (b. 1930), and of course Soriano, Luisa Valenzuela (b. 1938), María Luisa Puga (b. 1944), and Fernando del Paso (b. 1935).

Detective fiction in Latin America today pays a necessary tribute to the hard-boiled tradition. I don't believe that today it would occur to anyone to write classic detective fiction, which is why one can say that the hard-boiled genre has had a revolutionary influence on all Latin American narrative. In sum, the Latin

American writer also demands better living conditions, but money in his works are only a means, not an end or motivation. Corruption is not a deviation from the norm; the causes run deep and are almost never corrected. Power is neither flexible nor something that can be changed with hard work and tenacity; it is an objective to reach in order to change things. Politics is not a public service or charge; it is a passion born of desperation. And literature, of course, is not only evasion and entertainment: it can also be—and in many cases has been and is— an ideological weapon.

TRANSLATED BY DARRELL B. LOCKHART

Notes

1. Ricardo Piglia has pointed out, quite correctly, that "the English detective novel separates crime from its social motivation" ("Introducción" 8).

2. This is a, perhaps inadequate, translation for what in Latin American literature is called *Costumbrismo*. It does not refer to a specific literary movement such as Romanticism or Naturalism; rather, it is used to designate the tendency of writers to create a narrative of customs. That is, to describe in detail the customs, local habits, and general social environment of a given place and time—in effect, to "paint a portrait" for the reader.

3. Mention of this author requires a digression I feel is fundamental. Stephen Crane had an eventful though brief life (he died at age 29 of tuberculosis) but he left a profound mark on literature, particularly with his novel *The Red Badge of Courage* (1895). This novel is connected to the novels of chivalry and it is, aside from being a classic, a cornerstone of the literature of heroism and nationalism in the United States. Without a doubt, this work by Crane (who also wrote short stories, poetry, and two other novels) is the most complete study ever on human courage in the face of danger. Crane created a cult of bravery through his character Henry Fleming, a boy recruited by the Yankee troops to fight against the Southern Johnnies, who goes to war and participates in the battle of Chancellorsville, where in reality he confronts his own cowardice. He later realizes that he is nothing more than an outcast and deserts. In spite of the shame he feels, fate brings him back to his troop and in the end he becomes an authentic hero. Here, his renewed patriotism comes together: carrying the flag is symbolic in Crane. With an almost photographic realism amid poetic descriptions, the precise tracking of army positions and a vivid reproduction of battles, Crane created a true hero with which he helped to erect the myth of North American courage. The patriotic exaltations of Crane cannot help but anticipate the later bastardization of Hollywood when it became the great colonizing machine of ideological imperialism. It is impossible to know if this was Crane's intention, but *The Red Badge of Courage* must be recognized as one of the foundational works of North American nationalism and romanticism, which have created the cult of individuality and heroism. This epic literature nourished itself on personal daring as one of its basic elements, and could not help but impregnate a significant portion of subsequent literature, at least the "action" variant.

4. On this concept of postmodernism, see Giardinelli, "Variaciones sobre la posmodernidad, o ¿qué es eso del posboom latinoamericano," and also Giardinelli, *El país de las maravillas*, 15–34.

5. He also establishes an impeccable separation between the English and French novelistic traditions and explains how in the modern phase of the latter, Georges Simenon

acquires relevance with the incorporation of psychology. At the same time he shows how both are different from the North American school, which includes a respect for the truth, that is to say it provides credibility. From that point on, the genre is not just "what" (mystery) or "how" (reasoning), but what matters now is the "why."

6. On the concept of the West or Far West see, Juan Tébar, *Historias del Viejo Oeste* (1972).

7. There is scant bibliography on the existing relationship between both literatures. About the influence during these decades that the narrative of the United States exerted on Latin Ameican writers, the only existing record is that found in interviews or notes in which individual authors admit such an influence. Similarly, on the increasingly noticeable influence that in the last few decades (the 1980s and 1990s) Latin American authors exert on North Americans, there is virtually no research, at least, of which I am aware. However, the influence of the Latin American generation known as the so-called Boom is universally recognized today. One need only observe how the narrative strategies of the great Latin American writers are present in many North American, European, Asian, and African writers: John Irving (b. 1942), Toni Morrison (b. 1931), Milan Kundera (b. 1929), V. S. Naipul (b. 1932), and Salman Rushdie (b. 1947), among others.

8. It is obvious that television and cinema have served to strengthen this popularity during the twentieth and twenty-first centuries.

9. Concerning this categorization, which owes its name to the work published by the Paraguayan critic Juan Manuel Marcos in the early 1980s, I would like to propose what I think is a better term: "The literature of recovered democracies." See the books by Marcos and "Reflections of the Postboom" by Giardinelli.

10. The characteristic that I call "North-Americanness" has also influenced European writers of the genre: James Hadley Chase (1906–1985), Peter Cheyney (1896–1951), José Giovanni (b. 1923), P. D. James (b. 1920), Manuel Vázquez Montalbán (b. 1939), John Le Carré (b. 1931), and Dick Francis (b. 1920), among others.

11. In his introduction to *Kiss Tomorrow Goodbye* (*Dí adiós al mañana*), Juan Martini remarks: "The world in the work of McCoy is without doubt the same as in Hammett or Chandler, but his literary expression, ferocious and desperate, moves through a zone of hard-boiled literature in which it would not be going out on a limb to also situate Erskine Caldwell with *Tobacco Road* or Nathanael West with *Miss Lonelyhearts* or *The Day of the Locust*" (6).

12. From Argentina, other authors worth mentioning are Eduardo Goligorsky (b. 1931), Juan Sasturain (b. 1945), Rubén Tizziani (b. 1937), Sergio Sinay (b. 1947), Vicente Battista (b. 1940), Antonio Dal Massetto (b. 1938), José Pablo Feinmann (b. 1943), and Juan Carlos Martelli (b. 1934) to name just a few.

13. I have discussed these three authors at length in my *El género negro* (135–59).

References

Bermúdez, María Elvira. "Prólogo," in *Aventuras de Sherlock Holmes*, 2nd ed. Mexico City: Porrúa, 1982, 7–37.

Borges, Jorge Luis. "Prólogo," in *Bocetos californianos*, by Francis Bret Harte. Barcelona: Bruguera, 1979, 5–7.

Cernuda, Luis. "Prólogo," in *Cosecha roja* (*Red Harvest*) by Dashiell Hammett, 5th ed. Madrid: Alianza, 1981, 9–16.

Chandler, Raymond. *Selected Letters of Raymond Chandler*, ed. Frank MacShane. New York: Columbia University Press, 1981.

———. "The Simple Art of Murder" (1944), in *Popular Fiction: An Anthology*, ed. Gary Hoppenstand. New York: Longman, 1997, 498–508.

Coma, Javier. *La novela negra*. Barcelona: Ediciones El Viejo Topo, 1980.

Coto, María Rosa del. "El difícil arte de matar." *Arte y comunicación* (Buenos Aires) 2 (September 1982): 4.

Eisenstein, Sergei Mijailovich. "El género policíaco," in *La novela criminal*, 2nd ed., ed. Román Gubern (pp. 27–33). Barcelona: Tusquets, 1982.

Fuentes, Carlos. *La nueva novela hispanoamericana*, 4th ed. Mexico City: Joaquín Mortiz, 1974.

Giardinelli, Mempo. "Variaciones sobre la posmodernidad, o ¿qué es eso del posboom latinoamericano." *Puro cuento* 23 (1990): 30–32.

———. "Reflections on the Postboom." *Review: Latin American Literatures and Arts* 52 (1996): 83–87.

———. *El género negro*. Mexico City: Universidad Autónoma Metropolitana, 1996.

———. *El país de las maravillas*. Buenos Aires: Planeta, 1998.

Gramsci, Antonio. "Sobre la novela policial," in *La novela criminal*, 2nd ed., ed. Román Gubern (pp. 17–25). Barcelona: Tusquets, 1982.

Gubern, Román, ed. *La novela criminal*, 2nd ed. Barcelona: Tusquets, 1982.

Hoopes, Ned. E. "Introduction," in *Harte of the West, 17 Stories by Bret Harte*. New York: Dell, 1966, 7–9.

MacShane, Frank. *The Life of Raymond Chandler*. New York: E. P. Dutton, 1976.

Marcos, Juan Manuel. *Roa Bastos: precursor del Postboom*. Mexico City: Katún, 1983.

———. *De García Márquez al Postboom*. Madrid: Editorial Orígenes, 1986.

Martini, Juan. "Prólogo," in *Dí adiós al mañana* (*Kiss Tomorrow Goodbye*), by Horace McCoy. Barcelona: Bruguera, 1977, 5–7.

———. "Prólogo," in *Luces de Hollywood* (*I Should Have Stayed Home*), by Horace McCoy. Barcelona: Bruguera, 1977, 5–7.

———. "Presentación: un punto de partida," in *Dinero sangriento* (*The Big Knockover*), by Dashiell Hammett, 3rd ed. Barcelona: Bruguera, 1981, 5–8.

Narcejac, Thomas. "La novela policial," in *La novela criminal*, 2nd ed., ed. Román Gubern (pp. 49–80). Barcelona: Tusquets, 1982. Original in French as "Le roman policier," in *Histoire des littératures*, 3 vols., ed. Raymond Queneau (3:1644–70). Paris: Gallimard, 1956–58.

Narcejac, Thomas, and Pierre Boileau. *La novela policial*. Buenos Aires: Paidós, 1968.

Piglia, Ricardo. "Introducción," in *Cinco relatos de la Serie Negra*. Buenos Aires: Centro Editor de América Latina, 1979, 1–14.

Soriano, Osvaldo. Interview with Ross Macdonald. *La Opinión* [Buenos Aires] (1974).

Tébar, Juan. "La epopeya de un continente," in *Historias del Viejo Oeste*. Madrid: Ediciones Doncel, 1972, 7–16.

Torre, Guillermo de. *Claves de la literatura hispanoamericana*. Buenos Aires: Losada, 1968.

Valdivieso, Jaime. *Realidad y ficción en Latinoamérica*. Mexico City: Joaquín Mortiz, 1975.

Yates, Donald A. "Introducción," in *El cuento policial latinoamericano*. Mexico City: Ediciones de Andrea, 1964, 5–13.

Latin American Mystery Writers

Alvaro Abós (b. 1941)

ARGENTINA

Born in Buenos Aires, Abós has lived there all his life except for during the period of military dictatorship (1976–1983) when he lived in exile in Barcelona. A lawyer by profession, in Spain he worked as a journalist. Upon returning to Argentina, he contributed to the periodicals *El periodista* (The journalist), *Página 12* (Page 12), *Humor*, and he was a correspondent for the Barcelona newspaper *La vanguardia*. He also wrote several articles on labor unions and politics: *La columna vertebral* (The spinal column, 1983) and *El posperonismo* (Post-Peronism, 1986). In his creative writing, two works of fiction stand out as detective novels: *Restos humanos* (Human remains, 1991) and *El simulacro* (The simulacrum, 1993), for which he won the Spanish "Premio Jaén de Novela" (Jaén Prize for the Novel). In *Restos humanos*, Abós made use of a real event, widely exploited in the sensationalist press at the time, as the basis for the story. In brief, in 1955 the bookie Jorge Burgos murdered and dismembered a domestic servant, Alcira Methyger, and in packages distributed her remains around different parts of Buenos Aires.

However, Abós is not interested in focusing on the descriptive realism or the mystery surrounding the case. On the contrary, he is concerned mainly with elaborating the narrative point of view, the polyphony structured around the obsessive discourse of the narrator-murderer and the multiple popular and populist discourses of the time: radio, press, and other media. The central story is filtered through a perverse subjectivity that clashes with the kitschy rhetoric fired off by the news media. The narrator-murderer faces off with the embodiment of the law—at a time when Argentina is experiencing the last days of the Peronist government—in the figure of police commissioner José Ramoncino. The two meet in a face-to-face situation, the end result of which is anticipated from the very beginning. In the real case, the investigator was the famous commissioner Evaristo Meneses, portrayed previously in the detective comics of the well-known Muñoz–Sampayo duo. Nevertheless, the aesthetic concern of Abós is far from being formal. The point of view and the careful attention paid to language charge the text with meaning that not only raises questions about society in a decisive moment for contemporary Argentina, but also about the meaning of violence that appears and reappears as a stigma, marking private and public destinies.

El simulacro, published two years later, appears as a work that is more straightforward in its language and narrative design—again, from the outset. Two different plots are intertwined in the novel: one woven around detective Remo Invernizzi's surveillance of an adulterous woman; the other retraces the last moments in the life of the Italian writer Cesare Pavese before he committed suicide in a hotel in Turin. In these two narratives strands there are several narrators who each complete and alter facts and versions of events.

Abós is not a detective writer per se—at least he doesn't exclusively write detective fiction or adhere strictly to the genre. However, detective elements function in his works as a catalyst that allows one to examine the ultimate role of literature and writing in our society. Literature serves as means of rescuing human values, to extract poetry that seemingly fades and is lost, to later return and burst with a charge of truth that, in the end, addresses the interpretation of the binary opposition good versus evil.

Néstor Ponce

Works

"El triángulo de la obsesión." *Clarín, Cultura y Nación* (18 August 1994): 12.
Restos humanos. Buenos Aires: Ediciones de La Urraca, 1994.
El simulacro. Buenos Aires: Sudamericana, 1993.

Criticism

Rivera, Jorge. "El caso Burgos: crimen y ficción." *Restos humanos*, by Alvaro Abós, 155–62.

∼

Isaac Aisemberg (1918–1997)

ARGENTINA

Isaac "Isito" Aisemberg (author, screenwriter, and journalist) was born in General Pico, La Pampa in January 1918. He lived in the cities of Córdoba, Buenos Aires, Santa Fe, and La Plata, where he began his law studies, and he soon joined a long list of Argentine writers who were also lawyers. He never actually practiced law because he didn't feel it was his true calling: "You'll be what you must be or you'll be a lawyer," he used to say. He began to write at a very early age and published his first novel when he was only 16.

His first incursion into the detective genre was the novel *Tres negativos para un retrato* (Three negatives for a portrait, 1949), which clearly shows his fondness for Arthur Conan Doyle and Sexton Blake, created by Harry Blyth. The novel was published upon the recommendation of Manuel Peyrou by the Acme Agency, which in the 1940s and 1950s was attempting to meet the high demand for pulp literature by commissioning authors to write such books, many times under English-sounding pseudonyms. For example, Juan Jacobo Bajarlía wrote under the name John Batharly, and Alejandro Ruiz Guiñazú used the laughable Alexander Rice Guinness. Aisemberg chose for himself the pen name W. I. Eisen, though he sometimes also used Ismael Montaña. The enormous popular success of detective fiction caused it to be considered a second-class literary endeavor. Authors resorted to using pen names in an effort to avoid tarnishing their reputation as "serious" writers. The publisher Acme, like Hachette, used to print about 15,000 copies of a title (a huge number). In Aisemberg's case, there were some 7,500 additional copies printed.

Some of his other novels include *La tragedia del cero* (The tragedy of the zero, 1952), *Crimen en el río* (Crime at the river, 1978), *No hay rosas en la tumba del marino* (There are no roses on the sailor's grave, 1984), and *Es más tarde de lo que crees* (It's later than you think, 1985). In 1993, he tried his hand at political fiction with the spy novel *La guerra del cuarto mundo* (The war of the fourth world). Aisemberg's writing is characterized by his direct style, unhampered by excess but rich in images and impact.

Aisemberg was the nephew of the famous filmmaker Luis Saslavsky, so he was afforded close ties to the film world. After training as a screenwriter with Alejandro Casona, he wrote numerous scripts, of which the most famous is perhaps the movie version of "Hombre de la esquina rosada" ("Street Corner Man"), Jorge Luis Borges's short story, which he created along with Joaquín Gómez Bas and Carlos Adén for the film directed by René Múgica in 1962. He won two Martín Fierro prizes for his work in television, which included adaptations of novels from the famous *El Séptimo Círculo* (The seventh circle) series—the detective fiction collection created and edited by Borges and Adolfo Bioy Casares. He also won the Premio de Honor de Argentores (the most prestigious award given by the Sociedad General de Autores de la Argentina [the Argentine writers guild], the association of which he later became president). He taught at the Círculo de la Prensa School of Journalism, at Universidad del Cuyo, and the Universidad del Salvador. At the time of his death in December 1997, he was the director of the Centro de Experimentación y Realización Cinematográfica (Center for film experimentation and production.)

Of Jewish origin, Aisemberg was converted to Catholicism by his friend and colleague Leonardo Castellani, who was a priest and author of detective fiction. He admitted that this fact was important to his intellectual activity because he began to read Catholic authors such as Gilbert K. Chesterton and Graham Greene, whose influence is apparent in his works. In a yet-unpublished interview I conducted with him a year before he died, he assured me: "I find a profound relationship between religion and detective literature. On one hand there is the mystery implied by death, while on the other there is self-determinism and the problem of guilt."

In addition to the above-mentioned mystery novels, which sought to provide something more than merely satisfying market demand, Aisemberg also proved to be a skilled short-story writer. In fact, one of his stories, "Jaque mate en dos jugadas" ("Checkmate in Two Moves"), has become a classic of Argentine detective fiction. Regarding the origins of this formidable work, the author claimed that the idea came to him while he was waiting for Manuel Peyrou at the library of the *La Prensa* newspaper. He was browsing through a book on legal medicine when he found a note about a poison called coninine, a derivative of nicotine. The story was first published in the magazine *Leoplán* where Rodolfo Walsh read it and later included it in his ground-breaking anthology *Diez cuentos policiales argentinos* (Ten Argentine detective stories, 1953). It has been translated into 19 languages and widely anthologized. However, it was finally published in one of Aisemberg's own books in 1994. *Jaque mate en dos jugadas y otros cuentos* (Checkmate in two moves and other stories) contains the title story and seven others such as "Los tiempos de Ramón Acuña" (The times of Ramón Acuña) and "Las campanas de Sobrero" (The bells of Sobrero). The latter text is dedicated to Cornell Woolrich and is closer to being a hard-boiled narrative than a whodunit. It narrates a disturbing situation within the context of the violent 1960s in Argentina.

Juan José Delaney

Works

Crimen en el río. Buenos Aires: Acme, 1978.
Es más tarde de lo que crees. Buenos Aires: Galerna, 1983.
La guerra del cuarto mundo. Buenos Aires: Corregidor, 1993.
"Jaque mate en dos jugadas," in *Diez cuentos policiales argentinos*, ed. Rodolfo Walsh. Buenos Aires: Hachette, 1953; *El cuento policial latinoamericano*, ed. Donald A. Yates. Mexico City: Ediciones de Andrea, 1964, 107–14. English version published as "Check-

mate in Two Moves," in *Latin Blood: The Best Crime and Detective Stories of South America*, ed. and trans. Donald A. Yates. New York: Herder & Herder, 1972, 201–9.

Jaque mate en dos jugadas y otros cuentos. Buenos Aires: Corregidor, 1994.

No hay rosas en la tumba del marino. Buenos Aires: Atlántida, 1984.

"Los tiempos de Ramón Acuña," in *Cuentos policiales argentinos*, ed. Jorge Lafforgue. Buenos Aires: Alfaguara, 1997, 215–27.

La tragedia del cero. Buenos Aires: Acme, 1952.

Tres negativos para un retrato. Buenos Aires: Acme, 1949.

Criticism

Lafforgue, Jorge, and Jorge B. Rivera. *Asesinos de papel: ensayos sobre narrativa policial*. Buenos Aires: Ediciones Colihue, 1996.

Francisco José Amparán (b. 1957)

MEXICO

Francisco José Amparán was born in Torreón, Coahuila in 1957. He is part of a growing number of authors who live outside Mexico City (the traditional literary and cultural center) and who are responsible for making detective fiction a national phenomenon. Amparán is the recipient of several literary awards, among them the Latin American Short-Story Prize (1983) and the National Literary Award for a short story (1986). His first books, which include the short-story collections *La luna y otros testigos* (The moon and other witnesses, 1984) and *Cantos de acción a distancia* (Songs of action from a distance, 1988)—are characterized by the author's ability to portray life with vivid detail, irony, and elements of the fantastic.

With the publication of *Algunos crímenes norteños* (Some northern crimes, 1992) Amparán became known on a national level as a detective fiction writer. The book contains three novellas titled "El caso del industrial busca tesoros" (The case of the treasure-hunting industrialist), "El caso del maduro malinchista" (The case of the mature traitor), and "El caso del joyero politizado" (The case of the political jeweler). They were all written in 1987 and follow the model of the puzzle-novel more than the conventions of hard-boiled detective fiction, which most contemporary writers prefer. The setting is in Torreón and the detective is not a hardened private-eye or cop but a young engineer and professor. With a notorious sense of humor and mocking characterization of the typical inhabitants of his hometown, Amparán creates an ingenious sociological portrayal of provincial life.

Three years later, Amparán published his second book that continues the adventures of Francisco Reyes Ibáñez, the engineer-investigator. The novel, titled *Otras caras del paraíso* (Other faces of paradise, 1995), revolves around the search for a young girl that leads to the uncovering of a world of corruption and dirty dealings. In spite of the central plot-argument, the novel is infused with the author's characteristic humor, an element of Amparán that makes his detective fiction unique. In 1997, the author published *Tríptico gótico* (Gothic tryptic), which contains three stories that all begin with simple daily acts that turn into nightmarish situations: the murder of a neighbor, a ghost that lops off peoples heads, and the effect of a Oaxacan witch on a group of credulous criminals.

Like Hugo Valdés in Monterrey and Gabriel Trujillo in Mexicali, Amparán is a detective fiction writer who grounds his literature in his geographic environment—northern Mexico—and in a time when the culture of the drug trade and political scandals are the order of the day. His narrative is born from this peripheral view, where the center (Mexico City) has ceased to impose its conditions on culture-making, including the noir mythology of the detective genre.

Gabriel Trujillo Muñoz

Works

Algunos crímenes norteños. Puebla: Universidad Autónoma de Puebla, Universidad Autónoma de Zacatecas, 1992.

Otras caras del paraíso. Monterrey: Castillo, 1995.

Tríptico gótico. Playas de Tijuana, Baja California: Ediciones Yoremito, 1997.

Criticism

Segura, Gerardo. "Hay que pelear cada quien en su trinchera: interrogatorio a Francisco Amparán," in *Todos somos culpables: entrevistas con escritores policiacos mexicanos*. Saltillo, Coahuila: Instituto Coahuilense de Cultura, 1996, 23–31.

Roberto Ampuero (b. 1953)

CHILE

Born in 1953 in Valparaíso, Chile, Ampuero spent the 1970s and 1980s in Cuba, in the former East Germany, and in West Germany. He worked as a journalist in Berlin and Bonn where he also published his collection of short stories *Un canguru en Bernau* (A kangaroo in Bernau, 1984) and his children's book, *La guerra de los duraznos* (The war of the peaches, 1986). Upon returning to Chile, he collaborated with the press and television as a scriptwriter for a detective series. His first detective novel *¿Quién mató a Cristián Kustermann?* (Who killed Cristián Kustermann, 1993) won a prize awarded by *El Mercurio* (The mercury) newspaper and was translated immediately into several languages. He later published *Boleros en La Habana* (Boleros in Havana, 1994) and *El alemán de Atacama* (The German of Atacama, 1996).

With Ampuero, the Chilean detective novel earned the recognition of both the reading public and the critics, thus opening up new opportunities to a narrative genre that has traditionally remained at the margins of the literary canon. The three above-mentioned novels all revolve around the character of Cayetano Brulé, a Cuban detective who lives in Valparaíso, and of his confidant and employee, the Japanese-Chilean Bernardo Suzuki. Ampuero's narrative is characterized by his subtle use of parody, his carefree yet stark style that reveals the influence of the hard-boiled detective tradition, and his inclusion of local color and humor that provides ample criticism of late-twentieth-century Chilean life. His clever use of kitsch adds to an ironic distancing effect and links the reader to the characters on the fringes of society who resist the official rhetoric of the government, the police, and the corrupt public officials. In *Boleros en La Habana*, Ampuero broadens his critical register as Cayetano Brulé conducts his investigations not only in Chile but also in Miami, and above all in Havana. Ampuero uses humor to demythify the Cuban Revolution, contrasting it with a no-less-alienating Chilean reality.

Brulé, the protagonist of Ampuero's detective novels, is in his fifties, short, stocky, bald, and near-sighted. He likes bright colors and the bohemian lifestyle; clearly he is nothing like the typical young, athletic superhero. It is precisely through these distinctive though rather degrading traits that the author creates an authentic character the reader can relate to. As Ampuero states in an interview, "Lo único que no podía tener una novela policial chilena era un detective a lo James Bond" (The only thing a Chilean detective novel could not have is a James Bond–like detective [García-Corales 133]). However, the image of the superhero is not the only thing Brulé contradicts. The detective also opposes what he considers to be evil in general (drug-trafficking, and corruption for example). He is also, in a certain sense, in opposition to Chile itself, since he is a foreigner and thus represents the contrast between a series of value-charged dichotomies: hardship vs. opulence, emotion vs. coldness, loyalty vs. betrayal, and so on. He offers a picture of Latin American and European (German) societies through a narrative strategy that doesn't "limitarse al experimento de tipo deductivo o inductivo, sino mostrar un poco el espacio social dentro del cual se está moviendo la intriga" (limit itself to deductive or inductive experiments, but to show the social space in which the intrigue is taking place [Cárdenas 1995, 4]). At the same time he tries to do so "sin imponerle determinadas visiones al lector" (without imposing certain points of view on the reader [García-Corales 134]).

Néstor Ponce

Works

El alemán de Atacama. Santiago: Planeta Biblioteca del Sur, 1994.
Boleros en La Habana. Santiago: Planeta Biblioteca del Sur, 1994.
Un cangurú en Bernau. Berlin: Aufban Verlag, 1984.
La guerra de los duraznos. Berlin: Kinderbuchverlag, 1986.
¿Quién mató a Cristián Kustermann? Santiago: Planeta Biblioteca del Sur, 1993.

Criticism

Cárdenas, María Teresa. "Roberto Ampuero: 'Cayetano Brulé, el detective, me ganó.'" *El Mercurio, Revista de libros* 231 (3 October 1993): 1, 4–5. (Interview.)
———. "Roberto Ampuero: 'Me interesa ser entretenido.'" *El Mercurio, Revista de libros* 296 (8 January 1995): 1, 4–5. (Interview.)
Covarrubias Claro, María de los Ángeles. "Cuentos que se dictan solos." *El Mercurio, Artes y libros* (22 January 1995).
García-Corales, Guillermo. "La novela policial y la narrativa chilena de los noventa: una conversación con Roberto Ampuero." *Cuadernos Angers-La Plata* 2 (1998): 129–39.
I.P. "New Mystery Writers: Chile's Roberto Ampuero." *Buenos Aires Herald* (28 February 1995): 8.
Moody, Michael. "Roberto Ampuero y la novela negra, una entrevista." *Confluencia: revista hispánica de cultura y literatura* 15.1 (1999): 127–41.
Schenke, Josefina. "Quiero embrujar al lector." *Las últimas noticias* [Santiago] (29 January 1995). (Interview.)
Soto, Marcelo. "Intriga internacional." *Qué Pasa* [Santiago] (26 February 1994): 44.
Vargas Saavedra, Luis. "Roberto Ampuero, maestro del misterio." *El Mercurio, Revista de libros* 296 (8 January 1995): 5.

Enrique Anderson Imbert (1910–2000)

ARGENTINA

Enrique Anderson Imbert was born on 12 February 1910 in Córdoba, Argentina. He studied in La Plata before attending the University of Buenos Aires, where he received his Ph.D. in literature and philosophy under the direction of the famous literary critics Amado Alonso and Pedro Henríquez Ureña. He worked as a journalist and taught at several universities in Argentina before emigrating to the United States, where he taught at Michigan State University from 1947 to 1965. In 1965, Harvard University created a special chair for him and he remained there until 1980. Anderson Imbert was a prolific scholar of Latin American literature, publishing more than 20 books on the subject. Likewise, he was a productive literary author who wrote four novels and 13 collections of short stories. The majority of his works have been translated into English. Among his many stories are a handful that may be classified as detective fiction, at least one of which has become a classic. His detective fiction is modeled after the classic tradition of the puzzle-narrative, in which the author focuses on the intellectual game of solving a mystery through logic and reasoning. In this sense, his detective stories are similar to those of Jorge Luis Borges and Adolfo Bioy Casares.

Anderson Imbert's best-known detective tale is "El general hace un lindo cadáver" ("The General Makes a Lovely Corpse"), originally published in *El grimorio* (*The Other Side of the Mirror*, 1961). The story is a well-constructed satire of Peronism in Argentina. Again, this makes it similar to the kind of project Borges and Bioy Casares undertook in their *Seis problemas para don Isidro Parodi* (*Six Problems for Don Isidro Parodi*, 1942). There are numerous allusions to Perón throughout the text. Both Andrés Avellaneda and Amelia Simpson examine Anderson Imbert's story in this light. Typical of the author's style, the story is imbued with a good deal of irony and tinges of a clever but dark humor.

Another of Anderson Imbert's readily recognized detective stories is "Al rompecabezas le falta una pieza" (The puzzle's missing a piece), from *La botella de Klein* (Klein's bottle, 1975). What is interesting about this story, aside from its obvious entertainment, are the references included in the text. On the one hand, there are direct references to the famous detective characters Sherlock Holmes and Auguste Dupin as well as the premise of the story that Bolívar was the first American detective; on the other, is the main character, Harold Yates, a history professor from the United States, which is a fairly clear allusion to Donald Yates, the professor of Latin American literature and specialist in detective fiction, who knew Anderson Imbert very well at Michigan State.

A series of other stories that fit the detective model include "La bala cansada" (The tired bullet; *El grimorio*), "El detective" (The detective) and "El crimen perfecto" (The perfect crime) from *El gato de Cheshire* (*Cage with Only One Side*, 1965), "Francamente, no" (Frankly, no) and "Novela al revés" (Backward novel) from *La sandía y otros cuentos* (The watermelon and other stories, 1969), and "Murder" and "Novela que cambia de género" (Novel that changes genre) from *La locura juega al ajedrez* (Madness plays at chess, 1971). While, in general, Anderson Imbert's works have received a significant amount of critical attention, his detective fiction, as such, has to date not been adequately studied.

Darrell B. Lockhart

Works

"Al rompecabezas le falta una pieza," in *Cuentos policiales*, ed. Fermín Fevre. Buenos Aires: Kapelusz, 1974, 110–23.

La botella de Klein. Buenos Aires: P.E.N. Club Internacional, Centro Argentino, 1975.

El gato de Cheshire. Buenos Aires: Losada, 1965. English version published as *Cage with Only One Side*, trans. Isabel Reade. Reno, NV: West Coast Poetry Review, 1967.

"The General Makes a Lovely Corpse," trans. Isabel Reade, in *Latin Blood: The Best Crime and Detective Stories of South America*, ed. Donald A. Yates. New York: Herder & Herder, 1972, 149–72.

El grimorio. Buenos Aires: Losada, 1961. English version published as *The Other Side of the Mirror*, trans. Isabel Reade. Carbondale, IL: Southern Illinois University Press, 1966.

El leve Pedro. Madrid: Alianza, 1976. (Anthology of collected stories.)

La locura juega al ajedrez. Mexico City: Siglo XXI, 1971.

El milagro y otros cuentos. Buenos Aires: Kapelusz, 1985.

Narraciones completas, 6 vols. Buenos Aires: Corregidor, 1990–1999.

La sandía y otros cuentos. Buenos Aires: Galerna, 1969.

Woven on the Loom of Time, trans. Carlton Vail and Pamela Edwards-Mondragón, introduction by Ester de Izaguirre. Austin: University of Texas Press, 1990. (Anthology of stories from six different books.)

Criticism

Arancibia, Juana Alcira, ed. *Homenaje a Enrique Anderson Imbert*, special issue of *Alba de América* 18.33-34 (1999).

Avellaneda, Andrés. "Enrique Anderson Imbert: refutación y práctica del compromiso," in *El habla de la ideología*. Buenos Aires: Sudamericana, 1983, 170–207.

Azzario, Esther A., "La dialéctica creadora de Enrique Anderson Imbert en *La locura juega al ajedrez y La botella de Klein*." *Revista de estudios hispánicos* 16.3 (1982): 443–52.

Baker, Armand F. "La visión del mundo en los cuentos de Enrique Anderson Imbert." *Revista iberoamericana* 42 (1976): 497–516.

Coope, Marian G. R. "Autopsia del 'Lindo cadáver' de Enrique Anderson Imbert: divagaciones detectivescas alrededor de un 'whodunit' latinoamericano." *Explicación de textos literarios* 19.1 (1990–1991): 59–70.

Simpson, Amelia S. *Detective Fiction from Latin America*. Rutherford, NJ: Fairleigh Dickinson University Press, 1990, 131–34.

Roberto Arlt (1900–1942)

ARGENTINA

Roberto Godofredo Christophersen Arlt was born in Buenos Aires in 1900. His parents were both immigrants—his father from Germany and his mother from Trieste, Italy—who contributed to Argentina's surge in population at the turn of the nineteenth century. A tense relationship with his domineering father led Arlt to leave home at age 16. He likewise had to abandon his studies to work at an array of odd jobs, but he never put aside his interest in writing. In 1922, he married Carmen Antinucci in spite of her parents' objections. From this union their daughter, Mirta, was born a year later. His wife died in 1940 and the following year Arlt married Elizabeth Shine. In 1927, he worked for the newspaper *Crítica* (Critique), where he reported crime stories. A year later he moved to *El mundo* (The globe), where he published his famous short pieces known as *Aguasfuertes porteñas* (Buenos Aires etchings) until the time of his death. Arlt was a professional writer. He made a living from writing and found in the bustling publication industry of the time a steady source of work. In addition to the previously mentioned publications, Arlt also wrote for *La estrella* (The star), *Izquierda* (Left), *Ultima hora* (Last hour), *Don Goyo*, *Claridad* (Clarity), *Bandera roja* (Red flag), and *Argentina libre* (Free Argentina), among others.

Alongside his labors in journalism, Arlt cultivated and renovated both narrative and dramatic works. He was a master at writing about the urban experience and was among the first to do so in Latin American literature. Among his most well-known works are his novels *Los siete locos* (*The Seven Madmen*, 1929) and *Los lanzallamas* (The flame throwers, 1931), and his collection of short stories, *El jorobadito* (The little hunchback, 1933). Among his many plays, those that stand out are *Saverio el cruel* (Saverio the cruel, 1936), *El fabricante de fantasmas* (The ghost manufacturer, 1936), *La isla desierta* (The deserted island, 1937), and *La fiesta del hierro* (Celebration of iron, 1940). As a foreign correspondent, Arlt made trips to Uruguay, Brazil, Spain, and Chile. The precarious financial situation in which he always lived caused him to tinker with invention and experimentation in search of a "money-maker." The events of his own life are reflected in the sordid and chaotic representation of the modern city in his works. Arlt died of a heart attack on 26 July 1942.

Certain themes and discursive devices recurrent in much of Arlt's work can be found in his detective fiction. For example, the presentation of conflicts that lead to the polarization between the dominant and the dominated. These conflicts arise for reasons of money, love, and power and assume distinct characteristics between a man and a woman, given the presence of latent machista ideology. Crime and ingenuity are also commonly used as a means of ascending the social scale. There is frequent emphasis placed on the physical appearance of characters and the peculiarities of their bodies. Arlt constantly employs a surprise ending, and his writing is characteristically infused with a mixture of formal language and street slang. His sources of inspiration cover a wide range, from adventure novels and "penny dreadfuls" to television and film. Although somewhat toned down, the exaggeration and sensationalism of his crime reporting can be perceived in his short stories. Arlt combines traits of mystery writing and those of the hard-boiled novel with corresponding doses of violence and even parody. Indeed, through his use of parody he directly alludes to the detective genre as a literary device. The story "El crimen casi perfecto" (The almost perfect crime) is described as "una fantasía de novela policial" (a detective novel fantasy [*El crimen casi perfecto*, 105]), and in "Noche terrible" (Terrible night) one of the characters reads the novels of Edgar Wallace. In this last story, the crime committed is the abandonment of the bride just hours before the wedding. In other cases, the omniscient narrator offers too much information, as happens in "La pista de los dientes de oro" (The clue of the golden teeth) or "Un argentino entre gangsters" (An Argentine among gangsters). While in the classic detective novel emphasis is placed on the keen use of intelligence, in some of Arlt's stories the reasoning is naive and obvious, as in "El enigma de las tres cartas" (The enigma of the three letters) and "El crimen casi perfecto." In this last story, important clues are overlooked. On occasion, fantastic hypotheses are put forth to explain the crime. For example, the presumed guilt of an invisible man in "El misterio de los tres sobretodos" (The mystery of the three overcoats) or the intervention of a *deus ex machina* to solve the crime as is the case in "El enigma de las tres cartas."

Similarly, Arlt throughout his work deforms or animalizes his characters, often ridiculing them. This ridicule can play a major role in the text, overshadowing the solution of the mystery as in "El bastón de la muerte" (The cane of death). Another story that exemplifies this is "La pluma de ganso" (The goose feather) in which one of the characters is killed by making him laugh to death, tickling his feet with a goose feather. Arlt breaks with the majority of rules that govern the detective genre according to Jorge Luis Borges and Adolfo Bioy Casares (Lafforgue and Rivera 1996, 249–50) or S. S. Van Dine (pseudonym of Willard H. Wright) (Lafforgue and Rivera, 1996 261–62). Arlt does not seem to be concerned with creating a credible story.

Likewise, in many stories he deviates from strictly detective conventions and inserts other elements such as the fantastic in "El traje del fantasma" (The ghost's suit); psychological searching in "La jugada" (The play); the adventure tale in "La doble trampa mortal" (The double death trap); the romantic in "La pista de los dientes de oro"; and the supernatural in "El bastón de la muerte." In these texts, Arlt employs detective elements to sustain different types of discourse. In this sense, they can be classified as "false" detective stories.

Some of Arlt's recurrent motifs are condensed in "El misterio de los tres sobretodos." A series of petty thefts at a clothing store has the personnel in a state of alarm. The employees—who are poor and exploited—know that the guilty party is one of their own. A young girl, Ernestina, discovers the thief, but she does so by killing him. In other words, the detective is also the killer and her crime goes unpunished. Only she, the narrator—and on another level, the reader—know what happened. The narrator, who although he is a character has certain omniscient qualities, reconstructs the events as they were told to him, failing to mention that the only one who could have told him the secret to the story is Ernestina herself. A crucial detail in the mystery is the fact that the thief was missing a leg. Caricaturized as rats, the characters reveal the misery of the exploited worker in large cities.

In "Un argentino entre gangsters" a symbolic rivalry between Argentina—and by extension South America—and the United States, where the story takes place, is presented. A band of mafiosos kidnap an Argentine engineering student and ask him to invent a rigged roulette. In the end, the student's intelligence triumphs over the brute force of the gangsters, who are the Yankee versions of the protagonists in "Las fieras" (The wild beasts).

In Arlt, the conventions of detective fiction are a tool at the service of other themes and intentions removed from the genre. Even in the texts that seem more orthodox—"El crimen casi perfecto," "El enigma de las tres cartas"—Arlt distances himself from the detective genre. But in this, only purist readers would feel deceived.

Critical focus on Arlt's detective fiction is relatively new. Omar Borré, in his edition of Arlt's previously unpublished stories *"Estoy cargado de muerte" y otros borradores* (I am burdened by death and other drafts, 1984) included texts such as "Debajo del agua" (Under water), "La fuga" (The escape), "La jugada," and "Un error judicial" (A judicial error) that could be considered as belonging to the genre. Ten years later, Borré edited the volume *El crimen casi perfecto* (1994) that contains another eight stories that were previously unpublished. This volume was also published in Uruguay—minus "El bastón de la muerte"—under the title, *Un argentino entre gangsters*.

Domingo Luis Hernández's compilation *Narrativa corta completa* (Complete short narratives, 1995), and in particular volume 2, contains texts not previously compiled and broadens Arlt's detective fiction corpus under a section titled "Lo policíaco" (Detective stories). Stories under this heading include "El incendiario" (The arsonist) "La pluma de ganso," and "Jabulgot el Farsante" (Jabulgot the fake). Hernández also compiled texts that are more closely related to Arlt's crime chronicles and *Aguasfuertes*, under the generic heading "Otras prosas" (Other prose), which were originally published in *Don Goyo*. Among these texts, the ones that stand out are "El dinamitero" (The dynamite technician), "Epístola de un L.C. erudito al Jefe de Policía" (Letter of an erudite L.C. to the police chief), and "Nuestra policía, la mejor del mundo" (Our police, the best in the world).

Omar Borré and Ricardo Piglia filled a critical void by publishing Arlt's *Cuentos completos* (Complete short stories, 1996). Arranged chronologically, the volume contains detective stories such as "El resorte secreto" (The secret lever), "Espionaje" (Espionage), and "La venganza del médico" (The doctor's revenge), to name just a few. One could add to this list a few stories from *El jorobadito* such as "El traje del fantasma," "Las fieras," and "Noche terrible."

Compared with the critical studies of his work in general, analyses of his detective fiction are few and far between. Ricardo Piglia was one of the first to identify in Arlt's work a relationship to crime, embezzlement, robbery, and forgery (Piglia 1975, 136). He has written rather extensively on Arlt's detective fiction, making some interesting observations on the characteristics of the author's writing. In his "Homenaje a Roberto Arlt" (Homage to Roberto Arlt), Piglia manages to creatively fuse his own discourse with Arlt's together with criticism, literature, reality, and fiction.

Borré, in "Noticia" (Notes), seems to concur with Piglia by identifying robbery, crime, and informing as constant themes in Arlt's work, topics that provide fertile ground for the development of detective narratives. Borré points out Arlt's preference for action literature and its obvious relationship with hard-boiled and suspense novels. He also emphasizes the carelessness of critics who have overlooked the detective genre elements in Arlt's writing, and above all, the parodic aspects of this type of text (Borré 114–15).

Another approach taken by critics is to analyze Arlt's writing in relation to Borges and his own theories and texts on detective writing, particularly the classic puzzle-novel model (Rocca). Jorge B. Rivera, on the other hand, points to the popular-literature influences on Arlt, such as mass-market publications and pulp magazines that published adventure, suspense, and detective stories ("Arlt y el género policial"). As one can see, the detective genre elements in Arlt's work comprise an open field for investigation. The relationship of Arlt's detective fiction to the rest of his work and his place within Argentine detective fiction are but a few topics for study that could contribute to a better undertanding of the mysteries that still shroud the singularly original work of this writer.

José Alberto Bravo de Rueda

Works

Un argentino entre gangsters: cuentos policiales. Montevideo: Lectores de Banda Oriental, 1994.

Cuentos completos, 2nd ed., Ricardo Piglia and Omar Borré. Buenos Aires: Seix Barral-Espasa Calpe, 1996.

El crimen casi perfecto, ed. Omar Borré. Buenos Aires: Clarín/Aguilar, 1994.

El jorobadito. Buenos Aires: Espacio, 1993.

"Estoy cargado de muerte" y otros borradores, ed. Omar Borré. Buenos Aires: Torres Agüero, 1984.

Narrativa corta completa, 2 vols., ed. Domingo Luis Hernández. Canarias: Universidad de la Laguna, 1995.

Criticism

Borré, Omar. "Noticia," in *El crimen casi perfecto*, by Roberto Arlt, 109–15.

———. *Roberto Arlt: su vida y su obra*. Buenos Aires: Planeta, 1999.

Hernández, Domingo Luis. "Lo policiaco," in *Roberto Arlt, la sombra pronunciada*. Canarias: Universidad de la Laguna, 1995, 297–300.

Lafforgue, Jorge, and Jorge B. Rivera, eds. *Asesinos de papel: ensayos sobre narrativa policial.* Buenos Aires: Colihue, 1996.

Piglia, Ricardo. "Homenaje a Roberto Arlt," in *Nombre falso.* Buenos Aires: Siglo Veinte, 1975, 97–172.

———. "Sobre el género policial," in *Crítica y ficción.* Buenos Aires: Siglo Veinte-Universidad Nacional del Litoral, 1990, 111–17.

———. "Sobre Roberto Arlt," in *Crítica y ficción.* Buenos Aires: Siglo Veinte-Universidad Nacional del Litoral, 1990, 27–38.

———. "Prólogo," in *Las fieras: Arlt, Borges y otros*, ed. Ricardo Piglia. Buenos Aires: Clarín/Aguilar, 1993, 7–11.

Ponce, Néstor. *Diagonales del género: estudios sobre el policial argentino.* Paris: Editions du Temp, 2001.

Rivera, Jorge B. "Arlt y el género policial," in Jorge Lafforgue and Jorge B. Rivera, 137–40.

Rocca, Pablo. "Otro Arlt, idéntico a sí mismo." Prologue to *Un argentino entre gangsters: cuentos policiales*, by Roberto Arlt. Montevideo: Lectores de Banda Oriental, 1994, 7–12.

Saítta, Sylvia. *El escritor en el bosque de ladrillos. Una biografía de Roberto Arlt.* Buenos Aires, Sudamericana, 2000.

~

Velmiro Ayala Gauna (1905–1967)

ARGENTINA

Velmiro Ayala Gauna was born in the northern Argentine province of Corrientes. He worked for many years as a primary and secondary school teacher in Corrientes and Rosario, Santa Fe, where he also contributed to the periodical *La diligencia* (Diligence). He is primarily remembered as a regionalist writer whose literature—prose narrative and essay—focused on themes related to the rural provinces of Corrientes, Chaco, and Santa Fe. His writing documents in fastidious, folkloric detail life along the Paraná River, with a concentration on portraying the regional landscape, which he felt to be the essence of the national character.

He wrote two collections of short stories that stand out within his varied literary production as singular contributions to the detective genre in Argentina. His *Los casos de don Frutos Gómez* (The cases of Don Frutos Gómez, 1953) and *Don Frutos Gómez, el comisario* (Don Frutos Gómez, commissary, 1960) are unique in their approach and treatment of the detective model. The protagonist in the series, the rural commissary Frutos Gómez, works in Capibara-Cué, an imaginary small town in the northeastern province of Corrientes. The originality of Ayala Gauna's texts lies in the confluence of two systems of textual organization: the conventions of detective fiction, and his characteristic regionalism. The author injects the classic detective model with the mythemes of local folktales, the result of which is a constant challenge to the verisimilitude of circumstances, with a good deal of parody infused as well. Frutos Gómez serves as principal vehicle through which regional *criollismo* (rural native) values are expressed—values such as courage, *picardía* (craftiness), and generosity, which stand in stark contrast to big-city values that are always viewed in negative terms. This is also communicated symbolically through the town of Capibara-Cué that proudly displays its indigenous Guaraní origins—the complete opposite of the urban cosmopolitanism of Buenos Aires. Regional characters abound in the stories as archetypes used to illustrate provincial life: the rural school teacher, the Paraguayan exile, immigrants of all kind. These characters act as parodies, producing a distancing effect that underscores the conflicts among them. Humor and raillery generate a kind of carnavalization of situations marked by *quid pro quo* behavior, misunderstandings, and the exaggeration of traits and reactions. Marginalized for many years, Velmiro Ayala Gauna's work merits closer attention from critics and literary historians.

Néstor Ponce

Works

Los casos de don Frutos Gómez. Santa Fe, Argentina: Castellví, 1953. Reprint, Buenos Aires: Centro Editor de América Latina, 1967.

Don Frutos Gómez, el comisario. Rosario, Argentina: Hormiga, 1960.

"Early Morning Murder," in *Latin Blood: The Best Crime and Detective Stories of South America*, ed. Donald A. Yates. New York: Herder & Herder, 1972, 51–61.

"La justicia de don Frutos," in *El cuento policial argentino*, ed. Elena Braceras, Cristina Leytour, and Susana Pittella. Buenos Aires: Plus Ultra, 1986, 125–34.

"La pesquisa de don Frutos," in *Cuentos policiales argentinos*, ed. Jorge Lafforgue. Buenos Aires: Alfaguara, 1997, 181–91.

Criticism

Braceras, Elena, Cristina Leytour, and Susana Pitella. "Análisis de los elementos narrativos en 'La justicia de don Frutos' de V. Ayala Gauna," in *El cuento policial argentino*. Buenos Aires: Plus Ultra, 1986, 213–19.

Lafforgue, Jorge, and Jorge B. Rivera. *Asesinos de papel: ensayos sobre narrativa policial*. Buenos Aires: Colihue, 1996.

Ponce, Néstor. *Diagonales del género: estudios sobre el policial argentino*. Paris: Editions du Temps, 2001.

Vicente Battista (b. 1940)

ARGENTINA

Vicente Battista was born in Buenos Aires in 1940. His father, a carpenter, instilled in him a spirit of learning, although he wasn't particularly devoted to books himself. This led to Battista's vast and varied readings in his youth in the popular socialist library of Barracas, his neighborhood. Here he read Miguel de Cervantes, and translations of William Shakespeare, Jules Verne, Emilio Salgari, Jack London, and his beloved Mark Twain. These readings caused him to stray from the accounting studies he was taking in high school and decidedly take up literature. He then went on to study journalism in Buenos Aires. Beginning in 1961, he was on the editorial board of the literary magazine *El escarabajo de oro* (The golden scarab), together with the writer Abelardo Castillo. In 1970, with Gerardo Mario Goloboff, he founded and directed *Nuevos Aires* (New airs), a journal of fiction and critical thought.

His first published book was a collection of short stories titled *Los muertos* (The dead, 1968), which a year previously had been awarded the Cuban *Casa de las Américas* (House of the Americas) prize and National Fund of the Arts prize in Argentina. The recurring theme in the stories is that of betrayal, either private, as is the case in "El Bocha, le dicen" (They call him El Bocha), or political, as in "Esta noche, reunión en casa" (Tonight, a meeting at home). This story provides the title for his following book, also called *Esta noche, reunión en casa* (1973), which combines five stories already published in the previous volume with new ones. The story "Guillermo, él y una pared blanca y lisa" (Guillermo, him and a smooth white wall) describes a relationship of power in an almost phantasmagoric way. In "Mañana en Tribunales" (Tomorrow in Court), the protagonist, Enrique Alberto Barragán, attempts an impossible suicide. In 1972, Battista wrote the script of the movie *La familia unida esperando la llegada de Hallewyn* (The united family awaiting the arrival of Hallewyn), directed by Miguel Bejo, where political topics are mixed with the absurd. This film received the Grand Prize in the Festival at Manheinn, Germany. In 1973, he was invited to travel to Spain in order to pursue more screenwriting. Although he didn't create a single script he wrote two novels and remained in Spain for 11 years. During this time he lived in Barcelona and Las Palmas (Gran Canaria). In 1984, he returned to Buenos Aires, where he currently resides.

In Barcelona, Battista published *Como tanta gente que anda por ahí* (Like so many people who roam around, 1975), which brings together the stories of his two previous books and adds one new one, "La traición de Sandokán" (Sandokan's treason). This story shares elements of intertextuality with his first novel, *El libro de todos los engaños* (The complete book of tricks, 1984). In the novel, Battista parodies the modern detective genre as the mystery plot unfolds. The case revolves around the search for a mysterious volume known as *La Cátedra* (The cathedra), a book said to contain the real history of the world, and is considered as scripture by a religious sect led by Brother Silvio, who is the Universal Regenerator and Savior of the Sacred Worlds in Ascension. The protagonist of the novel is an Argentine exile who lives in Barcelona, although the narration of urban space clearly refers to Buenos Aires. False clues, chases, and useless information compose the narration, which contains traits of the hard-boiled mode.

A second novel, *Siroco* (Sirocco, 1985), adheres more strictly to the conventions of the hard-boiled detective novel. It is a story of fraud set in the Canary Islands in which the protagonist, who lives in Barcelona, is involved in a world of murder, violence, and the absence of morals. The character named Jordi—a friend of the protagonist—also appeared in *El libro de todos los engaños*. In the relationship between him and the protagonist, which is based on the classic model of two counterpart detectives, Jordi is the one who offers a pragmatic view to the investigation.

Battista returned to the publication of short stories with *El final de la calle* (The end of the street, 1992), which earned him the Municipal Award of Literature. The stories are divided into three sections titled "Sucesos argentinos" (Argentine events), "Coartada" (Alibi), and "Había una vez" (Once upon a time). The level of suspense builds as the stories progress, particularly in the second and third sections. In "Estaba escrito" (It was written), there is an intertextual game involving Dashiell Hammett's and Ross Macdonald's characters, Sam Spade and Lew Archer, respectively, whereas "Como absolutamente nada en el mundo" (Like absolutely nothing else in the world) treats the subject of the disappeared during the last Argentine military government.

He reached a crowning point in his career when he was awarded the Planeta Literary Prize in 1995 for his novel *Sucesos argentinos* (Argentine events, 1995). The protagonist is the same character as in *Siroco* and the novel is structured on autobiographical information and references to Argentine history relative to the period of military rule known as the Process of National Reorganization (1976–1983). The story focuses on the dirty business dealings involved in the construction of a new highway that intersects Buenos Aires. The main character (the same narrator-protagonist as in *Siroco*) is the Argentine representative of a Spanish corporation who travels from Barcelona, his place of residence, to Buenos Aires, after a long absence from his country. In this novel, corruption and murder set the violent tone—a constant in Battista's texts.

Battista's carefully crafted prose highlights the topic of deceit. Already apparent in his first book, he has developed the theme with increasing intensity throughout his works. Deceit, dishonesty, and dirty dealing go from the individual to the public level, reaching a point of maximum expression in his final novel. Furthermore, the topic of exile, in both its external and internal manifestations, opens up possible avenues of exploration for which the conventions of the hard-boiled novel, cast in its uniquely Argentine form, are especially well-suited.

María Alejandra Rosarossa

Works

"Caminaré en tu sangre," in *Escritos con sangre: cuentos argentinos sobre casos policiales*, ed. Sergio S. Olguín. Buenos Aires: Norma, 2003, 35–77.

Como tanta gente que anda por ahí. Prólogo de Noé Jitrik. Barcelona: Planeta, 1975.

Esta noche, reunión en casa. Buenos Aires: Centro Editor de América Latina, 1973.

El final de la calle. Buenos Aires: Emecé, 1992.

"Frente de tormenta," in *Cuentos policiales argentinos*, ed. Jorge Lafforgue. Buenos Aires: Alfaguara, 1997, 351–62.

El libro de todos los engaños. Barcelona: Bruguera, 1984.

Los muertos. Buenos Aires: Jorge Alvarez, 1968.

Siroco. Buenos Aires, Legasa, 1985. Reprint, Buenos Aires: Emecé, 1994.

Sucesos argentinos. Buenos Aires, Planeta, 1995.

Criticism

Gallone, Osvaldo. "Del texto policial hacia adelante: Originalidad de Vicente Battista." *El país cultural* (Montevideo) 166 (1993): 11.

Goloboff, Mario. "Review of Sucesos argentinos." *Cuadernos hispanoamericanos* 553–554 (1996): 287–88.

Graña, Rolando. "El thriller de las autopistas." *Página 12* (Buenos Aires) (15 September 1995): 28–29. (Interview.)

Malinov, Inés. "Las vacas gordas de Vicente Battista." *Suplemento literario de La Nación* (Buenos Aires) (24 September 1994): 2.

Russo, Miguel. "Escribir es un trabajo muy laborioso, que lleva mucho tiempo." *La Maga* (Buenos Aires) (20 September 1995): 17. (Interview.)

Serra, Alfredo. "La Argentina es una novela negra." *Revista Gente* (Buenos Aires) (28 September 1995): 70–71. (Interview.)

María Elvira Bermúdez (1916–1988)

MEXICO

María Elvira Bermúdez was one of the founders of the Mexican detective story. During her lifetime, she was the most prolific female detective fiction author in the Spanish-speaking world, one of the most innovative practitioners of the genre in Mexico and one of its most perceptive critics. Bermúdez also created the first female detective in Spanish American literature in three highly entertaining stories in which the unflappable María Elena Morán, *la detective*, solves crimes in a style very much her own.

Born in Durango, Durango, on November 27, 1916, María Elvira Bermúdez resided for most of her life in Mexico City. Receiving her law degree in 1939, she eventually served for many years as counsel to the Mexican Supreme Court, a job that afforded her many opportunities to learn firsthand about the machinations of the criminal mind and those of the Mexican legal system. In 1947, with the financial help of lawyer friend—a fan of the detective genre and later president of Mexico, Adolfo López Mateos—Bermúdez published the most ambitious detective novel up to that time in Mexico, *Diferentes razones tiene la muerte* (Death has different reasons, 1947). She was extremely knowledgeable about literature in general, and about the detective genre in particular. In the introduction to her 1955 anthology of detective fiction, *Los mejores cuentos policíacos mexicanos* (The best Mexican detective stories, 1955), she reveals an acute awareness of the history of detective fiction, from Edgar Allan Poe to Arthur Conan Doyle to Maurice Leblanc. This anthology was the first, and for many years the only, compilation dedicated exclusively to Mexican detective literature. She continued to write detective fiction during the succeeding 40 years of her life, publishing two short-story collections, *Detente, sombra* (Wait, shadow, 1961) and *Muerte a la zaga* (Death follows, 1985), but she also wrote stories of fantasy and mystery, numerous essays of literary criticism (authoring several prologues for Porrúa's *Sepan cuantos* . . . literary series) as well as a sociological essay, *La vida familiar del mexicano* (Family life of the Mexicans, 1955), which explores, among other things, gender roles in Mexican familial life. A feminist long before it was commonplace, María Elvira Bermúdez was for 50 years a unique voice in Spanish American detective fiction and criticism. Her contribution to detective fiction can generally be divided into two categories: her Armando H. Zozaya novel and stories, and her María Elena Morán stories.

Modeled after the American sleuth Ellery Queen, Armando H. Zozaya is an honest, logical journalist who first appears in Bermúdez's novel *Diferentes razones tiene la muerte*. Unlike his American counterpart, however, Zozaya makes his precise deductions in settings that are authentically Mexican: a village in Coyoacán, a street in the Roma colony, a Mexico City bus, Insurgentes Avenue, and many others. In *Diferentes razones*, Zozaya investigates two murders that have occurred at a gathering of the friends of Georgina Llorente's deceased husband. Zozaya solves the crime methodically, examining clues and fingerprints. Bermúdez usually adheres to the traditional "chess-problem" type of detective story. An interesting aspect of her works is the strength of her female characters. In this case, Georgina is an inveterate reader of detective fiction who is in many ways just as astute as Zozaya. In another Zozaya story, "El embrollo del reloj" ("The Puzzle of the Broken Watch," 1972), it is an acutely perceptive young girl, Rosita—not Zozaya—who notices that the incriminating broken watch does not belong to the accused, since its wristband is missing an extra hole for the pin of the clasp.

Bermúdez's first female detective story, "Detente, sombra," was published in 1961. Not one to do anything by halves, Bermúdez not only created the first female detective in Spanish American literature in this story, she also made its entire cast of a dozen or so characters women: the victim is a lesbian writer; the innocent, imprisoned suspect is a feminist literary critic; the judges, lawyers, and politicians are women who belong to the Union of Women; there is even a female taxi driver—an idea that is far ahead of its time even in today's Mexico. The detective, María Elena Morán, is an avid writer and reader of detective fiction. She is from Torreón and is widely respected for her sleuthing skills, having already solved a number of cases in Chihuahua and Mexico City. Obviously, this story—with the first female detective and an all-female cast—may be considered a self-consciously feminist detective story. Following Elaine Showalter's three stages of women's writing, it is simultaneously an imitation of a male literary model, a protest of patriarchal structures, and a discovery of the female self. María Elena Morán deduces the identity of the murderess by imitating the customary methods. The story wryly protests the male-dominated Mexican society and celebrates the female self by proudly showing that women are perfectly capable of performing any job they set their minds to: lawyer, judge, writer, critic, detective, reporter, or taxi driver. The attitudes expressed in this detective story are quite progressive, especially for a Mexican writer in 1961. The female reporter in the story, Lalita Sanromán, visits the jail regularly because she admires the women who have murdered their husbands, *las autoviudas* (self-made widows) as she calls them. Following the formula of many detective stories, there is a crime of passion, and here, since all the characters are women, Bermúdez does not hesitate to include the possibility of a lesbian crime of passion. Finally, the accused in "Detente, sombra" is a feminist literary critic who waxes eloquent about nineteenth-century Latin American women poets, and she compares herself to the original Mexican feminist, Sor Juana Inés de la Cruz, when she says that the latter was like a prisoner in her nun's cell. Interestingly, Bermúdez herself was quite passionate about Latin American women poets and later wrote a critical essay about Sor Juana.

Bermúdez's other two female detective stories are equally inventive. In "Las cosas hablan" (Things talk, 1985), Bermúdez is especially revealing about the uniquely feminine quality of María Elena Morán's method of sleuthing. Morán owes much of her detective abilities not only to cold, hard logic, but also to her restless, endlessly creative imagination. When she and her husband have car problems on the highway near Juárez and they seek assistance from a dark, foreboding, nearby mansion, María Elena's active imagination begins to make her suspect that the house has witnessed some evil event, which, of course, it has. In fact, María Elena is able to perceive the true nature of events and people by comparing things to people and people to things (thus, the story's title, "Las cosas hablan"). When she sees the mansion she compares it to a bitter old woman, and she knows that trouble is lurking within. María Elena's method of detection is by means of metaphor. She solves crimes by creating literature about them. Later in the story, after being introduced to the eventual villain, María Elena perceives that he is hiding something because, to her talented female sleuth's mind, he seems like an armoire. Bruno, who plays the role of the imperceptive male who is contemptuous of his wife's obsessive, female imagination, teasingly asks if she has "classified" the owner of the house, the eventual villain. María Elena's imaginings prove to be correct in the end, of course, when it is revealed that the owner has murdered his father-in-law and imprisoned his own wife. By confidently solving cases at times by means of associative imagination rather than by deductive analysis, María Elena Morán is creating her own female identity.

Bermúdez's third female detective story, "Precisamente ante sus ojos" (Right before your eyes, 1985), draws attention to another aspect of her originality: her ability to create self-referential, metafictional detective stories—that is, stories that comment on the fact that they are detective stories and on the detective genre as a whole. Female characters in Bermúdez's stories are often quite aware of the detective literary tradition, since they themselves are avid readers of detective fiction. María Elena Morán herself notes at the end of "Precisamente ante sus ojos" that the case is a kind of Mexican version of Edgar Allan Poe's "The Purloined Letter." In all three María Elena Morán stories, the female detective mentions that she also writes detective fiction, and she and her husband seem to be aware that she lives her life as a kind of detective story. Bermúdez's characters are aware of all the detectivesque clichés, and that is what makes her stories appealing. In "Precisamente ante sus ojos," Bermúdez pokes fun at herself and the entire genre when María Elena tries to tell her husband about her latest adventures in Mexico City. Since the detailed floor plan of a house often is crucial to the unraveling of a detective story, María Elena proceeds to give a detailed, room-by-room description of the house where the letter was stolen. Her husband is like a reluctant reader who has read one too many formulaic detective stories, and he asks his wife if it is absolutely necessary that he listen to the whole description of the house. María Elena responds that it is necessary, since this information sets the scene of the story. After her long and imaginative description, Bruno again complains (like a typical reader) that he will not be able to remember all the details. María Elena comforts him by telling him that he need only remember certain aspects of her description. In this way, Bermúdez, through her female detective, is communicating to the reader that she, too, is aware of the old clichés, that she is manipulating them in new ways, and that it will be worth it for the reader to finish the story. Bermúdez "quotes" certain elements of traditional detective fiction (such as the detailed floor plan), but does so ironically, in a self-conscious, postmodern way.

Bermúdez's detective fiction has not received the critical attention it deserves. In the 1950s, both her anthology and her first novel received favorable reviews. In 1956, Luis Leal commented in his history of the Mexican short story that Bermúdez's detective fiction was excellent and that Armando H. Zozaya was the most intellectual of Mexican detectives (Leal, 1956, 135–36). As early as 1960, Donald A. Yates pointed out the especially human quality of Bermúdez's characters. According to Yates, her stories involve people rather than two-dimensional automatons of plot. In the introduction to his collection of the best detective stories in Latin America (in Spanish, 1964; in English, 1972), Yates was the first critic to notice the particularly authentic nature of her detailed Mexican settings. Yates was also the first critic to point out Bermúdez's feminism, her creation of a female detective, and the unique contribution this made to Spanish American detective fiction. More recently, Ilán Stavans has presented a relatively negative view of Bermúdez in his history of the Mexican detective novel, *Antiheroes: Mexico and Its Detective Novel* (1997). Stavans declares that all of her detective stories are dull, conventional, and amateurish, since the same male detective, Armando H. Zozaya, always solves the crime in the same way. Apparently unaware of Bermúdez's María Elena Morán character, Stavans goes on to berate her for not creating a female detective in her works. Certainly, Bermúdez's detective fiction is deserving of a more extensive, balanced appraisal.

In all of Bermúdez's detective stories, but especially in her three María Elena Morán stories, she revisits past formulas with great ingenuity, never innocently. Far from conventional and dull, her characters are often quite original and multilayered. From the celebration of femaleness in "Detente, sombra" to the intricacies of the associative female imagination in "Las cosas hablan" to the postmodern metafiction of "Precisamente ante sus ojos," María Elvira Bermúdez constantly reinvented the Mexican detective story, making a unique contribution to the history of this genre in Mexico.

J. Patrick Duffey

Works

"Antea," in *Anuario del cuento mexicano 1960*. Mexico City: INBA, 1961, 38–40.

"La clave literaria," in *Los mejores cuentos policíacos mexicanos*, ed. and intro. María Elvira Bermúdez. Mexico City: Libro-Mex, 1955, 123–41.

"Cuando el río suena," in *Anuario del cuento mexicano 1954*. Mexico City: INBA, 1955, 53–71.

Cuento policiaco mexicano: breve antología, ed. and intro. María Elvira Bermúdez. Mexico City: Premiá, 1989.

Detente, sombra. Mexico City: Universidad Autónoma Metropolitana, 1984.

Diferentes razones tiene la muerte. Mexico City: Talleres Gráficos de la Nación, 1947. Reprint, Mexico City: Plaza y Valdés, 1987.

"El embrollo del reloj," in *El cuento policial latinoamericano*, ed. Donald A. Yates. Mexico
      City: Ediciones de Andrea, 1964, 67–78. Also in *El cuento policial mexicano*, ed. Vicente
      F. Torres. Mexico City: Diógenes, 1982, 43–56.
Los mejores cuentos policíacos mexicanos, ed. and intro. María Elvira Bermúdez. Mexico
      City: Libro-Mex, 1955.
Muerte a la zaga. Mexico City: Premiá, 1986.
"The Puzzle of the Broken Watch," in *Latin Blood: The Best Crime and Detective Stories of
      South America*, ed. and trans. Donald A. Yates. Englewood Cliffs, NJ: Prentice-Hall,
      1980, 94–109.

Criticism

Arellano, Jesús. Review of *Los mejores cuentos policíacos mexicanos*. Metáfora 5 (Novem-
      ber–December 1955): 36.
González Casanova, Henrique. "El libro de la semana: las razones de la muerte." *México en
      la cultura* 189 (November 2, 1952): 7.
Leal, Luis. *Breve historia del cuento mexicano*. Mexico City: Ediciones de Andrea, 1956,
      135–36.
Stavans, Ilán. *Antiheroes: Mexico and Its Detective Novel*, trans. Jesse H. Lytle and Jennifer
      A. Mattson. Teaneck, NJ: Fairleigh Dickinson Univeristy Press, 1997, 91–94.
Trujillo Muñoz, Gabriel. *Testigos de cargo: la narrativa policiaca mexicana y sus autores*.
      Tijuana, Mexico: CONACULTA/CECUT, 2000, 42–46.
Yates, Donald A. "The Mexican Detective Story." *Kentucky Foreign Language Quarterly* 8.1
      (1961): 42–47.

Rafael Bernal (1915–1972)

MEXICO

Rafael Bernal was born in Morelia, Michoacán in 1915. In his youth, his political activities landed him in jail or forced him to leave Mexico on several occasions. He traveled a great deal and lived for brief periods abroad, in several different countries. He wrote in a wide range of genres that included narrative, poetry, journalism, and television. Bernal died in Switzerland in 1972 (Stavans). The author of adventure novels and detective fiction, Rafael Bernal is the father of the hard-boiled genre in Mexico. His detective fiction consists of three books: *Tres novelas policiacas* (Three detective novels, 1946), *El complot mongol* (The Mongolian conspiracy, 1969), and *Un muerto en la tumba* (A dead man in the tomb, 1988). Bernal's works were essentially ignored by critics in Mexico. The posthumous publication of his main titles illustrate this oversight.

There are two aspects that stand out in his detective fiction: the use of parody, and the lack of direct social criticism. His amateur detective, the priest Teódulo Batanes, is modeled after G. K. Chesterton's classic Father Brown figure. Endowed with the virtues of Christian charity and a propensity to speak in series of synonyms, Batanes often clashes with reality, is seen as meddlesome by the police, and becomes involved in ridiculous situations. The stance of critical distance serves to highlight the regionalist descriptions and settings such that storytelling itself occupies a central position. *Un muerto en la tumba* takes up the, again classic, motif of the locked-room mystery. In this case, the locked room is an ancient Mayan tomb at Monte Albán, Oaxaca.

Bernal's masterpiece is *El complot mongol*, a pioneering text in Latin American detective fiction. Anticipating Carlos Fuentes's work in *La cabeza de la hidra* (*The Hydra's Head*, 1978), Bernal creates the secret agent Filiberto García, who becomes involved in an investigation in Mexico City's Chinatown in which the CIA and KGB are implicated. With world peace at risk, the agent—between melodramatic loves stories and mystery—deconstructs Mexican society of the 1960s.

Through local descriptions, Bernal's work acquires universal dimensions and invites reflection on the human condition. Several of his short stories are collected in anthologies of detective fiction, and he is considered to be one of the founding figures of the genre in Mexico, alongside María Elvira Bermúdez and Antonio Helú.

Néstor Ponce

Works

El complot mongol. Mexico City: Joaquín Mortiz, 1969.

"De muerte natural," in *Los mejores cuentos policiacos mexicanos*, ed. María Elvira Bermúdez. Mexico City: Libro-Mex 1955, 41–61.

"La muerte madrugadora," in *El cuento policial mexicano*, ed. Vicente Francisco Torres. Mexico City: Diógenes, 1982, 57–62.

"La muerte poética," in *Cuento policiaco mexicano: breve antología*, ed. María Elvira Ber-
    múdez. Mexico City: Premiá, 1987, 53–64.
Un muerto en la tumba. Mexico City: Jus, 1946. Reprint, 1988.
Tres novelas policiacas. Mexico City: Jus, 1946.

Criticism

Bermúdez, María Elvira. "Prológo," in *Cuento policiaco mexicano: breve antología*. Mexico
    City: Premiá, 1989, 7–27.
Stavans, Ilán. *Antiheroes: Mexico and Its Detective Novel*, trans. by Jesse H. Lytle and Jenni-
    fer A. Mattson. Cranbury, NJ: Associated University Presses, 1997, 95–99.
Taibo, Paco Ignacio, II. "La (otra) novela policiaca." *Los cuadernos del Norte* 8.41 (1987):
    36–41.
Trujillo Muñoz, Gabriel. *Testigos de cargo: la narrativa policiaca mexicana y sus autores*.
    Tijuana, Mexico: CONACULTA/CECUT, 2000, 46–52.

Adolfo Bioy Casares (1914–1999)

ARGENTINA

Born in Buenos Aires on September 15, 1914 to Adolfo Bioy and Marta Casares, both members of the land-owning upper-middle class, Bioy Casares grew up in a social milieu strongly influenced by French culture. To this familiar background he added a brief and incomplete stay at the university. He studied law at the University of Buenos Aires but soon switched to literature. As a consequence, his more significant formation comes from his contact with conspicuous elements of the Argentine intellectual élite and his readings of Hispanic classics and contemporary writers from all over the world.

Bioy began to write fantastic and detective fiction in his youth. In 1932, he became a member of the group of intellectuals associated with the prestigious literary magazine *Sur* (South), recently having been founded by Victoria Ocampo. It was at her house that he met Jorge Luis Borges, whose friendship would be recognized as a landmark in Bioy's literary career. Their long-lasting collaboration produced several thematic anthologies—*Antología de la literatura fantástica* (1940) (*The Book of Fantasy*, 1988), *Los mejores cuentos policiales* (The best detective short stories; 1943, 1951), *Cuentos breves y extraordinarios* (1955) (*Extraordinary Tales*, 1971), and *Poesía gauchesca* (Gaucho poetry, 1955)—and collections of original stories and miscellaneous pieces: *Seis problemas para don Isidro Parodi* (1942) (*Six Problems for Don Isidro Parodi*, 1981), *Dos fantasías memorables* (Two memorable fantasies, 1946), *Crónicas de Bustos Domecq* (Bustos Domecq's chronicles, 1967), and *Nuevos cuentos de Bustos Domecq* (Bustos Domecq's new short stories, 1977). Borges and Bioy also collaborated in editing the detective fiction series *El Séptimo Círculo* (The seventh circle), which was issued from 1944 onwards by the Buenos Aires publishing house Emecé.

Between 1927 and 1937, Bioy Casares wrote several books under the influence of surrealism that he later rejected: *Prólogo* (Prologue, 1929), which included short stories, reflective pieces, and a short comedy; *17 disparos contra lo porvenir* (17 shots against the future, 1933), short stories; *La nueva tormenta o La vida múltiple de Juan Ruteno* (The new storm, or, Juan Ruteno's multiple life, 1935); *La estatua casera* (The homemade statue, 1936), a collection of short stories, dreams, poems, and reflective pieces; and *Luis Greve, muerto* (Luis Greve, dead, 1937), short stories. During this period, Bioy also left unfinished two detective novels—*El problema de la torre china* (The problem of the chinese tower) and *La navaja del muerto* (The deadman's penknife). The literary writings that the author accepts as his valid work began with *La invención de Morel* (1940) (*The Invention of Morel*, 1964), recipient of the Buenos Aires First Prize for Literature in 1941 and, according to critics, his masterpiece and a classic of contemporary writing. From this moment on, Bioy wrote the short-story collections and novels that made him a leading figure in Argentine letters. His novels are *Plan de evasión* (1945) (*A Plan for Escape*, 1975), *El sueño de los héroes* (1954) (*The Dream of*

Heroes, 1987), *Diario de la guerra del cerdo* (1969) (*Diary of the War of the Pig,* 1972), *Dormir al sol* (1973) (*Asleep in the Sun,* 1978), *La aventura de un fotógrafo en La Plata* (1985) (*The Adventures of a Photographer in La Plata,* 1991), and *Un campeón desparejo* (An uneven champion, 1993). His major short-story collections are: *La trama celeste* (The celestial plot, 1949), *Historia prodigiosa* (A prodigious story; 1956), *Guirnalda con amores* (Love garland, 1959), *El lado de la sombra* (The shady side, 1962), which was awarded the Second National Prize for Literature, *El gran serafín* (The great seraph, 1967), First National Prize, *El héroe de las mujeres* (The women's hero, 1978), *Historias desaforadas* (Wild stories, 1986), and *La muñeca rusa* (1991) (*A Russian Doll,* 1992).

Bioy's narrative production has received some of the most important literary awards in the world. Besides significant Argentine recognitions such as the Sociedad Argentina de Escritores (Argentine association of writers) Prize of Honor (1975), the Platinum Konex Prize that he received twice (1984 and 1988), and the Brilliant Konex Prize (1994), Bioy was awarded the Mondello Prize to the best foreigner writer (Italy, 1984), the Prize of the Latin American Institute in Rome (1986), the Miguel de Cervantes Prize (Spain, 1990), the Alfonso Reyes Prize for Latin American Letters (Mexico, 1991), and the Roger Caillois Prize (France, 1995). In 1981, the French government distinguished Bioy's career by naming him a member of the prestigious Legion of Honor.

Bioy Casares's uncommon interest in detective fiction, which parallels a permanent enthusiasm for adventure novels, may be explained by the author's aesthetic compromise with a nonrepresentational style of writing. He was convinced that it was necessary to revitalize a narrative form characterized by a well-developed storyline, as opposed to the forms typical of psychological and traditional realism. According to Bioy's autobiographical writings, it was during the mid-1930s when he and Borges began experimenting with the detective short-story form. Both writers adhered to the basic English conception of the puzzle-novel, and the first examples of their collaborative efforts appeared several years later in *Sur*: "Las doce figuras del mundo" ("The Twelve Figures of the World") and "Las noches de Goliadkin" ("The Nights of Goliadkin"). These two short stories, signed under the pen name H. Bustos Domecq, were included in *Seis problemas para don Isidro Parodi* together with "El dios de los toros" ("The God of the Bulls"), "Las previsiones de Sangiácomo" ("Free Will and the Commendatore"), "La víctima de Tadeo Limardo" ("Tadeo Limardo's Victim"), and "La prolongada busca de Tai An" ("Tai An's Long Search").

The narrative framework of *Seis problemas* revolves around the barber Isidro Parodi, unjustly sentenced for a crime he did not commit, who spends his days in cell 273 at the National Penitentiary. Starting from the account of the events in which his visitors have been involved, Parodi is able to reorganize the information and scattered clues in order to find the hidden truth. In "Las doce figuras," for instance, the young journalist Aquiles Molinari pays Parodi a visit during which he confesses to having had a man killed. After telling his story in detail, the imprisoned detective gives a different interpretation of the events and concludes his retelling, convincing Molinari of his innocence. In this collection of short stories, it is simple to find all of the distinctive features of detective fiction, as it was codified by the nineteenth-century masters of the genre: in terms of the process of writing, the foreshadowed planting of clues, and the solution as well as the convention of "fair play" between writer and reader; in terms of the narrative structure, the idea of presenting the story from the viewpoint of several characters; and the final explanation in the form of a dialogue. However, Borges and Bioy did not subject themselves to a servile repetition of the code, but subverted it through parody and humor. As Lafforgue and Rivera have stated, Isidro Parodi's stories are characterized by "the deepening of the parodical dimension, of the ironic distance, of the play of thematic and formal conventions of the genre" (1996, 98).

Borges–Bioy's detective vein continues with *Un modelo para la muerte* (A model for death, 1946), published under the pseudonym B. Suárez Lynch. This story intensifies the baroque tendency apparent in the previous collection, emphasizing the complexity of the plot and developing long dialogs and secondary episodes. In the same year, Bustos Domecq published *Dos fantasías memorables*, including "El testigo" (The witness) and "El signo" (The sign).

In 1946, Bioy Casares published *Los que aman, odian* (Those who love, hate), a mildly parodic detective novel written in collaboration with his wife Silvina Ocampo. The novella, one of the first published in the *El Séptimo Círculo* collection, was written in a mainly ironic tone, interspersed with literary allusions that have nothing to do with the average reader of detective fiction—for example, the evocation of James Joyce's *Ulysses*, justified only by the proximity of the setting to the sea. The authors recreate the archetypal situation of a group of individuals, isolated in a secluded hotel by the sea. There, a mysterious murder arouses suspicion among the vacationers. The plot involves a series of unrequited loves, conflicting interests, the disappearance of precious jewelry, and the poisoning of several characters. The narrator, Doctor Humberto Huberman, a homeopath, finds himself involved in unexpected detective adventures that compel him to solve the mystery. Unlike traditional prototypes of the genre, the investigator of *Los que aman, odian* offers a chronicle of his mistakes and hasty conclusions.

Together with *La invención de Morel*, *Plan de evasión* is one of the exponents of a renewal of Argentine literature, distinguished by the exploration of new forms that conceived literature as a game of the intellect. According to Mauro, "these first novels share the same compositional techniques based on intertextuality and combining into a single plot elements of the adventure novel with detective, science-fiction, and fantastic stories" (1995, 37). In *Plan de evasión*, Antoine Brissac, a quasi-omniscient narrator, commenting on a testimonial text consisting of his nephew Enrique Nevers's letters, reconstructs the final months of the young man's life. Due to dark family problems, Nevers, a naval lieutenant, has been sent to the overseas French possessions in the Caribbean as an assistant to Pedro Castel, the local governor. As soon as he arrives in the islands, he perceives that there is something concealed, which he interprets as the preparation of an escape. The detective dimension of the novel emerges with a succession of unexplained murders, modeled on the archetypal circumstance of a crime committed in an enclosed room and under the strict surveillance of a character who cannot figure out a reasonable explanation. Finally, a document written by Castel is inserted in order to explain the situation through a description of his personal scientific experiment: the governor was trying to modify the prisoners' perception of reality through surgical procedures combined with a particular use of form and colors in their cells. In that way, he wanted to create in them a permanent sense of freedom despite the fact that they were concealed within the walls of the famous French penal colony on Devil's Island. Critics have noticed the influence of William James's experimental psychology, whose ideas on the perception of reality appear to be combined with the symbolist theory of correspondences in different passages of the novel.

Besides *Plan de evasión*, two short stories are especially decisive in assessing Bioy's contribution to the development of detective fiction in Latin America. Unquestionably, "El perjurio de la nieve" ("The Perjury of the Snow"), first published in Eduardo Mallea's *Cuadernos de la Quimera* and then included in *La trama celeste*, is one of Bioy's best short stories. In the 1967 Prologue, the author recalls that he had told Borges the plot of this story in 1932, but only 11 years later did he feel able to write it down. The attractiveness of the story is proved by the fact that the well-known Argentine film director Leopoldo Torres Ríos and his son Leopoldo Torre Nilsson released a film adaptation of "El perjurio de la nieve" under the title *El crimen de Oribe* in 1950.

The narration is organized as a dialogic play between a personal testimony, supposedly left by Juan Luis Villafañe, a journalist, and a narrative frame, signed by an "editorial" A.B.C. The embedded story is intended to explain the terrible events that mysteriously occurred in General Paz, a distant and isolated village in the south of the country, and that ended up with the killing of Carlos Oribe, a young and promising poet. Read by itself, Villafañe's report manages to convince the reader that the poet was the victim of a vengeful father. However, in the sequence of prologue and epilogue, A.B.C. comments on the inconsistencies of this version, proposes a different interpretation of the facts, and, by the same token, exposes the journalist as a perjurer. In light of this editorial intervention, it is clear that Oribe's murderer made a mistake and Villafañe himself played a major part in this tragic story. Obviously, in "El perjurio de la nieve," Bioy introduces a new turn of the screw in the traditional ending of detective stories, where the investigator explains the clues to his assistant, usually a less-than-clever character. Modifying the tacit reading contract, Bioy acts as a Sherlock Holmes who derives great satisfaction from providing for his Dr. Watson—the reader—a detailed account of the evidence he has missed or misunderstood.

Finally, in "Cavar un foso" (Digging a pit), from *El lado de la sombra*, Bioy exploits the schema of murder/guilt/self-accusation, following the structural pattern of Edgar Allan Poe's "The Tell-Tale Heart." A young couple in debt, Raúl and Julia Arévalo, owners of an inn by the sea, decide to take advantage of an opportunity to kill a wealthy woman who is traveling alone with the down-payment for her dream house. After the murder, they get rid of the body by pushing her car over a nearby cliff. When the crime is investigated by the local police, the couple manages to go on about their business without arousing suspicion. However, they commit a second crime out of guilt months later. Finally, an enigmatic character becomes a regular customer of the inn. During one of their occasional conversations, he identifies himself as a policeman who is on the verge of revealing the identity of the murderers. Consequently, they both realize that the happiness they seek will never be possible. Beside a meticulously constructed plot, in which no detail is superfluous, this story is a perfect example of the narrative virtuosity of the writer and his careful use of language.

Referring to Borges's short story "El jardín de senderos que se bifurcan" ("The Garden of the Forking Paths"), Bioy states that detective fiction "produced an ideal: the ideal of invention, of rigorousness, of elegance (in the sense of the word adopted for mathematics) of plots" and adds that "to highlight the importance of construction: that is, perhaps, the sense of the genre in literary history" (Zavala, 1996, 423). Even though detective fiction may arguably be considered an imported genre in Latin America, in the hands of perceptive writers such as Borges and Bioy it is not simply a model for imitation, but an opportunity to explore nonrealistic forms and reinvent their underlying codes. In the collaborative works, this innovative force is rooted in a glaring propensity to exploit parodic and humorous resources. In his own writings, Bioy deals with a major problem of detective fiction: that of the distance between the "facts" and the process of becoming aware in which the reader as a final recipient is involved. For this reason, he has employed countless resources of narrative mediation. In sum, the adoption of the genre is closely related to Bioy's straightforward commitment to fictionality as a superior literary form of expression.

Daniel Altamiranda

Works

The Adventures of a Photographer in La Plata, trans. Suzanne Jill Levine. New York: Dutton, 1989. Reprint, London: Bloomsbury, 1991.

Asleep in the Sun, trans. Suzanne Jill Levine. New York: Persea, 1978.

Diary of the War of the Pig, trans. Gregory Woodruff and Donald A. Yates. New York: McGraw-Hill, 1972. Reprint, London: Allison & Busby, 1989.

The Dream of Heroes, trans. Diana Thorold. London: Quartet, 1987. Reprint, New York: Dutton, 1988.

The Invention of Morel, and Other Stories from "La trama celeste," trans. Ruth L. C. Simms. Austin: University of Texas Press, 1964.

Obras completas, 5 vols. Buenos Aires: Norma, 1997.

A Plan for Escape, trans. Suzanne Jill Levine. New York: Dutton, 1975.

The Perjury of the Snow, trans. Ruth L. C. Simms. New York: Vanishing Rotating Triangle, 1964.

Los que aman, odian, in collaboration with Silvina Ocampo. Buenos Aires: Emecé, 1996.

A Russian Doll and Other Stories, trans. Suzanne Jill Levine. New York: New Directions, 1992.
Selected Stories, trans. Suzanne Jill Levine. New York: New Directions, 1994.

Criticism

Adolfo Bioy Casares. Premio de Literatura en Lengua Castellana "Miguel de Cervantes" 1990. Madrid: Anthropos/Ministerio de Cultura, 1991.
Bild, Rubén. *Tesis sobre Adolfo Bioy Casares.* London: King's College, 1975.
Camurati, Mireya. *Bioy Casares y el alegre trabajo de la inteligencia.* Buenos Aires: Corregidor, 1990.
Cossío, M. E. "Parody on Literariness: *Seis problemas para don Isidro Parodi.*" *Dispositio* 5–6.15–16 (1980–1981): 143–53.
Fichera, Marcella. *Filosofía, humorismo e ironía en la narrativa de A. Bioy Casares.* Milan: Università Comerciale Boccini, 1972.
Gallagher, David P. "The Novels and Short Stories of A. Bioy Casares." *Bulletin of Hispanic Studies* 52.3 (1975): 247–66.
Giacone, Lidia A. *Símbolo y mito en Adolfo Bioy Casares.* Buenos Aires: Agon, 1984.
Kovacci, Ofelia. *Adolfo Bioy Casares.* Buenos Aires: Ediciones Culturales Argentinas, 1963.
———. *Espacio y tiempo en la fantasía de Adolfo Bioy Casares.* Buenos Aires: Universidad de Buenos Aires, 1963.
Lafforgue, Jorge, and Jorge B. Rivera. *Asesinos de papel. Ensayos sobre narrativa policial.* Buenos Aires: Colihue, 1996.
Levine, Suzanne J. *Guía de Adolfo Bioy Casares.* Madrid: Fundamentos, 1982.
Mac Adam, Alfred J. *Modern Latin American Narratives: The Dreams of Reason.* Chicago: University of Chicago Press, 1977.
Martino, Daniel. *A–B–C de Adolfo Bioy Casares.* Buenos Aires: Emecé, 1989.
Mauro, Teresita. "Bioy Casares: La invención y la escritura." *A propósito de Bioy Casares y su obra.* Bogotá: Norma, 1995, 29–47.
Ponce, Néstor. *Diagonales del género: estudios sobre el policial argentino.* Paris: Editions du Temp, 2001.
Scheines, Graciela. "Las parodias de Jorge Luis Borges y Adolfo Bioy Casares." *Cuadernos hispanoamericanos* 505–507 (1992): 525–33.
Tamargo, María Isabel. *La narrativa de Bioy Casares.* Madrid: Playor, 1983.
Villordo, Oscar H. *Genio y figura de Adolfo Bioy Casares.* Buenos Aires: Eudeba, 1983.
Zavala, Lauro, ed. *La escritura del cuento.* Mexico City: Universidad Nacional Autónoma de México, 1996.

Jorge Luis Borges (1899–1986)

ARGENTINA

Borges is unquestionably the first and most significant promoter of detective fiction in Latin America. In his essay "Los laberintos policiales y Chesterton" ("Labyrinths of the Detective Story and Chesterton"), originally published in Victoria Ocampo's famous literary journal *Sur* in 1935, Borges offers an early vindication of the genre and its practitioners. Later, he indulges in a polemic with Roger Caillois, author of *Le Roman policier* (The detective novel, 1941). Reasserting the English and purely literary origin of the genre, Borges rejects Caillois's theory that detective fiction stems from particular circumstances in French history: namely, the creation of a secret police by Joseph Fouché in 1799. During the 1930s and 1940s, Borges published several reviews in which he examined both theoretical books like Nigel Morland's *How to Write Detective Novels* (1936) and Howard Haycraft's *Murder for Pleasure* (1942), and fictional pieces by G. K. Chesterton, Ellery Queen, John Dickson Carr, Anthony Berkeley, and Eden Phillpotts. With the collaboration of Adolfo Bioy Casares, he edited two series of *Los mejores cuentos policiales* (The best detective short stories, 1943, 1951). He was also co-editor of the prestigious collection *El Séptimo Círculo* (The seventh circle), which was issued from 1944 onwards by the Buenos Aires printing house Emecé.

Born in Buenos Aires, where he spent his childhood, Borges lived in Europe during World War I, attending school in Geneva. There he learned Latin, French, and German and read the contemporary classics of European literature. After the end of World War I, his family went to Spain, where Borges became a part of the local avant-garde movement. Back in Buenos Aires, he founded, with a group of young poets, the billboard review *Prisma* (Prism), followed immediately by the literary magazine *Proa* (Prow). Thus, by promulgating the avant-garde ideals that he had absorbed in Europe, Borges began to participate in the fervent intellectual life of the city. During this period, he published three books of poetry—*Fervor de Buenos Aires* (Fervor of Buenos Aires, 1923), *Luna de enfrente* (Moon across the way, 1925), and *Cuaderno San Martín* (San Martín notebook, 1929)—which he rewrote several times throughout his life. He also published three volumes of essays for which he never authorized a reprinting: *Inquisiciones* (Inquisitions, 1925), *El tamaño de mi esperanza* (The size of my hope, 1926), and *El idioma de los argentinos* (The language of Argentines, 1928). The recent publication of his *Textos recobrados* (Recovered texts, 1977), compiled by Irma Zangara (1997), opens a door to a reassessment of Borges's early writings.

In the 1930s, while working as an assistant librarian, Borges became a frequent contributor to *Sur* and published *Evaristo Carriego* (1930), an atypical biography of a popular poet, and two books of essays: *Discusión* (Discussion, 1932) and *Historia de la eternidad* (A history of eternity, 1936). More important for his career as a short-story writer is *Historia universal de la infamia* (A universal history of infamy, 1935), where he included narrative pieces previously published in the newspaper *Crítica* (Critique). During the next decade, Borges wrote the narrative prose that made him known worldwide as a master of modern fiction: *Ficciones* (Fictions, 1944) and *El Aleph* (The Aleph, 1949).

Vilified by his detractors and praised by his followers, Borges reached the height of Argentine literature. In the 1950s, he solidified his fame with *Otras inquisiciones* (Other inquisitions, 1952), essays, and *El hacedor* (The maker, *Dreamtigers* in the English edition, 1960), a compilation of brief pieces in prose and verse. Later, he published six books of poetry, two collections of short stories, and several literary and cultural essays in collaboration with Bioy Casares, Betina Edelberg, Margarita Guerrero, Alicia Jurado, María Kodama, María Esther Vázquez, and Esther Zemborain.

In his famous 1978 lecture on the detective story, Borges reminds us that the founder of the genre, Edgar Allan Poe, did not mean for it to adhere to realism. On the contrary, he developed an intellectual literary form based on something entirely fictional: a mysterious murder that must be solved by an abstract thinker and not through accusations or due to the murderer's negligence. Thus detective fiction, which is probably the most conventional of all literary genres, began with Poe's "The Murders in the Rue Morgue" in 1848, dealing with the situation of a crime committed in an enclosed room. Poe's story implies the logical unraveling of what seems to be purely illogical or inexplicable, and it would become a frequently revisited topic of detective fiction, as is evident in the long series of texts that followed such as G. K. Chesterton's "The Oracle of the Dog" (1926), Israel Zangwill's *The Big Bow Mystery* (1903), and Ellery Queen's *The Door Between* (1937). Contrary to Walter Benjamin's thesis, included in his study on Baudelaire's epoch where the constituents of French society—in particular, the *flâneur*—are described as historical referents of literary detectives, Borges insists on the conventionality of the central character.

A second vein, represented in "The Purloined Letter," consists of the treatment of the invisibility of the evident. According to Borges's summary, "the police of Paris, endeavored to find a missing letter, exploits in vain the resources of methodical research: the drill, the compass, the microscope. Meanwhile, the sedentary Auguste Dupin smokes his pipe, analyzes the terms of the problem, and visits the house that misled the police's examination. He enters the house and finds the letter immediately" (*Obras completas* 4: 246–47). Thus Dupin became the first in a long line of detectives who solved cases based on reason. According to Borges, Poe's detective is a Frenchman because the writer needed to establish a distance between his fictive agent and the world of references immediately available to his readers.

Finally, Borges finds all the basic characteristics of the genre fully developed in Poe's short stories, but observes that, in time, they have created a particular kind of reader: the suspicious one. This detective reader, according to Hernández Martín's terminology, "makes conjectures about the facts presented in the story and formulates questions about the relation between the signs of the text, what they express and what they do not, in order to generate from appearances the explanation that best accounts for the traces of mystery" (Hernández Martín 6–7).

In a review of Howard Haycraft's *Murder for Pleasure*, Borges states that "in every book, the detective solves the problem because the writer reveals the solution to him confidentially" (*Obras completas* 4: 67). Then, the method they follow is secondary and the problem itself is the essence of the genre. Borges also rejects the "scientific" solution of the mystery, based on technical knowledge—toxicology, ballistics, and the like—because that is information that the common reader usually does not have.

As an aesthetic form, Borges prefers the short story to the novel in detective fiction. Due to its length, the latter necessarily evolves into the psychological and characters require a life implying the development of details the plot itself does not need. In fact, as Borges observes, "it is ridiculous for a riddle to take three hundred pages" (*Obras completas* 4: 313). The short story, on the other hand, may have an exclusively detective nature—it may deal with just one particular problem and its explanation. That is a mark of superiority for Borges, who seems to set the surplus of the novelistic form in the limelight in his ingeniously conceived hoax "El acercamiento a Almotásim" ("The Approach to al-Mu'tasim"), from *Historia de la eternidad*, an essayistic text in which the author pretends to review a nonexistent detective novel written by the unknown Mir Bahadur Alí.

In an autobiographical passage, Borges writes:

> I have tried detective fiction at times; I am not particularly proud of what I did. I moved it to a symbolic level, but I am not sure if it is appropriate or not. I have written "Death and the Compass," some detective texts with Bioy Casares, whose stories are far better than mine: the stories of Isidro Parodi, a prisoner who solves crimes while in jail. ("El cuento policial" 197)

In fact, the friendship of Borges and Bioy Casares, which goes back to the early 1930s, produced several important works, besides the series *Los mejores cuentos policiales* and the thematic anthologies they prepared together. In 1942, under the pen name H. Bustos Domecq, they published *Seis problemas para don Isidro Parodi* (*Six Problems for don Isidro Parodi*, 1981), the first detective book to be written in Spanish. Their next two books, *Un modelo para la muerte* (A model for death, 1946) and *Dos fantasías memorables* (Two memorable fantasies, 1946) also belong to detective fiction, but the rest of their collaborative works explore different literary horizons: *Crónicas de Bustos Domecq* (Bustos Domecq's chronicles, 1965) and *Nuevos cuentos de Bustos Domecq* (Bustos Domecq's new short stories, 1977).

Only three of Borges's own short stories may be considered to be properly detective fiction: "La muerte y la brújula," "Emma Zunz," and "Abenjacán el Bojarí muerto en su laberinto" ("Ibn Hakkan al-Bokhari, Dead in His Labyrinth"). Some critics have contended that other pieces, such as "El jardín de senderos que se bifurcan" ("The Garden of Forking Paths," 1941), which was included in Rodolfo Walsh's *Diez cuentos policiales argentinos* (Ten Argentine detective short stories, 1953), "La forma de la espada" ("The Shape of the Sword," 1942), "Tema del traidor y del héroe" ("Theme of the Traitor and the Hero," 1944), and "La otra muerte" ("The Other Death," 1949) are to be included in a complete list of Borges's detective narratives. Considering its characters and structure, "El jardín de senderos que se bifurcan" belongs to the domain of the espionage story, and neither "La forma de la espada" nor "Tema del traidor y del héroe," whose main theme is treachery and denunciation set in the context of Irish independence movements, are detective fiction. As for "La otra muerte," the narrator states that this story corresponds to a scandal of reason, which translated in Borges's literary concepts refers to his classic idiosyncratic definition of the fantastic.

"La muerte y la brújula" was published in *Sur* in 1942 and included later in *Los mejores cuentos policiales* and *Ficciones*. This short story centers on two antagonistic characters: Red Scharlach, a well-known gangster who has threatened to kill Erik Löhnrot, a pure reasoner in the style of Auguste Dupin. As is suggested by the inclusion of the color red in both names (German *Scharlach* and *rot*), these characters are doubles but, since they are enemies, antithetical ones. The plot, designed as a clockwork, introduces a number of crimes, committed at a regular pace in the cardinal points of the city. Even though the geographical descriptions of the setting correspond to that of Buenos Aires, the narrator insistently proclaims the fictionality of his story. Finally, despite the perspicacity and concentration of the detective, which misled him to the conclusion that a Jewish sect of mentally unbalanced fanatics was carrying out a series of mystical sacrifices all over the city, it is the real murderer, Scharlach, who explains to Löhnrot the intricate plan that will end with the latter's imminent death.

In "Emma Zunz," published in *Sur* (1948) and included in *El Aleph*, the reader is confronted with a narrative that corresponds to what would be the impetus of a detective story: in order to avenge her father's death, young Emma sacrifices her virginity to a complete stranger and kills her boss, who was responsible for the elder Zunz's downfall. Both actions are interconnected, since she is planning to allege that the man had raped her and she killed him while defending her honor. At the end, the narrator comments: "Actually, the story was incredible, but it impressed everyone because substantially it was true." Detective fiction demands that the murder or offense adopt the form of a puzzle that someone is compelled to solve. In this case, Borges offers a fictional piece that, instead of revealing a mystery, highlights its construction. In other words, "Emma Zunz" presents the events that lead up to the point where the detective would begin his work.

Borges's last detective story, "Abenjacán el Bojarí muerto en su laberinto," was published in *Sur* in 1951 and included in the second edition of *El Aleph* (1952). Faraway in Cornwall, the "poet" Dunraven and the "mathematician" Unwin, two absentminded and keen young men, ponder the enigmatic death of Abenjacán el Bojarí, which occurred 25 years earlier. Although it is well-established that Abenjacán's cousin and unfaithful servant Zaid was responsible for his death, the circumstances are still obscure. The technique is masterfully exploited to underline and, at the same time, conceal the oral character of the narration by employing different presentation procedures. On the compositional level, the inclusion of metaliterary comments attracts the reader's attention: the characters discuss the idea of avoiding all unnecessary multiplication of mysteries, adopting Poe's "The Purloined Letter" as a paradigmatic example of simplicity, and they are fully aware of the conventions of the genre. In sum, in this short story Borges revisits the same parodic tone and structural situation explored in Isidro Parodi's narrations where the reader is invited to deal with two conflicting versions of the same events: the first one encoded in mystery, and the second as an elucidation of the previous one.

Borges's contribution to a Latin American development of detective fiction is both theoretical and practical. He despised the American hard-boiled novel and followed the classic detective narration with which he felt more comfortable not only due to his inclination toward intellectual games and the highlighting of reasoning, but also for the openly conventional nature of the so-called "whodunit." As "La muerte y la brújula" shows, Borges's ideal detective story implies the display of a purely geometrical problem that does not ignore the fallibility of human beings. Consequently, the greatest element of surprise is reached when the detective is the one who ends up being the victim in the case he analyzes.

Daniel Altamiranda

Works

El Aleph (1949), ed. and trans. Norman Thomas di Giovanni in collaboration with the author. New York: Dutton, 1970.

Atlas (1984), trans. Anthony Kerrigan. New York: Dutton, 1985.

Collected Fictions, trans. Andrew Hurley. New York: Penguin, 1999.

Elogio de la sombra (1969), trans. Norman Thomas di Giovanni as *In Praise of Darkness*. New York: Dutton, 1977.

Evaristo Carriego (1930), trans. Norman Thomas di Giovanni with the assistance of Susan Ashe as *Evaristo Carriego. A Book about Old-Time Buenos Aires*. New York: Dutton, 1983.

Ficciones (1944), trans. Anthony Kerrigan and others. New York: Grove Press, 1962.

El hacedor (1960), trans. Mildred Boyer and Harold Morland as *Dreamtigers*. Austin: University of Texas Press, 1964.

Historia universal de la infamia (1935), trans. Norman Thomas di Giovanni as *A Universal History of Infamy*. New York: Dutton, 1972.

El informe de Brodie (1970), trans. Norman Thomas di Giovanni in collaboration with the author as *Doctor Brodie's Report*. New York: Dutton, 1972.

Labyrinths: Selected Stories and Other Writings, ed. Donald A. Yates and James Irby. New York: New Directions, 1962.

El libro de arena (1975), trans. Norman Thomas di Giovanni as *The Book of Sand*. New York: Dutton, 1977.

Obras completas, 4 vols. Buenos Aires: Emecé, 1996.

Obras completas en colaboración. Buenos Aires: Emecé, 1979.

El oro de los tigres (1972), trans. Alastair Reid as *The Gold of the Tigers: Selected Later Poems*. New York: Dutton, 1977.

Otras inquisiciones (1952), trans. Ruth L. C. Simms as *Other Inquisitions, 1937–1952*. Austin: University of Texas Press, 1964.

A Personal Anthology, ed. Anthony Kerrigan. New York: Grove Press, 1967.

Seis problemas para don Isidro Parodi (1942), trans. Norman Thomas di Giovanni as *Six Problems for Don Isidro Parodi*. New York: Dutton, 1980.

Selected Poems, ed. Alexander Coleman. New York: Penguin, 1999.

Selected Poems 1923–1967, trans. Norman Thomas di Giovanni and others. New York: Delacorte Press, 1972.

Textos recobrados, 1919–1929, ed. Irma Zangara. Buenos Aires: Emecé, 1997.

Criticism

Agheana, Ion T. *The Prose of Jorge Luis Borges: Existencialism and the Dynamics of Surprise*. New York: Peter Lang, 1984.

———. *The Meaning of Experience in the Prose of Jorge Luis Borges*. New York: Peter Lang, 1988.

Aizenberg, Edna. *The Aleph Weaver: Biblical, Kabbalistic, and Judaic Elements in Borges*. Potomac, MD: Scripta Humanitatis, 1984.

———, ed. *Borges and His Successors: The Borgesian Impact on Literature and the Arts*. Columbia: University of Missouri Press, 1990.

Alazraki, Jaime. *La prosa narrativa de Jorge Luis Borges*, 3rd enlarged ed. Madrid: Gredos, 1983.

———, ed. *Critical Essays on Jorge Luis Borges*. Boston: Hall, 1987.

Balderston, Daniel, comp. *The Literary Universe of Jorge Luis Borges: An Index to References and Allusions to Persons, Titles, and Places in His Writings*. New York: Greenwood, 1986.

———. *Out of Context: Historical Reference and the Representation of Reality in Borges*. Durham, NC: Duke University Press, 1993.

Barnatán, Marcos Ricardo. *Conocer Borges y su obra*. Madrid: Dopesa, 1978.

Barrenechea, Ana María. *La expresión de la irrealidad en la obra de Borges*. México: El Colegio de México, 1957. Trans. Robert Lima as *Borges the Labyrinth Maker*. New York: New York University Press, 1965.

Becco, Horacio. *Jorge Luis Borges: Bibliografía total, 1923–1973*. Buenos Aires: Casa Pardo, 1973.

Bell-Villada, Gene H. *Borges and his Fiction: A Guide to His Mind and Art*. Chapel Hill, NC: University of North Carolina Press, 1981.

Benjamin, Walter. "El París del Segundo Imperio en Baudelaire." *Iluminaciones II*. Madrid: Taurus, 1972, 21–170.

Bloom, Harold, ed. *Jorge Luis Borges*. New York: Chelsea, 1986.

Burgin, Richard. *Conversations with Jorge Luis Borges*. New York: Holt, Rinehart and Winston, 1968.

Capdevila, Analía. "Una polémica olvidada. (Borges contra Caillois sobre el policial)," in *Borges, ocho ensayos*, Sergio Cueto et al. Rosario, Argentina: Beatriz Viterbo, 1995, 67–82.

Christ, Ronald. *The Narrow Act: Borges' Art of Allusion*. New York: New York University Press, 1969.

Ciocchini, Héctor. "Borges y el pretexto policíaco," in *Los héroes "difíciles": la literatura policial en la Argentina y en Italia*, ed. Giuseppe Petronio, Jorge B. Rivera, and Luigi Volta. Buenos Aires: Corregidor, 1991, 85–93.

Cossío, M. E. "A Parody on Literariness: *Seis problemas para Don Isidro Parodi*." *Dispositio* 5–6.15–16 (1980–1981): 143–53.

Echavarría, Arturo. "El intelectual y la violencia en dos hispanoamericanos: el (extraño) caso de la araña homicida en Borges y Martín Luis Guzmán." *La Torre, Nueva época* 2.8 (1988): 639–54.

Foster, David William. *Jorge Luis Borges: An Annotated Primary and Secondary Bibliography*. New York: Garland, 1984.

García, Guillermo. "Sobre la función del relato policial en la obra de Borges." *Proa. En las letras y en las artes Tercera época* 23 (1996): 165–67.

Gutiérrez Carbajo, Francisco. "El relato policial en Borges." *Cuadernos hispanoamericanos* 805–807 (1992): 371–88.

Helft, Nicolás. *Jorge Luis Borges. Bibliografía completa*. Buenos Aires: Fondo de Cultura Económica, 1997.

Hernández Martín, Jorge. *Readers and Labyrinths. Detective Fiction in Borges, Bustos Domecq, and Eco*. New York: Garland, 1995.

Holquist, Michael. "Jorge Luis Borges and the Metaphysical Mystery." *Mystery and Suspense Writers: The Literature of Crime, Detection, and Espionage*, 2 vols., ed. Robin W. Winks and Maureen Corrigan. New York: Scribner's, 1998, 1:83–96.

Jurado, Alicia. *Genio y figura de Jorge Luis Borges*, 3rd updated ed. Buenos Aires: Eudeba, 1980.

Lafforgue, Jorge, and Jorge B. Rivera. *Asesinos de papel. Ensayos sobre narrativa policial*. Buenos Aires: Colihue, 1996.

Lindstrom, Naomi. *Jorge Luis Borges. A Study of the Short Fiction*. Boston: Twayne, 1990.

Matamoro, Blas. *Diccionario privado de Jorge Luis Borges*. Madrid: Altalena, 1980.

Mac Adam, Alfred. "Un modelo para la muerte: la apoteosis de Parodi." *Revista iberoamericana* 46 (1980): 545–52.

Molloy, Sylvia. *Las letras de Borges*. Buenos Aires: Sudamericana, 1979. English version published as *Signs of Borges*, trans. Oscar Montero with the author. Durham, NC: Duke University Press, 1994.

Pastormerlo, Sergio. "Dos concepciones del género policial: una introducción a la narrativa borgeana," in *Literatura policial en la Argentina: Waleis, Borges, Saer*, ed. Néstor Ponce et al. La Plata, Argentina: Facultad de Humanidades y Ciencias de la Educación, Universidad Nacional de la Plata, 1997, 17–43.

Pérez, Alberto Julián. *Poética de la prosa de Jorge Luis Borges. Hacia una crítica bakhtiniana de la literatura*. Madrid: Gredos, 1986.

Ponce, Néstor. *Diagonales del género: estudios sobre el policial argentino*. Paris: Editions du Temp, 2001.

Rest, Jaime. *El laberinto del universo. Borges y el pensamiento nominalista*. Buenos Aires: Fausto, 1976.

Rodríguez Monegal, Emir. *Borges par lui-même*. Paris: Seuil, 1970. Spanish version, with a widely reelaborated anthology: *Borges por sí mismo*. Barcelona: Laia, 1984.

———. *Jorge Luis Borges: A Literary Biography*. New York: E. P. Dutton, 1978.

Sarlo, Beatriz. *Jorge Luis Borges: A Writer on the Edge*. London: Verso, 1993.

Scheines, Graciela. "Las parodias de Jorge Luis Borges y Adolfo Bioy Casares." *Cuadernos hispanoamericanos* 505–507 (1992): 525–33.

Stabb, Martin S. *Borges Revisited*. Boston: Twayne, 1991.

Sturrock, John. *Paper Tigers. The Ideal Fictions of Jorge Luis Borges*. Oxford: Clarendon Press, 1977.

Yates, Donald Alfred. "The Argentine Detective Story." Doctoral dissertation, University of Michigan, 1960.

María Angélica Bosco (b. 1917)

Novelist, short-story writer, essayist, translator (she published an excellent version of *Madame Bovary*), María Angélica Bosco was born in Buenos Aires in 1917. She has received numerous prizes and awards for her writings while being very active in public life as an instructor and later as director of the Fondo Nacional de las Artes (National fund for the arts) in Argentina. Her first novel was *La muerte baja en el ascensor* (Death takes the elevator), which won the Emecé prize in 1954. This book is a perfect model for Tzvetan Todorov's typology of detective fiction, which states that there must always be two stories in a single tale: the story of the crime and the story of the investigation. In *La muerte baja en el ascensor*, Bosco establishes the whodunit formula in neat, precise steps, first by introducing the murder victim and the characters who discovered the body, and then by tracking the investigation of the other suspects and relationships by the detective Ericourt and his young assistant, Blasi. A woman has been murdered and it is immediately apparent that all the suspects have secrets to hide.

If we compare this novel to those Bosco wrote later, we instantly notice her use of historical moment. Written after the war years, the book assembles all the ingredients of a classic detective novel, with echoes of the moral and psychic disjunctions occasioned by World War II. Many immigrants made their way to Argentina during the 1940s, and the German past haunted the survivors' memories. Most South Americans distrusted the Europeans that immigrated after the war, assuming they had something to hide.

The murder of Frida Eidenger takes place in a Buenos Aires apartment building that resembles the Pension Vauquer in Balzac's *Père Goriot*. All of the building's denizens are fascinating: even their names are enigmatic: Adolfo Luchter, Boris Czerbó. The detective traces the connections among the neighbors and discovers their secret vices and passions. Some of the suspects are eccentric, some merely sick or mentally feeble, and others are tormented by their past. Extortion and blackmail precipitate a dangerous situation.

Emphasis on police procedure is typical of this type of novel, and Ericourt the detective is a thorough investigator who patiently gathers evidence and conducts interviews, aided by his assistant sergeant. As he uncovers the facts in the case, Ericourt shows his readers his process of detection. Trying to make order out of the puzzle, he reasons logically, using the typical cause-and-effect sequence to fit everything together. The solution in this novel depends on something that happened during the war, and a woman's lipstick is an integral piece of the well-conceived plot. This is Bosco's classic detective fiction novel.

Her later novels do not depend as much on the detective's presence. They are well-presented narratives with intricate plots and a more psychological approach to suspects and victims. The settings of the books that follow *La muerte baja en el ascensor* also move in new directions: In *En la estela de un secuestro* (In the wake of a kidnapping, 1977), the sleepy landscape of the Paraná River delta provides a mysterious setting. It is a story about a father and son on the one hand and a kidnapping of a powerful figure on the other. Dr. Quintino Vestri, kidnapped while riding in his Mercedes-Benz and held for ransom, opens this story of passion and greed. The main character of the novel is Vestri's employee, a good man named Quintín who is the captain of Vestri's yacht. Quintín wants to help solve the case because his son Venanci is framed for robbery and murder. Father and son have to clear themselves of suspicion in the kidnapping.

En la estela de un secuestro is a curiously attractive novel. There is a murder at the end and a certain amount of action along the way, but Bosco relies mostly on character. There is also an attractive subplot about a boat that Quintín lends to a friend, and this seeming digression is actually an important clue in the resolution of the story. The author also criticizes the class system by showing how power is held by the upper classes while rougher justice is reserved for the lower ones. The procedural detail is realistic, and the characters have enough substance to support the subplots. This is a tale of corruption and family feuds resolved by the sympathetic Quintín.

Muerte en la costa del río (Death on the river bank, 1979) is set in Colonia, Uruguay. Tourists in several different boats are about to enjoy their holiday when a murder strikes and they all become suspects. The identity of the murder victim is the first shock. Ingenious alibis, misleading forensic information, and clues provide the necessary ingredients to keep the reader baffled. The protagonists are sharply delineated; some are warm and urbane, others are despicable. In this novel, the whodunit plot functions as a framework for the author's brilliant characterizations.

In *Muerte en la costa del río*, Bosco creates strong, believable female characters. Her earlier women were passive and reacted in an almost stereotypical fashion. In this novel, one of the characters, Betina, is a writer who wants to work along with the police detective, Sergeant Smith. Betina complains of not having the same opportunities as her husband and wants to use the case to give some sort of definition to her life. But her powers of detection are ineffective and usually misleading. She protects the wrong suspects. In this story, the mystery is not solved by the detective but by López, the "fatman," one of the many suspects. López dazzles the police with his unorthodox presentations. Not surprisingly, this character is fond of games; his boat is named the *Tarot*. In this novel, Bosco's parodic style echoes that of Manuel Puig (1932–1990).

La muerte vino de afuera (Death came from outside, 1982) calls into question those who administer justice. It takes place in Buenos Aires, where two criminals escape from prison. They had been sentenced to life, and those involved in the sentencing fear revenge. The characters here are well-drawn and the narrative provides interesting glimpses of certain segments of Argentine society.

In exploring the psychology of the protagonists, Bosco has the characters analyze themselves, providing complete autobiographies, with particular attention to their childhoods. But the real subject of this book is the death penalty. "Should the death of a criminal be the only compensation for irreversible damages? You kill, I kill, he kills. The evil circle of instincts, the animal circuit . . ." reflects the detective Tellez. His opinion clashes with that of the majority, which thinks that the death penalty is the only defense against certain crimes. Bosco has said that this book was born of a television debate about capital punishment.

These later detective fiction novels by Bosco are set in Argentina and Uruguay during the repression and political unrest of the 1970s and 1980s, but none of these events that we associate with this period enter into the stories. Paradoxically, the books are concerned with law and order, with the enforcement and preservation of the laws of the land to insure the safety of its citizens.

Bosco is a competent stylist with a good ear for dialogue. Her plots are original; some of the characters read Erich Fromm and Ortega y Gasset, revealing Bosco's own intellectual background. As Bosco indicates on the jacket-copy of *La muerte vino de afuera*, she is seriously committed to detective fiction and is a staunch defender of the genre:

> There is a fundamental prejudice that pigeonholes detective fiction—like children's literature—as literature's younger sister. I neither accuse nor excuse myself for my writings. I do not accuse those who believe in arbitrary hierarchies. I only want to explain that the detective genre attracts me: I prefer to create literary intrigues rather than project them into everyday life. I reject hypocrisy, and this is a common denominator in my work, as well as the desire to understand "the other" who is generally not very well understood.

In some of her later writings, Bosco has chosen to portray a historical landscape where women, moved by passion, are united in a tragic destiny, revealing different aspects of the human condition.

                                                                    Flora H. Schiminovich

Works

Las burlas del porvenir. Buenos Aires: Atlántida, 1993.
Cartas de mujeres. Buenos Aires: Emecé, 1975.
¿Dónde está el cordero? Buenos Aires: Emecé, 1966.
En la estela de un secuestro. Buenos Aires: Emecé, 1977.
Historia privada. Buenos Aires: Emecé, 1972.
La muerte baja en el ascensor. Buenos Aires: Emecé, 1954.
Muerte en la costa del río. Buenos Aires: Emecé, 1979.
La muerte soborna a Pandora. Buenos Aires: Emecé, 1956.
La muerte vino de afuera. Buenos Aires: Editorial Belgrano, 1982.
El sótano. Buenos Aires: Sudamericana, 1986.
Tres historias de mujeres. Buenos Aires: Vinciguerra, 1996.

Criticism

Campanella, Hebe. "La novela-enigma de María Angélica Bosco: ortodoxia y heterodoxia," in *Los héroes "difíciles": la literatura policial en la Argentina y en Italia*, ed. Giuseppe Petronio, Jorge B. Rivera, and Luigi Volta. Buenos Aires: Corregidor, 1991, 123–34.

Dunn, Kelly Anne. "Representative Detective Fiction Writers from Mexico and Argentina: Socio-Political Factors and Literary Context." Doctoral dissertation, University of Virginia, 1999.

Lafforgue Jorge, and Jorge B. Rivera. *Asesinos de papel: ensayos sobre narrativa policial*. Buenos Aires: Colihue, 1996.

Martella, Gianna M. "Pioneers: Spanish American Women Writers of Detective Fiction." *Letras femeninas* 28.1 (2002): 31–44.

Martínez, Victoria. "El acto de investigar: el rol de la mujer en la literatura policial de la Argentina y los Estados Unidos." *Primeras jornadas internacionales de literatura argentina/comparatística. Actas*. Buenos Aires: Facultad de Filosofía y Letras, Universidad de Buenos Aires, 1995, 425–30.

Orgambide, Pedro and Yahni, Roberto, eds. "María Angélica Bosco," in *Enciclopedia de la literatura argentina*. Buenos Aires: Sudamericana, 1970, 100-103.

Schiminovich, Flora. "Two Argentine Female Writers Perfect the Art of Detection: María Angélica Bosco and Syria Poletti." *Review: Latin American Literature and Arts* 42 (1990): 16–21.

Togno, María Elena. *Así escriben las mujeres*. Buenos Aires: Orion, 1975.

Martín Caparrós (b. 1957)

ARGENTINA

Martín Caparrós was born in Buenos Aires in 1957. He began his career as a journalist with the newpsaper *Noticias* (News) in 1973. From 1976 to 1983 he lived in Paris, where he earned a degree in history. Working in different print, radio, and television news media, Caparrós has been a sports, culture, food, political, and crime reporter. He also worked as an editor for the magazines *El Porteño* (The Buenos Aires resident) *Sal y Pimienta* (Salt and pepper) and *Cuisine & Vins* (Cuisine and wines), as well as editor-in-chief for *Página/30* (Page 30). Upon his return to Argentina, he published his novels *Ansay o los infortunios de la gloria* (Ansay, or the misfortunes of glory, 1984) and *No velas a tus muertos* (Don't mourn your dead, 1986). From April 1988 to March 1991 he directed, along with Jorge Dorio, the journal *Babel. Revista de libros* (Babel. Review of books), which gathered together a group of young authors who began to write and publish after the fall of the dictatorship: Daniel Guebel (b. 1956), Luis Chitarroni (b. 1958), Alan Pauls (b. 1959), Sergio Chejfec (b. 1953), C. E. Feiling (1961–1997), Sergio Bizzio (b. 1956), Matilde Sánchez (b. 1958), and Guillermo Saavedra (b. 1960), among others. The so-called *Grupo Shanghai* (Shanghai group) in which Caparrós participated proposed the autonomy of literature with regard to political and social issues, clearly in open argument against the literature of social commitment that characterized the writing of the 1970s. The body of literature produced during those years, reaffirming Borges's central position on the Argentine literary stage, was characterized by the use of nonreferential, exotic settings; by the creation of narratives where discourse is neither true nor false because it does not adhere to such categories but rather is viewed as a space to express doubt and uncertainty. Moreover, it was characterized by the mistrust of grandiose literary themes and a predilection toward fragmentation, narrative gaps, a rupture with linear structure, digressions, playing with literary genres, and constant literary referenciality.

In 1990, Caparrós published his first detective novel, *El tercer cuerpo* (The third body), which saw a second edition with minor punctuation and lexical corrections in 1997. This second edition places in motion, according to Caparrós, the idea of continuing the saga of Matías Jáuregui, the protagonist, "ya que en la úlitma escena de *El tercer cuerpo* le están por pegar un tiro, y yo supongo, ya que no está dicho en la novela, que fue en la pierna. Su vuelta depende de cuánto más se mantenga Fidel Castro en el poder en la isla de Cuba, ya que espero que la trama se sitúe allí" (since in the last scene of *El tercer cuerpo* he is about to get shot, in the leg, I suppose, since it is not mentioned in the novel. His return depends on how much longer Fidel Castro remains in power in Cuba because I hope to situate the action there [Russo]).

El tercer cuerpo is a novel that borrows features from detective fiction in order to narrate political crimes like the deals between bankers, colonels, and businessmen during the military dictatorship, the economic interests that led to the Falk-land/Malvinas Islands War, and the close relationships between members of the old Buenos Aires elite and drug dealers and para-police forces. The plot is sustained through the investigation of Matías Jáuregui, the wayward son of an old Argentine military family, who becomes a detective in order to make money. He discovers, almost by chance, some clues to solve the theft of three cadavers of illustrious families from the Recoleta cemetery, the resting place of the Argentine elite. Jáuregui constructs his identity from American detective novels, imitating gestures and modes of speech of the great literary detectives. Therefore, the text is replete with quotes that refer to the canon of detective literature with characters such as Phillip Marlowe and Mike Hammer. The truth of the plot in which he is caught, however, escapes him, and he cannot make sense of the unorganized clues provided by some of his informants. Only in the end does he discover the irrationality that his own investigation has uncovered.

The action takes place in Buenos Aires in January of 1989, a particularly conflictive moment in the political, social, and economic history of Argentina. For example, in December 1988 there was a military uprising headed by Colonel "Carapintada" Seineldín, who questioned the high ranks of the military because he considered them responsible for the defeat in the Falkland Islands War). Seineldín requested the pardon of convicted military leaders and called for the military to play its role again in the fight against subversion. In addition, in January 1989 there was a failed attempt to overtake the military headquarters of La Tablada, in the province of Buenos Aires, by a leftist commando group that (short in numbers and resources) was brutally repressed by the army in a shocking demonstration of force. Both events open a period of institutional instability. Besides this political instability, the country goes through an economic crisis during the first months of 1989 that placed it on the verge of social unrest. With the devaluation of the peso, a period of hyperinflation took place—a period whose dramatic effects turned into brutally repressed assaults and robberies of businesses and grocery stores.

El tercer cuerpo works with these materials and discourses from the political, economic and social arenas in order to create a Buenos Aires on the verge of social disintegration and upheaval. Within a climate of violence and degradation, there are explosions at embassies and courthouses, bonfires by homeless refugees in the city center, shortages, blackouts, car accidents, bombs exploding in currency-exchange offices, looting of grocery stores, and soup kitchens. Throughout the novel, a secret group, called *Lalengua* (The tongue), leaves disturbing and enigmatic graffiti messages on walls throughout the city, in which one of the enigmas of the novel appears in code by metaphorically referring to the trafficking of cadavers: "Los fiambres son para comérselos" (Dead meat is for eating [*fiambre* literally means "cold cuts" or "lunch meat," but is a slang term for a cadaver]), "La sangre no solo sirve para hacer morcillas" (Blood is not only used to make blood sausage), "Organicemos el hambre y todo será pan comido" (If we take care of hunger everything else will be solved). But *Lalengua* refers also, literally, to the secrets and lies that only lead to new deaths. At the end of the novel, after the kidnapping of one of the characters, Alberto Ferruci, a message on a wall reads, "Lalengua ya pagó" (The tongue already paid). Ferruci was murdered and his body found in a vacant lot with the tongue cut out.

Caparrós's novel belongs to a long line of Argentine literature that incorporates the conventions and codes of the hard-boiled novel in order to narrate the violence and corruption of the last military dictatorship. Therefore it goes back to the beginnings of the genre in which social and political corruption is placed at the center of the plot, the story runs parallel to the action, and the detective loses his immunity by risking his life to uncover the crime.

Sylvia Saítta

Work

El tercer cuerpo. Buenos Aires; Puntosur, 1990. Reprint, Buenos Aires: Norma, 1997.

Criticism

Russo, Miguel. "Tele, música, comida y cadáveres." *Radar libros* (Cultural supplement of the newpaper *Página/12*) (4 January 1998).

Leonardo Castellani (1896–1980)

ARGENTINA

In *Un modelo para la muerte* (A model for death, 1946), the novel by B. Suárez Lynch—pseudonym of Jorge Luis Borges and Adolfo Bioy Casares—there are multiple critiques of and mocking jabs taken at the cultural nationalism then in vogue. It was the period in Argentine history associated with the increasing fervor of Peronism in ascension, militarism and Catholicism. Suárez Lynch laid out a detailed verbal assault on those values defended by intellectuals such as Leopoldo Marechal, Leonardo Castellani, and José María Castiñeira de Dios. In fact, a certain "Father Gallegani," an unmistakable allusion to Father Leonardo Castellani, appears as a ridiculous defender of such ideas in the novel.

Castellani's work consists of the collection of short stories *Las muertes del padre Metri* (The deaths of Father Metri, 1942; definitive edition in 1975 that includes two additional stories), the novel *El enigma del fantasma en coche* (The enigma of the ghost in the car, 1958), and the stories contained in *El crimen de Ducadelia y otros cuentos del Trío* (The crime of Ducadelia and other stories of the Trio, 1959). The case of Castellani is interesting in the sense that his literary production offers several points in common with that of Borges, Bustos Domecq, and Manuel Peyrou , at the same time that it proposes a contradictory alternative model whose full potential has gone underexamined.

The intellectual environment of Buenos Aires during the 1940s expressed itself in the pages of the literary supplements of the leading newspapers *La Prensa* (The press) or *La Nación* (The nation), or in the journals *Sur* (South) and *Criterio* (Criterion). Borges and Bioy Casares could not ignore the detective tales that Castellani, under the pseudonym of Jerónimo del Rey, had been publishing in *La Nación* since the previous decade and that featured a rival of the famous fictional detective Father Brown by the name of Father Metri. Borges shared with Castellani an admiration for the British Catholic writer Gilbert K. Chesterton, whom Castellani had even personally met in Rome. Both Argentine intellectuals published reviews on the author of *The Innocence of Father Brown* (1911) in which their profoundly different ideological views are quite evident. Borges, in two articles in *Sur*, highlights the command of the hidden clues and the economy of resources ("En los relatos policiales de Chesterton todo se justifica: los episodios más fugaces y breves tienen proyección ulterior" [In Chesterton's detective stories everything is justified: the short, fleeting episodes have an ulterior projection] *Sur* 22 [1936]: 50). Furthermore, he points to the primacy of the how over the who, the shame of death, and the predominance of the intellectual game (the real detective avoids physical risk) over the referential clues ("Los lugares del crimen son admirables, como en todo libro de Chesterton, y cuidadosa y sensacionalmente falsos. ¿Ha alguien denunciado la afinidad entre el Londres fantástico de Stevenson y el de Chesterton?" [The crime scenes are admirable, as in every book by Chesterton, and carefully and sensationally false. Has anyone

denounced the afinity between the London of Stevenson and that of Chesterton?]
Sur 10 [1935]: 94). He also points out the use of humor and paradox to vindicate
Catholicism in a work that is apologetic in nature and doesn't use faith as a soci-
ological method, although he signals the risk of reducing the stories to mere para-
bles. In passing, Borges also defines his territory by recalling that "en Inglaterra
no hay el catolicismo petulante y autoritario que padece nuestra República"
(England doesn't have the petulant and authoritarian Catholicism that our
Republic has to suffer [*Sur* 22 (1936): 47]), which is precisely what he criticizes
Castellani for.

Castellani writes about Chesterton at the same time Borges does, between
1930 and 1940, and later combines his analyses in the essay "Gilbert K. Chesterton" (published in his *Crítica literaria* [Literary criticism, 1945]). In Chesterton's
detective fiction, he is interested in the quality of the mystery, the recurrence of
character types (protagonist-detective, antagonist-criminal, the intimacy of the
confidant, the incompetence of the police), the device of psychological notes,
philosophical ideas, local-color sketches, paradoxes, and the apologetic dimensions of the text. The detective genre offers an explanation of the catechism and
a way of understanding human nature (in this sense, the relation to Georges
Simenon's Commissioner Maigret of the 1930s is unavoidable): "¡El criminal! ¡El
criminal antagonista es convertido por el cura detective y se vuelve su confidente,
su Dr. Watson!" (The criminal! The antagonist criminal is converted by the priest
detective and becomes his confidant, his Dr. Watson!) ("Gilbert K. Chesterton").
Castellani underscores the didactic character of Chesterton's work, a quality that
clashed with Borges's line of thinking and that could only invite his rejection. In
this sense, we can read the Borges–Bioy Casares character Isidro Parodi (from
their *Seis problemas para don Isidro Parodi* [*Six Problems for Don Isidro Parodi*],
1942) as a parody of certain aspects of the detective created by Castellani, Friar
Hermete Demetrio Constanzi, alias Father Metri, especially given the exemplary
national character that the hero of the saga embodies. The didactic nature of his
detective fiction is connected with the necessity of founding an epic based on the
recovery of tradition, which facilitates the design of a relatively coherent narrative program.

Metri, the main character in all the stories, is constructed on the basis of lay-
ering the historic with the mythic and legendary. The result is a narrative voice
that manages to define the Franciscan as a saint-in-the-making that is voluntarily grounded in reality to produce a discourse in which the word of his ancestors
is cited as the certificate of authenticity for the adventures of the priest. In general, as is tradition in detective fiction, the stories present themselves as having
really occurred. To achieve this, the author claims to have changed some traits of
the priest for literary purposes, but he multiplies the apocryphal epigraphs that
mention Father Metri as a historical figure or confesses to having changed the
names of characters and places to protect the innocent. Affirming the historicity
of the character and establishing his epic nature strengthens the national character of the series.

The detective modalities of the British writer Chesterton were fairly easy to adapt to the Argentine environment and above all permit Castellani to introduce his nationalist thought through the conventions of the genre. The first latent difficulty of this parodic appropriation arose with the problem of how to adapt the Father Brown figure who carried out his mission in a kingdom plagued by conflict and religious debates with Protestantism. The use of humor and parody that both Borges and Castellani evoked in their commentaries relied on a critical distance accentuated by the defining characteristics of Brown as a sign: absent-minded, clumsy, simple, restrained, nearsighted, and stocky. Castellani's adaptation took up some of these qualities, but in the final product the character, in the interest of epic pretensions, tended much more toward heroic proportions.

Father Metri was a Franciscan priest, an Italian, who lived in the rural north of Argentina. Like Brown, he was part parish priest, part missionary whose primary characteristic was his marginal status. Up to this point, nothing new: the detective hero par excellence had always been, from the start, eccentric. Sherlock Holmes occupied himself with practicing the violin, Philo Vance with the contemplation of his art collection, and Sergeant Cuff loved to grow roses. Castellani's differed in an important way that represented a break from the social canon of the English detective tradition. Borges had pointed out in his essay, "Los laberintos policiales y Chesterton," that the English had two passions: the thirst for adventure, and an appetite for the law. And he added, Martín Fierro and Cruz (characters in José Hernández's nineteenth-century epic gaucho poem *Martín Fierro*) would laugh at the thought that the law was infallible. It is from this essential difference, this complicity with Fierro and Cruz, that distances him from Chesterton and the Anglo detective story in which Castellani creates his character Metri.

The priest operates during a decisive time in national history, the period of state formation at the end of the nineteenth century. If all fictions of the past are often a way for the author to examine the present, Metri's parables establish the basis, through the detective genre, for criticizing the dysfunction of a justice system caused by a state structure that from the beginning was built on a shaky foundation. Within this context, the social institutions of family, professional guilds, communes, corporations, and state institutions such as the university, the armed forces, and the Church are stripped of virtue in the strict sense. His criticism stems from the principle that there is a lack of national unity, generated by the absence of the state and a central authority (which is then assumed by the liberal oligarchy) in outlying provinces such as the Chaco region where the stories take place. When it is not absent, the state is poorly represented, as in the story "El degüello de San Antonio" (The slaughter of San Antonio) in which the arrogance of the military, represented by Major Ojeda, provokes a bloody uprising from the Toba Indians. Castellani undertakes a systematic critique of power, including the power of the church, which excommunicates the priest. Metri declares, "La justicia y la autoridad no existen sino como repugnante máscara" (Justice and authority existen only as a repugnant mask [166]) in "El caso de Ada Terry" (The case of Ada Terry, in *Las muertes del padre Metri*).

The social outlook implicit in the stories of this first stage relates the Metri series to the hard-boiled tradition. However, every genre requires the respect of certain stylistic guidelines. It is at this level, in our judgment, that the second difficulty with the parodic appropriation arises. Overall, is it undeniable that Castellani's literary production is linked with the detective mystery, at least in the tendency to organize the narration from the starting point of a double story—that of the crime, and that of the investigation.

Generally, the stories begin with the committing of the crime, usually taken to the extreme of murder. The mystery stands out for its complexity and for appealing to the need for the most rigorous process of logic and deduction. To the constant use of reasoning Castellani adds the handling of typological and structural codes that allow him in some stories to work with the principle of inversion, as in many of the masters of the genre. For example, in "El caso de Ada Terry" the killer turns out to be a policeman.

Castellani's innovation becomes evident in the pendular structure of his stories that, stemming from the detective mysteries of Chesterton, swing from the presentation to the development to the close of the mystery, with a series of introductory or complementary diversions on topics of philosophy, psychology, and so on. In his parodic appropriation, Leonardo Castellani makes substantial use of still-time, thus introducing a change in the structural format. "La muerte en el Majestic Hotel" (Death in the Majestic Hotel), for example, is organized around a triple story: the crime, the investigation, and what could be called a "delayed story" that explains the presence of Metri at the scene of the crime. This last story-line refers to Metri's stay in Buenos Aires in order to interview the president of the Republic and petition his intervention in the situation brewing in the Indian missions of the north, that live under the threat of rebellion provoked by the abuse of the authorities.

The use of still-time brings with it a third difficulty: the nature of these digressive fragments. If we return to Castellani's reading of Chesterton's poetics, we notice that the creation of local-color sketches (el costumbrismo) is directly related to psychology, in the sense that it facilitates the use of elements like the character and speech of country folk (and city dwellers), the concept of the family, the daily chores, festivals, religion, and folklore. The temporal and geographic setting emphasizes the national character, which is accentuated by the description of landscapes. The elaboration of these narrative spaces confers upon the writer the role of creator. The countryside—the interior of the country—is presented as the receptacle of tradition, while the urban capital—Buenos Aires—emerges as the territory of dispersion and disorder.

Meanwhile, of the 11 stories of the Metri series, only two take place away from the northern extreme of the Santa Fe province. "Hombre al agua" (Man overboard) occurs on an ocean liner, and it is the most Chestertonian of the collection. The other is the already-mentioned "La muerte en el Majestic Hotel," which takes place in the Buenos Aires neighborhood of Palermo, although, as we have described, the setting is defined in opposition to an absent and constantly refer-

enced space. In the Father Ducadelia series (another 11 stories), the action transpires mainly in Buenos Aires, but the values associated with the two spaces are
unchanged. In fact, one of the most common *costumbrista* traits is sobriety or
sternness, used by the narrator to describe the psychology of country folk (a characteristic of Isidro Parodi as well). This sobriety pertains to tradition—and the
detective protagonists adhere to tradition.

Another aspect that is painstakingly detailed is modes of speech. The narrator recreates local speech by phonetically transcribing regional variants, the
grammatical errors of Indians and immigrants, even those of Metri and Ducadelia, and opts for the local voseo (a second-person verb variation unique to the
region). Popular speech harbors a treasury of wisdom in the form of sayings and
refrains. The rural setting appears as a melting pot, the tranquil refuge of a population that merely needs to be guided and educated the way a priest guides and
educates his parishioners. The power of the word as an educational tool takes
center stage in the stories, and the reader and characters enter into a contract with
the text that is based on orality and conversation.

As we have seen, Castellani's appropriation in the Metri series fully meets the
goal of parody. This is achieved in the way that he, first, redistributes almost
mechanically the codified conventions of detective fiction as seen in Chesterton,
and, second, by generating a new proposal by inserting this style into an Argentine context. It is no coincidence that his generic model, which also comes from
a literary culture, runs parallel to that of Borges and Peyrou. Moreover, it continues in his later works as well as in the contributions of Velmiro Ayala Gauna and
Rodolfo Walsh, especially in the latter's Detective Laurenzi series. Likewise, it is
connected to the hard-boiled novel of the 1970s with which he shares a common
feeling of antiliberalism.

Metri sees his continuation in the figure of Father Ducadelia, protagonst of *El
crimen de Ducadelia y otros cuentos del Trío*. The "Trio" alludes to a "noncommer-
cial society" dedicated to reports and personal matters that is available at all hours
and that by definition belongs—as much for its activities as for the characteristics of its members—to the margins of society. The group is comprised of Father
Ducadelia, a Mocoví Indian chief, ironically named San Pablo (and who appeared
as an altar boy for Father Metri), and Alarcón, an ex-lawyer and ex-convict.

After having undertaken the nationalization of the genre, this second book of
stories incorporates new parodic elements, and even is a self-parody. Ducadelia is
formed from a succession of models. Like Brown, he is a priest, a detective, simple, nearsighted, and clumsy; like Metri, he is a priest, an Italian immigrant to
Argentina, a detective, and a polyglot. His way of thinking and acting reminds
one that investigations are a practical demonstration of the catechism. One of his
associates, San Pablo, stands out for his participation in the investigations in
which he proves his capability and qualities of observation and a surprising
"instinct" to arrive at the truth without overlooking the use of the most sophisticated techniques. He knows, for example, how to lift fingerprints. The allusions
to Holmes or Rouletabille are only thinly veiled: "Andaba a los garrones del indio

que se movía como un gato en el estrecho cuarto . . . mirando todo y oliscando todo." (He was right on the tail of the Indian who was moving about the cramped room like a cat . . . looking at everything, sniffing everything [37].) Obviously, his trait most readily mocked is that of being an Indian. In *Un modelo para la muerte*, Borges and Bioy Casares had satirized nationalism and ridiculed its vindication of autochthonous culture through the so-called Asociación Aborigenista Argentina (Argentine aboriginalist association), whose members used pseudonyms like Pincén or Catriel. In *El crimen de Ducadelia*, Castellani utilizes the same technique (inversely) and gives his Mocoví character the name San Pablo.

The Trio works principally in the Federal Capital, in an office downtown that serves a headquarters for an operation that reaches all over the country. For instance, "El caso del húngaro ahogado" (The case of the drowned Hungarian) takes place on a ranch in the province of Buenos Aires; "El crimen de Plauto Mendoza" (The crime of Plauto Mendoza) transpires in Reconquista, Santa Fe. The public space chosen by the protagonists to work in should not be confused with the private space the Trio inhabits—a marginal apartment building. In addition, Buenos Aires is defined as an unbalanced territory, like the gigantic head of an octopus that exploits the rest of the country.

The marginality of the main characters in *El crimen del padre Ducadelia*—greater than that of Father Metri, in the sense that they don't undergo a process of mythification—confirms the inherent disorder that frames the crimes. Therefore, it is futile to pretend that the actions of the investigators (Metri, Ducadelia, San Pablo, Alarcón) can restore a nonexistent order. This is why the theme of justice constantly reappears. In "El caso del húngaro ahogado" several characters successively declare themselves guilty of the crime so that in the end of the story the phrase "I am guilty" is left floating in the air like an unanswered question. As in reality, according to Castellani, in order to fight against disorder it is necessary to restore justice, by consolidating the Catholic religion, patriotism, and autocratic government.

While the hero of the North American hard-boiled novel speaks the same language, comes from the same social class, and lives in the same world as the criminal, this is not the case in Castellani. His detectives are different by being priests or a woman, but even more importantly, they do not operate with the same cultural codes as the victims, and in the case of Metri and Ducadelia, they are motivated by moral incentives (in spite of the fact that Ducadelia formed a commercial enterprise with Alarcón and San Pablo to make a living from their investigations). Moreover, Metri is mythified, Ducadelia is of noble origins (though fallen on hard times) and Marta Guevara Castellanos similarly admits to being the great-great-granddaughter of a two-time governor of Salta and official under Martín Güemes.

Metri acts without a confidant, although this role is at times played by a complicit narrator. By contrast, the Ducadelia series introduces a new element, since it operates with two confidants—who are not narrators—who share his same social register. *El enigma del fantasma en coche* introduces Marta Guevara Castellanos, a nurse at the Hospital de la Provincia, who is described among other

things as being nervous, energetic, and fairly good-looking. If Metri and Ducadelia are concerned with matters of the soul, Marta, buy virtue of her profession,
is responsible for bodily care and she is also adept at psychology. The catalyst that
initiates the investigation is a personal matter that will allow the mysterious disappearance of her sister Gladys to be linked to the alleged appearance of a ghost
in her sister's husband's car.

The figure of the woman here presents an image quite different than what appears previously in Castellani's works. Both priest-detectives and San Pablo sys-
tematically point out the malice and perfidy of the other sex. In this way, women
appear within a fictional hierarchy in three ways. The first is as the "Other," a figure of potential guilt as we see in the work of Raúl Waleis (pseudonym of Luis V.
Varela) or Eduardo E. Holmberg . The second is as a passive victim, incapable of
reaction when confronted with the power of the other sex. The third is the figure
of the assertive woman who is criticized as rebellious and too masculine.

El enigma del fantasma en coche, then, offers a new point of view in Marta
Guevara Castellanos, who is not only the heroine, but the detective and narrator
(similar to the hard-boiled model). At no time does she relinquish her role as the
creator of the story, although at times she delegates parts of the investigation to
her ex-boyfriend and permanent suitor, Police Commissioner Germán Valdés
Tristán, or to Dr. Jorge. Her condition as woman and narrator is connected to the
author's use of still-time, interweaving reflections on the feminine with the act of
narration. Marta defines herself, in direct contrast to men, with bold comments:
"La guerra que hacen los hombres no es nada al lado de las guerras continuas que
soportamos nosotras. En realidad las mujeres son más fuertes. Esa es la verdad."
(The war that men wage is nothing compared to the constant wars that we
women endure. In reality women are stronger. That's the truth [58].) Nevertheless, she will later affirm her marginality in an ironic twist that summarizes Castellani's position: "Creo que ni las mujeres ni los curas deberíamos ser novelistas."
(I believe that neither women nor priests should be novelists [77].) Self-referential parody makes an appearance in the character of Father Castell, ally and confidant of Marta. At one point, Valdés comments something to the effect that there
is a conspiracy between women and priests to derail the police.

The novelty of *El enigma* doesn't end with the figure of the narrator-detective,
but is further complemented by a host of characters. The feminine condition is
necessarily one of victim in the modest environment of life in the northern
province of Salta where the action transpires. The woman-victim is but one of a
group of disenfranchised figures that populate the stories of Metri and Ducadelia:
Toba Indians, peons, herders, woodcutters, and poor immigrants that constitute
a kind of portrait of the national body. Both priests are Italians but fervent
defenders of national(ist) values. However, the integration is never perfect, and at
the conclusion of the Ducadelia cycle the protagonist leaves for Spain, disillusioned and embittered by failure. The image of the immigrant serves to stir-up
friction. Castellani's extreme nationalism leads him to perceive the floods of immigrants as a threat to traditional Creole ways and values. In *El enigma*, a char-

acter lays the blame for the changes in Salta on inhabitants of Buenos Aires, Arabs, and Jews—all considered to be thieves. In addition, Castellani expressed such ideas outside his fiction as well, as can be seen in the declaration, "Un judío puede llegar a ser hombre de ciencia, difícil hombre de cultura. La cultura entraña una tradición, y el judío es esencialmente el hombre sin tradición patria. No digo sin tradición racial y religiosa" (A Jew can become a man of science, but hardly a man a culture. Culture entails a tradition, and the Jew is essentially a man without the tradition of a homeland. I don't mean to say without racial or religious tradition) (*Crítica literaria*, 366). Whatever the case, the initial disorder of his narratives—always the product of social confusion—is maintained and reinforced, including in the melodramatic happy ending of *El enigma* in which Marta and Valdés renew their romance.

The victimizers, meanwhile, are generally situated within structures of power, defined as state control, authority, and economic resources always characterized as *porteño* and masculine. The transgressive inversion of power thrives in this environment where agents of justice are easily transformed into criminals: the bourgeoisie, oligarchs, and politicians in "Hombre al agua" (Metri), "El crimen de Plauto Mendoza," "El caso del desaparecido" (The case of the missing man), and "El caso del enano del circo" (The case of the circus midget)—all from the Ducadelia series; wealthy foreigners in "La muerte en el Majestic Hotel"; the military and police in "El caso de Ada Terry"; scorned women who must take justice into their own hands in "El fusil que tira solo" (The gun that fires on its own) and "Montevideo su cerro" (Montevideo hill) or cruel women, "Los astericos de sangre" (Asterisks of blood); immigrants who are helpless in the face of state corruption, "La mosca de oro" (The golden fly); and fugitive or brutal immigrants in "La cabeza entre los libros" (The head among the books) (Metri), "El caso del húngaro ahogado" (Ducadelia), or the Hungarian Bela Kiss in *El enigma*. One shouldn't assume, however, that crime possesses a univocal social connotation; on the contrary, the context allows the narrator to advance the psychological descriptions and thus—returning to Chesterton—enter the criminal mind. This becomes explicit in the figure of the serial killer of women in *El enigma del fantasma en coche*.

The literary transcendence of Castellani's detective fiction poetics—elaborated in his 22 stories and one novel—contrasts with the scant repercussion his work has had on the genre in Argentina. The polemics of his ideology that place him in opposition to intellectual liberals and Marxists is not enough to account for his isolation. The circulation of discourse depends on multiple factors (artistic, political, ideological, commercial, and so on), but it would seem that in Argentina the notion of prestige played a major role. The practice of the genre lost its label as "popular," which allowed it to be picked up by the cultural/literary elite. The role of Castellani in this context should be revised.

Néstor Ponce

Works

"El caso de Ada Terry," in *El cuento policial latinoamericano*, ed. Donald A. Yates. Mexico City: Ediciones de Andrea, 1964, 51–66. Also in *Cuentos policiales argentinos*, ed. Jorge Lafforgue. Buenos Aires: Alfaguara, 1997, 95–114; and *Cuentos policiales*, ed. Fermín Fevre. Buenos Aires: Kapelusz, 1974, 87–109.

El crimen de Ducadelia y otros cuentos del Trío. Buenos Aires: Doseme, 1959.

Crítica literaria. Buenos Aires, Ediciones Penca, 1945.

El enigma de la muerte en coche. Buenos Aires: Ediciones Norte, 1958. Reprint Buenos Aires: n.p., 1976.

"Gilbert K. Chesterton," in *Crítica literaria*. Buenos Aires: Penca, 1945, 157–216.

Las 9 [nueve] muertes del Padre Metri. Buenos Aires: C.E.P.A., 1942. Definitive edition as *Las muertes del Padre Metri*. Buenos Aires: Ediciones Sed, 1952. Reprint, Buenos Aires: Dictio, 1978.

Criticism

Barcia, Pedro Luis. "Bibliografía de Leonardo Castellani." *El gato negro* 7 (1996): 42–46.

Delaney, Juan José. "Leonardo Castellani y el misterio." *El gato negro* 7 (1996): 34–41.

Lafforgue, Jorge, and Jorge B. Rivera. *Asesinos de papel: ensayos sobre narrativa policial*. Buenos Aires: Ediciones Colihue, 1996.

Lindstrom, Naomi. "The Argentine Reading of Chesterton." *Chesterton Review* 6 (1980): 272–79.

———. "Leonardo Castellani : Detective Fiction and Marginality." *Latin American Digest* 13.2 (1979) : 7–8, 10.

Ponce, Néstor. *Diagonales del género: estudios sobre el policial argentino*. Paris: Editions du Temp, 2001.

Romano, Eduardo. "Los parientes criollos del padre Brown," in *Los héroes "difíciles": la literatura policial en la Argentina y en Italia*, ed. Giuseppe Petronio, Jorge B. Rivera, and Luigi Volta. Buenos Aires: Corregidor, 1991, 257–80.

Simpson, Amelia S. *Detective Fiction from Latin America*. Rutherford, NJ: Fairleigh Dickinson University Press, 1990.

Zuleta Alvarez, Enrique. *El nacionalismo argentino (II)*. Bs. As., La Bastilla, 1975, 721–37.

Luiz Lopes Coelho (1911–1975)

BRAZIL

As a detective fiction writer, Lopes Coelho played a pivotal role in the development of the genre in Brazil. He was not the first Brazilian to create a literary detective. As Amelia Simpson points out, Jerônimo Monteiro, who wrote under the pseudonym Ronnie Wells, had already featured his detective, Dick Peter, in several works in the 1930s (Simpson 67). Both the author's pen name and his character's name signal the influence of foreign detective fiction in Brazil. Lopes Coelho, in contrast, is credited with being the first author "to create a truly autonomous, national interpretation of the genre" (Simpson 67). This is an important distinction to make, for it establishes the author's role as a foundational figure of a uniquely Brazilian brand of detective fiction. Medeiros e Albuquerque also comments that Lopes Coelho is to be recognized for having created "o primeiro detetive brasileiro de ficção. O Doutor Leite é, sobretudo, uma figura bem brasileira, que faz com que esqueçamos alguns dos muitos detetives estrangeiros" (the first fictional Brazilian detective. Doctor Leite is, above all, a very Brazilian figure, who helped us to forget some of the many foreign detectives) (Medeiros e Albuquerque 1973, 179).

Lopes Coelho wrote three detective-story collections, all of which feature his detective, Doutor Leite: *A morte no envelope* (Death in an envelope, 1957), *O homem que matava quadros* (The man who killed paintings, 1961), and *A idéia de matar Belina* (The plot to kill Belina, 1968). His stories may be characterized as following the classic model of the "whodunit" or puzzle-story where the detective is presented with a mystery, which is solved by applying principles of logic and deductive reasoning. Leite is described as an old—and therefore very experienced and wise—detective who solves the majority of the crimes presented to him by merely reconstructing the crime and unraveling the underlying logic of the mystery, mostly from his home or study or any other place that is distant from the crime scene itself. This is similar to the character Isidro Parodi, created by Jorge Luis Borges and Adolfo Bioy Casares, who solves crimes from his prison cell. There is also a bit of Sherlock Holmes in Leite, although with a very Brazilian twist. Likewise, there is the occasional wink and nod to other classic tales, as is the case with the story "Ninguem morre duas vezes" (No one dies twice) in *O homem que matava quadros*, in which Leite uses the lesson learned in Edgar Allan Poe's "The Purloined Letter" to solve the crime. Also, in "Seis homens e um brilhante" (Six men and a diamond) in *A morte no envelope,* Lopes Coelho recalls Owen Johnson's story "One Hundred in the Dark" to solve this classic locked-room case. Another locked-room mystery is the excellent "Só o crime estava na biblioteca" (Only the crime was in the library) in *A morte no envelope*. In this story, Leite, who is laid-up in the hospital with a broken leg, solves the murder of a millionaire killed in his library that was locked from the inside. A good example of a case of simple deductive reasoning can be found in "Whisky and Soda" in *A morte no envelope*, a story about a woman who poisons her husband at a dinner party. With all the suspects present, Leite considers the facts, evidence, and motives to eliminate them one by one until the murderer is identified.

While Lopes Coelho's stories are mainly intended to be entertainments with little or no social criticism, the author does touch on several more intellectual topics. In fact, the stories are clearly directed at a well-educated audience that will be able to follow his psychological, philosophical, artistic, literary, or pseudoscientific references. In several stories, the situation of the crime merely serves as a backdrop to discuss such issues. This is the case in "Seis homens e um brilhante," where the men sit around the dinner table in a heated philosophical debate. In "Vovô faz a gente de bôbo" (Grandpa makes fools of the guys) in *A morte no envelope*, where Leite, the grandpa, sits around with a group of young lawyers and entertains them with the story of a case and at the same time demonstrates the superior wisdom that comes with age. The story also revolves around the debate over whether the cause of criminal behavior is biological or sociological. Finally, in "O homem que matava quadros," the main subject is not discovering the culprit who is slashing paintings, but art and artistic movements and styles.

The stories in the last volume, *A idéia de matar Belina*, are not as clever or interesting as in the previous two collections. Nevertheless, Lopes Coelho's narratives are, in general, excellent examples of the early classic detective model adapted to a very Brazilian style that combines a good amount of humor and irony, local color and lore. There can be no question that the author is a cornerstone of the detective genre in Brazil.

Darrell B. Lockhart

Works

O homem que matava quadros. Rio de Janeiro: Editôra Civilização Brasileira, 1961.
A idéia de matar Belina. Rio de Janeiro: Sabiá, 1968.
A morte no envelope: contos policiais. Rio de Janeiro: Editôra Civilização Brasileira, 1957.

Criticism

Albuquerque, Paulo de Medeiros e. *Os maiores detetives de todos os tempos*. Rio de Janeiro: Civilização Brasileira, 1973.
———. *O mundo emocionante do romance policial*. Rio de Janeiro: Francisco Alves, 1979.
Simpson, Amelia S. *Detective Fiction from Latin America*. Rutherford, NJ: Fairleigh Dickinson University Press, 1990.

Hiber Conteris (b. 1933)

URUGUAY

Hiber Conteris was born in Paysandú, Uruguay, in September 1933. He later moved to Montevideo with his family and spent some of his formative years in Buenos Aires, Argentina. He gained vast theoretical grounding in the Humanities while studying in Buenos Aires and Montevideo. Furthermore, he pursued graduate studies in sociology and semiology in Europe, where he was a student of Lucien Goldmann, Roland Barthes, and Maurice Duverger.

In his native Montevideo he was an instructor of literature at the secondary level, as well as a professor of political science and the history of ideas at the Facultad de Derecho y Ciencias Sociales (College of law and social sciences). At the same time, he worked as a journalist for the prestigious weekly *Marcha*, where he wrote literary reviews and criticism.

The 1970s were tragic for Uruguay. A heavy-handed military dictatorship had been in power for well over a decade, and a large number of Uruguayan intellectuals—writers, actors, professors, dancers, and singers—were either incarcerated or forced into exile. Conteris spent more than eight years in prison, between 1976 and 1985. Shortly thereafter he migrated to the United States, where he presently resides. He has taught Latin American literature at the University of Madison at Wisconsin and chaired the Department of Foreign Languages at Alfred University in upstate New York for several years. Currently, he teaches literature and Latin American Studies at the University of Arizona (International College).

A prolific writer, he has had a brilliant career both as an author and playwright. His works include the novels *Cono Sur* (Southern Cone, 1963), *Virginia en flashback* (Virginia in flashback, 1966), *El nadador* (The swimmer, 1968), *La Diana en el crepúsculo* (Diana at twilight, 1987), *El diez por ciento de vida* (*Ten Percent of Life*, 1986), *El breve verano de Nefertiti* (Nefertiti's brief summer, 1996), *Round Trip* (1998), and *Oscura memoria del Sur* (Dark memory of the south; 2002) and short-story collections *Información sobre la ruta 1* (Information about route 1, 1987), and *La cifra anónima* (The anonymous cipher, 1988). He is also a prolific playwright and his dramatic production includes the works *Vila Anastacio* (1965), *El asesinato de Malcolm X* (The assassination of Malcolm X, 1969), *Enterrar a los muertos* (Burying the dead, 1959), *Este otro lado del telón* (This other side of the curtain, 1960), *El desvío* (The detour, 1963), *El socavón* (The pothole, 1963), *Berenice* (1972), *El intruso* (The intruder, 1987), and *Holiday Inn* (1988), among others. Many of these have been performed in Montevideo by local groups such as "El Galpón," "La Comedia Nacional," "La Máscara," and "La Farsa"; others have been staged in Chile, Cuba, Poland, Czechoslovakia, and the United States. Conteris has been awarded the Letras de Oro award (University of Miami, 1986), the coveted Casa de las Américas (Cuba, 1988), and a First Prize in Spain for *El breve verano de Nefertiti* (1994).

A second edition of *La cifra anónima* (1988), states on the back cover that the reader of this volume "will find the political, the detective story and the fantastic," recurrent themes in Conteris's literary corpus. What justifies the author's inclusion in this present volume, however, is his novel *El diez por ciento de vida* (originally published in Barcelona in 1986, and again in Montevideo in 1994). One of his most successful works to date, it has been translated into English, French, German, Italian, and Japanese.

"Ten Percent of Your Life" is the title of an essay written by Raymond Chandler in 1952 and published by the *Atlantic Monthly*. In it, Chandler discusses the basic immorality of literary agents who keep what he considers an excessive amount of the writer's hard-earned money. Conteris borrows the title and constructs an intriguing work that from the outset is presented as a homage to both the author of such masterpieces of the genre as *The Big Sleep* (1939), *Farewell, My Lovely* (1940), and *The Long Goodbye* (1954) and to his recurrent main character Phillip Marlowe. The novelty, of course, is that both Chandler and Marlowe are characters in Conteris's tightly controlled text.

Yensid Andress, a successful Hollywood agent, is found dead—a bullet in his head, a Colt 7.65 in his right hand. Although the evidence clearly points to suicide, Charles Morton, a seasoned reporter for the *Los Angeles Times*, cannot quite accept such a conclusion without further analysis, and he enlists his friend Marlowe, a private eye, to research the matter. Soon enough, Marlowe—and the reader—learn that somehow the pistol's locking mechanism has remained engaged, clearly indicating that someone other than the deceased might have operated it. In addition to that, through the mediation of Nulty, the "good cop" of the story, some important information is revealed: the weapon was fired from a distance, and the bullet's angle of penetration seems to prove that the gun was aimed down, a very awkward position for someone trying to blow his own brains out.

As in any "whodunit" worthy of such a name, once the crime has been revealed, the detective sets out to find the culprit(s). Although somewhat reluctantly, Marlowe embraces the challenge and quickly follows all possible leads. One such lead points to Velma Valento, the agent's business associate, a sultry lady who will eventually—and predictably—become romantically involved with Marlowe.

The text alternates between first-person narration (in this case the narrator is the protagonist, Marlowe) and the "traditional" omniscient third-person narrator. Let us also say that in Conteris's, novel Raymond Chandler plays himself and engages in lengthy discussions of the genre from a technical point of view, whereby he also considers the work of his colleagues, including the brilliant Dashiell Hammett, whom he repeatedly praises.

As might be expected, the plot thickens, and at Andress's funeral two shady characters appear, obviously concerned with the investigation and apparently targeting Marlowe. It is Morton, however, who reveals with his editor's enthusiastic approval that the alleged suicide is indeed a murder, and because of that, he himself is killed. Both Marlowe and Velma—who is after all, the one controlling everything related to Andress's business—might well be the next victims of these efficient thugs. Eventually, frustrating honest efforts by the police, and Nulty in particular, to protect them, Marlowe and Velma, also accompanied by the victim's son, are followed by the criminals. The magnificent car chase, masterfully narrated, ends up with the Oldsmobile driven by the criminals careening over a steep cliff. They survive, however, and at that moment the police finally arrive. In spite of Marlowe's desperate attempt at prevention, Nulty orders his men to fire and both suspects are instantly killed. Since it seems quite obvious that these two characters were hired killers, their deaths will forever hide the truth.

"Probably the biggest mistake a reader of Hiber Conteris's *El diez por ciento de vida* could make," writes Patricia Hart, "would be to think that such an obvious homage to Raymond Chandler must at the same time be an imitation" (Hart 1). Indeed it is not, especially in matters of writing style, but it is also important to see that in the novel, the one who actually gets closer to solving the case is Chandler, not Marlowe—it is crucial to read carefully page 191 of the second Spanish edition. What then is missing? Whodunit? We will never know. The frightening reality is that "The System" has assassinated the agent. The context is the witch-hunts of the McCarthy era, and one cannot but extrapolate from this clever text a strong and universal criticism of tyranny and oppression anytime, anywhere. Finally, worthy of mention is Conteris's eloquent essay (1999) on Chandler, "Hiber Conteris on Raymond Chandler," in which he examines the writer, his works, and his influence.

Horacio Xaubet

Works

La cifra anónima. Montevideo: Trilce, 1988. Reprint, Havana: Casa de las Américas, 1988; Mexico: El Juglar, 1989.
El diez por ciento de vida. Barcelona: Editorial Laia, 1986. Published as *10% de tu vida*. Montevideo: Editorial Fin de Siglo, 1994. English version as *Ten Percent of Life*, trans. Deborah Bergman. New York: Simon & Schuster, 1987.
"Hiber Conteris on Raymond Chandler," trans. Patricia L. Bornhofen, in *Mutual Impressions: Writers from the Americas Reading One Another*, ed. Ilán Stavans. Durham, NC: Duke University Press, 1999, 87–106.

Criticism

Colás, Santiago. "Un posmodernismo resistente en América latina: *El diez por ciento de vida* y la historia." *Nuevo texto crítico* 4.7 (1991): 179–96.
Hart, Patricia. "Revisiting Chandler and Recreating Marlowe in Hiber Conteris's *El diez por ciento de vida*." *Journal of the Midwest Modern Language Association* 23 (1990): 1–16.
Paul, Marcie. "Suspect Author: Hiber Conteris's *Ten Percent of Life*." *Latin American Literary Review* 35 (1990): 50–58.

Marco Denevi (1920–1998)

ARGENTINA

Born in Saénz Peña (in the province of Buenos Aires) on 12 May 1920, Marco Denevi is, strictly speaking, the author of only one detective novel, *Rosaura a las diez* (*Rosa at Ten O'Clock*, 1955) for which he won the then-prestigious Premio Kraft (Kraft literary award) in 1955. It was his first book and immediately became a bestseller that was translated into several languages. After 50 years it is still widely read and considered a classic of Argentine literature.

Modeled after the crime or mystery novel, *Rosaura a las diez* constitutes an effective example of a psychological investigation and of certain human behavior when love is at play. The novel is informed and clearly influenced by two memorable texts by master storyteller Wilkie Collins, *The Woman in White* (1860) and *The Moonstone* (1868). Denevi borrowed from them the technique of polyphonic discourse and the topic of switched identities (later a recurrent trait in his works), the trade of the love-struck character, and, to a certain extent, the ending. The effective and detailed writing style, the perfect presentation of the narrators, the revelation of their psychological motivation almost exclusively through their voices, and the subtle use of humor mixed with profound observations on art and life are all traits unique to Denevi's writing style. The influence of Luigi Pirandello is also evident in his portrayal of the characters, the issue of identity, and the concept of reality as a multifaceted phenomenon.

It is a text that exceeds the premises of the detective genre. In fact, if one takes into consideration the characterization of John Cawelti (the existence of a mystery, the fact that the story is structured around an investigation, and that the investigator is the center of it), *Rosaura a las diez* does not exactly fit the mold. The protagonist, Camilo Canegato, and his complex psychology constitute the axis of the story that explores a bigger mystery: that of life. It is within the scope of the written word, Denevi seems to indicate, that dreams, passions, and spiritual anxieties reach their ultimate expression and their revelatory potential that most approximates what is truly essential.

In addition to theatrical and television adaptations, *Rosaura a las diez* was made into a superb film in 1958 under the direction of Mario Soffici, with Juan Verdaguer, Susana Campos, and María Luisa Robledo in the leading roles. There were other foreign remake projects based on the text/film that never materialized. Nevertheless, Denevi wrote the script for another detective-like film, *Los acusados* (The accused), that was a sort of sequel to the first. Based on a real-life local event during the 1920s, it tells the story of the murder of an official, the investigation carried out by a judge, and of how politicians tripped up his efforts while the press distracted public opinion with deliberate lies. Obviously, the writer wanted to take advantage of his success as a detective-story writer at the same time he pursued other interests. His knowledge of law, from his frustrated career as a law student, helped him to elaborate the plot. But the fact of the matter is that *Los acusados*, meant to be a treatment of justice and the interests surrounding it, is not convincing due to its often grandiloquent discourse that doesn't always ring true.

Although *Rosaura a las diez* is Marco Denevi's only novel that is truly inscribed within the parameters of the detective genre, other of his subsequent works border it. For instance, *Ceremonia secreta* (*Secret Ceremony*, 1960) for which he won the "Life en Español" prize in 1960, was filmed by Joseph Losey in 1965 starring Elizabeth Taylor, Mia Farrow, and Robert Mitchum in the leading roles. In this novella, Denevi took up his favorite topic—that of identity-swapping. The main difference resides in the fact that, through greater verbal and stylistic economy, the author achieves a deeper and more dramatic examination of the behavior and dark motives that drive the characters. *Ceremonia secreta* belongs to the tradition of the gothic novel in spite of presenting a criminal act, a sort of investigation, a death, and certain echoes of Poe. Likewise, the novel *Los asesinos de los días de fiesta* (The holiday murderers, 1972) contains certain elements of the detective genre. The text was adapted to film by Damiano Damiani in 2001, and it has seen various reworkings in narrative form (*Asesinos de los días de fiesta* [1980], *Noche de duelo, casa del muerto* [Night of mourning, house of the dead man, 1994], and *Música de amor perdido* [Music of lost love, 1990]).

In 1976, Denevi wrote television scripts for an Argentine detective series called *División Homicidios* (Homicide division), a project he soon abandoned due to pressure from the producers. María Angélica Bosco and Plácido Donato, both detective fiction writers, took over the project. *División Homicidios* was a successful program that recreated real-life crime cases of the 1930s. Both Denevi's first novel and his scripts fall within the classic characterization of the genre. Marco Denevi was a candidate for the Nobel Prize in Literature in 1997. He died in Buenos Aires on 13 December 1998.

Juan José Delaney

Works

Asesinos de los días de fiesta. Buenos Aires: El Ateneo, 1980.
Los asesinos de los días de fiesta. Buenos Aires: Emecé, 1972.
Ceremonia secreta. 1960. Buenos Aires: Corregidor, 1999. English version as *Secret Ceremony*, trans. by Harriet de Onís. New York: Time, Inc., 1961.
Ceremonia secreta y otros cuentos, ed. Donald A. Yates. New York: Macmillan, 1965.
Música de amor perdido. Buenos Aires: Corregidor, 1990.
Noche de duelo, casa del muerto. Buenos Aires: Huemul, 1994.
Rosaura a las diez. Buenos Aires: G. Kraft, 1955. Reprint, Madrid: Alianza, 1993. English version as *Rosa at Ten O'Clock*, trans. Donald A. Yates. New York: Holt, Rinehart and Winston, 1964.

Criticism

Brant, Herbert J. "Camilo's Closet: Sexual Camouflage in Denevi's Rosaura a las diez," in *Bodies and Biases: Sexualities in Hispanic Cultures and Literatures*, ed. David William Foster and Roberto Reis. Minneapolis: University of Minnesota Press, 1996, 203–16.

Delaney, Juan José. *Marco Denevi y la sacra ceremonia de la escritura. Una biografía literaria*. Buenos Aires: Corregidor, 2003.

Feeny, Thoma. "The Influence of Wilkie Collins' *The Moonstone* on Marco Denevi's *Rosaura a las diez*." *Rivista di Letterature Moderne e Comparate* 31 (1978): 225–29.

Gotschilich, Guillermo. "*Ceremonia secreta* de Marco Denevi: enigma y ritualización." *Revista chilena de literatura* 33 (1989): 87–101.

Grove, Ivonne Reve. *La realidad calidoscópica de la obra de Marco Denevi*. Mexico City: B. Costa-Amic, 1974.

Gyurko, Lanin A. "Romantic Illusion in Denevi's *Rosaura a las diez*." *Iberoromania: Zeitschrift fur die Iberoromanischen Sprachen und Literaturen in Europa und Amerika/ Revista Dedica* 3 (1971): 357–73.

Lichtblau, Myron I. "Narrative Perspective and Reader Response in Marco Denevi's *Rosaura a las diez*." *Symposium: A Quarterly Journal in Modern Literatures* 40.1 (1986): 59–70.

Pardal, Inés. "Mujeres misteriosas en William Wilkie Collins y Marco Denevi." *El gato negro* 2 (1991): 28–34.

Piña, Cristina. "Marco Denevi: La soledad y sus disfraces," in *Ensayos de crítica literaria. Año 1983*. Buenos Aires: Editorial de Belgrano, 1983, 311–417.

Yates, Donald. "Marco Denevi: An Argentine Anomaly." *Kentucky Foreign Language Quarterly* 9.3 (1962): 162–67.

———. "Para una bibliografia de Marco Denevi." *Revista iberoamericana* 33 (1967): 141–46.

———. "Un acercamiento a Marco Denevi," in *El cuento hispanoamericano ante la crítica*, ed. Enrique Pupo-Walker. Madrid: Castalia, 1973, 223–34.

———. "Marco Denevi," in *Latin American Writers*, 3 vols., ed. Carlos A. Solé and Maria Abreu. New York: Scribner's, 1989, 3:1265–69.

Ramón Díaz Eterovic (b. 1956)

CHILE

Ramón Díaz Eterovic was born in 1956 in Punta Arenas, which is known for its claim to be the southernmost city in the world. His maternal grandparents were Croatian immigrants and his father's family was from the island of Chiloé in southern Chile. He lived en Punta Arenas until the age of 17, when he moved to Santiago to study. He obtained a degree in business administration from the University of Chile. From an early age he showed an interest in literature and while at the university he formed a small literary group in 1975 and directed a journal, which was short-lived due to censorship from the military dictatorship. He began his literary career as a poet, publishing two collections titled *El poeta derribado* (The defeated poet, 1980), and *Pasajero de la ausencia* (Passenger of absence, 1982). These volumes were followed by the short-story collection *Atrás sin golpe* (Backwards without incidence, 1985). In 1985, he wrote the first volume of his "Heredia" detective series, *La ciudad está triste* (The sad city), which was published in 1987. The series now (2004) includes a total of nine novels, plus two children's books. His works have earned him numerous literary honors and brought him into the fore as a major figure in contemporary Chilean narrative. He is also the editor of the volume *Crímenes criollos: antología del cuento policial chileno* (Creole crimes: anthology of Chilean detective stories, 1994), which contains stories by Poli Délano, Alberto Edwards, and René Vergara, among numerous other authors of the genre. Díaz Eterovic resides in Santiago, where in addition to his career as a writer, he works as a journalist.

As an author of hard-boiled detective fiction, Díaz Eterovic is one of the most prolific in Latin America. Moreover, he is one of the few writers whose works feature the same detective-protagonist, thus forming an ongoing series that narrates the adventures of Heredia (whose first name is never revealed) and his unusual sidekick Simenon, a cat. Heredia follows in the tradition of some of the most memorable literary detectives in the style of Hammett and Chandler, of course with his own Chilean idiosyncrasies. He is a native of Santiago who inhabits a small apartment in an old, bohemian neighborhood near the Mapocho River and the Plaza de Armas (the traditional square in the city center), which is imbued with history and representative of the city Santiago once was. Heredia demonstrates a profound knowledge of and love for his city and he serves as a social chronicler of its contemporary history as he walks through the streets observing a society devastated by years of military rule. He is also an avid reader who often quotes from literary texts. He is a somewhat typical private investigator in his melancholy solitude, dark humor, sardonic outlook on life, and skepticism. Likewise, he possesses a strong moral sense and personal code of ethics. Heredia is atypical, however, for the curious relationship he has with a stray cat he calls Simenon—a clear homage to Georges Simenon, the creator of the famous Inspector Maigret—with whom he imagines holding long, detailed conversations about life and the cases he is working on.

La ciudad está triste, the first book in the Heredia series, not only presents the detective but also clearly establishes his relationship with Santiago. The novel paints a rather grim though veridical portrait of the city ravaged by years of political oppression and economic depression. It is a city dominated and subdued by asphyxiating fear, extreme violence, lack of justice, and rampant corruption. In true hard-boiled style, the author mixes dirty realism with references to the sociopolitical situation of the country within the framework of a crime investigation in order to make an ideological statement. In this sense, Díaz Eterovic joins the ranks of other Southern Cone hard-boiled detective fiction authors such as Mempo Giardinelli, Juan Martini, and José Pablo Feinmann of Argentina who use the detective novel as a forum for political commentary and dissent, as well as speaking to the resiliency of the human spirit in the face of adversity. Many of the cases the detective is called upon to solve have to do with people who have been disappeared by the military, or in which the military is otherwise involved.

The series continues with *Solo en la oscuridad* (Alone in the dark, 1992), in which Heredia investigates the murder of flight attendant who unwittingly got herself caught up in drug-trafficking. It is in this book that Simenon makes his first appearance by showing up unexpectedly in Heredia's office and curling up for a catnap on the complete works of Georges Simenon, found among the many books the detective keeps in his personal library. From this moment on the cat will progressively become a more active participant in the novels. In *Nadie sabe más que los muertos* (No one knows more than the dead, 1993), the third novel, Simenon begins to speak with Heredia. The resulting dialogues make for some of the best components of this and subsequent books. In *Nadie sabe más que los muertos*, Heredia is asked to investigate the whereabouts of a child born in a detention center to a political prisoner. The plotline serves to elaborate on the corruption of power, dirty dealings, and abuse practiced by the military government. The child, not surprisingly, was "adopted" by a professional torturer. In *Angeles y solitarios* (Angels and lonely men, 1995), Heredia becomes involved in a case of arms-trafficking. This fourth novel in the series received the "Premio del Consejo Nacional del Libro y el Fomento a la Lectura" (National council on books and reading award), and the "Premio Municipal de Literatura" (Municipal literary award) for best novel. The next Heredia adventure is *Nunca enamores a un forastero* (Never let a stranger fall in love with you, 1999), in which Heredia travels to Punta Arenas to investigate the death of a young woman and the bombing of a local church. This was followed by the publication of *Los siete hijos de Simenon* (The seven sons of Simenon) in 2000. *El ojo del alma* (The soul's eye, 2001) earned the author his second "Premio Municipal de Literatura." As with previous cases, in this novel Heredia takes on the military and the dark shadow it cast upon Chilean history and society. Here he investigates the mysterious disappearance of a university friend suspected of being an informant for Pinochet during the dictatorship. With *El hombre que pregunta* (The man who asks, 2002), Díaz Eterovic departs from his usual narrative environment of the mean streets and sleazy bars of Santiago and enters the world of cultural institutions to investigate the murder of a literary critic. In the latest installment of the "Heredia" series, *El color de la piel* (The color of skin, 2003), the author returns to the underbelly of Santiago with a new twist. Heredia finds himself challenged to solve a case in "Lima chica" (Little Lima), an area of Santiago populated by Peruvian immigrants. The murder of a young indigenous Peruvian serves as the backdrop to raise issues of racism in Chilean society.

In an effort to involve his own children in his writing, Díaz Eterovic has penned two children's books that also feature his private investigator Heredia. *El secuestro de Benito* (The kidnapping of Benito, 2001) has Heredia helping a boy named Roldán discover what happened to Benito, a kidnapped dog. *"R y M" investigadores* ("R and M" investigators, 2002) is a reworking of the previous title. It features the sibling team of Roldán and Merced who, with the help of Heredia, solve the case of missing pets in their neighborhood.

Díaz Eterovic's works have been well-received in Chile by both readers and critics alike, and he has amassed a considerable following. Many of his books have been translated into other languages and published in Europe; none, however, has been translated into English yet. His work also has begun to receive much-deserved critical attention in recent years. The book *Poder y crimen en la narrativa chilena contemporánea: las novelas de Heredia* (Power and crime in contemporary Chilean narrative: the Heredia novels, 2002) by Guillermo García-Corales and Mirian Pino is clearly the most thorough examination of his narrative. It is not at all surprising that Díaz Eterovic's works (and not just his detective fiction) are stimulating academic interest. As a narrator, he has proven himself to be an uncanny observer of contemporary Chilean society. More specifically, his style of detective fiction comes across as a hybrid of classic authors such as Poe and Simenon, North American masters of the hard-boiled tradition such as Hammett and Chandler, and his Latin American counterparts such as those mentioned previously. From the unique perspective of Heredia, Díaz Eterovic provides insightful social commentary while at the same entertaining his reader with some of the best detective fiction being written in Latin America today.

Darrell B. Lockhart

Works

"Aficiones ocultas," in *Variaciones en negro: relatos policiales hispanoamericanos*, ed. Lucía López Coll. Bogotá: Norma, 2003, 185–208.

Angeles y solitarios. Santiago: Planeta, 1995. Reprint, Santiago: LOM Ediciones, 2000.

La ciudad está triste. Santiago: Sinfronteras, 1987. Reprint, Santiago: LOM Ediciones, 2000.

El color de la piel. Santiago, LOM Ediciones, 2003.

Crímenes criollos: antología del cuento policial chileno, ed. Ramón Díaz Eterovic. Santiago: Mosquito, 1994.

Ese viejo cuento de amar. Santiago: Mosquito, 1990.

El hombre que pregunta. Santiago: LOM Ediciones, 2002.

Nadie sabe más que los muertos. Santiago: Planeta, 1993. Reprint, Santiago: LOM Ediciones, 2002.

Nunca enamores a un forastero. Santiago: Caligrafía Azul, 1999.

El ojo del alma. Santiago: LOM Ediciones, 2001.

"Por amor a la señorita Blandish," in *Crímenes criollos: antología del cuento policial chileno*, ed. R. Díaz Eterovic, 57–67.

"*R y M" investigadores*. Bogotá: Norma, 2002.

Los siete hijos de Simenon. Santiago: LOM Ediciones, 2000. Reprint, Barcelona: Seix Barral, 2001.

El secuestro de Benito. Mexico City: CIDCLI/Consejo Nacional para la Cultura y las Artes, 2001.

Solo en la oscuridad. Buenos Aires: Torres Agüero, 1992.

Criticism

García-Corales, Guillermo. "Ramón Díaz Eterovic: reflexiones sobre la narrativa chilena de los noventa." *Confluencia: revista hispánica de cultura y literatura* 10.2 (1995): 190–95. (Interview.)

———. "Nostalgia y melancolía en la novela detectivesca del Chile de los noventa." *Revista iberoamericana* 65.186 (1999): 81–87.

———. "Ramón Díaz Eterovic." *Hispamérica* 88 (2001): 57–65. (Interview.)

———. "El espacio del deterioro en *Solo en la oscuridad* de Ramón Díaz Eterovic." *Chasqui: revista de literatura latinoamericana* 31.1 (2002): 28–37.

García-Corales, Guillermo, and Mirian Pino. *Poder y crimen en la narrativa chilena contemporánea: las novelas de Heredia*. Santiago: Mosquito, 2002.

Alberto Edwards (1873–1932)

CHILE

In April 1914, Alberto Edwards published the first Chilean detective story, "La catástrofe de la Punta del Diablo" (The catastrophe of Devil's Point), in *Pacífico Magazine* (issue no. 16), which he co-founded with Joaquín Díaz Garcés in 1913. The story had an eloquent subtitle in parentheses: "Román Calvo, el Sherlock Holmes chileno" (Roman Calvo, the Chilean Sherlock Holmes). It was a clear adaptation of the English poetics of storytelling based on a model of characters and exemplary situations as established by Arthur Conan Doyle. From the beginning, he had in mind the concept of a series based on the character Román Calvo, and he published 19 Calvo tales in *Pacífico Magazine*.[1]

Edwards stands out for the variety of his literary production, which includes historical and fantastic fiction, political essays such as *La fronda aristocrática en Chile* (The aristocratic frond in Chile, 1928), and his journalism. His first detective book was published in Spanish by Raymond L. Grismer and Mary B. Mac-Donald in New York. These editors translated other of Edwards's stories into English which appear in the volume *El tesoro enterrado y otros cuentos* (The buried treasure and other stories, 1952). Finally, the Santiago publishing house Editorial Pacífico published a collection of his stories under the title *Román Calvo, el Sherlock Holmes chileno* in 1953. This volume includes stories 3, 6, 9, 10, 15, and 16.

The first story establishes a model that serves to pattern the author's subsequent works. The protagonist, Román Calvo, is modeled after the examples of Dupin and Sherlock Holmes as a character that is somewhat quirky. He is a frail, eccentric individual who at first sight might be mistaken for a madman. Around 40 years old, he lives off a small income and dedicates his time to cultivating his

---

[1](1) "La catástrofe de la Punta del Diablo"; (2) "El hombre misterioso de la calle Santa Rosa" (The mystery man of Santa Rosa street [no. 17, May 1914]); (3) "El tesoro y la viudita" (The little widow's treasure [no. 18, June 1914, later called "El tesoro enterrado" [The buried treasure]); (4) "La locura de la verdad" (The insanity of the truth [no. 19, July 1914]); (5) "La guerra a bordo del Aragón. Román Calvo y el Capitán" (The war aboard the Aragón. Román Calvo and the captain [no. 21, September 1914]); (6) "El secuestro del candidato" (The kidnapping of the candidate [no. 27, March 1915]); (7) "La prenda perdida" (The lost article of clothing [no. 32, August 1915]); (8) "El misterio de La Cisterna" (The mystery of the cistern [no. 37, January 1916]); (9) "El despojo sangriento" (The bloody plunder [no. 41, May 1916]); (10) "La pista de don Antonio Pérez" (The clue of Don Antonio Pérez [no. 45, September 1916]); (11) "Sobre la pista del corsario" (On the clue of the pirate [no. 51, March 1917]); (12) "Los dos sobrinos" (The two nephews [no. 54, June 1917]); (13) "Una pesquisa en la luna" (An investigation on the moon [no. 56, August 1917]); (14) "El copihue blanco" (The white copihue plant [no. 63, March 1918]); (15) "La secretísima" (The big secret [no. 70, October 1918]); (16) "El marido de la señorita Sutter" (Ms. Sutter's husband [no. 75, March 1919]); (17) "Los enemigos misteriosos" (The mysterious enemies [no. 89, May 1920]); (18) "La señorita de Charce" (The young lady from Charce [no. 92, August 1920], later called "El robo de la nómina" [The theft of the list]); and (19) "El misterio de Tuqui" (The mystery of Tuqui [nos. 101–102, June 1921]).

interest in reading and study. He possesses a prodigious memory and shows a passion for collecting insects, chemistry experiments, genealogy, and heraldry. He has an uncommon power of observation and does not hesitate to disguise himself in order to go unnoticed and carry out his investigations. For example, dressed in beggar's clothes, he searches through the garbage to find a fake beard used by the criminal Mascayano during his crime. Calvo is an amateur detective, although he doesn't rule out the possibility of becoming a professional private investigator, since he perceives a healthy future for such a trade in Chile. The narrator in the series is a traditional confidant who, using the first person, relates the hero's feats as an amazed witness to Calvo's perspicacity, of which the narrator himself is hardly capable. The reader enters into a kind of capricious relationship with the narrator. On the one hand he identifies with his "normalcy" that prevents him from seeing what is going on around him, while on the other hand the reader distances himself from the narrator with whose ineptness he doesn't wish to identify. Román Calvo treats his narrator-friend much like Sherlock Holmes treats Dr. Watson, chastising him for not being observant or not showing the ingenuity to recognize and follow the clues that will lead to the resolution of the case.

The police in the stories are relegated a secondary status, seemingly impotent in the face of Calvo's skill and sharpness. They offer him strategic help and in the end depend on the detective's initiative, as in Auguste Dupin's case of "The Purloined Letter." This initiative stems from Calvo's deductive skills. He utilizes his power of observation and eye for detail, together with his vast knowledge of culture and photographic memory to discard all possible hypotheses until he discovers the culprit. Furthermore, he is perfectly familiar with the biography of Antonio Mascayano, his criminal nemesis, which allows him to determine the motive of the crime and propose an initial hypothesis on how Don Francisco and his children were murdered, for example. Later, he disregards one-by-one the criminal's alibis through an extremely logical procedure of deductive reasoning. His logic makes his arguments irrefutable when he confronts Mascayano and explains, in a dramatic way, how he murdered his relative in order to receive the inheritance.

The crime provokes—as the title indicates—a social catastrophe, and a chaotic situation ensues that must be resolved so that order may be restored. It is the worst of crimes, committed against a man and his three children. It provokes unrest in the community and is exploited by the yellow journalism eager to satisfy the public's sick curiosity and need to experience the strong appeal of another's pain. Solving the crime is synonymous with placing the detective's intelligence in the service of good, in opposition to the evil intelligence of the assassin, who presents clever alibis and has devised an elaborate ruse in order to make it look like an accident. From this struggle of opposites comes the synthesis of justice and confidence in the institutions that will ultimately mete out punishment upon the criminal and author of such disorder. The story is structured around the switching back and forth of narrative viewpoints, from the generic (portrayal of life in Santiago, introduction of the narrator and the detective) to the specific (the crime, the investigation, and Román Calvo's work to highlight the importance of the revelation). The story is a perfect illustration of the canonical model or schematic of a detective story in the puzzle- or enigma-story tradition.

Through his narratives, Edwards reveals to the reader a Chilean society that balances between modernism and traditionalism. However, the narrator is more interested in presenting a Santiago setting that lends itself to the development of detective elements than in painting a picture of society. In so doing, he lacks the irony of an Agatha Christie. Edwards exercised considerable influence on the detective genre in Chile. He made the conventions of the puzzle-narrative a viable option in Chile, which continued to be cultivated into the 1990s.

Néstor Ponce

Works

"The Case of the Travelling Corpse," in *Latin Blood: The Best Crime and Detective Stories of South America*, ed. Donald A. Yates. New York: Herder & Herder, 1972, 3–14.
Cuentos fantásticos, selección y prólogo de Manuel Rojas. Santiago: Zig-Zag, 1957.
La fronda aristocrática en Chile. Santiago: Imprenta Nacional, 1928.
Román Calvo, el Sherlock Holmes chileno. New York: Macmillan, 1946. Reprint, Santiago: Editorial del Pacífico, 1953.
"El secuestro del candidato," in *Crímenes criollos: antología del cuento policial chileno*, ed. Ramón Díaz Eterovic. Santiago: Mosquito Editores, 1994, 69–87.
El tesoro enterrado y otros cuentos, adapted from the Spanish with exercises, notes and vocabulary by Raymond L. Grismer and Mary B. MacDonald. Boston: Houghton, Mifflin, 1952.

Criticism

Rojas, Manuel. "La tragedia de Alberto Edwards." *Atenea* 20.86 (1932): 73–77.
Silva Castro, Raúl. *Don Alberto Edwards: Biografía y bibliografía*. Santiago: Imprenta Universitaria, 1933.

Enrique Fairlie Fuentes (b. 1915)

PERU

Enrique Fairlie Fuentes was born in Chile in 1915. In 1944, he married Ivonne Apablaza, with whom he had two children. After being exiled from his country by the government of Pedro Aguirre Cerda, he went to Bolivia, where he resided from 1952 until 1956; later he became a Bolivian citizen. In 1957, he arrived in Peru, where for more than ten years he worked in various media of communication.

Fairlie was a journalist with a wide-ranging career who had connections in high political circles. His work took him to practically every country in South America as well as to Mexico and the United States. Early in his career as a journalist in Chile, he collaborated with the following periodicals: *Las últimas noticias* (The latest news), *La Opinión* (Opinion), and *Las noticias gráficas* (Graphic news). In addition, he wrote for Colombia's *El Tiempo* (Time), Ecuador's *La Prensa* (The press), and Mexico's *Excélsior*, among other newspapers. During his long stay in Peru he worked for the following publications: *Vanguardia* (Vanguard), *La Crónica* (The chronicle), *La Prensa*, *El Comercio* (Commerce), and *Gente* (People). He also directed news programs and commentary on radio and television. In Peru, Fairlie received his doctorate in journalism and was a professor at the Universidad Femenina del Sagrado Corazón (Sacred Heart Women's University) in Lima.

Among the most outstanding of Fairlie's articles, of the hundreds that he wrote, are those on Lázaro Cárdenas, Charles de Gaulle, John F. Kennedy, Nikita Khrushchev, Marshal Montgomery, and Juan Domingo Perón, among others. His polemic style caused him problems on more than one occasion. To his already-mentioned exile from Chile, his expulsion from Ecuador by order of President Camilo Ponce Enríquez should be added, as well as his imprisonment in Colombia by order of General Gustavo Rojas Pinilla. Various interviews with Peruvian personalities were published in a book titled *Grandes reportajes* (Great interviews, 1970). Fairlie is also the author of *Cinco y medio: kilómetro del amor* (Five-and-a-half: Kilometer of love, 1970), short stories set in Peru's most famous brothel, as well as of *Periodismo fin y periodismo medio* (Journalism as end and means, 1970), a book of essays on journalistic ethics.

Fairlie's detective texts are collected in the volume titled *Cuentos policiales del Perú* (Detective stories from Peru, 1968). It is also necessary to consider the article "Confesiones del carterista más famoso del Perú" (Confessions of the most famous pickpocket in Peru), originally published in the journal *Vanguardia* and later included in *Grandes reportajes*. As the title indicates, the majority of the stories in *Cuentos policiales del Perú* are set in various locations within Peru—as many in the capital, Lima, as in the cities of the provinces. Fairlie's hero, the ex-police captain René Rodríguez Arenas—now dedicated to agriculture and the invariable narrator of the cases—is from Piura, a region located north of Lima. Fairlie's decentralized perspective is important, since he does not reduce Peruvian society to that of its capital. However, the opposition between big city and small town—with a noticeable contempt for the latter—is evident in the short stories "La llave" (The key) and "El error del Comisario" (The police chief's error). The opposition between city and rural town occurs at a symbolic level, by comparing Peru with more developed countries.

The characters of the short stories, policemen and criminals alike, are typical Peruvians, which is to say they are *criollos* or Creoles. *Criollos* is a term that, in the beginning, alluded to questions of origin (children of Spaniards born in the American continent), but it later assumed a different connotation related to a way of being defined as "Peruvian idiosyncrasy." Doing things "Creole style" implies a particular method: an unorthodox, informal manner although no less effective. In the short story "Asesinato en el jirón Camaná" (Murder on Camaná Avenue [a major thoroughfare in central Lima]), an explicit division is made between the Peruvian Creole methods and those of other countries, mainly Europe and the United States. For example, killing by poison, they say, is a typical European crime, whereas, "el criollo liquida sus problems con un par de tiros, dos o tres puñaladas y hasta usa dinamita" (the Creole eliminates his problems with a couple of gunshots, two or three stabs with a knife, and he will go as far as using dynamite [21–22]). According to the former police captain René Rodríguez Arenas, it is not unusual that Creole ingenuity is more effective than the scientific method. The character affirms that in Peru a crime rarely remains unpunished, while thousands of crimes go unsolved in the United States and Europe. Through this exaggeration, Fairlie highlights informality as an essential Peruvian characteristic. Yet the *criollo*, for his part, can be frowned upon within his own country. Once the crime is solved, the press does not give too much merit to the discoverers of the murderer because they have "nombres y apellidos criollos" (Creole names and surnames [24]). In this way, Fairlie reveals one of Peru's typical contradictions: it can simultaneously love and despise itself.

Other texts reveal a common problem in many Latin American countries: police corruption. In "La caída de Caifás" (The fall of Caifás), he paints a brutal portrait of a police captain who, through his actions, erases the difference between being a policeman and being a criminal. Likewise, in the article "Confesiones del carterista más famoso del Perú," the narrator condemns the cruelties of the Chilean and Argentine police whose methods include all the usual forms of torture. In the same way, "El error del comisario" shows that the line between honesty and crime is not always well-defined.

A chauvinist attitude can be perceived in the short story "Traición" (Treason), where a man turns to the police in order to denounce a case of adultery. Subsequently, upon the revelation that he is in fact not married to the woman, his honor is only "partly" stained and the cuckold turns out to be the lover. In the short story "Navidad de sangre en la Avenida Arequipa" (Bloody Christmas on Arequipa Avenue), the typical image of a Don Juan is presented.

Fairlie's texts vary between the short story and the journalistic note. *Cuentos policiales del Perú* includes short stories and several journalistic articles. This produces a tension between fiction and reality. The work of the journalist imposes on

Fairlie the necessity to distinguish between what is the truth and what is a lie. "Traición" is presented as being based on a true story, and the article "Confesiones del carterista más famoso del Perú" is supposedly true as well. In this last story, an elegant, refined thief who plays the piano and does not rob the poor tells of his life and his best robberies. In "La danza de la muerte" (The dance of death), following a clever reflection on fiction and reality, the narrator declares that his history equally contains both.

Some of the short stories include flights of imagination. The character in "El terrorista" (The terrorist) is a fortune-teller who upon the death of his son sees an angel pick him up. En "La danza de la muerte" the supernatural is in the form of the double. One of the characters attends a dance of skeletons and, at the end, cannot find his own body. Not all the stories are set in Peru. "La danza de la muerte" takes place in New York. "Traición" occurs in the Madrid of 1936 but the story makes no allusion is to the Civil War that devastated the Spanish nation. But "La carta" (The letter), set in Paris, offers a romantic vision of the Second World War in which love and friendship oppose death.

There is scarce criticism on Fairlie Fuentes's work. Emilio Armaza (1970), speaking of *Cuentos policiales del Perú*, highlights the realism of the texts in which the typical Peruvian is recognized in his characters. Armaza draws attention to Fairlie's journalistic style and maintains that his book fills a void in the practically nonexistent Peruvian detective literature. The apparent incompatibility between literature and journalism might be one cause of the critical disinterest of Fairlie. The abuse of commas and hyphens, with the abundance of intercalated sentences and eagerness to provide the most information possible (for example in "Navidad de sangre en la Avenida Arequipa" and in "La caída de Caifás") can be stylistically distracting. Nevertheless, these faults do not detract from the psychological, social, or even literary interest of Fairlie Fuentes's stories.

Fairlie portrays a contradictory Peru—therefore a real one. The oppositions between city and country, the autochthonous and foreign, excesses and morality, fantasy and reality interconnect in order to offer a portrait of Peru at the end of the 1970s, a portrait that, although partial, is no less truthful. The previous paradoxes are summarized in the fact that it has been a Chilean-born author who has written these Peruvian detective stories.

José Alberto Bravo de Rueda

Works

Cuentos policiales del Perú. Lima: n.p., 1968.
Grandes reportajes. Lima: n.p., 1970.

Criticism

Armaza, Emilio. "Libros nuevos: *Cuentos policiales del Perú*," in *Grandes reportajes* by E. Fairlie Fuentes. Lima: n.p., 1970, 297–98.

C. E. Feiling (1961–1997)

ARGENTINA

C. E. Feiling was born in Rosario on 5 June 1961 and died in Buenos Aires on 22 July 1997 at age 36 from leukemia, with which he was diagnosed in 1982. He attended secondary school at the Liceo Naval (Naval academy) and earned a degree in literature from the Universidad de Buenos Aires, where he also worked for a time as a professor of Latin and linguistics. He taught philosophy at the Universidad Nacional de Lomas de Zamora (National university of Lomas de Zamora) and at the Universidad de San Andrés and taught Hispanic literature at the University of Nottingham in England. In 1991, the British Council invited him to participate in the conferences in Walberberg, (Germany) and Cambridge. In 1994, Feiling received the Antorchas scholarship to attend the International Writing Program at the University of Iowa.

When Feiling moved away from academics, he began to write cultural journalism part-time. He was affiliated with a variety of national publications such as the newspapers *Clarín* (Bugle) and *Página 12* (Page 12) and the journal *Babel*. With the rest of his time, he dedicated himself to his own writing and produced three novels: *El agua electrizada* (Electrified water, 1992), *Un poeta nacional* (A national poet, 1995), and *El mal menor* (The lesser evil, 1996), which was a finalist for the Planeta, Biblioteca del Sur prize in 1995. Feiling also published a book of poems, *Amor a Roma* (Love of Rome, 1995), in which he demonstrates his profound relationship with poetry.

El agua electrizada is the only novel of the three that is related to the detective genre. Moreover, the author chose not to incorporate the genre fully, but rather use some of its devices in the creation of his text. This blending technique permits him to subtly and ironically manipulate a very careful use of language that goes beyond mere quotes in English and Latin, or the constantly recurring intertextuality and journey of searching for a conflictive past—a popular theme in Argentine literature.

The work is based on Feiling's desire to write a novel based on the actual suicide of a friend, and the choice of style is somewhat risky. He constructs the novel from two story-lines and uses one of them, the detective story, to tell the other—the one that really interests him, the one that needs to be told, and upon which the device story is based: the period of the military dictatorship in Argentina. Without a doubt, the device of the detective narrative takes the text to a different level where confusion favors the plot of this singular thriller—deviating from its own performance—in which the detective novel offers a solution not only to the mystery it attempts to solve, but also for itself.

The novel begins with the death of "el Indio" (the Indian) Juan Carlos Lousteau, a marine infantryman and ex-classmate of Tony, the protagonist, at the Naval Academy. Tony (Antonio Eduardo Hope) is now a professor of Latin at the University of Buenos Aires. The intrigue is structured around this inexplicable death, and Hope—not a "real detective"—undertakes the investigation. Over the course of his investigation, he fluctuates between the world of literature, philosophy, and painting and that of his search for the truth about his friend's death. Tony rejects the idea of suicide. If Juan Carlos had committed suicide, it would have been for the obvious reason of his illness. Nevertheless, "Juan Carlos no había tenido una recaída, puesto que los análisis estaban bien. La variedad de leucemia por la que lo habían tratado—¿linfoblástica aguda?—tenía un alto porcentaje de recuperación; llevaba más de dos años sin medicar, y del todo sano. Suicidio o accidente, las preguntas eran por qué y cómo" (Juan Carlos had not had a relapse and all his lab work was fine. The type of leukemia he was treated for—acute lymphoblastoma?—had a high survival rate. He had not had treatment for over two years and was perfectly healthy. Whether suicide or accident, the question was why and how? [16]). Tony also refuses to accept the idea of an accident because of two facts that don't add up according to his estimation: el Indio was an exemplary marksman: How could the gunshot wound to the head have been an accident, or a careless act with the safety mechanism of a regulation pistol? Moreover, Juan Carlos was right-handed: How could the pistol have been fired so effectively with his left hand?

The story begins with the burial of Juan Carlos in the Chacarita cemetery. There, Tony will become reacquainted not only with his past in the marines but also with his personal life: specifically, Irene Lousteau, Juan Carlos's sister. He wishes to be distanced from the former altogether, or at least pretends he does. As for the second, he tries to initiate a process of recuperation of time and memory. Irene will be his partner in the investigation, a sort of Watson to his imitation of Holmes. In addition, the discovery of some papers and an unreturned pornographic video provides possible clues to the alleged crime. Thus it initiates a plot in which the sharp deductions of Tony Hope will masterfully bring together the death of a friend and the case of two women that are found dead in a bathtub filled with water that had been electrified.

One has to reach the end of the novel, almost the last paragraph, to find out the truth. But in the meantime it is necessary to take the political past of Argentina into account and remember—something that is not far from the life of the protagonist—the horrors of the military government, of a police state in which power is equated with criminal acts. That is, a state that is responsible for the image of terror, not justice; a state in which the police are not an institution of the state, but rather the state itself; a state that will cause the Latin professor to think and show him his relationship to the events that have occurred.

Two stories co-exist in the novel: the crime and the investigation. In working with these two seemingly very different stories, the author also works with two different systems of causality. The intersection of the two stories provides a foundation for the creation of this narrative approximation to the detective genre. The first story is one of absence, a secret story that will keep careful watch over the way in which the narrator, from the protagonist's point of view, recounts the facts of the second story: the investigation. Juan Carlos's death, which could be considered a false crime, yields way to the real crime, the murder of the two women. This crime will weave the plot and lead the protagonist to discover more than one secret: the truth about Juan Carlos's death, and the truth about his own past as well as his present.

The detective genre in general is characterized by a set of basic, unchanging rules. However, the Argentine detective novel, especially after the military dictatorship, offers little evidence of ever having fully adhered to such guidelines. The Argentine detective novel is not produced within the traditional model of the genre, since it does not follow its rules or dogma. Rather, the Argentine version is inscribed on the margins of the genre. In general, Argentine detective literature, according to José Pablo Feinmann, "ha utilizado *lo policial* como elemento dinamizador del relato, como tensión, como mecanismo destinado a tironear la atención del lector" (has used detective elements to make the story more dynamic, to add tension, and as a device meant to grab the reader's attention [152]).

Feiling maintains that there is still a tradition within the British detective novel of choosing a subject as a detective that at first glance is seemingly not qualified to investigate a crime. Feiling's detective is one of these types. Hope, the Latin professor, will simultaneously perform the roles of professor and detective in this story. It is evident that this detective never dreamed of leaving his world of Latin literature, art, and poetry to become a private investigator: "Yo no hago policiales, querido" (I don't do detective work, dear [39]), he says to his friend Gustavo, although from this point on the reader is not so sure. In the beginning, when the doubt about Juan Carlos's death is a simple conjecture, an imprecise intuition, Tony, who only wants answers to his friend's death, doesn't even investigate, check the facts, or ask about the possible clues that might have been found at the crime scene. However, one could say—paraphrasing the words of Ricardo Piglia (1990)—that this detective who doesn't pay attention to details has been well-"translated"; that is, this character embodies certain typical characteristics, although the novel is not entirely inscribed within the conventions of the genre.

The investigation is started, as we have already mentioned, by Tony due to his refusal to believe that his friend Juan Carlos died by accident or committed suicide. Tony's imagination is incited by the detailed knowledge of the death, the finding of the paper and video, and he starts to look for a motive to the crime. Although with every clue there is an emendation, he goes in search of the truth. After coming across the "case of the two dead women in the bathtub," Tony will be in the presence of a "real" detective matter that will function as a dynamic element in the story; he will no longer be able to avoid his new role as investigator.

This event, which on the surface appears to be the stuff of a detective story, is immersed in a context that is far from that in which the original detective genre is developed. The murders that go hand-in-hand with the advancement of the plot will confirm our suspicions. They will be related to the facts and persons that pertain to a tragic past in Argentine history: the military state. The two women in one way or another have been associated with powerful men of that era: one woman is a collaborator in the crimes, and the other is the daughter of a torturer.

The protagonist, who in his youth was affiliated with the ranks of the marines and from which he now tries to distance himself through his university studies and professorship in the Department of Philosophy and Letters of the University of Buenos Aires, will have to remember. He will have to retrace his memory to realize and uncover what was not known at the time—although he could have guessed—about his friend, about himself, and the reality of a country subjected to the horrors of dictatorship.

Perhaps the need to have works pertain to certain genres brings up the question as to whether the novel is a detective story or a false thriller. It fact, it is neither. We have already stated that in Argentina, the deviation from the genre was necessary, and in the case of *El agua electrizada* this is evident. There are two stories: the first is one of absence, one of an apparent crime. It is this one that could make us think of the text as a false thriller. However, it is sustained by the same axis as the second story, an investigation that leads to a different crime, one that will unite, through these two different systems of causality, the points that construct the plot. The "noncrime" of Juan Carlos leads to the crime that propels the story—the murder of the two women. Through the course of the novel this story directs the reader to the real and much more horrific crime of genocide in Argentina. Perhaps one may conclude by stating that in this novel, one story illuminates, with great mastery, the secret truth of the other.

Claudia S. Hojman Conde

Work

El agua electrizada. Buenos Aires: Sudamericana, 1992.

Criticism

Feinmann, José Pablo. "Estado policial y novela negra argentina," in *Los héroes "difíciles"*: *la literatura policial en la Argentina y en Italia*, ed. Giuseppe Petronio, Jorge B. Rivera, and Luigi Volta. Buenos Aires: Corregidor, 1991, 143–53.

Lafforgue, Jorge, and Jorge B. Rivera. *Asesinos de papel: ensayos sobre narrativa policial*. Buenos Aires: Ediciones Colihue, 1996.

Piglia, Ricardo. *Crítica y ficción*. Buenos Aires: Siglo Veinte, Universidad Nacional del Litoral, 1990.

José Pablo Feinmann (b. 1943)

ARGENTINA

José Pablo Feinmann was born in Buenos Aires in 1943. He holds a degree in philosophy and taught at the University of Buenos Aires during the early 1970s. He is a journalist whose articles have appeared in several periodicals. A collection of his writings that originally appeared in *Página 12* (Page 12) between 1992 and 1994 was gathered and published in the book *Ignotos y famosos: política, posmodernidad, y farándula en la nueva Argentina* (The unknown and the famous: politics, postmodernity, and the frivolous in the new Argentina, 1994). He has written several influential books on politics and philosophy in Argentina. In addition, of course, he is a prolific author of fiction, whose works range from historical to detective novels. Furthermore, he is a talented screenwriter whose scripts have been made into successful films in Argentina and abroad, such as *Tango Bar* and *Play Murder for Me*. His body of detective fiction is comprised of four novels: *Ultimos días de la víctima* (The victim's last days, 1979), made into a film directed by Adolfo Aristarain (the film script is published in his *Escritos para el cine* [Writings for cinema, 1988]); *Ni el tiro del final* (Not even the last shot, 1981); *El cadáver imposible* (The impossible corpse, 1992), the first novel in the *La muerte y la brújula* (Death and the compass) detective series directed by Jorge Lafforgue; and *Los crímenes de Van Gogh* (The Van Gogh crimes, 1994). He also has written about the hard-boiled detective novel in Argentina in his essay "Estado policial y novela negra argentina" (The police state and the Argentine hard-boiled novel, 1991).

His first novel, born out of the turbulent years of military dictatorship, is typical of a generation of authors who saw in the hard-boiled model a form of narrative that was particularly suited to express the violence, corruption, lack of morality, and chaos that defined the period. As Amelia S. Simpson points out, the two epigraphs that are used to initiate the novel, one from Jorge Luis Borges and the other from Dashiell Hammett "link Feinmann's novel to two traditions: the North American hard-boiled detective model and Borges's philosophical, speculative fictions" (Simpson 141). *Ultimos días* is a thriller that functions on the concepts of doubling and inversion and results in a chilling game of cat-and-mouse in a violent, dehumanized environment. The main character, Mendizábal, is a paid assassin who receives an assignment to kill another man. Instead of quickly carrying out the assignment, he allows himself to become enthralled with his victim's life. During his early surveillance of the man, he takes photographs that he later blows up and hangs about his apartment. He becomes increasingly obsessed with the victim, arranging to meet his acquaintances, becoming familiar with his daily routine. The novel climaxes in a scene of absolute violence—and a twist. The man whom Mendizábal was sent to kill had also received the assignment to kill Mendizábal, which he does. The doubling of hunter and hunted in the end is designed to signal the fact that power is relative and random in a system where true power remains in the shadows and uses dispensable pawns to maintain a stronghold of fear and intimidation over individuals. This, Feinmann's first incursion in the hard-boiled genre, continues to be one of his best novels.

Ni el tiro del final follows in much the same vein as the previous novel. While the story, obviously, is different, many of the same narrative elements are present. The novel essentially describes the descent of three fairly common people—an intellectual, his girlfriend (a singer), and an architect—into a world of violence and psychological degradation. Their story runs parallel to the intercalated narrative of "El primo Matías" (Cousin Matías). While this latter story-line is presented as the tale of a Jack-the-Ripper type, it functions as an allegory of the violent period of the *Proceso* (the military dictatorship). *El cadáver imposible* likewise attempts a portrayal of violence in society in an effort to trace its origins and causes. The plot revolves around the case of a young girl who murders her mother and her mother's lover and then burns down the house. Consequently, she is remanded to a girls reformatory where her actions are scrutinized in an effort to understand what motivated her to such brutality. The originality of the text resides in its structure. The story is presented as a proposal that a writer sends to an editor, in which he first presents the circumstances of the story and then enters into the narration itself. There is a subtext running throughout the novel that provides and intersection between film and literature (revealing the author's interest in film as a cultural narrative). There are numerous footnotes in which the narrator diverges to make film references in relation to the story he is telling. In none of his first three detective novels does Feinmann actually include a detective. In this sense, they perhaps cannot even be strictly classified as detective fiction. However, the author does make use of the conventions of the hard-boiled novel in every other sense. All these texts, to some degree, reflect an overriding concern of approaching social issues through the vehicle of the detective/crime narrative.

His final novel in the genre also shares this concern; however, the approach is quite different. The tone of *Los crímenes de Van Gogh* is much more parodic, even humorous. Rather than utilizing the hard-boiled genre to address the topic of societal violence, Feinmann satirizes the genre itself. This is also the text in which Feinmann most clearly incorporates his interest in cinema—as an industry and as a powerful, popular-culture phenomenon. The basic premise of the novel is based on the desire of the protagonist, Fernando Castelli, to write the perfect film script and win the three-million-dollar prize offered by an international film company for best thriller. Castelli leads a boring life of drudgery and humiliation, both from his overbearing mother and at work. He holds two rather menial jobs as a video-store clerk and an assistant to a film-producer. He feels that this gives him a particular advantage. However, it is not until the ghost of Jack the Ripper appears to him that he receives the inspiration to devise a plan to make his film thriller as authentic as possible to ensure he wins the prize. His plan, suggested by Jack the Ripper, involves committing a series of actual violent murders to use as the subject for his film script. His simultaneous writing of the script over the course of the murders will lend his story the sense of authenticity that will guarantee his success. Castelli becomes known in the sensationalist media as the Van Gogh serial killer for his particularly macabre signature: he cuts an ear off his victim and uses it as a type of bloody brush to sign "Van Gogh" to his "work." This may be read as an obvious textual reference to Raymond Chandler's notion of the "art of murder," like so many other references to the classic hard-boiled model that the author parodies. In contrast to the previous three texts, there are in fact two people who separately investigate the crimes: the private-investigator Colombres (Colombo?) and the police detective Pietri. Together, they represent two sides of the same detective-figure coin. The novel includes all the major components of popular and mass-media culture in an ingenious narrative amalgamation that is both entertaining and timely in terms of making a satirical social commentary on the age of globalization, mass media, and the neoliberal policies of Argentina in the 1990s.

Feinmann is one of the most accomplished detective fiction writers in Argentina but, like so many others, his work has received scant critical attention. He has proven that the genre can evolve over time and still be a useful tool for examining the parameters of culture and society.

Darrell B. Lockhart

Works

El cadáver imposible. Buenos Aires: Clarín/Aguilar, 1992.

Los crímenes de Van Gogh. Buenos Aires: Planeta, 1994.

"Estado policial y novela negra argentina," in *Los héroes "difíciles": la literatura policial en la Argentina y en Italia*, ed. Giuseppe Petronio, Jorge B. Rivera, and Luigi Volta. Buenos Aires: Corregidor, 1991, 143–53.

Ni el tiro del final. Buenos Aires: Pomaire, 1981. Reprint, Buenos Aires: Legasa, 1988.

Ultimos días de la víctima. Buenos Aires: Legasa, 1979, 1987; Reprint, Buenos Aires: Seix Barral, 1996.

Criticism

Bosetti, Oscar. "Acerca de *Ultimos días de la víctima*, y 'lo policial' en la Argentina." *Crear* 2.9 (1982): 28–36.

Lafforgue Jorge, and Jorge B. Rivera. *Asesinos de papel: ensayos sobre narrativa policial.* Buenos Aires: Colihue, 1996.

Pardal, Inés. Review of *Los crímenes de Van Gogh. El gato negro: revista de narrativa policial y de misterio* (Buenos Aires) 5 (1994): 43–44.

Sablich, José. "Contextos reales y ficcionales en la novela negra argentina de la década del '70," in *Calibar sin rastros: aportes para una historia social de la literatura argentina*, ed. Jorge Torres Roggero and María Elena Legaz. Córdoba, Argentina: CONICET/CIFFyH, 1996, 157–85.

Simpson, Amelia S. "José Pablo Feinmann: *Ultimos días de la víctima*," in *Detective Fiction from Latin America*. Rutherford, NJ: Fairleigh Dickinson University Press, 1990, 141–46.

Rubem Fonseca (b. 1925)

BRAZIL

Rubem Fonseca was born in Juiz de Fora, Minas Gerais in 1925. From his early writings he established himself as one of the most acclaimed Brazilian novelists of his generation. After studying law and administration, he worked for years as a journalist and film critic, before finally dedicating himself to literature. While much of his writing can be classified as detective fiction, many of his books also are characterized by a strong erotic vein and in dealing with contemporary politics. Of his work that is more strictly political in nature, the novel *Agosto* (August, 1990) stands out. It is based on the historic events that resulted in the government crisis and suicide of President Getulio Vargas in 1954. Although the setting is eminently political, the novel can also be considered as a thriller, in that it combines violence, sex, power, and intrigue through the action of the characters.

Fonseca's love stories and works that are fundamentally erotic in nature include the short-story collection *Histórias de amor* (Love stories, 1997), the novella *E do meio do mundo prostituto só amores guardei ao meu charuto* (From the world of prostitution I only kept the love for my cigar, 1997), in addition to the short-story volumes *Romance negro e outras histórias* (Detective novel and other stories, 1992), and, in particular, *Feliz ano novo* (Happy new year, 1975). This latter was censored by the military government established in 1964 and the author was placed on a blacklist of writers prohibited by the authorities.

Among Fonseca's works that closely adhere to the detective fiction formula, one can name *Os prisioneiros* (The Prisoners, 1963 [short stories]), *A coleira do cão* (The dog collar, 1965 [short stoires]), *Lúcia McCartney*, 1969 [short stories]), *O caso Morel* (The Morel case, 1973 [novel]), *O homem de fevereiro ou março* (The man from February or March, 1973 [novel]), *O cobrador* (The tax collector, 1979 [short stories]), *Bufo & Spallanzini* (translated into English under the same title, 1985 [novel]), *O selvagem da ópera* (The savage of the opera, 1994 [novel]), *O buraco na parede* (The hole in the wall, 1995 [novel]), and above all, *A grande arte* (*High Art*, 1983 [novel]), which most critics agree is his most important work to date. *A grande arte* revolves around a series of murders in which the killer uses a knife to carve the letter "P" onto the face of the prostitutes he slays. The knife, then, becomes an instrument used to communicate meaning through the sign with which he marks his victims. By recovering an ancient Latin tradition, that letter, carved into skin, serves as an emblem of another matter, signaling the existence of a type of literature that hearkens to the past, appropriating textual practices and implementing the deconstruction of tradition. In general, his literature is characterized, like most hard-boiled fiction in Latin America, by unrestrained violence, crude language, and an overall adherence to dirty realism. His short story "Mandrake" (from *O cobrador*) merits mention here since it is his most widely anthologized text of the genre. The title is the name of the character, a private eye who appears in several of Fonseca's other texts, most notably in the novel *A grande arte*. Also, the short story "Romance negro," from the collection of *Romance negro e outras histórias* is an entertaining piece that plays mockingly with the conventions of detective fiction. Several of his other short stories also appear in anthologies of detective fiction, and the 1994 volume *Contos reunidos* (Collected stories) consists of six previous short-story collections gathered together.

Rubem Fonseca's work, which also includes texts that border the genre of essay such as *Vastas emoções e pensamentos imperfeitos* (*Vast Emotions and Imperfect Thoughts*, 1988), has earned him many important literary awards (Pen Club de Brasil; São Paulo Critics Association) and has been translated into several languages. His work has likewise made a lasting impact on subsequent generations of writers, and he has left a unique imprint on Brazilian literature. His work is the subject of numerous critical appraisals that analyze the author's intricate politico-criminal plots and narratives, taking into consideration the social and philosophical aspects of Fonseca's writing. Perhaps the best study of his work as a whole, and certainly as it pertains to the detective genre, is that of Deonísio da Silva (*Rubem Fonseca: proibido y consagrado*, 1996).

Hiber Conteris

Works

Agosto. São Paulo: Companhia das Letras, 1990.

Bufo & Spallanzini. Rio de Janeiro: Francisco Alves; 1985. English version as *Bufo & Spallanzini*, trans. Clifford E. Landers. New York: Dutton, 1990.

O buraco na parede. São Paulo: Companhia das Letras, 1995.

O caso Morel. Rio de Janeiro: Editora Artenova, 1973.

O cobrador. Rio de Janeiro: Editora Nova Fronteira, 1979.

A coleira do cão. Rio de Janeiro: Edições GRD, 1965.

Contos reunidos. São Paulo: Companhia das Letras, 1994.

"Crónica de sucesos," in *Cuentos policiacos*, ed. Zonia Nadhezda Truque and Mauricio Contreras Hernández. Bogotá: Magisterio, 1996, 111–17.

E do meio do mundo prostituto só amores guardei ao meu charuto. São Paulo: Companhia das Letras, 1997.

"El enano," trans. Assenio Cicero Sancristóbal, in *Variaciones en negro: relatos policiales iberoamericanos*, ed. Lucía López Coll and Leonardo Padura. Havana: Editorial Arte y Literatura, 2001, 257–70. Also in *Variaciones en negro: relatos policiales hispanoamericanos*, ed. Lucía López Coll. Bogotá: Norma, 2003.

Feliz ano novo. Rio de Janeiro: Editora Artenova, 1975.

A grande arte. Rio de Janeiro: Fracisco Alves, 1983. English version as *High Art*, trans. Ellen Watson. New York: Harper & Row, 1986.

Histórias de amor. São Paulo: Companhia das Letras, 1997.

O homem de fevereiro ou março. Rio de Janeiro: Editora Artenova, 1973.

Lúcia McCartney. Rio de Janeiro: Olivé Editor, 1969.

"Mandrake," in *New Tales of Mystery and Crime from Latin America*, ed. and trans. Amelia Simpson. Rutherford, NJ: Fairleigh Dickinson University Press, 1992, 62–88. In Spanish, *Breve antología de cuentos policiales*, ed. María Inés González and Marcela Grosso. Buenos Aires: Sudamericana, 1995, 187–228.

"Lonelyhearts," trans. Clifford E. Landers, in *A Hammock Beneath the Mangoes: Stories from Latin America*, ed. Thomas Colchie. New York: Plume, 1992, 224–36.

Os prisioneiros. Rio de Janeiro: Edições GRD, 1963.

Romance negro e outras histórias. São Paulo: Companhia das Letras, 1992.

O selvagem da ópera. São Paulo: Companhia das Letras, 1994.

Vastas emoções e pensamentos imperfeitos. São Paulo: Companhia das Letras, 1988. English version as *Vast Emotions and Imperfect Thoughts*, trans. Clifford E. Landers. Hopewell, NJ: Ecco Press, 1998.

Criticism

Brasil, Assi. "Rubem Fonseca y el cuento brasileño." *Nueva narrativa hispanoamericana* 1 (1973): 145–47.

Bueno, Eva. "'Languages' and 'Voices' in Brazilian Literature." *Revista de Letras* 36 (1996): 189–210.

Chiappini, Ligia. "A Questão da *Grande Arte*: Uma Faça de Dois Gomes." *Brasil/Brazil: Revista de Literatura Brasileira/A Journal of Brazilian Literature* 5.7 (1992): 47–60.

Coutinho, Afrânio. *O erotismo na literatura: O caso Rubem Fonseca*. Rio de Janeiro: Livraria Editora Cátedra, 1979.

Hastings, Kim Mrazek. "The Gaze." *Brasil/Brazil: Revista de Literatura Brasileira/A Journal of Brazilian Literature* 12 (1994): 83–95.

Paulino, Maria das Graças Rodrigues. "O Leitor Violentado." *Cadernos de Linguística e Teoria da Literatura* 2.4 (1980): 15–18.

Pereira, Maria Antonieta. *No fio do texto: A obra de Rubem Fonseca*. Belo Horizonte: Faculdade de Letras da UFMG, 1999.

———. "Signos em trânsito": *A Grande Arte* de Rubem Fonseca." *Letras & Letras* 6.99 (1993): 14–16.

Sant'ana, Sergi. "A propósito de *Lúcia McCartney*." *Nueva narrativa hispanoamericana* 1 (1973): 77–80.

Sarrias, Cristóbal. "Rubem Fonseca: literatura de denuncia en un Brasil conmocionado." *Razón y fe: revista hispanoamericana de cultura* 211.1041 (1985): 569–75.

Schnaiderman, Boris. "Vozes de barbárie, vozes de cultura: uma leitura dos contos de Rubem Fonseca," in *Contos reunidos*, by R. Fonseca. São Paulo: Companhia das Letras, 1994, 773–77.

Silva, Deonísio da. *O caso Rubem Fonseca: violência e erotismo em Feliz Ano Novo*. São Paulo: Editora Alfa-Omega, 1983.

———. *Rubem Fonseca: proibido y consagrado*. Rio de Janeiro: Relume-Dumará, 1996.

Silverman, Malcolm. *Moderna ficção brasileira 2: ensaios*. Rio de Janeiro: Civilização Brasileira, 1981.

Simpson, Amelia S. *Detective Fiction from Latin America*. Rutherford, NJ: Fairleigh Dickinson University Press, 1990.

Tolman, Jon M. "The Moral Dimension in Rubem Fonseca's Prose." *New World* 1.1 (1986): 61–81.

Vargas Llosa, Mario. "A *Grande Arte* da Paródia." *Jornal de Letras, Artes & Ideias* (Lisbon) 6.240 (1987): 8–9.

Vidal, Ariovaldo José. *Roteiro para un narrador: Uma leitura dos contos de Rubem Fonseca*. São Paulo: Ateliê Editorial, 2000.

Vieira, Nelson H. "'Evil Be Thou My Good': Postmodern Heroics and Ethics in *Billy Bathgate* and *Bufo & Spallanzini*." *Comparative Literature Studies* 28.4 (1994): 356–78.

Carlos Fuentes (b. 1928)

MEXICO

Born in Panama City to Berta Macías Rivas and Rafael Fuentes Boettiger, a Mexican diplomat, Carlos Fuentes spent most of his childhood and youth moving from one country to another. He attended Henry D. Cook Public School in Washington, D.C. and moved first to Santiago, Chile, where he studied at the Cambridge School and the Grange School, and later to Buenos Aires. During this period (1941–1944) he published his first articles and short stories in the *Boletín del Instituto Nacional de Chile*. Back in Mexico, he completed his basic formal education. Then he studied at the Institut des Hautes Études in Geneva, where he worked as a secretary in the Mexican delegation to the International Law Commission of the United Nations. Back in his native country in 1953, he became a collaborator on the preparation of the *Revista universitaria de México* while holding the post of assistant director of the cultural division at the UNAM (Universidad Nacional Autónoma de México).

Between 1956 and 1959, Fuentes served as director of International Cultural Relations for the Mexican State Department. At the end of this period he married the actress Rita Macedo and visited Cuba to celebrate the triumph of Castro's Revolution. During the following years he visited the island on several occasions and became a delegate to the congress in support of Cuba but, by the end of the decade, his political position changed due to the implementation of repressive intellectual policies by the revolutionary government.

During the 1960s, Fuentes lived in London, Paris, and Mexico City and, after divorcing Macedo, he married the journalist Sylvia Lemus in 1972. That same year he was appointed as a member of the prestigious Colegio Nacional de México. Two years later he received a fellowship at the Woodrow Wilson International Center for Scholars in Washington, D.C. He also served as Mexican ambassador to France from 1974 to 1977.

Fuentes's protean and polysemous work includes short stories, plays, cultural and political essays, and some of the most innovative and challenging novels that Latin American writers have produced in recent times. His appeal to popular and academic audiences, both through his writings and through his public appearances as a frequent figure in the media, made him an icon of the international, cosmopolitan intellectual, whose privileged viewpoint authorizes him to freely express his opinions on current issues and to be sensitive to the movements of human history, reevaluating the past and appraising the present.

In the earlier stage of his career, Fuentes was the object of political and, to a lesser extent, sociological criticism. As he recalls in *Geografía de la novela* (Geography of the novel, 1993), his first book of short stories, *Los días enmascarados* (The masked days, 1954), was criticized for failing to adjust to prevailing aesthetic and political principles among Mexican intellectuals during the 1950s: "It was a fantasy: it was not realistic. It was cosmopolitan: it turned its back on the nation.

It was irresponsible: it was not politically committed" (14). But when he published *La región más transparente* (1958; English translation, *Where the Air Is Clear*, 1960), the novel "was accused of exactly the opposite: it was too realistic, crude, violent. It dealt with the nation, but only to denigrate it. And its political commitment, revisionist and critical, was self-defeating" (14+).

In time, scholars began to build an ever-increasing body of critical writings that approach Fuentes's literary production from a wide range of perspectives, without necessarily leaving aside political concerns. The collection of articles edited by Helmy F. Giacomán in *Homenaje a Carlos Fuentes* (1971), the analysis of *Aura* (1962) by Manuel Durán in his *Tríptico mexicano* (1973), and studies like *La magia y las brujas en la obra de Carlos Fuentes* (1976; English translation, *The Archetypes of Carlos Fuentes: From Witch to Androgyne*, 1980) are milestones in the transition to a systematic study of his vast, versatile, and multidimensional work.

Fuentes's own literary criticism, which goes along with the constants and variations of his creative writings, may be divided into three periods: the initial "revolutionary" one (Williams 222) includes *La nueva novela hispanoamericana* (The Spanish American new novel, 1969) and the collection *Casa con dos puertas* (House with two doors, 1970); a second stage corresponding to the process of writing *Terra Nostra*, a process of historical and cultural concerns, materializes in *Cervantes; o, La crítica de la lectura* (English translation, *Don Quixote, or the Critique of Reading*, 1976); and a third one marked by the publication of *Valiente mundo nuevo* (A brave new world, 1990) and *Geografía de la novela* (Geography of the novel, 1993).

In 1967, his novel *Cambio de piel* (English translation, *A Change of Skin*, 1968) won the Biblioteca Breve Prize of the Barcelona publishing house Seix Barral, marking the beginning of his international recognition. He also received the Xavier Villaurrutia award (1975) and the Venezuelan Rómulo Gallegos prize (1977) for *Terra Nostra*. His literary production as a whole was recognized with the Alfonso Reyes award (1979) and the National Literature Prize in Mexico (1984). The long list of literary prizes he earned includes also the Miguel de Cervantes Prize (Spain, 1987), the Rubén Darío Prize (1988), the Instituto Italo-Latino Americano Prize (1988), the New York City National Arts Club Medal of Honor (1988), and the Order of Cultural Independence (Nicaragua, 1988).

During his stay at Dartmouth College in 1981, Fuentes began thinking of his narrative writings as a whole, in terms of an organic totality rather than the sum of individual pieces. In time, he drew up a distribution of both his previously published books and the future ones, leaving the pure chronology aside. This insight led to an outline, "La edad del tiempo" (The age of time), which was announced for the first time with the publication of the novel *Cristóbal Nonato* (1987; English translation, *Christopher Unborn*, 1989). Later, this first outline was slightly modified by the writer, and according to its most recent version that was included in the last pages of *Diana o la cazadora solitaria* (1994; English translation, *Diana, the Goddess Who Hunts Alone*, 1995), the initial core, called "El mal del tiempo" (The evil of time/the malaise of time), consists of four texts where Fuentes's aesthetic of the novel is encoded: *Aura* (1962; English version, 1965), *Cumpleaños* (Birthday, 1969), *Una familia lejana* (1980; English translation, *Distant Relations*, 1982), and *Constancia y otras novelas para vírgenes* (1989; English translation, *Constancia and Other Stories for Virgins*, 1990). The rest of his narrative production is organized following a more traditional chronological order: not that of the writing and publications, but that of the historical settings of the several different possible worlds that the author forged. Thus, the second cycle of "La edad del tiempo," which was named "Tiempo de fundaciones" (The age of founding/foundation), includes *Terra Nostra* (1975; English version, 1976), as a recognition of the central significance that this novel has reached both in the eyes of the writer and critics. The remaining narrations are sequenced in the following way: *La campaña* (1990; English translation, *The Campaign*, 1991); *Gringo viejo* (1985; English translation, *The Old Gringo*, 1985); *La región más transparente*; *La muerte de Artemio Cruz* (1962; English translation, *The Death of Artemio Cruz*, 1964); *Las buenas conciencias* (1959; English translation, *The Good Conscience*, 1961); *Zona sagrada* (1967; English translation, *Holy Place*, 1972); *Los días enmascarados*, *Cantar de ciegos* (Songs of the blind; 1964), *Agua quemada* (1981; English translation, *Burnt Water*, 1980); *La frontera de cristal* (1995; English translation, *The Crystal Frontier*, 1995); *La cabeza de la hidra* (1978; English translation, *The Hydra Head*, 1978); *Cambio de piel*; *Cristóbal Nonato*; *Diana o la cazadora solitaria*; and *El naranjo o los círculos del tiempo* (1993; *The Orange Tree*, 1994).

Even though Carlos Fuentes is not a detective fiction writer—critics agree that his narrations are either of a fantastic nature, with stories dominated by the themes of supernatural reincarnation, the double, and the survival of ancient Mexican myths, or of social and historical concerns, exploring the problems of national and personal identity—there is no doubt that the conventions of the genre influenced his writing to a certain extent. As stated by Cynthia Duncan for the case of "La muñeca reina" ("The Doll Queen") from *Cantar de ciegos*, several of his pieces are "similar in many ways to a classical detective story," establishing their relationship to this type of fiction "only to subvert the rules that are normally applied to the genre" (257). In fact, "La muñeca" can be read as a new twist to the detective story formula: the narrator, the romantic Carlos, takes on the detective role in order to solve the mysterious disappearance of Amilamia, a childhood friend. Another case in point is "Chac Mool," from *Los días enmascarados*: Filiberto, an obscure government clerk, a one-time promising individual who feels that he has become a failure in life, drowns in Acapulco. Before his suspicious death, he had bought a pre-Columbian stone idol that he put in his basement. While taking Filiberto's body back to Mexico City, the narrator, a close friend, reads his diary. Through this posthumous testimony he discovers that, during the rainy season, slime developed on the base of the idol and moss covered it. In time, the Chac Mool came back to life and subjected Filiberto to slavery. The story is a masterpiece of the fantastic, but the narrator's situation may be put on the same footing as that of many literary sleuths: he is confronted with a riddle that must be solved through reasoning.

Some elements of the detective genre may be identified in the "El mal del tiempo" novels. *Aura* combines elements from various literary traditions: on the one hand, the uncanny and obscure ambience characteristic of the gothic and fantastic novels, and on the other, experimental devices and techniques borrowed from the avant-garde prose and the French new novel. Although the opening paragraphs provide a primarily realistic representation of the protagonist—the young historian Felipe Montero—and his personal situation, the mysterious and nightmare-like atmosphere that dominates the rest of the novel begins as soon as he crosses the threshold of Consuelo Llorente's house in the old district of Mexico City. The woman is the widow of a general of the ill-fated Emperor Maximilian's army, who ruled the country from 1864 to 1867. She allegedly hires the historian to finish the memoirs of her husband, but the disturbing experiences Felipe is going to deal with in the house will give him, and the reader, an unusual perception of reality. During his stay there, he is seduced by Consuelo's beautiful young niece, Aura, who turns out to be a supernatural projection of the widow. Such a projection, the reader realizes, is a product of her sorcery. Victim of her magical powers, Felipe comes to acknowledge that he himself is a reincarnation of the dead general.

Even though there is no puzzling murder to be solved, Felipe is impelled to forge a rational explanation for his own circumstances. On this level, *Aura* represents a situation that highlights writing. Felipe is a historian, thus a writer, hired to both put in order another writer's papers and to finish his memoirs, compiling a book that would illuminate one of the crucial moments of Mexican history. This task, which he agrees to do only for the extraordinarily high wage offered, will prevent him from progressing in his own intellectual projects, which also have to do with the Mexican past. Following his Western academic formation, Felipe aspires to summarize all the dispersed chronicles of the discovery and conquest of America, make them intelligible, and find the historical correspondences that could contribute to understanding the past. In other words, he would like to make sense of the miscellaneous set of phenomena that combine to form history. Instead of achieving a rational recuperation of the past, he will undergo a unique experience of the supernatural that questions the prevailing linear conception of time and history.

A parallel situation to that of Felipe is exploited in *Cumpleaños*, perhaps the most enigmatic fictional text ever written by Fuentes, where a third-person omniscient narrator introduces an old man in confinement, accompanied by a woman and a cat. Later on, the reader finds out that the elderly man is Siger of Brabant (born c. 1235), an Averroist master at the University of Paris. This opening story is interrupted by a dotted line. At that point, another narrative sequence takes the reader to the present and to Hampstead, in London. A married couple, an architect named George and his wife, wake up on their only child's tenth birthday. After a brief return to the initial story, a third level in the plot begins with a shift in the narrative voice. Now, a character also named George, who seems to have an extraordinarily limited knowledge of himself and his circumstances, describes what he sees, feels, and does using the present tense. His lengthy discourse, which constitutes the main body of the novel, is often interrupted by ellipses that give the story a fragmentary pace. Through the denouement of the story, the reader becomes a sort of detective who must reorganize the dispersed clues and find a general sense to them.

But his most clear detective character is Whitby Hull, a 63-year-old physician in "Constancia," from *Constancia y otras novelas para vírgenes*. Set in Savannah, Georgia, the novella brings together three characters: Hull, his Sevillian wife, and an acquaintance of theirs, the Russian actor Mr. Plotnikov. From the very beginning, the novel introduces a mystery, which according to the imaginative logic developed by the writer, instead of leading to a solution that restores the confidence of the characters in their situation, is the lid of a Pandora's box, concealing a more complex and unsuspected reality: "The Old Russian actor Monsieur Plotnikov visited me the very day of his death. He told me that the years would pass and I would come to visit him on the day of my own death" (3). Despite the fact that Whitby and Constancia have lived together for 40 years, he knows nothing about her past until he realizes that he is a part of a peculiar love triangle—one he will have to acknowledge and interpret in its profound meaning. The evidence Whitby is brought face-to-face with does not respond to logic or common sense, and that is why he reluctantly accepts the existence of the inexplicable.

Although the fantastic shares with the detective narration—from their very beginning as literary forms in the nineteenth century—a common need of developing improbable stories, the acceptance of a strict definition for the latter is an obstacle hard to overcome when dealing with Fuentes's works. Clearly, one central element of detective narrative is the solving of an enigma whose nature may be reduced to the breaking of law—that is, a mysterious event pushing the legal bonding of society into crisis. This rupture of the conventional constitutive base of social life implies the appearance of a particular institutional order and its agents: police, judges, public opinion. In his short stories and novels, Carlos Fuentes provides ample evidence of his capacity to create possible worlds saturated with magic and suggestion, worlds that appear to be disturbing enigmas that the reader must actively deal with. There is no doubt that the issue of individual and social identity, the exploration and reconfiguration of the concept of history, and the necessity of creating new myths for modern writing can be traced throughout his narrative and are basic constituents of his aesthetics of the novel.

Daniel Altamiranda

Works

Agua quemada. Cuarteto narrativo. Mexico City: Fondo de Cultura Económica, 1981.
Aura. Mexico City: Era, 1962. English version trans. Lysander Kemp under the same title. New York: Farrar, Straus & Giroux, 1965.
Las buenas conciencias. Mexico City: Fondo de Cultura Económica, 1959. English version as *The Good Conscience*, trans. Sam Hileman. New York: Ivan Obolensky, 1961.

Burnt Water, trans. Margaret Sayers Peden. New York: Farrar, Straus & Giroux, 1980. Selected stories from his three short-story collections.

La cabeza de la hidra. Barcelona: Anaya, 1978. English version as *The Hydra Head*, trans. Margaret Sayers Peden. New York: Farrar, Straus & Giroux, 1978.

Cambio de piel. Buenos Aires: Sudamericana, 1967. English version as *A Change of Skin*, trans. Sam Hileman. New York: Farrar, Straus & Giroux, 1968.

La campaña. Mexico City: Fondo de Cultura Económica, 1990. English version as *The Campaign*, trans. Alfred Mac Adam. New York: Farrar, Straus & Giroux, 1991.

Cantar de ciegos. Mexico City: Joaquín Mortiz, 1964.

Casa con dos puertas. Mexico City: Joaquín Mortiz, 1970.

Ceremonias del alba. Madrid: Mondadori, 1991.

Cervantes; o, La crítica de la lectura. Mexico City: Joaquín Mortiz, 1976. *Don Quixote, or the Critique of Reading*. Austin: University of Texas Press, 1976.

Constancia y otras novelas para vírgenes. Madrid: Mondadori, 1989. English version as *Constancia and Other Stories for Virgins*, trans. Thomas Christensen. New York: Farrar, Straus & Giroux, 1990.

Cristóbal Nonato. Mexico City: Fondo de Cultura Económica, 1987. English version as *Christopher Unborn*, trans. Alfred Mac Adam. York: Farrar, Straus & Giroux, 1989.

Cumpleaños. Mexico City: Joaquín Mortiz, 1969.

Diana o la cazadora solitaria. Madrid: Alfaguara, 1994. English version as *Diana, the Goddess Who Hunts Alone*, trans. Alfred J. Mac Adam. New York: Farrar, Straus & Giroux, 1995.; Retitled as *Diana, the Lonely Huntress*. London: Bloomsbury, 1995.

Los días enmascarados. Mexico City: Los Presentes, 1954.

Una familia lejana. Mexico City: Era, 1980. English version as *Distant Relations*, trans. Margaret Sayers Peden. New York: Farrar, Straus & Giroux, 1982.

La frontera de cristal. Una novela en nueve cuentos. Mexico City: Alfaguara, 1995. English version as *The Crystal Frontier*, trans. Alfred Mac Adam. New York: Farrar, Straus & Giroux, 1997.

Geografía de la novela. Mexico City: Fondo de Cultura Económica, 1993.

Gringo viejo. Mexico City: Fondo de Cultura Económica, 1985. English version as *The Old Gringo*, trans. Margaret Sayers Peden and Carlos Fuentes. New York: Farrar, Straus & Giroux, 1985.

La muerte de Artemio Cruz. Mexico City: Fondo de Cultura Económica, 1962. English version as *The Death of Artemio Cruz*, trans. Sam Hileman. New York: Farrar, Straus & Company, 1964. Trans. Alfred Mac Adam under the same title. New York: Farrar, Straus & Giroux, 1991.

Myself with Others. Selected Essays. New York: Farrar, Straus & Giroux, 1988.

El naranjo o los círculos del tiempo. Mexico City: Alfaguara, 1993. English version as *The Orange Tree*, trans. Alfred Mac Adam. New York: Farrar, Straus & Giroux, 1994.

La nueva novela hispanoamericana. Mexico City: Joaquín Mortiz, 1969.

La región más transparente. Mexico City: Fondo de Cultura Económica, 1958. English version as *Where the Air Is Clear*, trans. Sam Hileman. New York: Ivan Obolensky, 1960.

Terra Nostra. Barcelona: Seix Barral, 1975. English version as *Terra Nostra*, trans. Margaret Sayers Peden. New York: Farrar, Straus & Giroux, 1976.

Tiempo mexicano. Mexico City: Joaquín Mortiz, 1971.

Tres discursos para dos aldeas. Mexico City: Fondo de Cultura Económica, 1993.

Valiente mundo nuevo. Épica, utopía y mito en la novela hispanoamericana. Madrid: Mondadori, 1990.

Zona sagrada. Mexico City: Siglo XXI, 1967. English version as *Holy Place*, trans. Suzanne Jill Levine. New York: E. P. Dutton, 1978.

Criticism

Albarracín Fernández, J. *La distorsión temporal en Carlos Fuentes y Mario Vargas Llosa*. Mérida, Venezuela: Universidad de los Andes, 1985.

Borel, Jean Paul, and Pierre Rossel. *La narrativa más transparente. (Contribución a un estudio de la relación entre Literatura y Sociedad, a propósito de tres novelas de Carlos Fuentes)*. Madrid: Asociación Europa de Profesores de Español, 1981.

Brody, Robert, and Charles Rossman, eds. *Carlos Fuentes: A Critical View*. Austin: University of Texas Press, 1982.

Carlos Fuentes: Premio "Miguel de Cervantes" 1987. Barcelona/Madrid: Anthropos/Ministerio de Cultura, 1988.

Duncan, Cynthia K. "'La muñeca reina' by Carlos Fuentes: A Detective Tale Turned Inside Out," in *Interpretaciones a la obra de Carlos Fuentes, un gigante de las letras hispanoamericanas*, ed. Ana María Hernández de López. Madrid: Beramar, 1990, 257–71.

Durán, Gloria. *La magia y las brujas en la obra de Carlos Fuentes*. Mexico City: Universidad Nacional Autónoma de México, 1976. English version as *The Archetypes of Carlos Fuentes: From Witch to Androgyne*. Hamden, CT: Archon Books, 1980.

Faris, Wendy B. *Carlos Fuentes*. New York: Frederick Ungar, 1983.

García Gutiérrez, Georgina. *Los disfraces. La obra mestiza de Carlos Fuentes*. Mexico City: El Colegio de México, 1981.

García Núñez, Fernando. *Fabulación de la fe: Carlos Fuentes*. Xalapa, Mexico: Universidad Veracruzana, 1989.

Giacomán, Helmy F., ed. *Homenaje a Carlos Fuentes. Variaciones interpretativas en torno a su obra*. New York: Las Américas, 1971.

González, Alfonso. *Carlos Fuentes: Life, Work, and Criticism*. Fredericton, NB, Canada: York Press, 1987.

Hernández de López, Ana María, ed. *La obra de Carlos Fuentes: Una visión múltiple*. Madrid: Pliegos, 1988.

———. *Interpretaciones a la obra de Carlos Fuentes, un gigante de las letras hispanoamericanas*. Madrid: Beramar, 1990.

Ibsen, Kristine. *Author, Text and Reader in the Novels of Carlos Fuentes*. New York: Peter Lang, 1993.

Lévy, Isaac Jack, and Juan Loveluck, eds. *Simposio Carlos Fuentes, Actas*. Columbia: University of South Carolina Press, 1978.

Moreno, Fernando. *Carlos Fuentes: "La mort d'Artemio Cruz", entre le mythe et l'histoire*. Paris: Editions caribéenes, 1989.

Ordiz, Francisco Javier. *El mito en la obra narrativa de Carlos Fuentes*. León: Universidad de León, Servicio de Publicaciones, 1987.

Ramírez Mattei, Aida Elsa. *La narrativa de Carlos Fuentes*. Río Piedras: Universidad de Puerto Rico, 1983.

Rodríguez Carranza, Luz. *Un teatro de la memoria. Análisis de "Terra Nostra" de Carlos Fuentes*. Buenos Aires: Leuven University Press/Vergara, 1990.

Simson, Ingrid. *Realidad y ficción en Terra Nostra de Carlos Fuentes*. Frankfurt: Vervuert Verlag, 1989.

Stavans, Ilán. *Antiheroes: Mexico and Its Detective Novel*, trans. Jesse H. Lytle and Jennifer A. Mattson. Madison: Fairleigh Dickinson University Press, 1997, 100–103.

Stoopen, María. *"La muerte de Artemio Cruz", una novela de denuncia y traición*. Mexico City: Universidad Nacional Autónoma de México, 1982.

Trujillo Muñoz, Gabriel. *Testigos de cargo: la narrativa policiaca mexicana y sus autores*. Tijuana, Mexico: CONACULTA/CECUT, 2000, 52–55.

Williams, Raymond Leslie. *The Writings of Carlos Fuentes*. Austin: University of Texas Press, 1996.

Mempo Giardinelli (b. 1947)

Mempo Giardinelli occupies a special place in the field of Argentine and Latin American narrative at this present turn of the century. His work is as admirable as it is varied; he moves comfortably between the short story, the novel, and the essay. His literary production to the present includes the novels *La revolución en bicicleta* (The revolution on bicycle, 1980), *El cielo con las manos* (Heaven in hand, 1981), *Luna caliente* (*Sultry Moon*, 1983 [winner of the Premio Nacional de Novela, Mexico]), *Qué solos se quedan los muertos* (How lonely are the dead, 1985), *Santo oficio de la memoria* (The holy office of memory, 1991 [winner of the Rómulo Gallegos award]), *Imposible equilibrio* (Impossible balance, 1995), and *El décimo infierno* (*The Tenth Circle*, 1999). Furthermore, his short-story collections include *Vidas ejemplares* (Exemplary lives, 1982), *La entrevista* (The interview, 1986), *Cuentos: Antología personal* (Stories: A personal anthology, 1987), *Carlitos Dancing Bar y otros cuentos* (1992), and *El castigo de Dios* (God's punishment, 1993). Among his essays, one must cite his outstanding *Así se escribe un cuento* (How to write a short story; 1992) and *El género negro* (The detective genre, 1984), with a revised edition published in 1996.

Giardinelli was born in Resistencia, Chaco in 1947, where he lived for a large portion of his life. Toward the end of the 1960s he established himself in Buenos Aires, where he began to work as a journalist and dedicate himself to making a living through writing. At this time, toward the end of his studies, he also abandoned plans for a career in law toward the end of his studies. His activities as a journalist as well as a militant within the writers union put him in direct contact with the political violence of the late 1960s and early 1970s in Argentina. Later, the military coup of 1976 that initiated one of the most tragic periods in Argentine history caused profound changes in the author's life. He went into exile in Mexico where he continued working in journalism. He soon became editor-in-chief of the journal *Expansión* (Expansion) and shortly thereafter was offered a teaching position at the Facultad de Periodismo y Comunicacion Social (College of journalism and communications) of the Universidad Iberoamericana (Iberoamerican University), which he held until 1984. Likewise, during the majority of his years spent in Mexico, he also contributed to the newspaper *Excélsior*. In 1983, he received the Premio Nacional de Novela de México (Mexican National Prize for the Novel) for his *Luna caliente*, the first time the award was given to a foreigner. In 1984, following the restitution of democracy, he returned to Argentina and again settled in Buenos Aires. The immediate publication of his works in Argentina, where they were previously unknown, led to his rapid recognition and participation in the Argentine cultural scene. Since then, he has maintained a constant presence as an established writer. He renewed his ties to the field of journalism in Buenos Aires and the interior of the country and many of his essays and articles were published in the leading Argentine periodicals (*Clarín* [Bugle], *La Razón* [Reason], *La*

Nación [The nation], and *Página 12* [Page 12]). In 1985, he founded the literary journal *Puro cuento* (Pure fiction), which he directed during the six years of its existence. That same year he published his fifth novel, *Qué solos se quedan los muertos*. In 1993, the author was honored with the prestigious Rómulo Gallegos award for his novel *Santo oficio de la memoria* (published in 1991).

One can identify the noticeable influence of the detective genre throughout Giardinelli's work. In fact, the author's relationship to this genre has a rather long history that is worth mentioning. It began in the 1950s with an impassioned reading of works by Arthur Conan Doyle and his subsequent discovery of the most important practitioners of the hard-boiled novel such as Dashiell Hammett, Raymond Chandler, and Ross Macdonald. This is the type of fiction, in the author's own words, that "se ocupa de la parte más sucia, generalmente la más sórdida, oculta y negada de toda la sociedad" (is concerned with the dirtiest, and generally the most sordid, hidden and denied elements of any society [*El género negro* 7]). Years later, while in exile in Mexico, he is given the opportunity to reflect on the genre in a more organized way through his contributions to the cultural supplement of the daily *Excélsior*. The success of these initial columns resulted in new invitations to elaborate his ideas on this literature in a more extensive format. His essays appeared in the journal *Comunidad Conacyt* (Conacyt community, published by the National Council of Science and Technology of Mexico) and the *Revista mexicana de ciencias políticas y sociales* (Mexican journal of political and social sciences) of the Universidad National Autónoma de México (National university of Mexico).

The fruit of this labor culminates in the two volumes of essays published under the title *El género negro* (1984), which gathers together the majority of texts written over the span of fours years. The corrected and revised edition, now in one volume, reveals the uninterrupted reflection that this genre has inspired in the author. The book consists of a well-argued and documented defense of the genre in which Giardinelli attempts to invalidate hierarchical academic canons and thus respond to those who still disdain the genre and disregard it as "serious" literature. The author frequently shows how the genre is an important venue for presenting certain social and ethical dilemmas. According to Giardinelli, the hard-boiled novel "tiene la capacidad extraordinaria para mostrar la sociedad de nuestro tiempo. . . . Es un medio estupendo para comprender, primero, y para indagar después, al mundo en que vivimos" (has the extraordinary capacity to show society in our times. . . . It is an excellent means of understanding, first, and for exploring second, the world in which we live [26]). Moreover, the mechanisms of detective fiction allow for the examination of power relations—according to the author, one of the primary foundational values of the genre—given that "siempre, las debilidades humanas son las que provocan el crimen, y siempre detrás de un crimen hay una manifestación de poder" (always, human weakness is what leads to crime, and alway behind a crime is a manifestation of power [30–31]). It is for this reason that it can be used as an effective critical instrument of social circumstances. For the author, the characteristic elements of the detective novel—crime and violence—allow for the codification of key indicators of a determined sociopolitical subtext. That is, the poetics of the genre allow authors to postulate, from a fictional space, an interpretive analysis of reality.

The research and reflections on detective fiction throughout the years has left a mark on Giardinelli's creative work. At this same time, he began to experiment with the discursive resources of the genre. In the stories "El tipo" (The guy) and "El paseo de Andrés López" (Andrés López's stroll) in *Vidas ejemplares*, his first anthology, one can perceive that Giardinelli turns to the diverse methods of detective fiction to create a sordid and enlightening portrait of violence. But it is not until *Luna caliente* that he fully adopts the narrative codes of the hard-boiled novel. Initially a short story in *Vidas ejemplares*, it was removed from the volume prior to publication and later rewritten as a *nouvelle*, as some critics prefer to call it. Aside from the aforementioned prize it earned in Mexico, *Luna caliente* enjoyed a warm reception among readers, and especially among academics. It was also a defining text for the author, since his name was finally incorporated into the panorama of Latin American literature during the 1980s. Likewise, the novel was translated into 13 languages, thereby helping the author to transcend the limits of the Spanish-speaking world. It is worth mentioning that the release of *Luna caliente* did not occur in Argentina until 1984. Its impact was the same it had the previous year in other places: it was on the best-seller list for several months and established the author as a major figure in Argentine intellectual circles, where he was virtually unknown due to his exile.

Luna caliente proposes a new way of fictionalizing the facts of the Proceso de Reorganización Nacional (Process of National Reorganization, as the military government referred to itself) through a simple but dense plot replete with multiple meaning and well-managed suspense. Ramiro, a young lawyer from Chaco, returns to his hometown (Resistencia) after having lived for a decade in Paris where he completed his studies. He soon meets Araceli, the sensual and mysterious adolescent (13 years old), daughter of friends of the family. The irresistible attraction that Ramiro feels for Araceli drives him to commit an abhorrent rape, and then to cover it up he suffocates the girl. Believing he was found out by the father, he decides to kill him as well. But it is not until the following day that he realizes, much to his horror, that the young girl is not dead. The novel presents classic situations of suspense. The police and military investigate the death of Araceli's father. Surprisingly, Ramiro is saved from going to jail thanks to the lies told by the girl. But her protection of him comes with a price. She demands he make love to her until she is completely satiated, which inverts the initial victim–victimizer relationship. Seeing himself trapped in a perverse game and in fear that the truth be discovered, Ramiro decides to strangle Araceli after another obligatory "encounter" filled with passion and violence. The epilogue presents Ramiro in Asunción, Paraguay, holed up in a hotel room and accosted by ghosts who tell him that life in hell will be eternal, as the last lines of the novel suggest.

Giardinelli makes use of the conventions of the hard-boiled novel to create a disturbing and dizzying story. An omniscient narrator establishes the narrative and emotional setting through a firm command of language, evident from the first statement: "Sabía que iba a pasar; lo supo en cuanto la vio" (He knew it was going to happen; he knew it as soon as he saw her [13]). The plot unfolds through a rapid succession of actions that generate an increasing sense of suspense and intrigue. The events, presented in chronological order, reveal a complex network of circumstances as the police and military try to uncover who committed the crime and why. The careful selection and linking of facts in the novel cause the action and time to pass quickly and dramatically, which lends to the building tension and structural economy of the text, characteristic of the genre. *Luna caliente* contains some of the fundamental premises of the hard-boiled novel. There is sexual violence, crimes, and an investigation, even if carried out by corrupt authorities. Nevertheless, there are important deviations from the classic model. From the beginning, it is known who the killer is and what the motives of the crime are. Aside from being a major difference, this also pushes the reader to undertake another kind of search to uncover the possible hidden meanings in the discourse and comprehend what is behind the appropriation of certain hard-boiled conventions while it deviates from others.

Luna caliente provides a perspective from which to interpret the real historical setting of the novel during the first stage of the Proceso in Argentina. While the novel seemingly remains distant from the collective social experience of the period, it implicitly proposes the decoding of certain clues that point directly at that bloody historical experience. One of these instances, for example, is found in the spatiotemporal setting: the summer (December) of 1977, in a subtropical region (Chaco). Without a doubt, the time and place of the action are condensed in an environment that is semantically charged for anyone familiar with the Argentine reality of the period. Likewise, the short but concise pieces of information offered by the narrator to poetically represent reality place the reader in the midst of the political intrigue of daily life in the Argentina of the 1970s: "este país es una mierda, Ramiro. Era hermoso, pero lo conviertieron en una mierda" (this country's a pile of shit, Ramiro. It used to be beautiful, but they've turned it into shit [41]). It is possible to perceive the climate of tension and fear that reigned during those years, the product of the societal confrontation between civilians and the military. For example, the participation of the police and members of the armed forces in the investigation allow the reader to enter a underworld where perversity, lies, manipulation, and violence make up the basic methodological principles for safeguarding social order. The double discursive codes emitted from the centers of power reveal the inner-workings of the ideological battle that was taking place in the country and that consisted of silencing, through violence, the dissident voices that "threatened" the social order. Thus, the reader discovers a world in which everything is out of place and, as for Ramiro, it all seems a cruel hallucination brought on by the intense heat of Chaco.

Giardinelli masterfully utilizes narrative strategies associated with the hard-boiled genre in *Luna caliente*. The most characteristic topics and elements such as violence, crime, investigation, sex, and death are all present. The filtered language of the narration and the narrative structure of brief, intense chapters contribute to the creation of an atmosphere of suspense, while the facts precipitously unfold toward a surprising climax (Buchanan, 159). Nonetheless, one of the most notable features of the text that the reader must face is the absence of anyone who solves the case and offers reparation for injustice, although societal ills cannot be eradicated. *Luna caliente* offers no reparation, and this absence defines the political implications of the text. Stated differently, there can be no justice served, precisely because those who administer it are the same ones who cover-up crimes on a daily basis. This is an essential and defining modification, since it reverses the dichotomy of criminal–victim. It is precisely this surprising reversal that underscores the political nature of the text, since the message of social indictment is so well-articulated.

Luna caliente is an undeniable allegorical text. The juxtaposition of the sexual with the political produces a highly suggestive metaphor of the political violence during 1970s Argentina. The country becomes metaphorized in the figure of Araceli, who is corrupted, raped, and perverse, but whose repeated reappearances constitute the return of a violent past that comes back to stalk its violators (Reati, 219–23). The "heat" of the subtropical region and of sexual desire, suggested in the title, transcend the physical to represent a concrete historical repertoire. In this way, the novel seeks to encapsulate, with all its intensity, the conflicts of a determined historical moment and prompts reflection on the crossroads and ambiguities of the Argentine national experience of the time. The appropriation of hard-boiled literary conventions permits the author to articulate a story that has the virtue of condensing, by metaphorical means, the ideological themes that the text insists on in the process of its critical examination.

Qué solos se quedan los muertos is a novel that also moves between detective and political elements through the amalgamation of amorous intrigue, the detective plot, and resistance journalism. Its characterization as a detective novel is obvious from the beginning. José Giustozzi, an Argentine journalist exiled in Mexico, responds to a plea for help from Carmen, his ex-lover. Her partner has been murdered and now she is in danger. Giustozzi finds an aloof Carmen in Zacatecas, who presents as many questions as the murder he is attempting to investigate. Over the course of the investigation, always hindered by the police, Carmen is also murdered. Money and drugs are the primary motives of the crime. Giustozzi's insistent investigations make him a threatening figure, for which he is attacked and followed, and other deaths occur around him. Thus, the novel appears to adhere to the fundamental codes of the hard-boiled genre. However, on this point, there is some disagreement among critics. For some, it is a detective novel in the best tradition of the hard-boiled genre (Kohut, Parsons); for others, the components of the genre allow the author to create a text capable of including the treatment of diverse themes that are of concern to him, such as exile, violence, and death (Marcos) and the dialogue with recent Argentine history with the concomitant psychoanalytical questioning of the narrator-protagonist (Gutiérrez Mouat). Giardinelli undoubtedly appropriates the codes of the hard-boiled novel, but he transgresses and reformulates them also. The most remarkable deviation is to be found in the markedly essayistic intratext that subverts the hard-boiled codes and gives the text a novel–essay narrative profile. While the detective undercurrent of the novel indeed stands out, it is more appropriate to speak of the novel as a hybrid text, related to the detective novel, the *bildungsroman*, testimony, and journalistic writing, and even to a love story.

The first signs of rupture in *Qué solos se quedan los muertos* are found in its literary allusions. Juan Rulfo's classic novel *Pedro Páramo* (1955) is the most obvious example. There are numerous references to the voices of the dead, the winds of Comala, and to Susana San Juan (a main character in *Pedro Páramo*). There are also remarkable similarities between the experiences of Giustozzi in Zacatecas and those of Juan Preciado in Comala in that they both confront memories and their unconscious, which is a cemetery of solitude where the protagonists are obligated to dig-up the past (Gutiérrez Mouat 112–13). These allusions are suggested from the very beginning in the verse that Giardinelli borrows from Gustavo Adolfo Bécquer to title the novel. Similarly, the epigraphs to the parts the novel is divided into suggest a transgression of the hard-boiled codes and signal the dialogue that the novel invokes with other literary texts. In other words, the detective model impels the narrative action and serves as a pretext. The narrator presents this idea himself when he states "este texto, contra lo que pudiera parecer, no es ni pretende ser una novela policial" (this text, contrary to however it may seem, is not nor pretends to be a detective novel [132]). Giustozzi—an avid reader of Virgil, Bécquer, Rulfo, and Octavio Paz—is very different from the average detective or private investigator in detective fiction. That difference is most noticeable in his contemplative nature that leads him to reflect on the history of Mexico (without overlooking its tastes, customs, and idiosyncrasies) and, equally, on Argentine history (specifically of the 1970s). In these narrative fragments, the text is transformed into a statement of protest, a painful lament for the dead, the disappeared, the exiled, and political prisoners. As Giustozzi comments on Carmen's death, "me ha removido todo y me ha metido en esta especie de laguna estigia de lamentaciones y dolores" (it has scrambled everything up for me and thrown me into this hellish lagoon of lamentation and pain [102]). In addition to the loss of a beloved woman are added an endless number of collective losses. Thus, unraveling Carmen's murder allows him to weigh some possible answers for all those other senseless deaths. In this way, Giustozzi's inquiries are transformed at times into an up-front appeal to the history of his country. His self-critical vocation results in a truly scathing analysis of the Argentine reality of the 1970s.

The essayistic intratext of *Qué solos se quedan los muertos* is one of the most significant strategies in the text used to subvert the conventions of the detective story. In these sections, the novel loses all narrative force, and behind the voice of Giustozzi one can hear that of the author himself. If the questioning of and appeal to history are constants in Giardinelli's novelistic production, never before had they been formulated with such straightforward signs and with such a pronounced political voice. Moreover, it's obvious that the essayistic discourse pretends to fill the void left by other intellectual and political discourses. Nonetheless, Giradinelli's writing does not become exhausted either by allusion or denouncement. In fact, it chooses to place everything on center stage, action after action, to construct an asphyxiating atmosphere of fear and persecution (typical of the genre) so that the reader may judge with his own eyes and thus be able to form a critical-interpretive analysis of society's ills. That is, it appeals to the conventions of the hard-boiled novel in order to provide testimony of the offenses and crimes that are committed from centers of power that are connected to the underworld of delinquency and drug-trafficking. The appropriation of the thematic and stylistic elements of the detective story allows for the establishment of similarities between the traits of violence in fiction and violence in reality. In other words, it functions as a tool for thinking about violence, to question it, to resist it, and, in fact, to also reject it, and from whence comes the political statement that is perceived in the text. But it is a statement that is not always easy to identify due to the interweaving of genres, the frequent literary allusions, and the metanarrative commentary that complicate the process of deciphering the embedded message. Nevertheless, the importance of the detective undercurrent is easily recognized in the novel, since its system of codes is transgressed and reformulated to guide the reader through the details of the story to the historical analysis.

Luna caliente and *Qué solos se quedan los muertos* are texts of social and political commitment. In both texts, social criticism and protest—implicit and explicit alike—constitute the basic ingredients that come together in the appropriation of the conventions of the hard-boiled genre. With its power to question and irreverent attitude, the genre facilitates a more-free examination of and commentary on the different aspects related to the problem of institutionalized violence and political repression. Both texts make use of the conventions of the hard-boiled novel in particular to enable a dialogue with history and propose other possible constellations of meaning. In this way, the author reaffirms the power of literature in general, and of the hard-boiled novel in particular, to dispute truth by presenting provocative and destabilizing readings of conventional models of reality. Marked by a violence that exposes the bloody face of Argentine reality during the 1970s, both *Luna caliente* and *Qué solos se quedan los muertos* are trenchantly critical texts in the sense that criticism and protest—even when only suggested— constitute the basic ingredients of literary practice. The conventions of hard-boiled fiction in both texts become essential elements in connecting the stuff of narrative to external reality. The conventions of the hard-boiled genre that the author utilizes to construct fictional worlds permit him to transform the sociopolitical events of history, without detracting from them, so that they become pertinent examples of the solidarity between ethical and aesthetic values that come together in the narratives of Mempo Giardinelli.

Alicia Rolón

Works

Así se escribe un cuento. Buenos Aires: Beas Ediciones, 1992.

Carlitos Dancing Bar y otros cuentos. Buenos Aires: Almagesto, 1992.

El castigo de Dios. Buenos Aires: Norma, 1993.

El cielo con las manos. Hanover, NH: Ediciones del Norte, 1981.

El cielo con las manos: edición definitiva. Buenos Aires: Seix Barral, 1997.

Cuentos: antología personal. Buenos Aires: Puntosur, 1987.

Cuentos completos. Buenos Aires: Seix Barral, 1999.

El décimo infierno. Buenos Aires: Planeta, 1999. English version as *The Tenth Circle*, trans. Andrea Labinger. Pittsburgh: Latin American Literary Review Press, 2001.

La entrevista. Madrid: Almarabu, 1986.

El género negro, 2 vols. Mexico City: Universidad Autónoma Metropolitana, 1984; 2nd ed., 1996, 1 vol. Also, Córdoba, Argentina: Op Oloop Ediciones, 1997.

Imposible equilibrio. Buenos Aires: Planeta, 1995.

Luna caliente. Mexico City: Oasis, 1983, Buenos Aires: Bruguera, 1984. Reprint, Buenos Aires: Seix Barral, 2000, Madrid: Alianza, 2002. English version as *Sultry Moon*, trans. Patricia J. Duncan. Pittsburgh: Latin American Literary Review Press, 1998.

Qué solos se quedan los muertos. Buenos Aires: Sudamericana, 1985. Reprint, Buenos Aires: Seix Barral, 1997.

La revolución en bicicleta. Barcelona: Pomaire, 1980.

Santo oficio de la memoria. Bogotá: Norma, 1991.

"El tipo," in *Variaciones en negro: relatos policiales iberoamericanos*, ed. Lucía López Coll and Leonardo Padura. Havana: Editorial Arte y Literatura, 2001, 61–70. Also in *Variaciones en negro: relatos policiales hispanoamericanos*, ed. Lucía López Coll. Bogotá: Norma, 2003, 89–104.

Vida ejemplares. Hanover, NH: Ediciones del Norte, 1982.

Criticism

Alvarez Insúa, Carlos. "Entrevista con Mempo Giardinelli." *Piel* [Mexico] (14–16 June 1984): 39–40.

Buchanan, Rhonda. "El género negro como radiografía de una sociedad en *Luna caliente* de Mempo Giardinelli," in *Narrativa hispanoamericana contemporánea: entre la vanguardia y el posboom*, ed. Ana María Hernández de López. Madrid: Pliegos, 1996, 155–66.

Campos, Marcos Antonio. "*Luna caliente*, de Mempo Giardinelli." *Proceso* [Mexico] (February 1984): 56–57.

Dunn, Kelly Anne. "Representative Detective Fiction Writers Writers from Mexico and Argentina: Socio-Political Factors and Literary Context." Doctoral dissertation, University of Virginia, 1998.

Espinoza, Pilar. "*Luna caliente* de Mempo Giardinelli y *Lolita* de Vladimir Nabokov." *Atenea: revista de ciencia, arte, y literatura de la Universidad de Concepción* 475 (1997): 187–97.

García Chichester, Ana. "Jerarquía de los géneros sexuales en *Luna caliente* de Mempo Giardinelli." *Romance Notes* 34.2 (1993): 169–76.

Granrose, Kathleen. "Mempo Giardinelli." *Hispamérica* 84 (1999): 59-69. (Interview.)

Gutiérrez Mouat, Ricardo. "Texto e intertexto en la narrativa de Mempo Giardinelli," in Kohut 101–18.

Kohut, Karl, ed. *Un universo cargado de violencia. Presentación, aproximación y docu-*

mentación de la obra de Mempo Giardinelli. Frankfurt am Main: Vervuert Verlag, 1990.

Marcos, Juan Manuel. "La narrativa de Mempo Giardinelli." *Escritura: revista de teoría y crítica literarias* [Caracas] 8.16 (1983): 217–22.

———. "Mempo Giardinelli, del discurso provinciano a la ciudad del exilio," in *De García Márquez al postboom*. Madrid: Editorial Orígenes, 1986.

———. "Mempo Giardinelli in the Wake of Utopia." *Hispania* 70.2 (1987): 240–49.

———. "El género popular como meta-estructura textual del post-boom latinoamericano." *Monographic review/Revista monográfica* 3.1–2 (1987): 268–78.

Martul, Luis. "*Qué solos se quedan los muertos*: convenciones narrativas y transgresiones interpretativas," in *Convergencias Hispánicas: Selected Proceedings and Other Essays on Spanish and Latin American Literature, Film, and Linguistics*, ed. Elizabeth Scarlett and Howard B. West. Newark, DE: Juan de la Cuesta, 2001, 197–206.

Mathieu, Corina. "Visión paródica de la realidad argentina en *Imposible equilibrio* de Mempo Giardinelli." *RLA: Romance Languages Annual* 10.2 (1998): 715–18.

Méndez-Faith, Teresa. "Entrevista con Mempo Giardinelli." *Discurso literario* 5.2 (1988): 313–21.

O'Connell, Patrick L. "Narrating Memory and the Recuperation of Identity by Mempo Giardinelli: 'Una historia sin olvido.'" *Confluencia* 15.1 (1999): 46–57.

Parsons, Robert A. "Mempo Giardinelli's *Qué solos se quedan los muertos*: An Investigation of Argentina in Mexico." *Proceedings of the Philological Association of Louisana* (1990): 21–32.

Pellón, Gustavo. "Ideology and Structure in Giardinelli's *Santo oficio de la memoria*." *Studies in Twentieth-Century Literature* 19.1 (1995): 81–99.

Piña, Cristina. "La narrativa argentina de los años setenta y ochenta." *Cuadernos hispanoamericanos* 517–519 (1993): 121–38.

Planells, Antonio. "Mempo Giardinelli: el narrador en la tormenta." *Chasqui* 17.2 (1989): 79–88.

Reati, Fernando. *Nombrar lo innombrable. Violencia política y novela argentina: 1975–1985*. Buenos Aires: Legasa, 1992.

Roffé, Reina. "Entrevista a Mempo Giardinelli." *Cuadernos hispanoamericanos* 615 (2001): 81–92.

Rolón, Alicia. "*Luna caliente* de Mempo Giardinelli: de la violencia textual a la violencia sexual." *Romance Languages Annual* 8 (1996): 648–54.

———. "Relectura y reescritura de la Historia: La novelística de Mempo Giardinelli entre 1980 y 1991." Doctoral dissertation, University of Colorado, 1996.

———. "(Sub)versiones de la historia: la novelística de Mempo Giardinelli entre 1981 y 1991." *Alba de América* 17.32 (1999): 209–22.

Ruffinelli, Jorge. "Mempo Giardinelli al encuentro de territorios posibles," in Kohut 93–99.

Sablich, José. "Contextos reales y ficcionales en la novela negra argentina de la década del 70," in *Calibar sin rastros: aportes para un historia social de la literatura argentina*, ed. Jorge Torres Roggero and María Elena Legaz. Córdoba, Argentina: Solsona, 1996, 155–85.

Stone, Kenton V. "Mempo Giardinelli and the Anxiety of Borges's Influence." *Chasqui* 23.1 (1994): 83–90.

Torres, Vicente Francisco. "El trabajo literario de Mempo Giardinelli." *La palabra y el hombre* [Mexico] 61 (1987): 89–94.

Antonio Helú (1900–1972)

MEXICO

Antonio Helú, born in San Luis Potosí in 1900, is considered to be the first writer to create a recurring Mexican detective figure in literature (Trujillo Muñoz 31). It is important to clarify, however, that while the character, Máximo Roldán, solves crimes, he is not a detective or private investigator in the traditional sense. Máximo Roldán, this uniquely Mexican incarnation of the detective figure, does not work for or represent any official agency of the law. In fact, he is a minor criminal. The pioneering critic of Latin American detective fiction, Donald A. Yates, pointed out long ago that "Roldán" is a an anagram of *ladrón* (thief [12]). That a detective—theoretically a crime fighter—is a thief should not come as a surprise. As Yates points out, the so-called law in many parts of Latin America is part of the criminal element, and given the Mexican penchant for sticking up for the lowly underdog who finds himself the victim of the system (Yates 9). Furthermore, Helú's Mexicanization of the Anglo detective model is a rather ingenious narrative—and ideological—maneuver. As Amelia Simpson states, "Helú's creation of a rogue-detective hero who profits from crime, makes fools of the police, and disregards the law establishes a type of detective fiction that parodies the genre's conventions and favors the individual against the system" (84).

Helú first began writing fiction during the mid-1920s. His *Pepe Vargas al teléfono* (Pepe Vargas on the phone, 1925), published as a small pamphlet of 29 pages, is billed as novel. The author has at least three other short-story-length texts that are also called "novels." The previously mentioned text, along with *El centro de gravedad* (The center of gravity) and *Los predestinados* (The predestined), both written in 1925, have been collected, along with the one-act play *La comedia termina* (The comedy ends), in *3 novelas, 1 cuento y una comedia* (3 novels, 1 story and one comedy, 1965) and also in *El centro de gravedad y otras cosas* (The center of gravity and other things, 1969). Helú co-authored with Adolfo Fernández Bustamante one of the few Latin American dramatic pieces that is described as a work of detective fiction. The play, *El crimen de Insurgentes: comedia policiaca en tres actos* (The Insurgentes crime: A detective comedy in three acts), debuted in the Teatro Abreu on August 20, 1935 (the date of the published text is unknown). The story "Un día antes de morir" (A day before dying), included in the two previously mentioned books and in the anthology of collected works *La obligación de asesinar* (The obligation to murder, 1997), is one of Helu's best-crafted detective stories. It is told in the first person by a man who has been condemned to death for a double murder, only one of which he actually committed. The day before he is scheduled to be executed he decides to narrate the story, in the form of a written confession, so that the truth be known regarding the circumstances of the case. The story is told with great precision and attention to detail in order to logically lead the reader through the series of events in which the narrator found himself both involved and entrapped. He plots to murder his one-time best friend but when he actually goes to carry out his carefully devised plan, he discovers that someone has beat him to it. What's more, the murderer has obviously left signs to frame him for the crime. Given his lack of trust in the justice system—a common theme in Helú—he does not contact the police. Rather, after deducing who the murderer is, he plans to confront and blackmail him. When he does so a struggle ensues and the narrator ends up killing the murderer in self-defense. When he is arrested, he tries to explain it all to the police who, of course, do not believe him and charge him for both murders.

In spite of the quality of texts such as "Un día antes de morir," Helú is best-remembered for his Máximo Roldán series of stories published in the original *La obligación de asesinar* (1946). There are seven stories in all that follow a somewhat chronological order, one building on the previous. The first tale, "Un clavo saca otro clavo" (One good turn deserves another), initiates the story of Roldán and describes his transformation from regular working man to criminal. More than conscious choice, Roldán enters a life of crime as a victim of circumstance. As will become a common occurrence—and as we saw happen to the narrator of "Un día antes de morir"—Roldán finds himself in the wrong place at the wrong time, a situation that forces him to choose survival over upholding the law, as well as affording him the opportunity to make some money on the side. The story ends with his arrest, which is where the next story, "El hombre de la otra acera" (The man on the opposite sidewalk), picks up. Here, Roldán outwits the feebleminded police who have him in their custody by exhibiting his talent for verbal virtuosity, which he uses to confound the officers and convince them (deceive them, really) to let him go. Ilán Stavans is quite right in comparing the Roldán character to the popular film-actor Cantinflas, who utilized the same technique in his many comedic films: "Both characters utilize language in order to persuade and confuse, to elaborate upon personal reality, and to oblige their fellow men to interact with them on their own terms" (75–76). Of the other stories in the series "El fistol de corbata" (The tie pin), "Piropos a medianoche" ("Piropos at Midnight"), and "Las tres bolas de billar" (The three billiard balls) are perhaps the most representative, especially given that they are the most anthologized of Helú's stories. In fact, the author's work is included in the groundbreaking detective fiction anthologies of María Elvira Bermúdez and Donald A. Yates (both in Spanish and in English). The story, "La obligación de asesinar," which of course gives the title to the entire collection, is the longest and in fact is often considered to be one of Helú's short novels. Curiously, Roldán does not appear in this story, although he is mentioned. The main character is Roldán's sidekick (the Watson to his Holmes) Carlos Miranda, who, as is typical, finds himself quite by accident in a sticky situation in which he is falsely accused of murder. The story is a classic locked-room puzzle-narrative in which the crime is solved through logic and deductive reasoning.

Helú's detective stories are classics. In fact, Stavans calls him the "cornerstone of detective letters in Mexico" (75). His work has been enthusiastically endorsed by Xavier Villaurrutia (a major figure in Mexican literature), who wrote the prologue to *La obligación de asesinar*. Likewise, the Mexican writer and cultural critic Carlos Monsiváis wrote the introduction to the most recent anthology of Helú's works, titled *La obligación de asesinar: novelas y cuentos policiacos* (1997). This same volume has a foreword by Helú's nephew.

Antonio Helú not only wrote detective fiction, but he was an active promoter of the genre as well. He edited the volume *El cuento enigmático* (The mystery story, 1968), which contains classic tales by Mark Twain and Nathaniel Hawthorne, among others, in Spanish translation. Furthermore, he founded the magazine *Selecciones policiacas y de misterio*, the official Spanish-language version of *Ellery Queen's Mystery Magazine*. The contribution of Helú to Mexican, and in a broader sense Latin American, detective fiction is among the most significant in the history of the genre. He played a pioneering role and made a lasting impact with his unique style and unforgettable character, Máximo Roldán, one of the first genuinely Latin American detective figures.

Darrell B. Lockhart

Works

El centro de gravedad y otras cosas. Mexico City: Secretaría de Educación Pública, Cuadernos de Lectura Popular, 1969. (Contains the same texts as *3 novelas 1 cuento y una comedia*.)

El crimen de Insurgentes: comedia policíaca en tres actos (with Adolfo Fernández Bustamante). Mexico City: Sociedad General de Autores de México, n.d.

El cuento enigmático (edited by Helú). Mexico City: Secretaría de Educación Pública, Cuadernos de Lectura Popular, 1968.

"El fistol de corbata," in *El cuento policial mexicano*, ed. Vicente Francisco Torres. Mexico City: Diógenes, 1982, 31–42.

La obligación de asesinar. Mexico City: Albatros, 1946. Reprint, Mexico City: Novaro, 1957; Consejo Nacional para la Cultura y las Artes, 1991.

La obligación de asesinar: novelas y cuentos policiacos, foreword by Alfredo Harp Helú, introduction by Carlos Monsiváis. Mexico City: Miguel Angel Porrúa, 1997 (2nd ed., 1998). (This volume is an anthology of the author's work that includes his three "novelas" and six of the Máximo Roldán stories.)

Pepe Vargas al teléfono. Mexico City: El Universal Ilustrado, 1925.

"Piropos a medianoche," in *El cuento policial latinoamericano*, ed. Donald A. Yates. Mexico City: Ediciones de Andrea, 1964, 29–36. English version as "Piropos at Midnight," in *Latin Blood: The Best Crime and Detective Stories of South America*, ed. Donald A. Yates. New York: Herder & Herder, 1972, 81–91.

"Las tres bolas de billar," in *Los mejores cuentos policiacos mexicanos*, ed. María Elvira Bermúdez. Mexico City: Libro-Mex, 1955, 25–39.

3 [Tres] novelas, 1 [un] cuento y una comedia. Mexico City: Editorial Enigma, 1965. (Contains "Pepe Vargas al teléfono," "El centro de gravedad," "Los predestinados," "Un día antes de morir," and "La comedia termina.")

Criticism

Simpson, Amelia S. *Detective Fiction from Latin America*. Rutherford, NJ: Fairleigh Dickinson University Press, 1990.

Stavans, Ilán. *Antiheroes: Mexico and Its Detective Novel*, trans. by Jesse H. Lytle and Jennifer A. Mattson. Cranbury, NJ: Associated University Presses, 1997, 75–79.

Trujillo Muñoz, Gabriel. *Testigos de cargo: la narrativa policiaca mexicana y sus autores*. Tijuana, Mexico: CONACULTA/CECUT, 2000, 31–35.

Yates, Donald A. "Introducción," in *El cuento policial latinoamericano*, ed. Donald A. Yates. Mexico City: Ediciones de Andrea, 1964, 5-13.

Juan Hernández Luna (b. 1962)

MEXICO

Juan Hernández Luna was born in Azcapotzalco, Distrito Federal in 1962. His father, a policeman, moved the family to Netzahualcóyotl in 1968 in search of better living conditions, which turned out to be the same or worse. As he explains in an interview with Gerardo Segura, his childhood was marked by violence, crime, death, and a good deal of fear. Hernández Luna now lives in Puebla, where the majority of his stories are situated. His first publication was the collection of short stories *Crucigrama* (Crossword puzzle, 1988), followed by *Unico territorio* (The only territory, 1989), which won the National Award for novel. However, his reputation as a detective fiction writer didn't begin until 1991 with the publication of *Naufragio* (Shipwreck), which was followed by three other detective novels: *Quizás otros labios* (Perhaps other lips, 1994), *Tabaco para el puma* (Tobacco for the puma, 1996), and *Tijuana dream* (1998).

In his fiction, Hernández Luna seeks to tell the dark stories of the other Mexico, bringing together the pieces of a somber but authentic vision of the turbulence, outbursts, and anger of the country. In defiance of the practice established by previous generations of detective fiction writers to concentrate on Mexico City as the only viable setting for crime fiction, the author is determined to change this tendency and write from alternate spaces. In his particular case, from Puebla, as he states in an interview: "Por mi parte yo quiero contar Puebla, a mí me gusta Puebla, dénme chance de contar Puebla, ya contaron todos el Distrito Federal." (For my part, I want to narrate Puebla, I like Puebla, give me the chance to narrate Puebla, everyone has already written about Mexico City [Segura 50].)

Indeed, his stories take place in the city of Puebla de los Angeles. In each, there is an element of calling into question certain criminal activities or political corruption, which is always a constant. Nevertheless, what stands out in his writing is the careful elaboration of the characters that populate his stories, from the circus dwarfs in *Quizás otros labios* to the spies in *Tabaco para el puma*. But the real protagonist of his books is the criminal act itself and its consequences in society. For example, the suicide who hurls himself headfirst from the Cathedral tower in Puebla. This act allows the author to initiate the story and weave a narration from the perspective of the different reactions caused by such a death in a sacred spot for the inhabitants of the city. Hernández Luna's message is that no one is innocent of the death of another, that violence is the responsibility of the city where it occurs and of the citizens who live there. No matter if they are indifferent to it or appalled by it, crime is a matter of concern for every citizen.

For Hernández Luna, detective fiction is not about the crime—the who, how, and why it is committed. Rather, its great contribution in Mexico is to narrate the city where it occurs, the lifestyle that supports such crime and criminals. In other words, the network of social relations that allows for, encourages, and protects criminal activity. Thus, his short stories and novels paint a true-to-life portrait of the many Mexicos that exist: different in habits, accents, and customs, but united in the eternal marriage of victims and victimizers, official (those who make and enforce the law) and unofficial (those outside the law) thugs.

As part of a generation that followed that of Paco Ignacio Taibo II, instead of the revolutionary epic of 1968 and the literature of political commitment, Juan Hernández recognizes his belonging to a "sandwich" generation that arrived too late for the great battles of history. For him, literature offers a space for freedom and commitment to the reader. In a Mexico of perpetual crisis, in an unending transition to democracy, Hernández's characters are not different or special with regard to Mexican society in general. They only want to get through life in one piece with the least amount of damage possible. Also, and more importantly, they are willing to defend their rights, maintain their sanity, and decide for themselves their own life and death. It is the least they can accept as Mexicans at the end of the millennium, as witnesses and protagonists of the dark history of our country.

Gabriel Trujillo Muñoz

Works

"¡Al ganso las plumas!," in *Variaciones en negro: relatos policiales iberoamericanos*, ed. Lucía López Coll and Leonardo Padura. Havana: Editorial Arte y Literatura, 2001, 199–216.
Naufragio. Guadalajara: EDUG [Universidad de Guadalajara], 1991.
Quizás otros labios. Mexico City: Martínez Roca, 1994.
Tabaco para el puma. Mexico City: Martínez Roca, 1996.
Tijuana dream. Mexico City: Selector, 1998.
Yodo. Mexico City: Times, 1998.

Criticism

Segura, Gerardo. "El crimen es un pretexto para contar la ciudad: interrogatorio a Juan Hernández Luna," in *Todos somos culpables: entrevistas con escritores policiacos mexicanos*. Saltillo, Coahuila: Instituto Coahuilense de Cultura, 1996, 43–52.

Jorge Ibargüengoitia (1928–1983)

MEXICO

Jorge Ibargüengoitia is a prolific essayist, playwright, poet, novelist, short-story writer, translator, and literary critic. He studied civil engineering and literature at the Universidad Autónoma de México (the Autonomous University of Mexico). He received various scholarships from different institutions and nonprofit organizations over the course of his studies. He also worked as a freelance writer for several newspapers and cultural journals such as the Mexican literary journal *Revista de la Universidad de México* (Literary magazine of the University of Mexico) and the Mexican newspaper *El Excélsior* (from 1969 to 1976). In addition, Ibargüengoitia worked as a professor of Spanish American literature with a specialty in drama and theater. He received several awards for his literary production, particularly for his novels and plays. In 1960, his play *La conspiración vendida* (The sold conspiracy) was awarded the Premio de Teatro, Ciudad de México (theatrical prize of Mexico City), and in 1963 his drama *El atentado* (The threat) earned the Premio de Teatro from Casa de las Américas (Casa de las Américas theater award), one of the most prestigious accolades. In 1964, his novel *Los relámpagos de agosto* (Lightning in August) won the Premio de Novela from Casa de las Américas (prize for a novel), and in 1975 another of his novels, *Estas ruinas que ves* (These ruins you see) earned the Premio Internacional de Novela, México (International prize for a novel). In addition to those mentioned, his novels include *Maten al león* (Kill the lion, 1969), *Las muertas* (*The Dead Girls*, 1977), *Dos crímenes* (*Two Crimes*, 1979), and *Los pasos de López* (López's steps, 1982). His only collection of short stories is *La ley de Herodes* (Herod's law, 1967).

Ibagüengoitia is often described as an abstruse author only understood by himself, an idiosyncrasy that has contributed to the ambiguous image with which many of his readers view him. He has also been perceived as a solitary person whose child-like spirit would occasionally reveal itself, bringing out a mischievous sense of humor that is evident both in his personal life and throughout his writings.

Ibargüengoitia's literature encompasses a wide range of styles, resources, and themes that include humor, irony, parody, polyphony, colloquial language, oral testimony, the picaresque, official history, national heroes, and myths, as well as the denunciation of social, political, economical, ideological, historical, and gender issues in Mexican society. A constant in the author's work is his use of dark humor as a defining literary device and as an effective tool for debunking official versions of history and national myths. Moreover, through a skillful wielding of his acerbic wit, he manages to mock Mexican naiveté, criticize provincial double standards, and denounce political corruption.

There is relatively scant critical appraisal of Ibargüengoitia's detective fiction, and for some scholars only one of his novels, *Dos crímenes*, actually belongs to the detective genre. Notwithstanding, the novel *Las muertas* may also be included in that group. *Las muertas* narrates the notorious, factual case of *Las poquianchis*—a nickname used to describe Angela and Serafina Balastro, the female pimps who also operated brothels—who provoked a national scandal in Mexico during the early 1960s. The two women received the maximum sentence in 1964 for the multiple crimes they committed: pimping, physical abuse, torture, corruption of minors, kidnapping, and most serious of all, the murder of several female prostitutes employed by them.

The majority of criticism has perceived *Las muertas* as a sort of tabloid or crime-chronicle story, rather than as a detective novel. Nevertheless, the text contains many of the qualities that Mempo Giardinelli identifies in his *El género negro* (The detective novel, 1984) as pertaining to the detective novel. These elements include the evaluation and criticism of traditions and of political systems, the exercise of justice, the presentation of the opinions of both victims and perpetrators, the listing of motives for violence caused by greed, the abuse of power and sex, and last but not least, the use of crude and vulgar language. In *Las muertas*, the critique of Mexican society consists of the denunciation of the exploitation and prostitution of women, political corruption, police injustice, and crime, especially the murder of women at the hands of the *Poquianchis* and their accomplices.

The narrative structure of *Las muertas* can be characterized as a collage of diverse literary artifacts that range from various textual examples (reports, newspaper clippings, interviews, photographs, legal documents) to the heteroglossic discourse of the different voices present in the text. The lack of an easily recognizable single narrator, together with the mixture of fiction and reality, is not intended to confuse the reader. Rather, it is used to create a text that enables the reader to contemplate the problems that ail society and to judge the characters as they see fit.

According to scholar Vicente Francisco Torres, the four fundamental components of this type of novel are the city, a concern for social problems, the use of rough or vulgar language, and the description of sordid places (no-tell motels, brothels, and assorted other dives). In *Las muertas*, one finds all these elements present. The fictitious city is Mezcala (the city where the crimes actually took place is Guanajuato). The social problems of prostitution and violence are centered in the brothels El México Lindo and El Casino del Danzón. The language in the novel is largely humorous, crude, colloquial, and sarcastic slang. The sordid places are the rooms where women are forced to work and live. It is significant to mention that in the case of the women working for the Balastro sisters, these rooms have the added plight of being extremely precarious and unhealthy.

Even if Ibargüengoitia appears to use a tabloid, yellow-journalism style in *Las muertas*, that does not necessarily indicate that the novel lacks the elements to classify it as a detective novel. If one takes into consideration the conceptualization and characteristics of this genre as proposed by Giardinelli and Torres, then one must accept that *Las muertas* is indeed a detective novel. In fact, this novel includes even more than the above-mentioned elements. It forces the reader to confront the disturbing reality of society and to demand justice for the exploitation of human beings, especially women. In sum, *Las muertas* is a text that sensitizes the reader, especially the Mexican reader, to issues regarding the lack of education and the problems of unemployment and economic crisis, particularly in rural areas located outside the capital, that are common in the country.

If in *Las muertas* the motive for murder is women, money, and power, in *Dos crímenes* the motive is money and revenge. *Dos crímenes* is a novel that narrates the killing—by poisoning—of an old man, Ramón, and his niece, Lucero, at the hands of their own family members who conspire in their deaths in order to be the sole inheritors of Ramón's fortune. The novel also portrays the behavior, customs, and greed for money and power of the residents of a fictitious province in the center of Mexico called Plan de Abajo (Plan from beneath).

Through humor, sarcasm, irony, flashbacks, advertisements, and letters, Ibargüengoitia introduces the themes of indigenous identity, submission, revenge, resentment, private history, seduction, the exploitation of women, the struggle for power, greed, popular culture, and women's erotic needs. It is also important to stress that the novel has two narrators: Marcos (Ramón's nephew) and José (Ramón's best friend). As the initial narrator of the novel, Marcos is in charge of telling the story from the beginning to midpoint. Although the action is slow in this section of the novel, the purpose is to set the scene for events that will follow in the second half. This is achieved through the use of clues and by way of foreshadowing future events. In the second part of the novel, the narrator is José. This section of the text deals with the first murder—Ramón's poisoning—with its motives and suspects, as well as with the second murder, which occurs by accident at the very end of the story.

The existence of two narrators functions as a mechanism to present two different levels of narration, two spaces (Mexico City and Plan de Abajo) and two opposite ideologies (liberal and conservative). The first argument is represented by Marcos, his wife, and friends who reside in Mexico City, whereas the second one is represented by Marcos's relatives in the Mexican province of Plan de Abajo.

There is no specific detective in *Las muertas*; in *Dos crímenes*, the characters José and Canalejas are portrayed as amateur detectives who discover that their friend Ramón did not commit suicide but was murdered by his own family. Canalejas, a doctor, is the first one to suspect that Ramón was poisoned and consults José, a pharmacist, in order to confirm his suspicion. Canaleja's concern for the circumstances that led to Ramón's death arouses José's suspicion regarding the disappearance of Marcos, an event that coincides with his uncle's death.

José, as a narrator and detective, not only recounts Ramón's story and that of his family and his former life, but also discovers Ramón's murderer after putting together all the pieces of the puzzle. José's role as private detective is accidental, in that he is motivated by his curiosity with regard to Marco's behavior and attitude toward his uncle Ramón. The reasons that lead José to consider Marcos as Ramón's killer are his sudden arrival in town, his business relationship with Ramón—they are partners in a mining company—his dissimulation about his stay in town, his knowledge of the place where his uncle stored the poison, and finally his abrupt disappearance. All these clues lead José to undertake an investigation in which Marcos's whereabouts are discovered and a meeting to reveal the truth about Ramón's death is discussed. Up to this moment, José is convinced of Marcos's guilt, but it is not until Marcos goes to the hospital due to a poisoning that José reconsiders his position toward his first suspect and begins to have second thoughts regarding the death of his friend. Marcos's trip to the hospital for poisoning is important, since in addition to saving his life, it establishes his innocence.

Once Marcos is declared innocent, he has to face a new series of problems that he had left behind in Mexico City—mainly his political woes. José, "the new detective," blackmails the police in order to exonerate Marcos from political accusations. With such behavior as this, José contributes to the problem of corruption in Mexican law, but the outcome of this so-called "blackmail" is positive.

Dos crímenes, as a detective novel, not only deals with the issues of murder and violence, but also with the portrayal and evaluation of the social, ideological, economical, political, and moral models that exist in patriarchal society. Ibargüengoitia uses the detective genre in order to show how greed and the abuse of power and the consequences of societal "progress" and "modernization" are responsible for humankind's shortcomings.

According to Giardinelli, the Latin American detective novel goes beyond dealing with the typical traits and elements of the genre, because it also takes into consideration the crude and sordid reality of Latin American countries. In conclusion, in *Las muertas* and *Dos crímenes*, Ibargüengoitia, like other Latin American writers, utilizes the detective genre in order to portray and critically evaluate society's crude and painful reality, showing the reader the conflicts and struggles of his homeland, Mexico.

Juan Antonio Serna

Works

El atentado. Mexico City: Joaquín Mortiz, 1978.

Dos crímenes. Mexico City: Joaquín Mortiz, 1979. English version as *Two Crimes*, trans. Asa Zatz. Boston: D. R. Godine; New York: Avon Books, 1984. Also, London: Chatto & Windus, 1984.

Estas ruinas que ves. Mexico City: Organización Editorial Novaro, 1975. Reprint, Mexico City: Joaquín Mortiz, 1994.

La ley de Herodes. Mexico City: Joaquín Mortiz, 1967.

Maten al león. Mexico City: Joaquín Mortiz, 1969; 1992.

Las muertas. Mexico City: Joaquín Mortiz, 1977. English version as *The Dead Girls*, trans. Asa Zatz. London: Chatto & Windus/Hogarth Press, 1981. Also, New York: Avon Books, 1983.

Los pasos de López. Mexico City: Océano, 1982.

Los relámpagos de agosto. Mexico City: Joaquín Mortiz, 1965.

Criticism

Campbell, Federico. "Ibargüengoitia: la sátira histórico-política." *Revista iberoamericana* 55.148–149 (1989): 1047–55.

Clark, Stella. "Testimonio, historia y ficción: *Crónica de una muerte anunciada y Las muertas.*" *Texto crítico* 15.40–41 (1989): 21–29.

———. "The Novel as Cultural Interpreter: The Case of 'Las Poquianchis' in Mexico." *North Dakota Quarterly* 58.4 (1990): 205–14.

Giardinelli, Mempo. *El género negro: ensayos sobre literatura policial.* Mexico City.: Universidad Autónoma Metropolitana, 1984.

González, Alfonso. "La sátira en los escritos breves de Jorge Ibargüengoitia." *La palabra y el hombre* 87 (1993): 135–41.

Guerrero, Elisabeth. "The Plotting Priest: Jorge Ibargüengoitia's *Los pasos de López.*" *Hispanófila* 133 (2001): 103–21.

Lorenzo, Jaime. "La pareja profana: historia y humor en la obra de Jorge Ibargüengoitia." *La palabra y el hombre* 78 (1991): 287–97.

Mathieu, Corina S. "El humor en *Los pasos de López* de Jorge Ibargüengoitia." *Alba de América* 16.30–31 (1998): 315–22.

Rehder, Ernest. "Ibargüengoitia's *Estas ruinas que ves* as a Neo-costumbrista Novel: In the Spanish Tradition." *Hispanic Journal* 11.1 (1990): 61–76.

Sklodowska, Elzbieta. "Transgresión paródica de la fórmula policial," in *La parodia en la nueva novela hispanoamericana (1960–1985).* Purdue University Monographs in Romance Languages. Amsterdam/Philadelphia: John Benjamins Publishing, 1991, 111–39.

Stavans, Ilán. "Jorge Ibargüengoitia," in *Antiheroes: Mexico in Its Detective Novel*, trans. Jesse H. Lytle and Jennifer A. Mattson. Madison, NJ: Fairleigh Dickinson University Press, 1997, 131–38.

Torres, Francisco Vicente. *Esta narrativa mexicana: ensayos y entrevistas.* Mexico City: Leega, S.A., 1991.

Trujillo Muñoz, Gabriel. *Testigos de cargo: la narrativa policiaca mexicana y sus autores.* Tijuana, Mexico: CONACULTA/CECUT, 2000, 56–60.

Miriam Laurini (b. 1947)

ARGENTINA

Miriam Laurini was born in Argentina in 1947. Due to persecution by the military regime, she left the country in 1976, accompanied by two of her children and husband, fellow writer and political militant Rolo Diez. A third son remained behind in Argentina and was subsequently disappeared during the government's "dirty war" against its own citizenry. Following several years of hardship in Brazil, Italy, and Spain, she was granted official refugee status by an agency of the United Nations and in 1980 she and her family took up residence in Mexico City, where she has been employed by various newspapers and journals, forming part of the so-called Argen-Mex community. Her first novel, *Morena en rojo* (Dark woman in red), appeared in 1994. Several shorter versions of the same work have appeared in anthologies of detective fiction, namely, "La nota roja que no existió: cuerpo muerto" (The police beat report that didn't exist: dead body) and "Lost Dreams." She has also had several stories published in Germany and the Czech Republic, and in 1989 was awarded first prize for a short story in the *Semana Negra* festival held in Gijón, Spain.

Morena en rojo is set in contemporary Mexico and details the adventures of a provincial journalist—Laurini's alter ego—in her vocational and personal endeavors. Professionally, against the wishes of the police, she investigates first the murder of a federal officer, second the substandard living conditions endured in the *maquiladoras* (border factories), and finally the activities of a kidnapping ring implicated in child-labor abuses, prostitution and black-market organ selling. On a personal level, the journalist known only as "La Morena" is divided among shielding a murderess, dodging old lovers, administering to the psychologically and physically battered half of a lesbian couple, making amends with an ailing mother who disapproves of her life choices, and pursuing the man of her dreams who is "sort of" married and is certainly involved in illicit activities. Her research and romances have her literally traversing the four corners of Mexico—from Mérida to Tijuana, Guadalajara to Veracruz—and encountering a wide spectrum of characters designed to represent the diversity and heterogeneity that are the Americas of the late twentieth century.

Both the novel and its main character comprise a blending of traditions, cultures, and histories. Argentine detective fiction in the 1970s and 1980s tended toward the hard-boiled style, with an emphasis on action over analysis, and a willingness to reflect and portray the violence and corruption pervasive in political and social institutions. Resulting from this exposé of institutional corruption is a critical, often cynical view of society as a whole. La Morena resembles her hard-boiled counterparts in her use of slang, her sexual activities, and her propensity toward a corporeal or visceral approach over an intellectual one to investigating. Mexican detective fiction, on the other hand, developed in a different direction, tending toward caricature and parody, critical self-contemplation, loss of innocence, the fallibility of the detective, the importance of intuition, and the predominance of passion. There is usually a distinct national orientation by which the author expresses and explores Mexico's cultures and problems. While Laurini's use of parody is not as acute as that of her contemporaries such as Paco Ignacio Taibo II, one may certainly discern exaggerations in the portrayal of La Morena's personality, attitude, and actions. And true to form, intuition and passion combine to play a pivotal role in the denouement of the novel. A gut feeling draws her to the site of the crime, but passion blinds her to the fact that the criminal is her lover.

Laurini would appear to have taken to heart the suggestions proffered by Kathleen Gregory Klein in that female authors of crime fiction first open their writings to explore and expose social crimes other than murder; second, that there be more open-ended uncertainty to the novels, suggesting that not all of the problems encountered have been solved; and third, that private investigators be replaced by a wide range of plausible women. The scope of *Morena en rojo* opens beyond the investigation of a simple murder to encompass the social crimes and abuses suffered by women and children in Mexico and worldwide. Her protagonist is not a private investigator but rather a journalist, certainly a more plausible profession. And only one crime is solved, La Morena having had little if anything to do with the final outcome. Nevertheless, she is not a failure. She was not dissuaded by the male authority figures demanding that she step aside, and gives every indication that she will continue to investigate social crimes. As one of the few female detective figures in Latin American literature, she should be seen as the prototype for the next wave of detective and crime fiction.

Linda S. Zee

Works

"Lost Dreams," trans. William I. Neuman, in *Women on the Case*, ed. Sara Paretsky. New York: Dell, 1996.

Morena en rojo. Mexico City: Joaquín Mortiz, 1994.

"La nota roja que no existió: cuerpo muerto," in *Cuentos policíacos mexicanos: lo mejor del género en nuestro país*, ed. Paco Ignacio Taibo II and Víctor Ronquillo. Mexico City: Selector, 1997, 39–55. Also in *Variaciones en negro: relatos policiales iberoamericanos*, ed. Lucía López Coll and Leonardo Padura. Havana: Editorial Arte y Literatura, 2001, 71–83; and *Cuentos policiacos*, ed. Zonia Nadhezda Truque and Mauricio Contreras Hernández. Bogotá: Magisterio, 1996, 93–108.

Criticism

Caputo, Iaia, and Laura Lepri. "Miriam Laurini: Cronaca de una vita esiliata," in *Conversazioni di fine secolo: 12 interviste con 12 scrittrici contemporanee*. Milan: La Tartaruga, 1995, 85–104.

Caccuci, Pino. *Camminando: Incontri di un viadante*. Milan: Feltrinelli, 1996.

Vicente Leñero (b. 1933)

MEXICO

Vicente Leñero, born in Guadalajara in 1933, is of the same generation of Mexican writers as Carlos Fuentes (b. 1928). He has distinguished himself and built a solid reputation as an author by excelling in three essential areas of Mexican cultural production: journalism, narrative, and dramaturgy. In 1963, he won the Premio Biblioteca Breve, a prestigious award sponsored by the Spanish publishing house Seix Barral, for his novel *Los albañiles* (The bricklayers, 1964) that was later adapted to the theater and film. Following the pattern of the French novel of the time, he published *Estudio Q* (Studio Q, 1965) and *El garabato* (The scribble, 1967). In 1978, he denounced the government crackdown on the newspaper *Excélsior* in his *Los periodistas* (The journalists). His contemporary allegory of the passion of Christ, *El evangelio de Lucas Gavilán* (*The Gospel of Lucas Gavilán*), was published in 1979. In the 1980s, Leñero returned to the detective genre with a noncriminal investigation—the lack of water at his house—in *La gota de agua* (The drop of water, 1983), and the investigation of the Flores Muñoz (a married couple) murder titled *Asesinato* (Murder, 1985).

Leñero, as a Catholic writer, shows a passion for the struggle of good and evil, although in his works, evil often triumphs, even if only temporarily. His prose is characterized by an exacerbated realism—that of a journalist with an eye for detail and documentation. Viewed as a whole, his works contain in varying degrees elements that can be attributed to the detective genre in that they depend on a structure of suspense, mystery, false clues, and the testimony of witnesses and victims as well as the evidence at hand. In *El evangelio de Lucas Gavilán*, the reader familiar with Catholic doctrine will recognize in Lucas Gavilán a new (or the same?) redeemer who must pass through each stage of his suffering. The force of Leñero's narrative is found not so much in the facts he relates as the structure that lends them weight and purpose. Something very similar occurs in *La gota de agua*. The simple lack of water in the author's home leads him to uncover a world of fragile connections in which some people profit from the lack of water while the majority of the population in urban Mexico City always ends up losing.

Victims and victimizers appear in stark contrast in *Los albañiles* and *Asesinato*. The first is an allegory, once again, of a community betrayed by its own egotism and ambition. The novel presents a metaphor of Christianity that revolves around the murder of Don Jesús, the nightwatchman at a construction site in Mexico City. The victim's name, of course, makes it possible to draw a parallel between him as an ordinary man and Jesus Christ (both an ordinary man and divine being). Both are caught up in the machinations of the power structure of their time and both end up sacrificed. In *Asesinato*, Leñero follows the model of the true crime novel in the manner of Truman Capote's *In Cold Blood* (1966). The book deals with the real-life case of the murder of an old and powerful Mexican politician and his wife. The crime is attributed to his young grandson, and the author uses this fact to suggest that the entire trial is set-up from the beginning by the Mexican judicial system portrayed as a bureaucratic machine whose interest is not justice but in bringing a quick close to the case.

One can conclude by saying that Leñero's detective novels provide a broad view of the human condition, the detailed descriptions of a conscience that seeks the truth, which cannot be carried out to its ultimate end. Like the rest of Mexican society, Leñero can observe crimes that occur right before his eyes and arrive at his own conclusions with regard to assigning guilt or innocence, but without being able to prove anything one way or the other. Leñero offers up the cadaver of Mexican-style power, the fingerprints that prove that all are guilty, by action or omission, of the state of things and of a situation stymied by a decaying legal, judicial, and ethical system.

Gabriel Trujillo Muñoz

Works

Los albañiles. Barcelona: Seix Barral, 1964.
Asesinato. Mexico City: Plaza & Janés, 1985.
El evangelio de Lucas Gavilán. Barcelona: Seix Barral, 1979. English version as *The Gospel of Lucas Gavilán*, trans. Robert G. Mowry. Lanham, MD: University Press of America, 1991.
El garabato. Mexico City: Joaquín Mortiz, 1967.
La gota de agua. Mexico City: Plaza & Janés, 1983.

Criticism

Anderson, Danny J. *Vicente Leñero: The Novelist as Critic.* New York: Peter Lang, 1989.
Figuerola, Luciana. "Los códigos de veridicción en *El garabato* de Vicente Leñero." *Semiosis* 4 (1980): 31–59.
Garavito, Lucía. "La narrativa y la focalización como base para un análisis de la novelística de Vicente Leñero." *Semiosis* 4 (1980): 61–82.
Kellerman, Owen L. "*Los albañiles* de Vicente Leñero: estudio de la víctima." *Hispanófila* 70 (1980): 45–55.
Lipski, John M. "Vicente Leñero: Narrative Evolution as Religious Search." *Hispanic Journal* 3.2 (1982): 41–59.
Ludmer, Josefina. "Vicente Leñero, *Los albañiles*. Lector y actor," in *Nueva novela latinoamericana*, ed. Jorge Lafforgue. Buenos Aires: Paidós, 1969–72, 1:194–208.
McMurray, George R. "The Novels of Vicente Leñero." *Critique* 8.3 (1966): 55–61.
Martínez Morales, José Luis. "Leñero: ficción de la realidad, realidad de la ficción." *Texto crítico* 29 (1984): 173–87.
———. "Asesinato, la novela del lector." *Texto crítico* 36–37 (1987): 54–67.
Prieto, Angélica. "Componente discursiva y estructuras profundas en *Los albañiles*." *Semiosis* 16 (1986): 73–98.
Robles, Humberto E. "Aproximaciones a *Los albañiles* de Vicente Leñero." *Revista iberoamericana* 73 (1970): 579–99.
Segura, Gerardo. "Uno escribe para emocionar a los lectores: interrogatorio a Vicente

Leñero," in *Todos somos culpables: entrevistas con escritores policiacos mexicanos*. Saltillo, Coahuila: Instituto Coahuilense de Cultura, 1996, 53–62.

Simpson, Amelia S. *Detective Fiction from Latin America*. Rutherford, NJ: Fairleigh Dickinson University Press, 1990, 146–52.

Stavans, Ilán. *Antiheroes: Mexico and Its Detective Novel*, trans. by Jesse H. Lytle and Jennifer A. Mattson. Cranbury, NJ: Associated University Presses, 1997, 124–30.

Szmetan, Ricardo. "*Los albañiles* de Vicente Leñero dentro de las novelas de detectives." *Confluencia* 4.2 (1989): 67–71.

Sauli Lostal (dates unknown)

ARGENTINA

Sauli Lostal is the author of the "Primera gran novela argentina de carácter policial" (first great Argentine detective novel), *El enigma de la calle Arcos* (The enigma of Arcos street). It was first published in the Buenos Aires newspaper *Crítica* (Critique) in serial form between October 30 and November 30, 1932. The second edition was published in book form by the Am-Bass publishing house in one volume of 245 pages, illustrated by Pedro de Rojas, the illustrator for *Crítica*. It appears as the "Segunda edición corregida" (second corrected edition). Given its characterization as a "second edition" is established in relation to the first publication in *Crítica* (for which the date of completion as indicated at the end of the last installment is June–August 1932), there are few changes. For example, each installment is divided into subtitles that do not appear in the book, the placement of adjectives and the use of certain nouns are modified, but most importantly the ending is different. While in the *Crítica* version the ideological author of the crime, Yvette Repeport, ends up in jail with a life sentence, in the book, her death is narrated after a "purifying" repentance. In 1996, the novel was reedited by the Simurg Publishing House.

The principal (still unresolved) "enigma" that the book posits is the identity of the writer hidden behind the pseudonym Sauli Lostal. At the time it first appeared, the novel was attributed to Luis Diéguez, who worked as a journalist at *Crítica* and who signed his name to the prologue of the book in the brief review that appeared in the journal *Literatura Argentina* (Argentine literature) in July of 1933. The republication of this work by the Simurg publishing house in 1996 generated new controversy about the authorship, mainly from Juan-Jacobo Bajarlía, who maintains that the novel was written by Jorge Luis Borges. Bajarlía guarantees that Ulyses Petit de Murat, co-director along with Borges of the journal *Multicolor de los Sábados* (a Saturday supplemental review of *Crítica*), confessed to him that the novel was written by Borges in order to try his hand at this new genre. Although Enrique Anderson Imbert and Gonzalo Moisés Aguilar have both alluded to the existence of textual similarities between Borgesian literary style and that of *El enigma de la calle Arcos*, proof of such has never been demonstrated. Tomás Giordano, in a letter to the editor sent to the newspaper *Clarín* (Bugle, February 27, 1997), claims that "Sauli Lostal es Luis A. Stallo a'l'anvers' y fue el seudónimo adoptado por el autor para firmar el mencionado relato." (Sauli Lostal is Luis A. Stallo, who adopted the anagramatic pseudonym to sign the work in question.) Giordano goes on to make credible claims regarding his personal acquaintance with Stallo who, according to him, wrote the text in response to a literary contest sponsored by *Crítica*. The purpose of the contest was to induce readers to create a better ending to *El misterio del cuarto amarillo* (The mystery of the yellow room) by Gastón Leroux. Although Alejandro Vaccaro has corroborated the existence of a Luis Stallo in the telephone books of the period, it has not been possible to confirm the existence of the contest mentioned by Giordano or that Stallo was in fact the author of the novel.

In the quest to attribute a text to a certain author, Michel Foucault indicates in "What Is an author?"—taking up the *Desiris illustribus* of San Jerónimo—that it is necessary to exclude works that are written in a different style, with words and twists that are not typically found from the author's pen. In this sense, there is nothing further from the lexicon and style of Borges than *El enigma de la calle Arcos*, in which the author uses an abundance of colloquial language and frequently resorts to the use of *lunfardo* (slang) and the modulations and rhythms of *porteño* (native Buenos Aires) speech-patterns not to mention the genre—the novel—in which Borges never demonstrated an interest.

In "El acercamiento de Almotásim" ("The Approach to al-Mu'tasim"), Borges seems to allude to *El enigma de la calle Arcos* in code, stating that "el papel era casi de diario; la cubierta anunciaba al comprador que se trataba de la primera novela policial escrita por un nativo de Bombay City" (the paper it was printed on was similar to newsprint; the cover announced to the buyer that it was the first detective novel written by a native of Bombay City [414]). Over the years, this has attained mythic proportions in Argentine literary criticism, beginning with the article by Anderson Imbert, which points to the novel's intertextuality with Borgesian literature. The issue has been more fully addressed by Sylvia Saítta, and specialists of the genre concur that the novel, regardless of authorship, should be considered as one of the founding texts of Argentine detective fiction.

In its role as a founding text of the genre in Argentina, *El enigma de la calle Arcos* is placed in the long tradition of the "locked-room mystery," first formulated by Edgar Allan Poe in his "The Murders in the Rue Morgue" (1841). It is a narrative device that has been employed with great success in subsequent works. The principal proponents of this tradition have been Arthur Conan Doyle with "The Adventure of the Speckled Band" (in *The Adventures of Sherlock Holmes*, 1882), Israel Zangwill with *The Big Bow Mystery* (1895), and Gastón Leroux with *The Mystery of the Yellow Room* (1907), a novel that quickly became well-known in Buenos Aires through its 1908 publication in the newspaper *La Nación* (The nation). As indicated by Boileau and Narcejac, the locked-room is a problem par excellence in detective literature because it is a scandal of logic, the triumph of magic and the irrational. At the same time, the locked-room is an evident artifice, a powerful device used to produce a determined effect, since it is designed to highlight a character and not a man.

El enigma de la calle Arcos refers to the classic detective texts in which the principal enigma is to determine how the criminal left a room that is locked from the inside, and, as with all puzzle-novels, two stories are narrated simultaneously: the tale of the crime and the story of the investigation carried out by two characters, the detective and the reporter who know the rules of investigation and use their professional experience to solve the crime. In spite of the obvious similarity that this novel has with Leroux's *El misterio del cuarto amarillo*, Sauli Lostal introduces something new into the well-known formula—a set of references familiar to the *porteño* reader. The isolated castle of Glandier located in the forests of Saint-Geneviève, Paris, yields way to an old mansion in the Belgrano neighborhood of Buenos Aires. Likewise, the brilliant reporter-cum-detective who risks his personal pride to unravel the enigma becomes someone in danger of being fired by the editor of the newspaper to whom he must answer. In addition to the detective plot, this novel exhibits an internal mechanism of the modern press whose protagonist is a reporter who, within the framework of the competitive news industry, must demonstrate to the editors, his fellow journalists, the police, and the judge the truth of his hypothesis. Thus the inside workings of crime reporting are framed within a fictional narrative.

This newly proposed narrative that follows the most rigid rules of the genre is uniquely *porteño* in nature. The setting of the action, the characters, and the use of colloquial language comprise a well-crafted intrigue by maintaining the suspense and resolving the enigma without resorting to supernatural, fantastic, or implausible means. As the book cover states, it is the first Argentine detective novel that at the same time presents the role of mass-market newspapers and reporters within the environment of its highly competitive industry. The pressures of this business, the need to be the first to cover or uncover the story, to have the best and most accurate information, and to obtain that information from the police, lawyers, and judges trains in a roundabout way, the reporter to be an able detective. Here, a crime reporter risks his job and personal safety and challenges the police and the rest of his colleagues but manages, in spite of negative public opinion, to successfully solve the mystery. Therefore in this first detective novel it is possible to detect a highly productive interaction between a textual strategy from one culture that is inserted into a much different cultural reality. The conventions of the European detective novel allow for the narration of the popular urban *porteño* experience through a format in which the chaos of the criminal world is organized by the rationality of a reporter who offers a sense of much-needed order to the facts that pile up on his newsdesk.

Sylvia Saítta

Work

El enigma de la calle Arcos. 1st edition, *Crítica* (30 October to 30 November 1932); 2nd, corrected edition, Buenos Aires: Am-Bass, 1933; 3rd edition, Buenos Aires: Simurg, 1996 (with prologue by Sylvia Saítta).

Criticism

Aguilar, Gonzalo Moisés. "*Proa* en los libros: Sauli Lostal *El enigma de la calle Arcos.*" *Proa* 25 (tercera época, September–October 1996).

Anderson Imbert, Enrique. "Nueva contribución al estudio de las fuentes de Borges." *Filología* 8.1–2 (1962).

Bajarlía, Juan-Jacobo. "La novela de Borges." *Radar; Ocio, cultura y estilos* [Suplemento de *Página 12*] 14 (17 November 1996).

———. "La enigmática novela de Borges." *Suplemento Cultura de La Nación* (13 July 1997).

Borges, Jorge Luis. "El acercamiento a Almutásim," in *Obras completas*, vol. 1. Buenos Aires: Emecé, 1996, 414–18.

Diéguez, Luis. Review of *El enigma de la calle Arcos*. Literatura Argentina 59 (July 1933).

Kolesnicov, Patricia. "Discuten si son de Borges una novela y varios artículos." *Clarín* (28 September 1997).

Saítta, Sylvia. "Informe sobre *El enigma de la calle Arcos*," in *Asesinos de papel: ensayos sobre narrativa policial*, ed. Jorge Lafforgue and Jorge B. Rivera. Buenos Aires: Colihue, 1996, 235–46.

Vaccaro, Alejandro. "El fin de un enigma." *Proa* (tercera época, March–April 1997).

Jorge Manzur (b. 1949)

ARGENTINA

Jorge Manzur was born on 26 July 1949, in Luján, in the Province of Buenos Aires, Argentina. His parents were both teachers and he was educated by the Marist Brothers. He also studied guitar, but moved to the capital in 1967 to study law. After four years, he gave up law in favor of music. In 1972, he published a volume of poetry, *Poemas libres* (Free poems), and shortly after also made a record. By 1977, however, with the publication of his first volume of short stories, *Riesgos nocturnos* (Night risks), Manzur had turned to narrative. He had also begun to earn a living as a journalist—beginning as a music critic—and has since contributed regularly to several Argentinean periodicals and dailies, including *La Voz*, *La Razón*, and *Somos*, as well as participating in several television programs.

Since the appearance of *Riesgos nocturnos* in 1977, Manzur has published eight other books. These include an anthology of his newspaper writings, *Tapen al minotauro que hay niños* (Cover up the minotaur, there are children present, 1988); three novels, *Tinta roja* (Red ink, 1980), *Crónica de amor, de locura y de muerte* (Chronicle of love, madness and death, 1986), and *El simulador* (The simulator, 1990); and four anthologies of short stories, *Bajo palabra* (On parole, 1980), *Tratos inútiles* (Useless dealings, 1984), *Serie negra* (Crime series, 1987), and *Función privada* (Private function, 1992). However, only three of the more recent books—the novel *El simulador* and the two anthologies *Serie negra* and *Función privada*—are fully relevant for a consideration of Manzur's contribution to detective fiction. Most of the more significant earlier writings by him in this vein are re-edited in the two anthologies along with newly published texts.

To say that Jorge Manzur has contributed to detective fiction requires some clarification. There are a few detectives in his writing, but his investigators are less likely to be professional crime-fighters than ordinary individuals in search of truth or the solution of a mystery. There are also crimes aplenty told in the hard-boiled, noir tradition of North American fiction and film, which was extraordinarily popular in mid-twentieth-century Argentina. His stories are set mainly in Buenos Aires and are peopled primarily by alienated inhabitants of a modern urban environment. Crimes, committed by hired killers and underworld criminals among others, are motivated by greed, power, and infidelity and may be either a product of individual passion or the coldly calculated act of the state. But Manzur's detective fiction is not in the classic mode. He has no dominant figure in the Holmes/Poirot/Marlowe/Spade tradition who re-appears from one story to another and whose activities are a key structural element in the narrative with respect to both the discovery of a crime and the solution of its mysteries. Manzur writes what may best be described as "new detective fiction"—narratives written within and against the traditional genre, which maintain it as a constant point of reference, but that treat its conventions quite loosely. In view of these characteristics, his contribution to detective fiction will perhaps be best understood through consideration of aspects of his transgressive or deconstructive approach to the genre, an attitude that tends to turn his writing into an exploration of its limits or a continuing essay on the nature of the genre itself.

"Riesgos nocturnos," the title story of Manzur's first anthology—one of the texts not republished in a later anthology—already shows elements from which some of the constants of his writing would emerge. It is the story of the betrayal and ambush of a criminal gang told with an emphasis on the violent lives of its members and their alienated existence. The narrative does not therefore represent a disturbance in an ordered reality caused by a mystery that enshrouds a crime and is removed only when the crime is solved and order is restored through judicial sanction. The reader is not kept in the dark about who has committed the crimes, and these are part of an inherently disordered world, affirming the notion underlying a number of Manzur's stories that crime and disorder are intrinsic elements of social life. In some instances, his stories are concerned only with the narration of a crime, not with its discovery and punishment; in others, a mystery remains unsolved, as if reflecting the impenetrable anarchy of social life.

In "El aparecido" (The spectre)—first published in *Tratos inútiles* and, like "Riesgos nocturnos," not anthologized again later—a wandering youth who has been kidnapped, ill-treated, and abandoned on a highway is picked up by a driver named Reynal. The young man has amnesia and only recalls fragments of his past, but he remembers enough to be able, with Reynal's help, to return to the place from which he was kidnapped, only to be taken again and find Reynal lying bleeding and beaten on the back seat of the car into which he is forced. Reynal and the youth assume the role of detectives as they follow a trail through an urban night in an attempt to illuminate the past, but their quest uncovers little and leads only to a further crime. Here, using the features of noir fiction to describe the political violence of Argentina during the 1970s and early 1980s, Manzur also shows his tendency to re-direct the conventions of detective writing.

This practice of redirecting the convention is especially evident in stories that take an unexpected turn. In "Cambio de frente" (Change of front), for example, the narrator is contracted by a rather disagreeable client to kill Ana. Instead, he falls for her, begins an affair, and ends by murdering his wife Marguerite so that he is free to begin a new life with Ana in Europe. In "Un cliente bien informado" (A well-informed client), a man named Luis Delbono seeks out a private detective, Manuel Asturiano, in his office and somewhat self-consciously narrates the discovery of his wife's infidelity. The detective listens rather dismissively to Delbono's plight, but has the tables turned on him in the end when Delbono pulls out a gun and shoots him after revealing that his discovery has led him to Asturiano's office and to the knowledge that the detective is his wife's lover.

Both stories contain a reversal, which is implied in the first one by its title, and is evident in the content of the second through the story of a client who sleuths his own case, following a trail that leads him to a detective, eventually turning the latter from hunter to hunted. Moreover, although both stories entail an element of mystery that is gradually resolved as the story proceeds, there is nothing mysterious about the murder narrated in the last lines of each of them. Not only is the reader immediately privy to all its circumstances, but the narration of the crime is not framed by any form of judicial sanction, as if the objective of the stories was to narrate the crime as a social phenomenon for its own sake rather than to assert the primacy of a social order sustained by the discovery and punishment of wrongdoing.

Similar concepts are at play in "Cuando se apagan las luces" (When the lights go out), the final story of *Función privada*. With more than a touch of black humor, it tells of a security guard who ingratiates himself with the inhabitants of the streets he patrols at night by staging a series of increasingly serious, but equally fake, crimes from which he claims to have saved them in the course of his duty. He not only creates expectations among the people he protects with respect to the criminal environment in which they live, but also a sense of dependence on him as their protector, a process that leads to his being hired by a notary, one of the pillars of the community, to terrorize his wife in exchange for a large sum of money. In addition to the reversal of roles similar to that noted in other stories—the upholders of the law are its violators and sources of social disorder, making the story a critique of graft and corruption in police services—"Cuando se apagan las luces" also draws attention to the creativity of crime and the artistry of the criminal. Like the security guard in this story, the criminal creates reality, not only through activities that change lives, but through the subterfuges that cover his crimes and are comparable in their way to the elaboration of a fiction.

The title story of *Función privada* is especially eloquent in this respect. It is the tale of a film director, Sebastián Carmona, whose one and only film is mercilessly pilloried by the critics. Eleven years later he takes his revenge by killing them off and, with a certain sense of poetic justice, makes the computer or typewriter at which they write their reviews the instrument of his revenge. In this instance, the affinity between the artist and criminal is not only present in the identity of Carmona as a filmmaker, but in the artistry with which he executes his crime. It is also noteworthy that the mystery of Carmona's crimes is uncovered by a writer, Washington Robles, whose long years as a critic and his knowledge of the archive allow him to reconstruct the past and understand what Carmona has created in the present. Since he is also one of the critics targeted by Carmona, the trail he follows in pursuit of an explanation of the murders will ironically also lead to his own death by guiding him to the typewriter that will be the instrument of his demise.

The connection between writing and crime—present in a rather understated way in "Función privada"—has a much more prominent place in a number of other stories, where the border between the real and the imaginary is readily transgressed. It should be noted, however, that Jorge Manzur is a particularly "literary" writer. His stories are inserted in a world circumscribed by literature. Many carry a dedication to or an epigraph taken from well-known Argentinean or international writers, and there are numerous references to other authors in his writing. Jorge Luis Borges occupies an especially significant place, as will be seen, and the world of detective fiction with which Manzur's writing has a particular affinity is well-represented through direct and implied references to Raymond Chandler and Dashiell Hammett. His crime fictions are often about writing and frequently have an autobiographical veneer—a genre that already confuses fictional and real constructions. He uses them to confront the ontological status of the world represented through a text in a process that may become, in turn, a way of questioning the status of the real world. The idea is iconographically conveyed on the cover of the Sudamericana edition of *Serie negra* in a design that would not disgrace the cover of a pulp fiction by Mickey Spillane: a woman reclines provocatively on a table, leaning on one hand, the other resting on the back of her head where it holds back her hair from her face; on the same table in front of her is a pile of books bound in black, with a dagger stuck into the top one so that blood oozes out of it and trickles down the side of the pile onto the table; in the foreground, contemplating this tableau, is the male gaze of the detective, represented by the back of a trilby hat from under which a whisp of cigarette smoke emerges. This picture, which also has the *chiaroscuro* lighting of a scene set in the interior of a gloomy office, represents several elements of noir fiction, but the transformation of the books into the bleeding victims of a crime is a significant change. It emphasizes the literary world of crime, further attested by the title (*Serie negra*) of Manzur's book, which was also the title of an important Argentinean crime fiction series of the 1960s and 1970s. But the anthropomorphic image of the bleeding books already represents that fluidity between the fictional and the real that is the subject of several of his stories.

In "La florista" (The flower woman), which has an epigraph from Augusto Roa Bastos, a narrator describes his tendency to imagine the lives of people he sees on the subway or in the streets. In particular, he tells the story of a flower-seller whom he has seen at her sidewalk stall from a favorite vantage point through a window in a bar that looks out onto the street. Imagining the continuation of her life, he elaborates a detailed story that culminates in the stabbing death of the woman, whom he has christened "Inés." A month later, he returns to the bar for the first time since he has imagined the story and when he looks out the window, notices that the woman is no longer at her post. When he inquires about her, a waiter, referring to her as Inés, the same name as that imagined by the voyeur, replies that, after years of being on the street every day, she suddenly stopped coming on the same day that the narrator was last in the bar. In view of this reply, contained in the last line of the story, the reader is left to wonder whether what was imagined by the narrator was not in fact real, and to what extent reality is therefore as much a construction as a narrative text.

A comparable situation arises in "En defensa propia" (In self defense), also in *Serie negra*, in which a writer (Manzur!) is confronted by a gun-waving character from one of his own compositions and reproached for how he has degraded him and other characters in his stories. The intruder then turns the tables on the author by submitting him to an equally humiliating situation. Such rebellions by fictional characters have had a place in modern fiction in Spanish since the revolt by the character Augusto Pérez against his creator, Spanish author Miguel de Unamuno in *Niebla* (1914), but in Manzur's writing it is the predicament of the writer that is the subject of some of his more interesting stories. Such is the case of "Serie negra," the title story of his 1987 anthology, and "Triste Marlowe" (Sad Marlowe), which was published in *Tratos inútiles* and is included, with "Serie negra," in *Función privada*. Both are longer than Manzur's other stories and have a disaffected writer as their protagonist. "Serie negra" is dedicated to the Argentinean writer Juan Carlos Martini and is a story of rivalry between two journalists who are also crime writers; one of them, Minelli, is named for a character from Martini's fiction, while the other is an evident representation of Manzur himself. They are approached by a publisher for a story to contribute to a volume that is also to contain work by other Argentinean authors, including Borges, Adolfo Bioy Casares, and Rodolfo Walsh. However, the text must be delivered within a few days and is not to exceed 151 lines. While Minelli is not disposed to pursue the project, his colleague, known as Turco, who is in need of the payment he would receive for his work, pretends that he has a text already available that only needs to be finished off. Needless to say, Turco is unable to conform to the demands of the publisher and abandons the assignment, but not without giving Minelli a copy of what he has written. Two months later, he finds a copy of the proposed anthology of crime stories, now newly published. It includes, of course, a completed version of the story Turco could not finish, written by Minelli in 302 lines and published under the same title, "Serie negra," which Turco had proposed for his own text.

"Serie negra" (Manzur's story) is a rather playful work in which Minelli's plagiarism should not perhaps be taken too seriously, not just because it is something of a practical joke between friends, but because it is a metaphor of the relations established among writers and their texts. The concepts of influence, styles, and modes of writing is a topic of conversation between Turco and Minelli, and the title "Serie negra" figures as part of a structure that illustrates the principle of textual relations. Thus, "Serie negra," the story co-written by Turco and Minelli, is embedded and cited extensively in "Serie negra," the story written by Manzur in homage to his contemporary Martini. Manzur's story is, in turn, published in a volume titled *Serie negra*, a phrase that, as the design on the cover so eloquently affirms, refers us to the particular genre to which all these texts are related. Manzur's writing thereby consciously activates a complex, hierarchical system of signification whereby the author of one text inevitably refers us to other authors and other texts.

It is this system and the frequency of Manzur's overt exploitation of it that gives his fiction much of the "literary" quality alluded to earlier. Not only is his writing often about writing, but his representation of the world often relies on configurations derived from other authors. This facet of his work is quite blatantly present in "Dama sofisticada" (Sophisticated lady), a story dedicated to Julio Cortázar and essentially a rewriting of his "Continuidad de los parques" (Continuity of the Parks, 1964). On the day before she is murdered, a woman interrupts her reading of Cortázar's *Rayuela* (*Hopscotch*, 1963) in order to engineer a meeting between Cortázar and Duke Ellington in ringside seats during a title fight in Luna Park in Buenos Aires. The meeting and brief exchange that occurs between them is an effect of juxtaposition wrought by the woman in response to her reading the novel while listening to a jazz recording. As a homage to Cortázar, the story recognizes the capacity of artists, whether writers or musicians, to create a world that engages those who receive their work. Moreover, as a version of "Continuidad de los parques," it also presents a trajectory that begins with reading and ends with the murder of the reader. However, by comparison with "Dama sofisticada," Manzur's "Triste Marlowe" offers a more intense exploration of these concepts.

Like "Serie negra," "Triste Marlowe" might well be considered a novella rather than a short story. It has an epigraph taken from Borges, but, as its title suggests, is a homage to Chandler. Marlowe in this instance refers to the narrator, a disaffected writer and journalist whose name is eventually revealed as Manzur. He has been investigating the case of Luis Martel, also a writer and journalist, who disappeared while writing about the circumstances of the murder of Hugo Serrano, for which Serrano's widow has been convicted. At a moment when Manzur's life has reached an *impasse*, he meets a woman named Patricia in a bar and, with utter spontaneity, assumes the identity of Martel. They begin an affair, but their relationship becomes complicated when Patricia reveals Manzur's true identity to him and then tells him not only that she is Martel's second wife, but that Martel was responsible for the death of Serrano and the framing of his widow. Martel had since felt some remorse but rather than confess his guilt, had begun to show a public interest in the case, somewhat in the style of *Crime and Punishment*, in the hope that the police would realize the innocence of the woman who had been convicted. In the end, however, the narrative seems to lead nowhere. Patricia is committed to looking after Martel, who is now terminally ill, while she and Manzur seem unable either to continue or end their affair. As the story concludes, Manzur is as disaffected as at its beginning and is about to commit a murder in imitation of the one committed earlier by Martel.

In comparison with other narratives in which Manzur explores the concept of literary relations, "Triste Marlowe" is an intensely pessimistic treatment of the subject. The writer has become almost incapable of independent action. He not only assumes the identity of another writer and falls for the same woman, but ends by plotting a similar crime. It is a bleak story and the figure of Manzur is, like Marlowe, an alienated individual who becomes entrapped in the crime he is investigating, in part because the woman with whom he becomes involved— to use phrases that Marlowe himself might have spoken—"doesn't give it to him straight and plays him for a sap." As an allegory of literary dependence, it is the story of a writer unable to find himself.

The figure of the writer is redeemed somewhat in Manzur's only detective novel, *El simulador*, perhaps because the writer in this instance is no less a figure than Borges. The kernel of the plot developed in the novel is contained in an earlier short story dedicated to Borges and titled "Otra versión" (Another version). It is an account of two robberies at the same bank, the first in 1976 when, in addition to a large sum of money, thieves also took an incomplete and unpublished novel by Borges. Nine years later, in 1985, during a parallel robbery, Borges's manuscript is returned to the safety-deposit box from which it was taken. Like the police and customers of the bank, Borges reflects on the parallels between the two robberies, but unlike them, who can only speculate about them, he is able to see an authentic connection. Since he did not reveal the loss of his manuscript in 1976, he also stays silent about its return in 1985. In view of these facts, but also, as the story makes clear, because of his status as a poet and sage, Borges occupies a privileged position, denied to others, as one able to see the hidden meanings of reality. In this respect, as one who knows about the nature of events and the connections between them, he is in the same situation as the criminal.

In *El simulador*, the story becomes a tale of international intrigue that follows the fortunes of the manuscript during the time it is missing. On its trail are a professor of literature, Tomás Blake, who turns out to be as self-interested and unprincipled as any criminal, and an Argentinean policeman, Inspector Montalbán, who is after the mastermind behind the bank robberies, a man known, among other aliases, as "El Oriental." Of course, it is Borges, the writer, and El Oriental, the master criminal, who know the full story and hold all the answers. The inspector and the professor are outsiders who are led on a dance and are both eventually killed, a fate which is not unexpected given that of similar characters in Manzur's writing, and that preserves the secrets of both the writer and the criminal and their privileged view of reality. The simulator mentioned in the title of the novel is therefore the one who knows the truth but who fakes reality or covers it up so that none can learn its true shape or meaning. He is therefore both the writer and the criminal, a point made by Jorge Lafforgue (*Función privada* 185) at the same time as he noted that the real "simulador" is in Manzur himself.

For all his simulation, however, Manzur never seems quite able to create his own disguises. The figure of the writer trapped by the influences of his own readings and how he has dealt with them in his own writing emerges again in the story "El Oriental" (The Uruguayan), published in *Función privada*, in which Manzur revives the character of the criminal he had developed more fully in *El simulador*. Here, a writer (Manzur again!) is struggling to complete a book of short stories for which the publisher has given him a final deadline. He is contacted by El Oriental, whom he recognizes, of course, as a character from his own writing and who offers him a notebook containing ideas for stories that he claims to have stolen from Gabriel García Márquez in 1978. In this very situation, the fictional Manzur finds the solution to his immediate problem: in the story of the stolen notebook and how he came by it he will find the very story he needs in order to meet his publisher's deadline. In this situation, however, there is an allegory of the limitations of the writing of the real Manzur. He has some clever plots and often resists the closure characteristic of traditional crime writing, but his writing is frequently too self-consciously intertextual. Both tendencies (the open text and its overtly intertextual nature) are features of much contemporary writing, but Manzur does not always successfully transcend them. His writing is too often like that of the writers he represents in his fiction—in "Triste Marlowe," "Serie negra," "La florista," "En defensa propia," or "El Oriental," for example—in which authors struggle with their work against the tradition in which they are writing and who, in the end, do not really succeed in finding their own voice.

Richard Young

Works

Bajo palabra. Buenos Aires: Galerna, 1980.
Crónica de amor, de locura y de muerte. Buenos Aires: Sudamericana, 1986.
Función privada. Buenos Aires: Clarín/Aguilar, 1992.
Riesgos nocturnos. Buenos Aires: Galerna, 1977.
Serie negra. Buenos Aires: Sudamericana, 1987.
El simulador. Buenos Aires: Planeta, 1990.
Tapen al minotauro que hay niños. Buenos Aires: Puntosur, 1988.
Tinta roja. Buenos Aires: Legasa, 1980.
Tratos inútiles. Buenos Aires: Legasa, 1984.
"Triste Marlowe," in *El relato policial en la Argentina*, ed. Jorge B. Rivera. Buenos Aires: EUDEBA, 1986, 175–220.

Criticism

Lafforgue, Jorge, and Jorge B. Rivera. *Asesinos de papel: ensayos sobre narrativa policial*. Buenos Aires: Colihue, 1996, 161–64.
Young, Richard. "La sombra de la tradición: continuidad y transgresión en el cuento argentino (Fresán, Manzur, Saccomano)," in *Culturas del Río de la Plata (1973–1995): transgresión e intercambio*, ed. Roland Spiller. Frankfurt: Vervuet Verlag, 1995, 141–54.

∼

José Martínez de la Vega (1908–1954)

MEXICO

José "Pepe" Martínez de la Vega occupies a special position in the history of Mexican detective fiction. Not only is he one of the founders and first practitioners of the genre in Mexico, but his detective character, Péter Pérez, is one of the most memorable. His stories, collected in *Péter Pérez, detective de Peralvillo y anexas* (Péter Pérez, detective of Peralvillo and surroundings, 1952), have been included in some of the most important anthologies of Mexican and Latin American detective fiction. His story "El secreto de la lata de sardines" (The secret of the sardine can), for example, has become a classic. Amelia Simpson and Eugenia Revueltas both single out this story as his most representative, and consider parody to be the distinguishing characteristic in Martínez de la Vega's stories. He is considered to be a uniquely Mexican detective type, transforming the conventions of the detective story to the context and reality of Mexican society. Pérez is a typical *pelado*, a poor man who must eke out a living by his wits. Gabriel Trujillo Muñoz likens him to El Periquillo Sarniento, the eponymous hero of the classic nineteenth-century novel by José Joaquín Fernández de Lizardi [39]). Like his compatriot Máximo Roldán (the detective created by Antonio Helú), Péter Pérez lives on the margins of society. As Ilán Stavans points out:

> In the forties, Peralvillo was usually one of the poorest neighborhoods in Mexico City, in which vendors wandered the streets and illicit transactions were carried out. Police raids, arrests, and prosecutions occurred with frequency, even though the gendarmes and bailiffs were apprehensive about venturing into the district. Even suggesting that the protagonist is a Peralvillo detective is a joke from the start. (Stavans 88)

However, unlike Roldán, Pérez is not a rogue or thief. While Roldán solves crimes for his own benefit, not out of any sense of justice or commitment to the law, Pérez seems genuinely interested in upholding and enforcing the law, though he may be at odds with it at times. But above all, Péter Pérez is, as Simpson states, "an observer who criticizes, but does not actively defy, the system" (88). Most remarkable in the adventures of Pérez is the biting humor, unleashed like a comic whip mostly against the ruling political party, the PRI (Partido Revolucionario Institucional [Institutional Revolutionary Party]). The narrator—Pérez typically does not narrate the stories—is constantly taking jabs at the ruling party with statements like "Péter Pérez, el genial detective de Peralvillo, estaba comiendo, porque también los ciudadanos que no pertenecen al PRI comen de vez en cuando." (Péter Pérez, the brilliant detective of Peralvillo, was eating, since citizens that don't belong to the PRI also eat once in a while [*Péter Pérez, detective de Peralvillo y anexas*, 1993, 51]). Pérez's intelligence, cleverness, and shrewdness are repeatedly reinforced throughout the stories. Likewise, the excesses and advantages of the wealthy are placed in direct contrast with the needs of the underprivileged, of which Pérez is one. His cases are simple and brief, most no more than a few pages long, and follow the basic model of the enigma- or puzzle-story to the point of being overly, and purposely, obvious, as in "El cuarto cerrado" (The locked room). But in those few pages the author manages to create entertaining tales that offer the reader the stimulation of mystery, the entertainment of humor and irony, and insightful observations and social commentary.

Pérez Pérez was an extremely popular character. Not only did he appear in written stories that were widely read, but there was also a successful radio series in which dramatizations of his cases were broadcast to the eager listening public. Four such scripts are included in the 1993 edition of *Péter Pérez, detective de Peralvillo y anexas.*

Darrell B. Lockhart

Works

"The Dead Man Was a Lively One," in *Latin Blood: The Best Crime and Detective Stories of South America*, ed. Donald A. Yates. New York: Herder & Herder, 1972, 173–82.

"El muerto era un vivo," in *Los mejores cuentos policiacos mexicanos*, ed. María Elvira Bermúdez. Mexico City: Libro-Mex, 1955, 63–73.

Péter Pérez, detective de Peralvillo y anexas. Mexico City: Talleres Gráficos de la Nación, 1952; 2nd ed., Mexico City: Joaquín Mortiz, 1993.

"El secreto de la lata de sardinas," in *El cuento policial mexicano*, ed. Vicente Francisco Torres. Mexico City: Diógenes, 1982, 71–76.

Criticism

Revueltas, Eugenia. "La novela policiaca en México y en Cuba." *Cuadernos americanos* [Nueva época] 1.1 (1987): 102–20.

Simpson, Amelia S. *Detective Fiction from Latin America.* Rutherford, NJ: Fairleigh Dickinson University Press, 1990.

Stavans, Ilán. *Antiheroes: Mexico and Its Detective Novel*, trans. by Jesse H. Lytle and Jennifer A. Mattson. Cranbury, NJ: Associated University Presses, 1997, 88–90.

Trujillo Muñoz, Gabriel. *Testigos de cargo: la narrativa policiaca mexicana y sus autores.* Tijuana, Mexico: CONACULTA/CECUT, 2000, 39–42.

Juan Martini (b. 1944)

ARGENTINA

Juan Martini was born in Rosario, Argentina in 1944. He has lived in Argentina, either in Rosario or in Buenos Aires, all his life, except for a period of almost ten years (1975–1984), which he spent in Barcelona as an exile. In Spain, he worked for the Bruguera publishing house and directed their important *Serie Novela Negra* (detective novel series). He currently lives in Buenos Aires where he writes, works as a journalist, and is a chief editor for a major publishing house. Martini began publishing his books under his full name, Juan Carlos Martini Real. He then shortened it to Juan Carlos Martini, and now uses Juan Martini. He is the author of some 15 works of fiction, both short-story collections and novels. In 1986, he received a Guggenheim Fellowship to write his novel *La construcción del héroe* (The construction of the hero), which was published in 1989 and won the Buenos Aires Municipal First Prize for a novel. Of his extensive literary oeuvre—which has continued to grow at a steady pace up to the present—three novels written during the 1970s stand out among the best of Argentine detective fiction: *El agua en los pulmones* (Water in the lungs, 1973), *Los asesinos las prefieren rubias* (Murderers prefer blondes, 1974), and *El cerco* (The siege, 1977). These established Martini as a master of the hard-boiled novel. The three titles were later collected in the volume *Tres novelas policiales* (Three detective novels, 1985).

Martini was just one of many Argentine authors who were turning to the hard-boiled detective genre during the 1970s. They were influenced by the North American hard-boiled classics they had grown up reading, and they discovered that the genre, adapted to the context of Argentina, provided an excellent vehicle for addressing the violent social upheaval of the 1970s and early 1980s that was occasioned mainly by the neofascist military dictatorship. *El agua en los pulmones*, set in the city of Rosario, features the detective Simón Solís as he works on a confusing case that involves international intrigue, danger, corruption, and a hearty dose of violence. The title is derived from the type of torture Solís receives at the hands of his enemies. Almost all the critics who have commented on the novel mention the influence of the North American models established by authors such as Raymond Chandler and Dashiell Hammett. Amelia S. Simpson, for example, observes that Simón Solís "is very much like the detective heroes of Chandler and Hammett—a populist individualist, he distrusts all forms of institutional authority and follows his own private code of honor to maintain his integrity and to exact a measure of justice in an unjust world" (Simpson 54).

If *El agua en los pulmones* appropriates, quite successfully, the hard-boiled novel of the North American tradition, *Los asesinos las prefieren rubias* goes one step further. The action takes place across two different time periods and geographic locations: Hollywood of the 1950s and Buenos Aires of, mostly, the 1970s. The added ingredient of the influence of Hollywood films, the figure of Marilyn Monroe as the murder victim, and the participation of other recognizable Hollywood figures in the novel, though in bizarre new roles, makes the text an obvious parody. The two detectives, for example, are named Sinatra and Brando. Martini plays with the parallels between fantasy and reality until the lines become blurred and the reader seems to be watching a film made from the mixed-up reels of two separate stories. Simpson analyzes the device of doubling in the novel, which makes it possible to read the text on several different levels. *Los asesinos las prefieren rubias* is typical of the kind of detective fiction being written at the time. The use of foreign models and references to talk about Argentine reality becomes a kind of clever technique utilized by authors like Martini, José Pablo Feinmann, Osvaldo Soriano, Pablo Urbanyi, and several others who wrote detective fiction during this time.

In *El cerco*, Martini returns to a more direct approach, and the intensified violence of the novel reflects that of the country. Written in 1975 and published in Spain in 1977, *El cerco* makes little effort to disguise the fact that it is a harsh criticism of the events that lead up to the military coup d'état of 1976 and the major figures and institutions (like José López Rega and the Triple A [Argentine anticommunist association]) that played keys roles in the dismantling of Argentine society and unleashing institutionalized violence the likes of which the country had never experienced. The novel essentially narrates the story of a man, Stein, who, finding himself suddenly on the outside of the power structure, spirals into a world of fear, paranoia, and the sense of imminent death (Feinmann 146). In fact, the two epigraphs used by the author to frame the novel both make clear, almost chilling references to death. One is by Jorge Luis Borges and the other is by Franz Kafka, both of which serve to situate the text in a specifically Argentine context while at the same time foreshadowing the absurdity of the circumstances that will be narrated. The novel is not in the traditional sense a detective story, since there is no detective really, but clearly Martini continues to make use of the hard-boiled model. In this case, it is not the use of parody or the imitation of types, but more the violent atmosphere, the sense of imminent danger that defines the novel, and as well, of course, as the social commentary that the novel provides.

While the author has written three volumes of short stories, few could be classified as belonging to the detective genre. Nevertheless, his story "Obelisco" (Obelisk) has been anthologized in two important collections of Argentine detective fiction. Although Martini seems to have pretty much abandoned the genre to pursue other avenues of expression, his later works are still imbued with tinges of his early detective fiction. No matter where his writing takes him in the future, Juan Martini has secured himself a spot as one of the best and most influential of the Argentine hard-boiled detective fiction writers. His works are already considered classic examples of the boom in hard-boiled literature that began during the 1970s in Argentina.

Darrell B. Lockhart

Works

El agua en los pulmones. Buenos Aires: Juan Goyanarte, 1973.
Los asesinos las prefieren rubias. Buenos Aires: La Línea, 1974.
El cerco. Barcelona: Bruguera, 1977.
"Las cosas como son," in *Escritos con sangre: cuentos argentinos sobre casos policiales,* ed. Sergio S. Olguín. Buenos Aires: Norma, 2003, 151–70.
"Obelisco," in *El relato policial en la Argentina,* ed. Jorge B. Rivera. Buenos Aires: EUDEBA, 1986, 147–74. Also in *Cuentos policiales argentinos,* ed. Jorge Lafforgue. Buenos Aires: Alfaguara, 1997, 291–314.
Tres novelas policiales. Buenos Aires: Legasa, 1985. (*El agua en los pulmones*; *Los asesinos las prefieren rubias*; *El cerco.*)

Criticism

José Pablo Feinmann. "Estado policial y novela negra argentina," in *Los héroes "difíciles": la literatura policial en la Argentina y en Italia,* ed. Giuseppe Petronio, Jorge B. Rivera, and Luigi Volta. Buenos Aires: Corregidor, 1991, 143–53.
Lafforgue, Jorge, and Jorge B. Rivera. *Asesinos de papel: ensayos sobre narrativa policial.* Buenos Aires: Colihue, 1996.
Lagmonovich, David. "Gandolfo, Gorodischer, Martini: Tres narradores jóvenes de Rosario (Argentina)." *Chasqui: revista de literatura latinoamericana* 4.2 (1975): 18–28.
Sablich, José. "Contextos reales y ficcionales en la novela negra argentina de la década del '70," in *Calibar sin rastros: aportes para una historia social de la literatura argentina.* Ed. Jorge Torres Roggero and María Elena Legaz. Córdoba, Argentina: CONICET/CIFFyH, 1996, 157–85.
Simpson, Amelia S. *Detective Fiction from Latin America.* Rutherford, NJ: Fairleigh Dickinson University Press, 1990.

Leonardo Padura Fuentes (b. 1955)

CUBA

Leonardo Padura Fuentes was born in Havana in 1955. He is representative of a new generation of detective fiction writers in Cuba who are trying to move away from the simplistic type of crime fiction that has been promoted by the Ministry of Interior since the 1970s. In addition to being a fiction writer and literary critic, he has also worked as a journalist and screenwriter. He is currently the chief editor of *La Gaceta de Cuba*, one of the leading literary and cultural journals in the country. His first fictional text was the novel *Fiebre de caballos* (Horse fever, 1988) and it was followed a year later by a collection of short stories, *Según pasan los años* (As the years go by, 1989). Both texts are centered in a world of childhood, youth, and memory—topics to which Padura frequently returns in his detective fiction. As a literary critic, he has published studies on Garcilaso de la Vega, magical realism, and Alejo Carpentier. In 1991, after years of criticizing the lack of quality crime fiction written in Cuba, Padura decided to write his first detective novel, *Pasado perfecto* (Past perfect, 1991). Set during December 1988, it tells the story of detective Mario Conde, who is given the task of finding a prominent member of the Cuban government whose disappearance on New Year's Eve puzzles everyone. The novel takes place during the Cuban winter, the first volume of a projected tetralogy in which each novel corresponds to a season of the year. His second novel, *Vientos de cuaresma* (The winds of lent, 1994), about the mysterious murder of a high school teacher won an annual award given by the UNEAC (Unión de Escritores y Artistas de Cuba [Cuban Artists and Writers Union]).

The importance of Padura's work for the short literary history of the genre in Cuba is immediately evident when we compare his books to the detective fiction that began to be written during the early 1970s. These novels were too simplistic in their structure: at their core was the basic conflict of the good guys—represented by the local police or anyone defending the revolutionary government—versus the bad guys, who were normally spies or individuals working for the CIA. The detective working for the government was always portrayed as an almost-perfect hero. The CIA agents or counterrevolutionary criminals who they were trying to capture or discover, on the other hand, were often not very intelligent (Taibo 13; Epple 55). Padura's novels, in contrast, are much more complex in plot and character development than their predecessors. The so-called good guy, for instance, Mario Conde—the main character in Padura's two novels—is not perfect, to say the least. He is a drunkard who is constantly stereotyping Cubans of African and Asian descent. He does not always follow official procedures and has frequent doubts about the socialist political system. Conde also dreams of becoming a writer, but he has been unable to write even a single line in a long time. He is obviously Padura's alter ego, and the description of the character's past is probably full of autobiographical references.

One of Padura's main topics—one can almost call it an obsession, because it appears in almost all his books and short stories—is the effect that decisions made in the past (by the characters in the book or by the government) have on the rest of one's life. Among the memories that his characters constantly revert back to (flashback is Padura's favorite narrative technique in *Pasado perfecto*) are those connected to their days as students in the *pre-universitario* or high school. The *"Pre"* days in Padura's books invariably symbolize (both in his crime novels and other fiction) a period of time when there is hope of realizing one's dreams, when one still holds great expectations for the future. Most of the characters in Padura's narratives, however, have not been able to achieve any of the things that they were planning to do with their lives after high school, including, of course Conde himself who has not become the writer he wanted to be. But there is more than a mere fixation with the past here: Conde's high school days (early 1970s) represent a period in which there were still a lot of people inside and outside of Cuba who believed in the future of the socialist revolution. Thus, the failures of Conde and his friends are in part an allegorical allusion to the problems that the creation of a socialist society in Cuba begins to face towards the 1970s. Moreover, the fact that Conde's best friend in high school, *el flaco* (skinny) Carlos, who was shot while fighting in the Angolan civil war and is now paralyzed, becomes a clear symbol of the present paralysis of the revolutionary process. But Conde also knows that after Carlos's mother dies, he will take care of his friend, and this action thus clearly expresses Padura's own position of never abandoning Cuba, even as the political/economic situation worsens (Epple 66). Another clear reference to the political events of the 1970s is the incident that Conde and his friends call the *"Waterpre."* A young literature teacher who had just started working at the *Pre* wanted to publish a literary magazine with contributions written by her students. They were all enthusiastic about the project, especially Conde, because he was going to see his first short story published. The magazine is never released into circulation; it is censored by the school's principal because of its alleged subversive content. Conde is criticized for writing an innocent story dealing with a religious topic that, read out of context, is taken to be counterrevolutionary. Although the name *"Waterpre"* alludes to the Watergate scandal, the story is in reality a veiled reference to the Heberto Padilla case that during the early 1970s made so many artists and intellectuals from other countries distance themselves from the Cuban government and condemn its cultural policies (Epple 50).

Another characteristic of Padura's new fiction is that the detective is no longer looking for some sort of CIA-directed plot as the solution to a mystery, nor are the victims presented as being totally innocent. The criminals and the victims, on the contrary, are usually highly regarded individuals who, although they appear to be supporters of the revolution and model citizens, are really corrupt people who have taken advantage of their positions to benefit themselves. The idea that the "enemy is within"—that instead of worrying about some outside force threatening to overthrow the system of government, the Cuban detective narratives should be more concerned about local and everyday problems—is a recurrent one in Padura. In fact, most of the time solving the mystery in his novels is not the central aspect of the text. Most of the author's (and the main character's) attention is focused on people or groups of people marginalized by the socialist government, on the decay of Havana or the lowering of the standard of living there, the lack of a sense of direction in the younger generations, and the illegal ways in which people try to improve their personal situations.

The detective Mario Conde returns, in spite of being retired, to investigate a new case in *Adiós, Hemingway* (Goodbye, Hemingway, 2003) that involves the discovery of a skeleton at Finca Vigía, Ernest Hemingway's old house in Havana. The victim died from two gunshot wounds sometime between 1957 and 1960, the period when Hemingway was living in Cuba and just shortly before his suicide in 1961. In the course of his investigation, Conde makes some surprising revelations and paints an unexpected portrait of the famous author, of whom he is a great admirer.

For Padura, this de-emphasizing of the solution in a detective novel is an aspect of his fiction that could be related to postmodernism. And it is true that the absence of a *telos* is part of the postmodern detective fiction, as in the case of Thomas Pynchon's *The Crying of Lot 49* (1966). But the impression that we get from Padura's main characters is that they still have a clear goal (contribute to improving their society), even if they are a bit skeptical about the possibility of achieving it. However, there are other characteristics in his texts that we can perhaps examine in relation to postmodernism, the most interesting ones being the nostalgia for a recent past (the early 1970s), self-reflection (Conde even reads Padura's novel, *Fiebre de caballos*), and the attempt to turn a mass-culture literary genre into "high" culture. But it would seem that if anything is really postmodern in his work, it is the rejection of global solutions—or to put it another way, the desire to find local solutions to local problems. In this sense, it is useful to contrast Padura's own fiction with the work of the famous Cuban novelist Alejo Carpentier, about whom Padura has written a critical study. Carpentier was always interested in creating characters that symbolized Latin American people or countries. His novels are highly allegorical texts dealing with lofty topics such as the circularity of time, the contradictions of historical processes, and so on. Padura, on the other hand, is not interested in writing about and for the whole of Latin America, but only for Cubans and about the problems they face in everyday life.

José Eduardo González

Works

Adiós, Hemingway. Bogotá: Norma, 2003.
"Mirando al sol," in *Variaciones en negro: relatos policiales hispanoamericanos*, ed. Lucía López Coll. Bogotá: Norma, 2003, 237–54.
Pasado perfecto. Guadalajara: EDUG, 1991.
Vientos de cuaresma. Havana: Unión, 1994.

Criticism

Braham, Persephone. "Machismo, travestismo y revolución en dos novelas policiacas cubanas," in *Pensamiento y crítica: los discursos de la cultura hoy*, ed. Javier Durán, Rosaura Hernández Monroy, and Manuel F. Medina. East Lansing: Michigan State University, University of Louisville, Centro de Cultura Casa Lamm, 2000, 437–44.

Castells, Ricardo. "La novela policíaca en la Cuba del período especial: *Pasado perfecto* de Leonardo Padura Fuentes." *South Eastern Latin Americanist* 41.3–4 (1998): 21–35.

Epple, Juan Armando. "Leonardo Padura Fuentes." *Hispamérica* 71 (1995): 49–66. (Interview.)

Pérez, Janet. "Intertextuality, Homosexuality, Marginality and Circularity as Subversion in Novel Permutations of the Detective Genre." *Hispanófila* 135 (2002): 73–88.

Rosell, Sara. "La (re)formulación del policial cubano: la tetralogía de Leonardo Padura Fuentes." *Hispanic Journal* 21.2 (2000): 447–58.

Smith, Verity. "Leonardo Padura habla de sus libros." *Torre de Papel* 8.1 (1998): 105–17. (Interview.)

Taibo, Paco Ignacio, II. "Introduction," in *Pasado perfecto*, by Leonardo Padura. Guadalajara: EDUG, 1991, 13–14.

Adolfo L. Pérez Zelaschi (b. 1920)

ARGENTINA

Adolfo Luis Pérez Zelaschi was born in Bolívar, Province of Buenos Aires in 1920. He studied literature, law, and sociology at the university, but didn't complete a degree in any subject. He later went on to work as a journalist, editor, and in publicity. His is the author of over 20 books that include novels, short stories, and poetry. His literature has earned him numerous prizes and awards both in Argentina and abroad. Of his broad literary production, only a few of his books are within the detective fiction genre: the short-story collections *Con arcos y ballestas* (With bows and crossbows, 1968), *Divertimiento para revólver y piano* (Divertimento for pistol and piano, 1981), and *Mis mejores cuentos policiales* (My best detective stories, 1988), and the novel *El caso de la muerte que telefonea* (The case of the phone call from death, 1939). Pérez Zelaschi published the majority of his stories in popular magazines—mostly *Vea y Lea* (See and read)—before they were gathered together in book form. He is considered one of the main practitioners of the detective genre in Argentina in its first phase. Many of his stories are included in anthologies dedicated to detective fiction from Argentina and Latin America, one of which is "Las señales" (The signs, 1964). Jury members Jorge Luis Borges, Adolf Bioy Casares, and Manuel Peyrou selected it to win first prize for detective fiction awarded by *Vea y Lea*.

Pérez Zelaschi created a memorable and unique character in his police commissioner Leoni. He indicates that the character was based on a friend of his who died in 1970 (*Mis mejores cuentos policiales*, 202). In fact, the nine stories that feature Leoni and comprise *Con arcos y ballestas* (the title derives from weapons used in the stories) are structured around the device of an ongoing dialogue between the two friends. Pérez Zelaschi's stories follow the classic detective model of the "whodunit" in which a mystery is presented and then solved through clever techniques of deduction to reveal the culprit in the end. What makes Leoni unique is not only his rough Argentine character but his philosophy of justice, which does not always side with the law. For instance, in the story, "El caso del orangután malabarista" (The case of the juggling orangutan), the murderer is discovered in the end by Leoni's adept reasoning skills but is not turned over to the authorities. This story is also of note for the several intertextual elements that inform it, whether openly or through allusion. Leoni himself recognizes that there is a striking similarity between the case he is involved in and "The Murders in the Rue Morgue" (1841) by Edgar Allan Poe, though he doesn't accept it as plausible. Moreover, in Leoni's case, the murderer is in fact human, not simian. One cannot help but see an allusion to Leopoldo Lugones's story "Yzur" (1906) and Horacio Quiroga's *El mono que asesinó* (The monkey that murdered, 1909) as well. Another clever intersection with Argentine literature is seen in the story "El caso de la suerte de Martín Fierro" (The case of Martín Fierro's luck). While José Hernández's famous literary figure doesn't appear as a character in Pérez Zelaschi's story, he does provide the philosophy behind it. Other stories that showcase Leoni include "El caso de la callada muerte" (The case of silent death), a well-crafted tale about the murder of a tyrannical father in which all the children are suspects (again, though the murderer is revealed in the end, she gets away with it); and "El caso del callejón de las Tunas" (The case of Tunas alley), which features another Argentine detective writer, Rodolfo Walsh and his *Variaciones en rojo* (Variations in red, 1953). The Leoni series must necessarily be counted among the best Argentine detective fiction of the time, and for creating a lasting character in Leoni himself.

Pérez Zelaschi also wrote several stories that did not feature his famous detective. Worth mentioning are "El piola" (The wise guy) about a would-be criminal who tries to pull off a con-job and ends up being conned himself; "El banquero, la muerte y la luna" (The banker, death, and the moon), a complicated but intriguing story of separated twins, astrology, and fratricide; and finally, "Las señales," a gangster-inspired story about a bar owner who unwittingly becomes involved in a dangerous twist of fate.

There is virtually no critical appraisal of Pérez Zelaschi's work to date, aside from reviews and brief mentions. Lafforgue and Rivera include him in their valuable resource *Asesinos de papel* (Paper murderers, 1996), but fail to provide an indepth analysis of his work. Nevertheless, his texts remain some of the best examples of early homegrown Argentine detective fiction and continue to be entertaining reading.

Darrell B. Lockhart

Works

"Alias el Gringo," in *Tiempo de puñales*. Buenos Aires: Seijas y Goyanarte, 1964, 29–41.

El caso de la muerte que telefonea. Buenos Aires: Manuel Láinez, 1939.

"El caso de la suerte de Martín Fierro," in *Cuentos policiales*, ed. Fermín Fevre. Buenos Aires: Kapelusz, 1974, 165–75.

"El caso de los crímenes sin firma," in *El relato policial en la Argentina: antología crítica*, ed. Jorge B. Rivera. Buenos Aires: Eudeba, 1986, 119–34.

Con arcos y ballestas. Buenos Aires: Ediciones Paulinas, 1967.

Divertimiento para revólver y piano. Buenos Aires: Editorial Ofra, 1981.

Mis mejores cuentos policiales. Buenos Aires: Ediciones Lucanor, 1988.

"El misterio de la muerte del capitán Robles," and "Fuga," in *El cuento policial argentino: una propuesta de lectura productiva para la escuela secundaria*, ed. Elena Braceras, Cristina Leytour, and Susana Pittella. Buenos Aires: Plus Ultra, 1986, 175–90, 191–97.

"Las señales," in *El cuento policial latinoamericano*, ed. Donald A. Yates. Mexico City: Ediciones de Andrea, 1964, 122–33. Also in *Cuentos policiales argentinos*, ed. Jorge Lafforgue. Buenos Aires: Alfaguara, 1997, 199–214; and *Tiempo de puñales*. Buenos Aires: Seijas y Goyanarte, 1964, 13–28.

Criticism

Lafforgue, Jorge, and Jorge B. Rivera. *Asesinos de papel: ensayos sobre narrativa policial*. Buenos Aires: Ediciones Colihue, 1996.

Manuel Peyrou (1902–1974)

ARGENTINA

Manuel Peyrou was born in San Nicolás de los Arroyos in 1902. In 1915, his father—a lawyer—moved the family to Buenos Aires. In 1920, Peyrou entered law school, more to satisfy his father's wishes than his own. He obtained his degree in 1925 but never practiced law. Instead, he initiated a career in journalism and eventually turned to creative writing and became involved with the group of writers associated with the literary journal *Sur*, founded by Victoria Ocampo. Through *Sur* he met Jorge Luis Borges, who became his mentor and helped Peyrou publish his first story in 1932 in the supplement *Crítica* (Criticism), which Borges directed. Peyrou subsequently published a series of short stories in the daily *La Prensa* (The press) between 1935 and 1942. He published his first book, the collection of short stories *La espada dormida* (The sleeping sword), in 1944, for which he received the Municipal Prize for literature in 1945. In 1947, he began working for *La Prensa*, where he remained until 1951 when it was shut down by the Peronist regime. Peyrou's work, like that of other *Sur* writers, is markedly anti-Peronist. This is particularly true of his novels *Las leyes del juego* (The laws of the game, 1959), *Acto y ceniza* (Act and ash, 1963), and *Se vuelven contra nosotros* (They're turning against us, 1966). Both Rodolfo Borello and Raúl Castagnino have analyzed the critical stance of Peyrou in regard to Peronism. These texts, however, are not related directly to detective fiction in any concrete way.

Peyrou initiated his detective fiction with the publication of *La espada dormida*, a volume of six short stories that feature the amateur detective figure Jorge Vane, of the British Ministry of Information. The British setting and very Anglo-sounding names of the characters are perhaps one of the most defining characteristics of the book. The influence of English detective fiction is clearly evident in the style as well. Beatriz Borovich draws a convincing parallel between Vane and G. K. Chesterton's Father Brown character. Vane solves crime strictly through the intellectual exercise of deduction, reasoning, and the keen intuitive ability to see clues where others don't. The stories "El agua del infierno" (Hells' water) and "La espada dormida" are the most representative of the volume, having been widely studied and anthologized. The volume appeared just two years after *Seis problemas para don Isidro Parodi* (*Six Problems for Don Isidro Parodi*, 1942) by Borges and Adolfo Bioy Casares, largely considered to be the first detective fiction book *per se* published in Argentina. The influence of Borges is evident here and elsewhere in Peyrou's stories (several of which are strikingly similar to his mentor's).

The author published *El estruendo de las rosas*, his only detective novel, in 1948. It was part of the famous detective fiction series *El Séptimo Círculo* (The seventh circle), directed by Borges and Bioy Casares and one of the first texts by an Argentine author. Like Peyrou's later novels, mentioned above, *El estruendo* also offers a rather biting critique of Peronism, though in a much less obvious way (Ponce; Avellaneda; Simpson). The novel was translated into English as *The

Thunder of Roses (1972) by Donald A. Yates and carries an enthusiastic preface by Borges. Nevertheless, the novel is not Peyrou's best example of detective fiction.

Peyrou's subsequent short-story collections contain his best detective fiction: *La noche repetida* (The repeated night, 1953), *El árbol de Judas* (The Judas tree, 1961), for which he won the Ricardo Rojas Prize (1963), and *Marea de fervor* (Rough tide, 1967). In *La noche repetida* there is no central character. Each story stands alone and the narrator and setting vary, though many of the stories do take place in Argentina. Moreover, only a few of the stories can be classified as belonging to the detective genre; that which most stands out is "Julieta y el mago" (Julieta and the magician). *El árbol de Judas* is a volume of five detective stories that feature the detective Pablo Laborde and his godson Juan Carlos. The stories are markedly more Argentine in nature, as is made evident not only in the main characters but also by being grounded in the local culture and history. The stories are structured around the device of dialogue between the young man and his much older and wiser godfather. In spite of the regionalist elements in the stories, one can still clearly identify the influence of the English model. In fact, Borovich calls Laborde a "Sherlock Holmes criollo" (Creole, native Argentine, Sherlock Holmes [18]). In *Marea de fervor*, Laborde and his young disciple return in two stories, "El crimen de don Magín Casanovas" (The Crime of Don Magín Casanovas) and "Uno en dos" (One in two), and are in fact the only two detective stories in the volume. Jorge Lafforgue places Peyrou's detective fiction within the foundational generation of writers who introduced the genre in Argentina following the classic English model of the puzzle- or enigma-story (109). Other writers of this same category include Leonardo Castellani, Jorge Luis Borges, Adolfo Bioy Casares, and Enrique Anderson Imbert.

Manuel Peyrou died on 1 January 1974, but there are two important short-story collections that appeared posthumously. *El crimen de don Magín Casanovas* (1976) contains 15 stories taken from the previous four volumes, most of them detective stories. The volume also contains a useful survey by Alberto Blasi of Peyrou's short fiction. The best examination of the author's detective writing is found in *Los mejores cuentos policiales de Manuel Peyrou* (The best detective stories by Manuel Peyrou, 1993), edited by Beatriz Borovich. The critic provides a thorough survey of Peyrou's work in general and then an in-depth analysis of some of his best detective stories. The volume includes ten stories gathered from *La espada dormida*, *La noche repetida*, and *El árbol de Judas*. Borovich and Néstor Ponce provide the most complete analyses of the author's work to date.

Darrell B. Lockhart

Works

Acto y ceniza. Buenos Aires: Emecé, 1963.

"El agua del infierno," in *Cuentos policiales argentinos*, ed. Jorge Lafforgue. Buenos Aires: Alfaguara, 1997, 153–64.

El árbol de Judas. Buenos Aires: Emecé, 1961.

El crimen de don Magín Casanovas. Buenos Aires: Huemul, 1976.

"La Delfina," in *El cuento policial argentino: una propuesta de lectura productiva para la escuela secundaria*, ed. Elena Braceras, Cristina Leytour, and Susana Pittella. Buenos Aires: Plus Ultra, 1986, 137–47.

La espada dormida. Buenos Aires: Sur, 1944.

"La espada dormida," in *Breve antología de cuentos policiales*, ed. María Inés González and Marcela Grosso. Buenos Aires: Sudamericana, 1995, 99–115.

La espada dormida y otros cuentos. Buenos Aires: Losada, 2003.

El estruendo de las rosas. Buenos Aires: Emecé, 1948. Reprint, Buenos Aires: Fabril, 1969; Buenos Aires: Colihue, 2001. English version as *Thunder of Roses*, trans. Donald A. Yates, introduction by Jorge Luis Borges. New York: Herder & Herder, 1972.

"Julieta y el mago," in *El cuento policial latinoamericano*, ed. Donald A. Yates. Mexico City: Ediciones de Andrea, 1964, 79–87. English version as "Juliet and the Magician," in *Latin Blood: The Best Crime and Detective Stories of South America*, ed. Donald A. Yates. New York: Herder & Herder, 1972, 29–41.

Las leyes del juego. Buenos Aires: Emecé, 1959.

Marea de fervor. Buenos Aires: Emecé, 1967.

Los mejores cuentos policiales de Manuel Peyrou. Selección, estudio preliminar y notas, Beatriz Borovich. Buenos Aires: Corregidor, 1993.

"Muerte en el Riachuelo," in *Cuentos policiales*, ed. Fermín Fevre. Buenos Aires: Kapelusz, 1974, 78–86.

La noche repetida. Buenos Aires: Emecé, 1953.

Se vuelven contra nosotros. Buenos Aires: Emecé, 1966.

Criticism

Avellaneda, Andrés. *El habla de la ideología.* Buenos Aires: Sudamericana, 1983, 43–47.

Blasi, Alberto Oscar. "Los cuentos de Manuel Peyrou," in *El crimen de don Magín Casanovas*, by M. Peyrou. Buenos Aires: Huemul, 1976, 11–32.

Borello, Rodolfo A. "Borges y los escritores liberales argentinos: visión narrativa del período peronista (1944–1955)." *Ottawa Hispanica* 3 (1981): 59–89. Also in his *El peronismo (1943–1955) en la narrativa argentina.* Ottawa: Dovehouse Editions, 1991, 158–65.

Borovich, Beatriz. "Estudio preliminar," in *Los mejores cuentos policiales de Manuel Peyrou.* Buenos Aires: Corregidor, 1993, 13–45.

Capano, Daniel A. "Matriz diegética y topografía dantescas en 'El agua del Infierno' de Manuel Peyrou." *Primeras jornadas internacionales de literatura argentina comparatística. Actas.* Buenos Aires: Facultad de Filosofía y Letras, Universidad de Buenos Aires, 1995, 355–62.

Castagnino, Raúl H. "Manuel Peyrou: el testimonio novelesco de una época argentina." *Revista de la Biblioteca Nacional* [Montevideo] 2.3 (1983): 21–34.

Lafforgue, Jorge, and Jorge B. Rivera. *Asesinos de papel: ensayos sobre narrativa policial.* Buenos Aires: Ediciones Colihue, 1996.

Ponce, Néstor. *Diagonales del género: estudios sobre el policial argentino.* Paris: Editions du Temp, 2001, 96–104.

Romano, Eduardo. "Los parientes criollos del padre Brown," in *Los héroes "difíciles": la literatura policial en la Argentina y en Italia*, ed. Giuseppe Petronio, Jorge B. Rivera, and Luigi Volta. Buenos Aires: Corregidor, 1991, 257–80.

Simpson, Amelia S. *Detective Fiction from Latin America.* Rutherford, NJ: Fairleigh Dickinson University Press, 1990.

Ricardo Piglia (b. 1940)

ARGENTINA

Ricardo Emilio Piglia Renzi was born in Adrogué, Buenos Aires in 1940 to a family of Italian origin. He completed his elementary education there and then his father, a Peronist, made the decision to leave the town in 1955 for political reasons. The family moved to the seaside resort town of Mar del Plata, where Piglia began to show an interest in literature. His personal, handwritten diary (never published and which he continues to keep) and an American friend named Steve Ratliff (writer, adventurer, and reader of Melville, who will later appear as a character in his short stories) are the first literary stimuli for Piglia at around 1956. However, at that time he was not yet thinking of literature as a profession.

He completed a degree in history at the Universidad de la Plata, which later led him to literature and criticism and eventually he began teaching at the university level. In 1967, he published his first book, *La invasión* (The invasion) and moved to Buenos Aires, where he joined other intellectuals of his generation. By 1962 he had already won a prize sponsored by the magazine *El escarabajo de oro* (The golden scarab) for one of his short stories. This marked the beginning of a series of achievements that peaked with his winning of the prestigious *Premio Planeta* (Planeta literary award) in 1997 for his novel *Plata quemada* (Burnt money). Based on a true event, the novel recreates, in a rather documentary fashion, a bank heist that took place in 1965. There is also a film version of the novel under the same title.

Nombre falso (*Assumed Name*), the short-story collection that includes the famous "Homenaje a Roberto Arlt" (Homage to Roberto Arlt), was published in December 1975. The same year, the story "La loca y el relato del crimen" ("The crazy woman and the story of the crime") was one of five winners of the *Primer Certamen Latinoamericano de Cuentos Policiales* (First Latin American detective short story contest), sponsored by the magazine *Siete días* (Seven days). All five stories were published in the book *Misterio 5* (Mystery 5).

From 1969 to 1976 Piglia worked for several different publishing houses. While he was at Tiempo contemporáneo (Contemporary time) he edited an important collection of theoretical works that led to the translation and diffusion of New Criticism in Buenos Aires, especially the works of French structuralism. He also edited the collection *Cuentos policiales de la Serie Negra* (Detective stories of the hard-boiled series), which published translations of works by Raymond Chandler, Horace McCoy, José Giovanni, and Dashiel Hammett among others. Piglia signed his name as "Emilio Renzi" to the foreword of the first volume of the detective collection, which started in 1969. Emilio Renzi (Piglia) appears from then on as a narrator, detective, and a journalist by trade. Emilio Renzi is the journalist who travels to Mar del Plata to attend his father's death in "El fin del viaje" (End of the road), the first story in *Nombre falso*. Renzi is also the chronicler for *El mundo* (The world) newspaper (a reference to Roberto Arlt) who covers the standoff between the police and the robbers in *Plata quemada*. And Renzi is also the nephew of Marcelo Maggi, the researcher of Enrique Ossorio's testimonies (and of Argentine history) in *Respiración artificial* (*Artificial Respiration*). *Respiración artificial* appeared in 1980 and won the *Premio Boris Vian* (Boris Vian prize) in 1981. It was a major bestseller in the Argentine and Latin American markets. As a metaphor of national woes, *Respiración* was, without a doubt, one of the books that best represented the problems of Argentine historical roots and identity during that time. In *Prisión perpetua* (Life sentence, 1988) and *La ciudad ausente* (*The Absent City*, 1992), Piglia returns to this topic from a different narrative angle. *Prisión perpetua* consists of the re-edition of *Nombre falso* plus "La loca y el relato del crimen" and other new stories such as "En otro país" (In another country), which narrates Piglia's experience in the United States where he has been a university professor on several occasions since 1977. He currently teaches at Princeton University.

The novel *La ciudad ausente* presents a textual detective mystery around Macedonio Fernández's theory of the novel in *Museo de la novela Eterna* (Museum of the novel of eternity, 1967). While *Respiración* can be considered a reflection on Argentine literature and a tribute to Jorge Luis Borges, *La ciudad ausente* is a tribute to Macedonio Fernández, to his "narrative machine," or even a continuation of Fernández's novel. Piglia, however, also returns in *La ciudad ausente* to Borges's vision of the world as an Aleph, an idea also present in Italo Calvino's *Le citté invisibili* (The invisible cities, 1972). In *La ciudad ausente*, Emilio Renzi is again a journalist who investigates and follows the hidden clues in the text.

As a novelist and critic, Piglia experiments through his own narrative with the topic of the detective genre as a twofold story: that of the crime through the clues given to the reader, and that of its reconstruction narrated through the detective's interpretation. This double story, the foundation of the genre, has been used by postmodernist writers in order to reflect the narrator's own conscience about the artificiality of what has been narrated. This artificiality or self-referential aspect of literature is Piglia's main topic, especially when referring to Argentine literature, of which it forms a part.

Respiración artificial becomes, in part, a study of literature through the long conversation (lesson) between Emilio Renzi (Piglia) and one of the characters in the novel. Here we see an early version of many of the concepts later developed by Piglia in his book of theory, *Crítica y ficción* (Criticism and fiction, 1990). His ideas on detective fiction comprise one of those concepts. In *Crítica y ficción*, Piglia states that the definition of the detective genre must be sought in "The Murders in the Rue Morgue" (1841), Edgar Allan Poe's story that first establishes the rules for puzzle-narratives. Piglia's vision of the genre defines textuality as the space where the clues to the mystery are hidden. Thus, Piglia states in "Homenaje a Roberto Arlt" that "un crítico literario es siempre, de algún modo, un detective que persigue sobre la superficie de los textos, las huellas, los rastros, que permiten descifrar su enigma" (a literary critic is always, in some way, a detective who pursues in the text the tracks, the clues, that lead to the deciphering of their enigma

[*Prisión perpetua* 136]). For the narrator and detective, the most interesting part is the enigma. Emilio Renzi, both narrator and detective, is aware of the fictional structure of narrative as he unravels the mystery of the text. This knowledge points to the device of a "story within a story," since the solving of the riddle functions as another story whose referent is the fictional story being told.

On the other hand, as indicated by Jorge B. Rivera, an Argentine expert in the genre, the function of the narrator journalist who solves a mystery through language is already present in Rodolfo Walsh's detective story "La aventura de las pruebas de imprenta" (The adventure of the printer's proofs, included in *Variaciones en Rojo* [Variations in red, 1953]). The detective hero in the story, journalist Daniel Hernández, resurfaces in other stories by Walsh. His name is clearly symbolic: Daniel, for the Biblical prophet, and Hernández for José Hernández, the author of *Martín Fierro* (1872, 1879) the most famous poem in Argentine literature. Emilio Renzi and Daniel Hernández thus function as local creations of Holmes, Poirot, Watson, or Dupin, following the parodic deconstruction of the detective novel in *Seis problemas para don Isidro Parodi* (*Six Problems for Don Isidro Parodi*, 1941), by Jorge Luis Borges and Adolfo Bioy Casares, published under the pseudonym of H. Bustos Domecq. In *Seis problemas*, the detective Parodi ends up solving the crimes through the use of logic from his prison cell. Piglia discusses Borges (as well as Poe and others) and the detective genre in his *Crítica y ficción*.

In "La loca y el relato del crimen," Piglia's first detective story, the crime is solved thanks to Emilio Renzi's knowledge of sociolinguistics. He deciphers the story of the crime hidden in the madwoman's speech (random words and unrelated sentences within a psychotic repetition). If in Walsh's story, Daniel Hernández solved the enigma through language by calculating time—that is, the logical way—in Piglia's story, some Freudian elements of psychoanalysis are incorporated in order to solve the crime. The use of semiotics and psychoanalysis makes the process modern, although they do not take away from the traditional rules of the logical and scientifically oriented detective genre. Piglia's break with the rules consists of the story referring to itself, becoming apparently independent from the narrator (like the psychotic discourse of the madwoman, which works by itself), which produces a distancing effect. The process is quite original, with its mixture of intratextuality and the traditional rules of the genre that points to the self-conscious nature of the text that is paradigmatic of postmodern literature.

In "La loca y el relato del crimen," the character Rinaldi also appears. Rinaldi, a Uruguayan as revealed in "La caja de vidrio" (The glass box), also keeps a diary and is present throughout Piglia's work. In "La loca," Rinaldi is the parodied investigator, the detective who can't read, as opposed to Renzi. But in "Homenaje a Roberto Arlt," Rinaldi corrupts an innocent youth, Letiff, by taking charge of his criminal education. Between "Homenaje a Roberto Arlt" and "La loca y el relato del crimen" there are many of the same sentences repeated as individual pieces of a great labyrinth of writing. Their goal is to mark the inherent intratextuality of any discourse, and in a broader sense to show plagiarism as a constituent characteristic of literature.

One can say that Piglia's detective fiction poetics can be summarized into three main elements: (1) the parody of the genre, following Borges, both in its rational, classic form and in its "hard-boiled" form; (2) following Borges and Poe, the significance of the detective genre in its intersection with the problematic of narrative construction, of the relationship between history and fiction; and (3) the relationship between money, detective fiction, and writing as a capitalist product. Regarding this last problem, Piglia quotes Bertolt Brecht: "What is to rob a bank compared to founding it?" (*Crítica y ficción* 117). Piglia affirms that crime is always caused by money: murder, robbery, fraud, extortion, kidnapping, the chain is always economic (*Crítica y ficción* 116).

Undoubtedly, Piglia's first short stories are mostly characterized by their parodic nature, while his novels seek to develop and broaden his theoretical concerns. However, his novel *Plata quemada*, although it condenses his theoretical point of view shown throughout his works as a starting point, it evolves clearly as a hard-boiled thriller. Piglia first wrote the novel in 1970 about a bank robbery that occurred 1965. He researched all the details of the event in Buenos Aires and Uruguay, compiled materials, wrote the novel, and in the end did not like it, so he kept it in a box for two decades. The published text is a revised version of the original. Narrative elements that are new to the last few decades (and previously unseen in his own works) are readily noticeable in *Plata quemada*, such as a homoerotic theme, the underworld of drugs, the use of street slang, and the presentation of delinquency. The novel moves at the fast pace of a thriller, with no literary digressions. In this sense, the text more closely approximates the writing of hard-boiled author José Pablo Feinmann. It also highlights Piglia's concern with the money–literature relationship and, in a broader sense, with the value of money in a capitalist society. The robbers of *Plata quemada* burn the money they stole when they realize they are going to die. With this act, the criminals sublimate their condition as delinquents and bring the system to its knees. The novel, then, becomes symbolic and self-referential with the evaporation of the object, of its causality; in other words, with the characteristic decentered nature of the postmodern detective novel and its utopian discourse. *Plata quemada* thus become a puzzle-novel, as Piglia states: "los crímenes son 'gratuitos', justamente porque la gratuidad del móvil fortalece la complejidad del enigma" (crimes are gratuitous, precisely because the gratuity of the motive strengthens the complexity of the enigma (*Crítica y ficción* 116).

Clearly, Piglia's detective fiction and essays comprise one of the most important contributions to the genre as it is being currently developed in Argentina and throughout Latin America. In his fiction, one may observe the evolution of detective fiction from early models to postmodern parodies that signal the blurred boundaries of reality and fiction, history and narrative. In addition to his own fiction and essays, he also compiled one of the most important anthologies of Argentine detective fiction. His *Las fieras* (The beasts, 1993) was published as volume 6 of the *La muerte y la brújula* series edited by Jorge Lafforgue. His revised and much-expanded anthology *Las fieras: antología del género policial en la Argentina* (The beasts: Anthology of Argentine detective fiction) appeared in 1999.

Cristina Guzzo

Works

La ciudad ausente. Buenos Aires: Sudamericana, 1992. English version as *The Absent City*, trans. Sergio Gabriel Waisman. Durham, NC: Duke University Press, 2000.

Crítica y ficción. Buenos Aires: Siglo Veinte; Universidad Nacional del Litoral, 1976, 1990. Reprint, Buenos Aires: Seix Barral, 2000; Barcelona: Anagrama, 2001.

Las fieras, ed. R. Piglia. Buenos Aires: Clarín/Aguilar, 1993.

Las fieras: antología del género policial en la Argentina, ed. R. Piglia. Buenos Aires: Alfaguara, 1999. (Expanded version of previous item.)

"La loca y el relato del crimen," in *Cuentos policiales argentinos*, ed. Jorge Lafforgue. Buenos Aires: Alfaguara, 1997, 281–89. Also in *Variaciones en negro: relatos policiales iberoamericanos*, ed. Lucía López Coll and Leonardo Padura. Havana: Editorial Arte y Literatura, 2001, 97–106. English version as "The Crazy Woman and the Story of the Crime," in *New Tales of Mystery and Crime from Latin America*, ed. and trans. Amelia Simpson. Rutherford, NJ: Fairleigh Dickinson University Press, 1992, 23–30.

Nombre falso. Buenos Aires: Siglo XXI, 1975. Reprinted, Buenos Aires: Seix Barral, 1994. English version as *Assumed Name*, trans. Sergio Gabriel Waisman. Pittsburgh: Latin American Literary Review Press, 1995.

Nombre falso: edición definitiva. Buenos Aires: Seix Barral, 1997.

"Nota preliminar," (signed Emilio Renzi), in *Cuentos policiales de la Serie Negra.* Buenos Aires: Tiempo Contemporáneo, 1969.

"Notas sobre Macedonio en un diario." *Clarín, Suplemento Cultura y Nación* (12 September 1985): 1–3.

Plata quemada. Buenos Aires: Planeta, 1997. Reprint, Barcelona: Anagrama, 2000.

Prisión perpetua. Buenos Aires: Sudamericana, 1988.

"La prolijidad de lo real." *Punto de vista* 3 (1978): 26–28.

Respiración artificial. Buenos Aires: Pomaire, 1980. Reprint, Buenos Aires: Sudamericana, 1988; Barcelona: Anagrama, 2001. English version as *Artificial Respiration*, trans. Daniel Balderston. Durham, NC: Duke University Press, 1994.

"Roberto Arlt: la ficción del dinero." *Hispamérica* 3.7 (1974): 25–28.

"La vida está llena de cosas así," in *Variaciones en negro: relatos policiales hispanoamericanos*, ed. Lucía López Coll. Bogotá: Norma, 2003, 139–52.

Criticism

Avelar, Idelber. "Cómo respiran los ausentes: la narrativa de Ricardo Piglia." *MLN* [Modern Language Notes] 110.2 (1995): 416–32.

Balderston, Daniel. "'La verdad de la historia': History and Fiction in Ricardo Piglia's *Respiración artificial*," in *El Cono Sur: Dinámica y dimensiones de su literatura. A Symposium*, ed. Rose S. Minc. Upper Montclair, NJ: Montclair State College, 1985, 82–86

Berg, Edgardo. "La búsqueda del archivo familiar: notas de lectura sobre *Respiración artificial* de Ricardo Piglia." *Confluencia* 10.1 (1994): 45–56.

Bravo, Víctor. "El relato policiaco postmoderno: tres novelas argentinas contemporáneas." *Espéculo: revista de estudios literarios* 9 (1998): n.p.

Colás, Santiago. "Resuscitating History in *Respiración artificial*," in *Postmodernity in Latin America. The Argentine Paradigm*. Durham, NC: Duke University Press, 1994, 121–57.

De Grandis, Rita. "Enmendar la lectura," in *Polémicas y estrategias narrativas en América Latina*. Rosario, Argentina: Beatriz Viterbo, 1993, 121–48.

Fornet, Jorge. "'Homenaje a Roberto Arlt': o, la literatura como plagio." *Nueva revista de filología hispánica* 42.1 (1994): 115–41.

Gandolfo, Elvio. "Entrevista a Ricardo Piglia." Suplemento *Radar. Página 12* (13 October 1996).

Gnutzmann, Rita. "Ricardo Piglia o la crítica literaria como relato detectivesco," in *Literatura como intertextualidad: IX Simposio Internacional de Literatura*, ed. Juana Alcira Arancibia. Buenos Aires: Instituto Literario y Cultural Hispánico, 1993, 523–31.

Iglesia, Cristina. "Crimen y castigo: las reglas del juego. Notas sobre *La ciudad ausente* de Ricardo Piglia." *Filología* 29.1–2 (1996): 95–103.

Kaplan, Marina. "Between Arlt and Borges: An Interview with Ricardo Piglia." *New Orleans Review* 16.2 (1989): 64–85. (Includes excerpt of *Artificial Respiration*.)

Kolesnicov, Patricia. "El dinero y la literatura, según Ricardo Piglia." *Clarín* (6 November 1997): 26. (Interview.)

Link, Daniel. "Carta de Argentina: historia y novela negra." *Cuadernos hispanoamericanos* 575 (1998): 109–18.

Maristany, José Javier. *Narraciones peligrosas: Resistencia y adhesión en las novelas del Proceso*. Buenos Aires: Biblos, 1999, 55–105.

McCraken, Ellen. "Metaplagiarism and the Critic's Role as Detective: Ricardo Piglia's Reinvention of Roberto Arlt." *PMLA* 106 (1991): 1071–82.

Newman, Kathleen. "Historical novel in the Post-Boom Novel," in *The Historical Novel in Latin America*, ed. Daniel Balderston. Gaithersburg, MD: Hispamérica, 1986, 209–19.

Rivarola, José Luis, and Susana Reisz de Rivarola. "Semántica del discurso referido," in *Homenaje a Ana María Barrenechea*, ed. Lía Lerner Schwarz and Isaías Lerner. Madrid: Castalia, 1984.

Rivera, Jorge B., ed. "Introducción," in *El relato policial en la Argentina*. Buenos Aires: Eudeba, 1986, 9–41.

Roffé, Reina. "Entrevista a Ricardo Piglia." *Cuadernos hispanoamericanos* 607 (2001): 97–111.

Romano-Thuesen, Evelia. "Macedonio Fernández: su teoría de la novela en *La ciudad ausente* de Ricardo Piglia." *Alba de América* 12.22–23 (1994): 213–26.

San Miguel, Ana López. "La Historia en *Respiración Artificial*." *Hispanic Journal* 15.2 (1994): 321–33.

Spiller, Roland. "Tres detectives literarios de la nueva novela argentina: Martini, Piglia, Rabanal," in *Río de la Plata: Culturas* 11–12 (1991): 361–69.

Mónica Plöese (b. 1962)

ARGENTINA

Mónica Plöese was born in Buenos Aires in 1962. She studied literature at the Universidad del Salvador, and she is the author of, so far, two novels that form part of a projected detective series called "Los Crímenes del Zodíaco" (The crimes of the zodiac). As the title of the series suggests, each novel is based on one of the zodiacal signs. The first two books are *El muerto quiere saber de qué se trata* (The dead man wants to know what it's all about, 1999) and *La curiosidad mató al hombre* (Curiosity killed the man, 1999). Plöese's narrative project represents several innovations in Argentine, and by extension Latin American detective fiction. In addition to being one of very few women who write in the genre, and the only one (of whom I am aware) who so far has written exclusively detective fiction, she is the creator of Irene Adler, perhaps the first recurring woman-detective character. Furthermore, the premise of her fiction, that crimes are both related to and can be solved through astrology, is also a fairly original approach to the genre in Latin America. This topic has been presented in the past; one instance that immediately comes to mind is Adolfo Pérez Zelaschi's story "El banquero, la muerte y la luna" (The banker, death, and the moon), which like Plöese's second novel also involves twins. However, Plöese is the only Latin American author whose entire detective series is based on astrology.

Each novel provides a list of the cast of characters, which is helpful because there are many and they are all either related or connected in some way. Many characters in the first novel, in addition to Adler, reappear in the second. There are 28 characters listed as participants in *El muerto quiere saber de qué se trata.* The somewhat complicated relationships between them all give the book an almost soap opera–like quality. There are scattered footnotes throughout to help the uninformed reader decipher the astrological signifiers in text. As *El muerto* is the first book of the series, the reader is introduced to Adler, who herself is introduced to the world of crime-solving when her mentor, Fernando Soria, dies in an accident in Buenos Aires. Soria was a Spanish psychoanalyst who specialized in criminal profiling through astrology. He was also, like Adler, a member of the Asociación para la Recuperación de la Memoria (Association for the recovery of memory), founded by the psychologist Stella Campos, another of the characters. This mystery surrounding his death leads to a series of successive events that motivate Adler to solve the case, of course using her training in astrology.

In *La curiosidad mató al hombre*, Irene Adler picks up essentially where the last novel left off. Not only do characters from the previous novel reappear, but there are also references to the previous mystery. Again, there are more footnotes to guide the reader and, in addition, there are a number of textual references and even quotations from other authors' works. For example, one of the characters, Celina Stern, a psychologist, quotes Marcos Aguinis's text *El elogio de la culpa* (In praise of guilt, 1993) in an essay she is preparing on her computer. The most interesting aspect of the text is the way Plöese manages to combine astrology and Greek mythology with indigenous mythology. As the second book, *La curiosidad* is associated with the sign of Gemini, the twins. The theme of twins, then, runs throughout the text. The author melds the Greek legend of the Dioscuri (Castor and Pollux, the twins sons of Leda who were transformed into the constellation Gemini) and the Guaraní legend of the twins Kuarahy and Jasy. The mystery takes place between Buenos Aires and Asunción, which explains the Guaraní influence, since Paraguayan culture is imbued with Guaraní tradition. The cast of characters is again lengthy. The majority belong to the Adler, Chornik, and Stern families—all relatives of Irene Adler. The structure of the novel is quite different from the first. *La curiosidad* takes place over the span of one month, July. Time is carefully registered over the course of the narration, which has much to do with the development of the novel. The text is divided into brief narrative sections that are headed by the place, date, and time. For example, the novel begins on 3 July at 8:00 in Asunción, and ends on 1 August at 6:30 in Asunción, as Adler waits for her plane. In between, the action takes place among Asunción, Areguá, and Buenos Aires.

The novels do not adhere to the hard-boiled tradition. There is none of the violence, underworld ambience, rough language, or mistrust of authority that are characteristic of the hard-boiled novel. While they may be described as light-reading entertainment, this should not be construed as a negative. One can emphasize, again, that Plöese's texts are innovative contributions to Latin American detective fiction, even a refreshing change-of-pace.

Darrell B. Lockhart

Works

La curiosidad mató al hombre. Buenos Aires: Norma, 1999.
El muerto quiere saber de qué se trata. Buenos Aires: Norma, 1999.

Syria Poletti (1921–1991)

ARGENTINA

Syria Poletti was born in Italy but moved to Argentina in 1945. Her childhood was described as magical, marked by sudden changes and peopled with unusual beings. Her adolescence was affected by illness and poverty. Her first experiences in rural Argentina made her aware of the difficulties faced by the Italian immigrants in Argentina. She later moved to Buenos Aires. In the big city, she began her career as a journalist. She is the author of several novels, short stories, children's books, and numerous essays. When her novel *Gente conmigo* (People with me) was published in 1962, it became a bestseller and won Poletti two distinguished prizes. Her short story "Rojo en la salina" (Red in the salt pit) was one of Jorge Luis Borges's favorite stories.

Poletti is one of the first Latin American authors who wrote about the conflicts of Italian immigrants in Argentina: the way family relationships are affected by the loss of tradition, separation of family members due to the workplace, the condition of women in the new society, the problems of adaptation. Older women become important characters in her fiction, providing a role model for the younger generations. Her narratives also include children, their voices providing an important point-of-view in the stories.

Syria Poletti was one of the first women in Latin America to write detective fiction, and she used the genre to reflect on the problems faced by women and immigrants in Argentina after the Second World War. Her short story "Rojo en la salina" first appeared in 1964 in a collection that included works by Borges, Donald Yates, and Adolfo Bioy Casares, among others. Poletti's story has an interesting cinematic style and, despite sharp differences, recalls Julio Cortázar's short story "Blow Up." In Poletti's story, a painting done by a twelve-year-old girl becomes the plot's principal clue. Here the author follows the classic conventions of the detective story: the crime, the clues, the suspects, and the puzzles are there, but never the solution. Like the antidetection stories of Borges and Robbes-Gillet, "Rojo en la salina" underscores the limits of knowledge, and supports Poletti's contention that "intelligence and reasoning alone are not enough to solve any mystery. What is needed is a keen knowledge of human nature, as a fundamental perception of the complexities of human foibles and experiences." The author states in an interview:

> My stories are not real detective stories in the classical or traditional sense but rather psychological tales. In the collection *Historias en rojo* (Stories in scarlet) there is a common denominator: to investigate who was responsible for the crime in order to reveal the mysteries of being. It is more important to know why one kills rather than knowing how a crime is discovered. (*Taller de imaginería*; my translation)

"Rojo en la salina" is set in Patagonia, the Argentine desert. It is a story of love and deceit, a study in blindness, a dark-sided version of married life. The protagonist is a woman who becomes her own private detective, and her detection leads to self-revealing truths that simultaneously open up for the reader a world of ambiguities and a sense of the complexities of human relationships. While the protagonist's young daughter Yessy becomes an important accomplice in the unraveling of events that led to the murder, the woman's tragedy at the end is that she must blind herself to the truth she has just gleaned. The sad experiences shared by mother and daughter bond them together, transforming the traditional detective fiction plot into something altogether different.

The other stories in this collection also investigate not only murder but life as it is lived on many levels. Poletti is particularly fond of portraying adolescent and adult female characters. She has stated in *Taller de imaginería*: "In particular, I am interested in mysteries of women and adolescents. They are the constants of my work" (my translation). In the short story "Mala suerte" (Bad luck), murder and those suspected of murder open a young adolescent's eyes to the sordid and violent side of life. Here again, a mother is the victim of secret vices and passions that surface in violence. As in some of the other stories, in "Mala suerte" Poletti presents the uneasy relations among family members, usually Italian immigrants living in Argentina. They are passionate characters who struggle to endure life, and while managing to keep one another's spirits up, they create and try to preserve something out of the pieces of their lives, to establish connections with others.

Poletti's protagonists are sturdy. They have to come to terms with change and loss resulting from violent murder, and yet they always struggle to preserve something from life. The police usually reach the wrong conclusions here, so the families must protect themselves from danger. In "El hombre de las vasijas de barro" (The man of the clay vessels), the prime suspect is mentally retarded, and even when the case seems closed, an older woman, who tries to prove that the poor man is innocent, finds out herself who the real killer and rapist is. The young women or adolescents who narrate these stories try to find answers to both the criminal and existential matters that have been puzzling them.

Historias en rojo is an intelligent, sympathetic, and sometimes ironical look at life in Argentina and its struggle with the past. Poletti skillfully weaves her plots so that we constantly suspend judgment. She is a perceptive reader of character, with a broad understanding of human behavior. As British detective fiction writer P. D. James is quoted as saying: "What gives any mystery writer the claim to be regarded as a serious novelist is the power to create a sense of place and to make it as real to the reader as his won living room-and then to people it with characters who are suffering men and women, not stereotypes to be knocked down like dummies in the final chapter" (*New York Times Book Review*, January 28, 1990).

Poletti has written many works for children: we should mention *El juguete misterioso* and *El misterio de las valijas verdes*. Although written for a younger audience, these books have all the elements of detective fiction: mystery and suspense being the most important ones. Poletti had a special sensitivity for writing children's stories and she successfully combined her different styles and inclinations. The author died in Buenos Aires in 1991.

Flora H. Schiminovich

Works

Gente conmigo. Buenos Aires: Losada, 1962.
Historias en rojo. Buenos Aires: Calatayud, 1967. Reprint, Buenos Aires: Losada, 1978.
El juguete misterioso. Buenos Aires: Sigmar, 1977.
El misterio de las valijas verdes. Buenos Aires: Plus Ultra, 1978.
"Rojo en la salina," in *Cuentos policiales*, ed. Fermín Fevre. Buenos Aires: Kapelusz, 1974, 124–50.
Taller de imaginería. Buenos Aires: Losada, 1977.

Criticism

Castelli, Eugenio. "La palabra-mito en las novelas de Syria Poletti." *Sur* 348 (1981): 101–7.
Correas de Zapata, Celia. *Ensayos hispanoamericanos.* Buenos Aires: Corregidor, 1978.
Dunn, Kelly Anne. "Representative Detective Fiction Writers from Mexico and Argentina: Socio-Political Factors and Literary Context." Doctoral dissertation, University of Virginia, 1999.
Gardini, Walter. *Syria Poletti, mujer de dos mundos.* Buenos Aires: Dante Alighieri, 1994.
Hernández-Araico, Susana. "Syria Poletti," in *Spanish American Women Writers*, ed. Diane E. Marting. Westport, CT: Greenwood Press, 1990, 461–71.
Martella, Gianna M. "Pioneers: Spanish American Women Writers of Detective Fiction." *Letras femeninas* 28.1 (2002): 31–44.
Martínez, Victoria. "El acto de investigar: el rol de la mujer en la literatura policial de la Argentina y los Estados Unidos," in *Primeras jornadas internacionales de literatura argentina/comparatística. Actas.* Buenos Aires: Facultad de Filosofía y Letras, Universidad de Buenos Aires, 1995, 425–30.
Mathieu, Corina S. "Syria Poletti, intérprete de la realidad argentina." *Sin nombre* [Puerto Rico] 13.3 (1983): 87–93.
Schiminovich, Flora. "Two Argentine Female Writers Perfect the Art of Detection: María Angélica Bosco y Syria Poletti." *Review: Latin American Literature and Arts* 42 (1990): 16–21.
Tcachuk, Alexandra. "Conversación con Syria Poletti." *Hispania* 65.1 (1982): 125–27.
Titiev, Janice Geasler. "Structure as a Feminist Statement in the Fiction of Syria Poletti." *Letras femeninas* 15.1–2 (1989): 48–58.

Rafael Ramírez Heredia (b. 1942)

MEXICO

An essayist, playwright, novelist, short-story writer, chronicler, and professor, Rafael Ramírez Heredia began writing during 1962–63 while studing accounting. As a freelance author, he wrote for the Mexican publications *Excélsior*, *Unomásuno*, and *Ovaciones*. He has also been a professor of Mexican history and Spanish literature, and he currently directs several literary workshops. Ramírez Heredia's own literary production has been influenced by writers as diverse as Henry Miller, Ernest Hemingway, Franz Kafka, James Joyce, Chester Himes, Malcolm Lowry, Gabriel García Márquez, Julio Cortázar, Jaime Sabines, Juan Rulfo, Agustín Yáñez, Carlos Fuentes, Vicente Leñero, and Ramón López Velarde. His first book, *El enemigo* (The enemy) was published in 1965. Ramírez Heredia has won several prestigious literary prizes, including the Juan Rulfo (1984), the Juan Ruiz de Alarcón (1990), and the Rafael Bernal (1993).

Ramírez Heredia claims that at the beginning of his literary career he was neither popular nor well-known and that his books were only published in Mexico. However, following the publication of *El Rayo Macoy* (Rayo Macoy, 1984) he began to gain more recognition and his books began to sell. According to the author, his novels *Trampas de metal* (Metal traps, 1979) and *Muerte en la carretera* (Death on the highway, 1985) belong to the thriller genre. Furthermore, he claims that his "detective-thriller" literary production belongs to a marginal period when he was writing such books merely for entertainment. Nevertheless, critics such as Reinhard Teichmann and Vicente Francisco Torres seem to agree that these two texts may be classified as detective novels.

Ramírez Heredia frequently uses such literary devices and topics as humor, irony, sarcasm, parody, vulgar and colloquial language, flashbacks, provincial settings (particularly Tamaulipas), travel motifs, political figures, and film legends to portray underground and corrupt spaces, to denounce political dishonesty, and to reprimand the exploitation of marginalized, subaltern individuals who are utilized as commodities and myths in society.

According to Teichmann, in *Trampas de metal* and *Muerte en la carretera*, Ramírez Heredia introduces one of the first literary Mexican detectives in the character of Ifigenio Clausel. Clausel is portrayed as an individual who loves tacos, alcoholic beverages, and women. He is described as a detective and individual who lacks both intuition and intelligence, but who is very agreeable and very different from the typical American and British detectives.

Muerte en la carretera narrates the murder of a congressman, Silvino Arruza. The novel portrays the Mexican ideology of power and the corruption of politicians. Furthermore, it depicts the need to uncover the truth and determine the inner workings of the judicial and political systems. By way of using a narrator who also participates in the story, flashbacks, and humor, the author is able to present the themes of travel, class struggle, political conflicts (among the diverse

Mexican political parties), corruption, political blackmail, issues of identity, popular culture, and environmental criticism. As a detective fiction writer, Ramírez Heredia makes reference in *Muerte* to other Mexican detective novels such as *El complot mongol* (The mongol plot, 1969) by Rafael Bernal and *La cabeza de la hidra* (*The Hydra Head*, 1978) by Carlos Fuentes. In addition, Ramírez Heredia discusses the role of a private detective within this genre. Following Mempo Giardinelli's definition of the detective genre, *Muerte en la carreterra* is a novel that meets all the requirements that constitute a typical detective novel.

In *Muerte*, private detective Ifigenio Clausel is hired by Justino Cabrera, a congressman, to investigate a murder case. Clausel plays the role of a detective who is not afraid of showing his vices nor his virtues. He is portrayed as humorous, violent, tranquil, astute, observant, and an extremely meticulous investigator. These personality traits are inferred in the text by Clausel's actions: his constant use of a pen to jot down notes, his obsession with observing the time, his careful descriptions, his attention to detail, and his suspicions and intuitions.

As a novel of social criticism, *Muerte* exposes the dirty and corrupt world of politics in which individuals are willing to go to any length (even murder) in order to maintain power. Clausel discovers this by talking to the character Cabrera, who states, "En política todo es posible" (Everything is possible in politics [64]). The characters Silvino Arruza and Justino Cabrera bring to life all the problems of the contemporary Mexican political system. These two men symbolize the corrupt and unscrupulous government to which they belong.

Muerte may be considered a detective novel according to Torres's definition, because it includes an urban setting, a concern for social problems, vulgar language, and a sordid environment. The cities in the text are Mexico City, Pachuca, Tampico, Madero, and a few towns located in the state of Chiapas. The social concerns presented are pollution, corruption, class struggle, and discrimination against homosexuals. Billingsgate is reflected through plays on words, colloquial slang, and language that is replete with idiosyncrasies that reflect the educational level and social class of the speaker. The sordid spaces are the nightclubs and underground places where corruption, seduction, blackmail, violence, eroticism, drugs, and alcohol are always present.

The fact that Clausel is both a character and narrator functions to create a novel with constant tension, adventures, action, road trips, and conundrums. In addition, this technique demystifies the role of the detective and reveals the author's concern for an obsolete social, ideological, economical, moral, and political system. In sum, Ramírez Heredia uses the detective genre to judge and analyze the way in which Mexican society deals with its problems, struggles, and conflicts.

In "Junto a Tampico" (Near Tampico), a short story from *De tacones y gabardina* (In high heels and a raincoat, 1996), Ramírez Heredia invents a new detective, named Gurrola. "Junto a Tampico" was awarded the Detective Short Story National Prize. It narrates the story of a serial killer and his victims in the port of Tampico, Mexico. As in his other detective works, the author uses humor, flashbacks, mass media, irony, parody, tension, and colloquial language to depict provincial society, to ridicule the role of private detectives, and to introduce the crimes against young women at the hand of a sadistic individual. The most readily identifiable elements in the story include feminine discourse, gender struggle, political corruption coupled with crime, identity issues, regionalist points of view, provincial scenery, the oppressive heat of the setting, and the demand and hope for social justice. It is important to highlight that in this work, Ramírez Heredia allows women to acquire a voice and attain rights that seem to be silenced and ignored in his other detective works.

Like *Muerte*, "Junto a Tampico" belongs to the detective genre because it includes an eccentric detective protagonist and offers a statement of social criticism. Gurrola, as the only private detective in town, is in charge of investigating the murder of two women killed in a sordid area of the city. Both victims were in their early twenties and were killed in a similar manner, by having their throats cut. Gurrola is portrayed as a humorous, dull, and tranquil individual who falls into his own trap. By doing so, the author elaborates an ingenious conclusion to the story as revealed in the line, "alguien lo tomó por el cuello y antes de caer al río supo que el cuchillo de pescador había hecho un corte limpio" (someone took him by the neck and before he fell into the river, he realized that the fisherman's knife had made a clean cut [51]). By having the detective Gurrola killed, Ramírez Heredia not only pokes fun at and parodies the role of detectives, but also questions their ability and cleverness to solve crimes.

As a social critique, "Junto a Tampico" represents a feminine struggle for social justice and personal safety in the city. It is women who take to the streets and protest to demand the capture of the murderer. Nevertheless, on an allegorical level, what these events truly symbolize is the acquisition of a feminine voice. Furthermore, it shows how murder is utilized to exercise hegemony over marginalized groups such as women and the indigent. In sum, "Junto a Tampico" is a detective story that in spite of its inverted circumstances, is an evaluation of Mexican politics and crime. Thus, the two elements are seen to go hand-in-hand.

If in *Muerte en la carretera* the author presents a national murder case and in "Junto a Tampico" a local one, in *Con M de Marilyn* (With an M as in Marilyn, 1997) he goes on to narrate an international conspiracy. In addition, Ramírez Heredia's detectives have in common a passion for women. In *Muerte*, Clausel is infatuated with Rosaura, while Gurrola in "Junto" has a sexual fixation on Esthela and José Baños in *Con M* is obssessed with Marilyn Monroe. However, the case of Baños allows one to see how men tend to idealize women and be dumbfounded by their feminine beauty.

Con M is a novel that narrates Marilyn Monroe's visit to Mexico in 1961 and that depicts the Mexican film industry, its movie stars and legends. Ramírez Heredia utilizes the myth of Marilyn Monroe to create a detective novel whose narrative structure is based on the use of flashbacks, humor, history, films, and popular culture. The narration is carried out on two levels: on one, the reader is afforded the biography and frustrations of marginalized individuals like Baños, who at first is depicted as sort of a loser, but who later is given recognition thanks to his supposed friendship with the "Goddess"; on a second level, the reader becomes aware of the personal and mysterious life of Marilyn Monroe and begins to question the real reasons behind her death.

Con M de Marilyn is a text full of conspiracies, lies, sex, drugs, clues, and spies. It is also a novel in which the reader is taken on a tour through the past, particularly through the social, economical, political, and ideological era of the early 1960s in three different countries: the United States, Mexico, and Cuba. The only perspective provided throughout the novel is that of José Baños, whose point-of-view not only identifies Marilyn Monroe as a bimbo, but which demythifies the stigma of being considered a rather dumb and promiscuous woman. Thus, *Con M* not only serves to deconstruct the ideal image of Marilyn Monroe on a textual level, but on a metaphorical level, it deconstructs the image and voice of women in postmodern Mexican society.

The protagonists of *Con M* are the new detective José Baños and the famously controversial icon and sexual symbol of American popular culture, Marilyn Monroe. Both Baños and Monroe are used by a third protagonist, the American government. Baños is exploited by becoming a spy whose task is to reveal secrets and political writings that are found in the personal diary of the "Goddess," whereas Marilyn Monroe is exploited by becoming a commodity of the American president and film directors.

As a fan of Marilyn Monroe, Baños uses his contacts as a journalist to obtain a personal interview with her. Through the interview, Baños has the opportunity to get acquainted with Marilyn Monroe and this leads him to have a fictional affair with her. However, what he does not realize is that he is being used and set up by the American government that hopes to uncover the political denunciation Marilyn Monroe has written in her diary and which she has planned to make public at a press conference once she returns to the United States. By doing so, Marilyn wants to be heard and taken seriously concerning politics. She is also aware of the U.S. government's plans against Cuba and, therefore, she feels compelled to speak in support of Cubans. Needless to say, the government does not allow it to happen and thus is implied to be behind her mysterious death. Marilyn Monroe and José Baños are silenced when both tried to reveal a conspiracy against Cuba.

As a novel of social critique, *Con M* functions to denounce the abuse of women's bodies in order to satisfy the erotic and lascivious needs of patriarchal capitalist societies (American and Mexican). It also censures the exploitation of marginalized individuals such as Baños, the use of popular myths (Marilyn Monroe) as a mechanism of exercising control over the masses, the corruption of politicians, and the struggle for power in order to silence and dominate individuals who lack that power and voice (José Baños and Marilyn Monroe).

In addition, the narrator allows Baños to acquire a voice whose intention is to offer the reader his own point-of-view about the Mexican film industry and the mysterious death of Marilyn Monroe. Thus, one is privy only to Baños's hypotheses and conclusions regarding the reasons underlying the alleged suicide of Marilyn Monroe. Through his novel, Ramírez Heredia presents the voice of a victim—Baños—as an allegory of individuals who have been victims of political corruption and capitalist society. It also depicts the exploitation of women's bodies as well as their weaknesses and the way in which human beings are repressed when they dare to transgress the status quo.

In conclusion, Ramírez Heredia utilizes the detective genre as a literary resource to portray a crude reality that truly reflects the idiosyncrasies of contemporary Mexican society, namely violence, vulgar language, a seedy underworld culture, class struggle, economic crisis, political corruption, the use of women as commodities, the exploitation of subaltern individuals, repression, degradation, dehumanization, and ideological and moral crisis. Furthermore, one perceives that the solitude of Ramírez's detectives on an allegorical level represents a lack of integration into a society that does nothing but repress and silence the needs and rights of human beings, as well as a lack of trust in the Mexican political system.

Juan Antonio Serna

Works

Con M de Marilyn. Mexico City: Alfaguara, 1997.
De tacones y gabardina. Mexico City: Alfaguara, 1996.
El enemigo. Mexico City: Costa-Amic, 1965.
"Eso dicen," in Variaciones en negro: relatos policiales iberoamericanos, ed. Lucía López Coll and Leonardo Padura. Havana: Editorial Arte y Literatura, 2001, 229–42.
Muerte en la carretera. Mexico City: Joaquín Mortiz, 1985.
El Rayo Macoy. Mexico City: Joaquín Mortiz, 1984.
"No son, pero son," in Cuentos policiacos mexicanos: lo mejor del género en nuestro país, ed. Paco Ignacio Taibo II and Víctor Ronquillo. Mexico City: Selector, 1997, 17–32.
Trampa de metal. Mexico City: Editorial Universo, 1979.

Criticism

Giardinelli, Mempo. El género negro: ensayos sobre literatura policial. Mexico City: Universidad Autónoma Metropolitana, 1984.
Segura, Gerardo. "La parábola del detective: interrogatorio a Rafael Ramírez Heredia," in Todos somos culpables: entrevistas con escritores policiacos mexicanos. Saltillo, Coahuila: Instituto Coahuilense de Cultura, 1996, 63–71.
Serna, Juan Antonio. "Marilyn Monroe: la política del cuerpo en Con M de Marilyn de Rafael Ramírez Heredia," in Pensamiento y crítica: los discursos de la cultura hoy, ed. Javier Durán, Rosaura Hernández Monroy, and Manuel F. Medina. East Lansing: Michigan State University, University of Louisville, Centro de Cultura Casa Lamm, 2000, 264–69.
Teichmann, Reinhard. De la onda en adelante: conversaciones con 21 novelistas mexicanos. Mexico City: Editorial Posada, 1987.
Torres, Vicente Francisco. Esta narrativa mexicana: ensayos y entrevistas. Mexico City: Leega, S.A., 1991.
Trujillo Muñoz, Gabriel. Testigos de cargo: la narrativa policiaca mexicana y sus autores. Tijuana, Mexico: CONACULTA/CECUT, 2000, 67–71.

Bertha Recio Tenorio (b. circa 1950)

CUBA

Bertha Recio Tenorio was born in Bayamo, Cuba. She studied journalism at the University of Havana and has worked as a journalist and interpreter. Her incursion into the field of detective fiction writing appears to have been concentrated during the 1980s when she enjoyed a reasonable measure of success. In 1980, her novel *Una vez más* (One more time) was awarded first prize in the Concurso Aniversario de la Revolución (Anniversary of the revolution literary contest) sponsored by MININT (Ministry of the interior). And in 1986, *Cuentos para una noche lluviosa* (Stories for a rainy night) received top honors for short stories in the same state-sponsored competition, while *Un hombre honorable* (An honorable man) received first honorable mention in the short-story category. Her literary efforts earned her the Raúl Gómez García medal from the Sindicato Nacional de Trabajadores de la Cultura (National cultural workers union). Her work, to date, has not been translated into English.

Recio Tenorio's works conform strictly to the tenets set by MININT, in that all works in the detective genre should be didactic in nature and further awareness, and prevention, of all antisocial and counterrevolutionary activities, and whose basic theme should be the struggle against manifestations of social inadequacy and the persistence of vices from the past. Both the novel and short stories explore criminal activities set against the backdrop of actively mobilized, vigilant masses; the transgressors stand out immediately due to their nonconformist ways.

Una vez más may be characterized as a testimonial novel in which presumably real documents, reports, records, interviews, and court proceedings are intercalated so as to better reconstruct the story, lending an air of documentary authenticity. The novel is divided into an alternating number of sections corresponding to the voice of the first murder victim, the written and oral reports of the anonymous investigator, the written and oral reports of the informant coerced into cooperation by the Department of State Security, and transcripts of the judicial hearings of the defendants. Documents are carefully numbered and chronology is meticulously metered. The introduction of each character is immediately followed by an evaluation by the investigating official and his co-workers (this is, as are most Cuban fictional crime investigations, a collaborative effort) as to his or her appearance, personality, work habits, and social conduct. The classification of protagonists is Manichean in nature—characters are good, upstanding Socialists or degenerate, foreign-affiliated antirevolutionaries. This most dogmatic of her writings ends with a final report and summation by the collaborator: "Before me lay a new path, thanks to the generosity of the Revolution, which had pardoned my sins."

Her short stories are more polished in their structure and development and are connected through the recurrence of detective figure Lt. Dionisio Darias. Darias is a somber and efficient policeman who provides little commentary as to how the various cases are progressing. Evidence is gathered, witnesses and suspects are questioned, informants' claims are considered, and the case is solved, usually with the guilty party becoming unraveled or being felled by a karate chop to the neck. Resolution of the case is invariably the result of a collaborative effort by Darias, nameless colleagues, and concerned vigilant citizens whose observations about their neighbors are accepted unquestioningly by the authorities. Crimes as disparate as murder and stolen chickens are dealt with uniformly: each is an expression of antirevolutionary behavior motivated by a morally corrupt attitude.

Linda S. Zee

Works

Aterrizaje forzoso (with Carmen González). Havana: Letras Cubanas, 1981.
Cuentos para una noche lluviosa. Havana: Letras Cubanas, 1989.
Un hombre honorable. Havana: Letras Cubanas, 1985.
Una vez más. Havana: Letras Cubanas, 1980.

Víctor Ronquillo (b. 1959)

MEXICO

Víctor Ronquillo was born in Mexico City in 1959. He holds a degree in Spanish language and literature from the Universidad Nacional Autónoma de México (National autonomous university of mexico). In 1984, he began work as a journalist for the cultural section of the newspaper *El Nacional* (The national). He has also worked for *El Universal* (Universal), doing special reports and reviews of rock music, the magazine *Memoria de papel* (Paper memory), and finally the newspaper *Reforma* (Reform). Likewise, he works for T.V. Azteca and other television stations doing special reports on national life, and on violence in all its manifestations. His experience as a journalist has led him to specialize in the dynamics of violence in contemporary Mexico. His investigations have led to books such as *La muerte viste de rosa* (Death wears pink, 1994), about the murder of gay men in southern Mexico, the compilation *La nota roja de los años 50s* (Red journalism in the 1950s, 1993), which gathers the principal police cases of the decade; *La guerra oculta. Historias de impunidad y abusos de poder* (The hidden war. Stories of impunity and abuses of power, 1996), on the ties between power and crime and the traffic of influence; and *Las muertas de Juárez* (The dead women of Juárez, 1998), which addresses the most famous Mexican case of a serial killer (or band of killers) that for years has preyed on the border city.

In each of his investigations, Ronquillo has brought to light crimes that have been purposely overlooked by the authorities because, in the majority of cases, the structures of power have been involved. His first book, *El caso Molinet* (The Molinet case, 1992)—written with Paco Ignacio Taibo II—is a firm denouncement of the Mexican judicial system that prefers to create scapegoats instead of recognizing its errors and ignorance. The case of Pablo Molinet—a famous cause that united a large number of Mexican intellectuals and human-rights organizations—revolved around his unjust and illegal arrest, trial, and imprisonment. He was accused of murdering the household maid because heavy-metal music and Stephen King novels were found in his room. Ronquillo closely followed the case and detailed its progress until Molinet was finally freed and completely exonerated two years later.

In 1997, Víctor Ronquillo was chosen as the Mexican representative of the International Detective Fiction Writers Association. In that capacity he compiled—again, with Taibo—the collection of stories *Cuentos policiacos mexicanos* (Mexican detective stories, 1997). It is the first anthology that brings together contemporary writers of the genre; that is, the generation of Taibo and the one that followed (authors born after 1955). The anthology contains stories by both Taibo and Ronquillo in addition to Rafael Ramírez Heredia, Myriam Laurini, and Gabriel Trujillo Muñoz, among others.

Ronquillo accepts that his fascination with the dark side of life—murder, suicide, crime—is an inexhaustible source for his literature in which all Mexicans can contemplate their reflection—the collective face of Mexico and its identity.

Gabriel Trujillo Muñoz

Works

El caso Molinet (with Paco Ignacio Taibo II). Mexico City: Difusión Editorial, 1992.

Cuentos policiacos mexicanos (edited with Paco Ignacio Taibo II). Mexico City: Selector, 1997.

La guerra oculta. Historias de impunidad y abusos de poder. Mexico City: Espasa-Calpe Mexicana, 1996.

"La mala broma de 'El Colombiano,'" in *Cuentos policiacos mexicanos*, 131–45.

Las muertas de Juárez. Mexico City: Planeta, 1998.

La muerte viste de rosa. Mexico City: Ediciones Roca, 1994.

La nota roja de los años 50s. Mexico City: Diana, 1993.

Criticism

Segura, Gerardo. "La belleza de la amistad: interrogatorio a Víctor Ronquillo," in *Todos somos culpables: entrevistas con escritores policiacos mexicanos.* Saltillo, Coahuila: Instituto Coahuilense de Cultura, 1996, 73–80.

Juan Sasturain (b. 1945)

ARGENTINA

Juan Sasturain, born in Adolfo González Chaves (Province of Buenos Aires) in 1945, is an active participant in several different areas of Argentine cultural production. He is a professor of literature, having taught at the University of Buenos Aires and the University of Rosario. However, he has mostly earned a living as a journalist—becoming one of the most prominent in the profession by working in one capacity or another, from freelance contributor to editor. His articles on a vast array of topics, have appeared in practically all the major newspapers of Buenos Aires including: *Clarín* (The bugle), *La Opinión* (Opinion), *Tiempo Argentino* (Argentine times), and *Página 12* (Page 12), to name a few. In addition to journalism, he has also made an impact in areas of popular culture, working extensively in comics and graphic humor. Most notable in this area is his *Perramus* (1982–89), the comic he created together with the illustrator Alberto Breccia. It has been collected in four volumes, published in many different countries in Europe and in the United States, and in 1988 won an award from Amnesty International. He is also the author of *El domicilio de la aventura* (The domicile of adventure, 1995), a history of graphic humor in Argentina. Moreover, he is a fiction writer whose works include four detective novels: *Manual de perdedores 1* (Manual for losers 1, 1985), *Manual de perdedores 2* (1987), *Arena en los zapatos* (Sand in the shoes, 1989), and *Los sentidos del agua* (The direction of water, 1990). In addition, he is the editor of a volume of classic detective fiction stories titled *Los mejores cuentos policiales* (The best detective stories, 1997), which includes texts by Edgar Allan Poe, Arthur Conan Doyle, and G. K. Chesterton, among others.

The *Manual de perdedores* books first appeared, in part, in serial form. Over the course of a few months in 1983—roughly March to May—daily episodes appeared in the newspaper *La voz* (The voice). These were later gathered into book-form, which comprise part of *Manual 2*. In tune with Sasturain's interest in graphic popular genres, the stories include illustrations by Hernán Haedo, drawn especially for the series, along with a few comic illustrations taken from other strips. *Manual de perdedores* features the adventures of the private investigator (and former policeman) Etchenaik and his assistant, the one-time waiter Tony García. The narrative follows the classic conventions of the hard-boiled novel and is even self-referential in terms of its relation to the genre, making the text a parody more than an imitation. The characters often refer to other fictional detectives such as Mike Hammer, and there are multiple intertextual references to both North American and Argentine detective fiction writers. Etchenaik is an avid, almost obsessive reader of hard-boiled novels, and he carries his readings into life in absurd ways that often lead to ludicrous situations. Jorge Lafforgue compares him to Don Quijote who filled his head with tales of chivalry and lived in a fantasy world disconnected from his surroundings, but who nevertheless offered a critical view of reality (Lafforgue 158). The two men are weathered private investigators whose cases take them throughout Buenos Aires, from the most sordid spaces of the underworld to the centers of power. Sasturain weaves a telling narrative of the Argentine social fabric that is marked by violence, melancholy, and corruption. In the best tradition of hard-boiled fiction, the narrative is sparse and fast-paced, but not without a good deal of irony and black humor. The language is exaggeratedly the rough, unpolished talk of the street. Etchenaik and García continue their adventures in *Arena en los zapatos*. In Sasturain's 2002 novel, *La lucha continúa* (The struggle continues), Etchenaik also makes an appearance as a minor character among the many who populate this pastiche of contemporary social life.

Sasturain and his family lived in Barcelona between 1989 and 1992, which may be seen as having inspired his novel, *Los sentidos del agua*. It was initially published as the third volume in the *La muerte y la brújula* (Death and the compass) detective series edited by Jorge Lafforgue. The characters of the novel are entirely new and the action transpires in Barcelona. The "detective" (he's not a detective in the traditional sense of the word) in this case is Spencer Roselló, a native of Uruguay who lives with his wife in Barcelona. Billing himself as "the fastest translator in the West," he makes a living interpreting for Unesco until he's fired. He then sets up a booth in Las Ramblas where he and Joya, his wife, do translations on the spot for people on the street. All good hard-boiled detectives have at least one character flaw, and Roselló's is his weakness for gambling. The intrigue in the novel begins when Roselló accepts a job to translate a series of adventure books on Vietnam. The plot, however, is used only as means to present a variety of other topics that range from exile and military dictatorships to the global position of the Third World. With his characteristic humor, Sasturain inserts a multiplicity of popular culture and literary referents into the text. The character Alicia—a.k.a. "El Topo," or The Mole—serves as the main vehicle for the political elements of the text, at least those that refer to the *Proceso* (the last military dictatorship in Argentina 1976–83). Blind as a result of the torture she underwent, Alicia (Joya's cousin) sells birds in Las Ramblas. *Los sentidos del agua* also adheres to many aspects of the hard-boiled novel.

Sasturain has also written a number of short stories, most of which are collected in *La mujer ducha* (The skillful woman, 2001) His "Con tinta sangre" (With blood ink) won first prize in the Concurso Internacional Semana Negra de Gijón (1990), a competition sponsored by the international group of detective fiction writers and critics that meets each year in Gijón, Spain. He has also twice been a finalist for the Premio Hammett (Hammett award), awarded to the best detective novel written in Spanish. The story "Versión de un relato de Hammett" (Version of a Hammett story) is an excellent, condensed version of Sasturain's work, with his typical inclusion of the detective genre mixed with graphic humor, even if only as a cultural referent (in this case Mafalda). Furthermore, the author presents a powerful expression of the consequences of military dictatorship and its effect on the individual in both pyschological and physical terms. As in *Los senti-dos del agua*, the story also deals with translation, or more specifically here, a false translation. Two stories are interwoven in this brief narrative in an ingenious way: the story of a man writing a story that purports to be the translation of a lost Dashiell Hammett text, and the story of a family dealing with the repercussions of the military dictatorship. Jorge Lafforgue included "Versión de un relato de Hammett" in his anthology of Argentine detective fiction. A third story, "Sub-juntivo" (Subjunctive), is unique in that it is written entirely in the subjunctive. Sasturain makes an important contribution to Argentine detective fiction with his highly original works and memorable characters. In spite of this fact, to date his work has received very little critical attention.

Darrell B. Lockhart

Works

Arena en los zapatos. Barcelona: Ediciones B, 1989; Buenos Aires: Ediciones Grupo Zeta, 1989.
La lucha continúa. Buenos Aires: Sudamericana, 2002.
"Lengua larga," in *Escritos con sangre: cuentos argentinos sobre casos policiales*, ed. Sergio S. Olguín. Buenos Aires: Norma, 2003, 171–90.
Manual de perdedores 1. Buenos Aires: Legasa, 1985.
Manual de perdedores 2. Buenos Aires: Legasa, 1987.
Manual de perdedores. Barcelona: Ediciones B, 1988. (The two volumes together.)
Los mejores cuentos policiales, ed. Juan Sasturain. Buenos Aires: Ameghino, 1997.
La mujer ducha. Buenos Aires: Sudamericana, 2001.
Los sentidos del agua. Buenos Aire: Clarín/Aguilar, 1990. Reprint, Buenos Aires: Sudamer-icana, 2002.
"Versión de un relato de Hammett," in *Cuentos policiales argentinos*, ed. Jorge Lafforgue. Buenos Aires: Alfaguara, 1997, 363–71.

Criticism

Lafforgue, Jorge, and Jorge B. Rivera. *Asesinos de papel: ensayos sobre narrativa policial*. Buenos Aires: Ediciones Colihue, 1996.

Enrique Serna (b. 1959)

MEXICO

Enrique Serna was born in Mexico City in 1959. He began his career in writing with his satirical column "Las caricaturas me hacen llorar" (Caricatures make me cry) in *Sábado* (Saturday), a supplement of the newspaper *Unomásuno* (Oneplus-one). As a fiction writer, Serna is known for his novels *Uno soñaba que era rey* (Dreams of being king, 1989), *Señorita México* (Miss Mexico, 1993), and *El miedo a los animales* (Fear of animals; 1995); the short-story collection *Amores de segunda mano* (Second-hand love, 1996); and the collection of essays *Las caricaturas me hacen llorar* (1996). Serna is without a doubt one of the most innovative young writers in Mexico, reaching new creative heights with a perspective on national life that is tremendously disturbing, insightful, and vengeful.

To date, his only work of detective fiction is *El miedo a los animales*, in which he goes head-to-head with national culture in a bitingly critical way. The journalist-turned-investigator in the novel must confront corruption as well as intellectual stumbling blocks in order to uncover the real culprit, instead of finding an easy scapegoat as is usually done. With a dark sense of humor and a solid foundation of knowledge about the inner workings of the literary establishment in Mexican culture, the investigator Evaristo Reyes dismantles the myths of intellectual superiority. The image of writers goes from admiration to disgust as the narrative progresses. Serna uses the plot of a hard-boiled novel not to tell the story of a crime, but the criminal story of a cultural medium that operates, like politics, on secret arrangements and treachery to achieve 15 minutes of fame. In this world where honesty and integrity are scarce, Reyes is an angel compared to those who surround him: painters, poets, novelists, and art critics. The title of the novel takes its name from the fact that, according to Serna, truly important writers are the most generous, since they don't envy you and they don't need to bad mouth you because their talent speaks for itself. The bad ones are envious and afraid. Fear that the other will be successful leads to panic and murder, which translates in Serna's novel as a battle of angry beasts that destroy each other in their fight to achieve literary fame among a sea of mediocrity and jealously worthy of a cheap soap opera.

El miedo a los animales was well-received by the very literary community it satirized and became one of the most widely read detective novels of the 1990s in Mexico. Its portrayal of the world of art and culture as tantamount to the machinations of organized crime transforms Mexican fine arts into the perfect murder—an impeccable detective story.

Gabriel Trujillo Muñoz

Work

El miedo a los animales. Mexico City: Joaquín Mortiz, 1995.

Criticism

Galván, Delia V. "Un judicial intelectual y un narcopoeta en *El miedo a los animales* de Enrique Serna." *Alba de América* 20.37–38 (2001): 523–30.

Sergio Sinay (b. 1947)

ARGENTINA

Sergio Sinay was born on August 10, 1947 in Buenos Aires. He has worked as a journalist since age 19 and has contributed to, edited, or directed a wide array of periodicals that include *Siete días* (Seven days) and the Sunday supplement of *Clarín* (Bugle), one of the principal newspapers in Buenos Aires. He has worked in film and television as a scriptwriter and has also written comic strips.

He initiated a career as a fiction writer in 1975 with his promising first novel *Ni un dólar partido por la mitad* (Not even a dollar ripped in half), published just shortly before the military coup of 1976 and the installation of the neofascist dictatorship known as the *Proceso* (Process [of National Reorganization] 1976–83). It revolves around the kidnapping of an American executive in Buenos Aires and underscores the relationship between social politics and the hard-boiled novel— in the process making a strong denunciatory statement. *Sombras de Broadway* (Shadows of Broadway, 1984), his best book, was written while Sinay was living as an exile in Mexico. Set in New York City, the novel features an Argentine detective, Felipe Rafaelli. Following closely the North American hard-boiled model, it draws the reader into a world of intrigue, danger, and, of course, murder. The transplantation of the character to a foreign setting and consequent dislocation of identity allow for a sharp critique of reality in an environment of Italian immigrants and Argentine journalists missing in Manhattan. In *Dale campeón* (Go champ, 1988), Sinay attempts to blow the top off the scandal generated by the imprisonment of the Argentine boxing champion Carlos Monzón—though not identified in the text, he is easily recognizable. *Es peligroso escribir de noche* (It's dangerous to write at night, 1992) is volume 4 in the detective fiction series *La muerte y la brújula* (Death and the compass), edited by Jorge Lafforgue. In this his fourth novel, Sinay incorporates strong erotic elements linked to the Argentina of the 1990s, where money rules and morality has been discarded as a weakness of the past.

Néstor Ponce

Works

Dale campeón. Buenos Aires: Puntosur, 1988.
Es peligroso escribir de noche. Buenos Aires: Clarín/Aguilar, 1992.
Ni un dólar partido por la mitad. Buenos Aires: Ediciones de la Flor, 1975.
Sombras de Broadway. Buenos Aires: Ediciones de la Pluma, 1984.

Criticism

Lafforgue, Jorge, and Jorge B. Rivera. *Asesinos de papel: ensayos sobre narrativa policial*. Buenos Aires: Ediciones Colihue, 1996.

Juan José de Soiza Reilly (1879–1959)

ARGENTINA

The life story of Juan José de Soiza Reilly—journalist, narrator, and at times play-wright—reads much like a detective novel. Upon piecing together his biography, unknown and forgotten both in the Río de la Plata (River Plate) and abroad, one encounters some initial stumbling bocks. The matter of his birthplace and given name presents somewhat of a mystery from the outset. The confusing details beg to be unraveled and rewritten. His name appears in several variations: Juan José de Soiza Reilly, Juan José Da Soiza Reilly, Juan José (de) Soiza Relly, Juan José Da Soiza O´Reilly, and Souza Reilly. This type of fluid variation also applies to his works that have undergone multiple editions, corrections, and revisions, in which either the date, the publisher, titles, contents, a chapter here, a story there come and go, change, disappear, and reappear in a seemingly random fashion. Likewise the details of his birthplace: he was either born in Paysandú, Uruguay, on May 19, 1879 or Concordia, Entre Ríos (Argentina); no one, not even his descendants, remembers exactly which place it was. As with the Uruguayan-born writers Horacio Quiroga—with whom he shares several traits—and Florencio Sánchez, the weak definition of geographical borders ended up making him an Argentine. The fact that he worked primarily in Buenos Aires serves to reinforce such an identity. His works, depending upon the period in which he was writing, reveal traces of both origins. His early texts would lead one to infer his Uruguayan origin. However, from the 1930s on, such textual clues disappear from his writing. He may have had political motives or simply more convenient cultural reasons to proclaim himself Argentine, though other possibilities do exist. In any case, Concordia and Paysandú are border towns—with all that that implies. Soiza Reilly's birth certificate is Uruguayan, although he used to smile and say that he was the only Argentine with an Argentine citizenship card. One of his favorite words in his chronicles and fiction is "mystery." The circumstances of his birth—in large part made up by the author himself—hold true to the concept. His death, on the other hand, holds no mystery: it occurred on March 19, 1959 in Buenos Aires.

His background was doubly European, having descended from Portuguese and Irish immigrants. His parents were Juan José de Soiza and Catalina Reilly, who settled in Uruguay and worked in meat-salting plants. He was the fifth of ten children and the first male. When Juan José was very young, his family moved to Buenos Aires. In 1908, he married Emma Martínez Lobato. In 1909, his first son was born and named Rubén Darío, after the famous modernist poet. In 1919, a daughter was born and named after her mother. He completed his education as a teacher at a normal school in Entre Ríos. In 1921, he became secretary of the Founding Convention of Santa Fe (Convención Constituyente de Santa Fe) and later was the director of the library for the Facultad de Ciencias Jurídicas y Sociales de la Universisad del Litoral (School of justice and social sciences at the university of the Litoral). In 1923, he began to teach history at the Dr. A. Bermejo

School in Buenos Aires. He is also known to have performed a variety of odd jobs, from newspaper vendor to security guard to justice of the peace, which afforded him the streetwise experience that will later surface in his writing.

He worked for the famous magazine *Caras y caretas* (Faces and masks) in Europe where he covered the First World War, thus becoming a top-notch Argentine reporter, one of the first foreign correspondents from the country. He went on to specialize in journalism and interviews. He worked as a war correspondent for the newspaper *La Nación* (The nation) as well. In addition, Soiza Reilly contributed to *La Razón* (Reason) and *Crítica* (Critique) and belonged to the "Círculo de la Prensa" (a press organization).

Meanwhile, he also met with success abroad with his books, which were translated into several languages. In San Francisco in 1910, he won the gold medal for *El alma de los perros* (The soul of dogs, 1907) at the California World's Fair. Furthermore, he was made "Caballero de la Corona de Italia" (Knight of the crown of Italy), a country to which he often paid tribute in his writings, and a country where he lived and made many friends as a war correspondent.

Soiza Reilly was an important figure in the literary life of the 1920s. Although he didn't practice the aesthetics of the avant-garde, he was part of the bohemian crowd and his involvement and influence was mostly due to his early introduction into the mass media. His circle of friends or influences can be traced through the many prologues he wrote for others: from the introductions to books by the anarchist Alejandro Sux and Nicolás Granada to the prologues to *La luna del bajo fondo* (The moon of the underworld) and *Abierto toda la noche* (Open all night) by the tango singer/composer Enrique Cadícamo. This bohemian setting, between anarchism and tango, was where he felt most at home. The environment of the *boedistas* (members of the bohemian Boedo literary/artistic group), the night, prostitution, the marginalized and the poor, pulp editions of books, and hospitals defined his world. He knew Buenos Aires very well. He lived at one time in the La Recoleta neighborhood, close to the famous cemetery where Argentina's patrician families are buried. This setting would appear frequently in his stories and chronicles, which pay attention to the details of the urban *porteño* (Buenos Aires) layout and know very well of the dead.

Soiza Reilly is not, strictly speaking, a detective fiction writer in the classic sense of the term. His greatest contribution rests on the fact that he approaches literature from the journalistic chronicle and helps to define a genre that had already been in the making in Argentina since at least Eduardo Holmberg. Contemporaries of Soiza Reilly, such as Horacio Quiroga and Nicolás Olivari, among others, seduced by the streets, guns, and death, cover the same territory. Obvious differences aside, if one had to define Soiza Reilly's narrative style, it may be characterized as having a good deal in common with North American hard-boiled fiction. This is true in the sense that Soiza Reilly doesn't place emphasis on the mystery itself, but focuses on the underlying social circumstances of the crime. In Soiza Reilly, we can see the making of yellow journalism, the use of a pathos effect that attempts to reach the reader by conjuring up emotion. He is a moralist who disdains moralizing. He looks at the society that surrounds him with a scrutinizing eye and portrays what he observes with the double goal of social commitment and literary creation. He is an unwitting participant in the realist narrative vein of the early twentieth century that begins with Manuel Gálvez.

His theme is not so much the discovery of murder, but suicide. The motive of death in the majority of his works has to do unavoidably with money (another link to the hard-boiled tradition). People kill or kill themselves as a consequence of misery or as a consequence of the vices (gambling, drugs, and so on) that are only made possible by the overabundance of money. There is an aristocracy of the knife, as the narrator states in "Un crimen vulgar" (A common crime, in *Crónicas de amor, de belleza y sangre* [Chronicles of love, beauty, and blood, 1911; the title is a clear reference to a similar title used by Horacio Quiroga]). In Soiza Reilly's texts, the crime is more often thievery than murder. The classic image of the detective is overshadowed by the journalist who is not investigating the crime in the present for the reader, but revealing to him what he knows as a result of already having been at the scene.

There are types of criminal behavior that consist of inducing others to commit suicide. In "Historia humana de dos balas perdidas" (The human story of two stray bullets, in *Crónicas de amor, de belleza y de sangre*), Soiza Reilly even portrays himself in a supposed (and probable) autobiographic episode in which a youth is encouraged to kill himself. There also exist cases of homicides turned into suicide, or desires of suicide transformed into possible homicides as in the example of *La mujer de fuego* (The woman of fire, 1921). Furthermore, there are crimes that end up in suicide like that of the character in "La filosofía de las almohadas" (The philosophy of pillows, in *El alma de los perros*). Many of these texts first appeared in magazines of the time, mostly in *Caras y caretas*, and later were compiled into books.

Soiza Reilly creates his own conventions derived from his readings of newspaper crime reports and foreign literature. The pursuit of an aesthetics of death becomes a recurrent theme in his work. The tension generated among different elements is sometimes macabre, sometimes mocking. This type of satirical treatment is presented in the narration of the death, wake, and burial of an archetype figure in "El final de don Juan Pérez" (The end of Juan Pérez, in *El alma de los perros*). There is a certain delight to be perceived in the rough, even bloody vocabulary and descriptions in some stories. In contrast, a more dramatic effect is offered in *Mujeres de carne y hueso* (Women of flesh and blood, 1928), in which the protagonist, upon regaining consciousness, realizes that he has been castrated by his lover's husband; or in "La historia de Luisita" (The story of Luisita, in *La ciudad de los locos* [The city of the insane, 1914]), where the title character is shot and killed by her husband, Don Graciano, in the last sentence. Soiza Reilly also deals with death in historical episodes where crime is validated by the laws of war, as in the case of *El apóstol del Ayuí* (The apostle of Ayuí, 1918) in reference to General Artigas, a famous figure in Argentine history.

The book *Criminales* (Criminals, 1926) contains more than one surprise in its presentation of a whole spectrum of crime. It is divided into six chapters titled "Criminales sin corazón" (Heartless criminals), "Criminales de amor" (Criminals of love), "Criminales a la sombra" (Criminals in the shadows), "Criminales del olvido" (Criminals of forgetting), "Criminales contra el talento" (Criminals against talent), and "Criminales de dolor" (Criminals of pain), which reinforce the book's title. However, the end result is less of an emphasis on actual crime than in books with less obvious titles. Instead of examining more-or-less possible crimes, he re-semantizes the language of crime and crime fiction to call attention to, for example, an "an advancing enemy," which is nothing other than the threat of leprosy. Thus the importance of the volume's subtitle: "Almas sucias de mujeres y hombres limpios" (Dirty souls of clean men and women). Nevertheless, among the "Criminales a la sombra," one can find criminals who commit crimes in the traditional sense even though the focus is on showing how they are inevitably victims of circumstance.

The paradigms of health and illness allow Soiza Reilly an avenue for analyzing society and proposing romantic and positivist views through which to demythify traits of so-called sanity in the average human being and idealize psychosis. The madman and the murderer carry within themselves the inherent advantage of geniality, which inspires reflection and admiration in the narrator. In his portrayals of crime, he criticizes science—which fascinates him—for its inadequacy and above all its hypocrisy. The familiarity with death developed by medicine becomes a temptation to experiment with death and blurs ethical boundaries. In the struggle with mortality, Soiza Reilly's characters spare no resource in pushing the limitations of nature in pursuit of perfection and longevity for failing bodies. The story "La embalsamada" (The embalmed woman), from *Pecadoras* (Sinful women, 1924–25), eerily prefigures the saga of Eva Perón and offers a glimpse at events that were still three decades off but would enter the realm of myth in the social imagination.

Soiza Reilly's texts present cadavers that are alive as well as dead. Among the threats posed by different illnesses, perhaps none is as feared as deformity. Insanity has a certain prestige and other pathologies their dignity, since the assault on the aesthetic parameters of the physical is neither total nor categorical. The deformed appear as monstrous beings who assail the harmony of beauty and the possibilities of a positive existence; for example, the series of events unleashed by the one-eyed character Pisa-huevos (Egg-stomper) in the story "El dolor de un niño" (A child's pain, in *No leas este libro. El amor, las mujeres y otros venenos* [Don't read this book: Love, women, and other poisons, 1925]). Likewise, the example of "El niño que se cayó de la cuna" (The child who fell from the crib, in *Crónicas de amor, de belleza y de sangre*), who was in actuality deliberately thrown from the crib by his father. This last story can be read in relation to Horacio Quiroga's famously dark tale "La gallina degollada" ("The Decapitated Chicken"). The system of analogies presented by Soiza Reilly emphasizes a set order of virtues and defects. School can be an educational institution or a prison (the prison in *La escuela de los pillos* [The school of scoundrels, 1920])—both are a place of learning. Differences between the mental institution and the social club become erased. The hospital is compared to the cemetery. Drugs are medicines and hallucinogens sought after for pleasure. There is no lack of doctors (like the one in *La muerte blanca* [White death, 1926]) who prescribe drugs not as a remedy but as a vice. There are dead people who seem alive as in the already-mentioned "La embalsamada" or "La cabecita rubia" (The little blondie, in *La escuela de los pillos*), and living who look dead. Murderers and madmen can be as brilliant as artists or scientists. Mystery enters Soiza Reilly's literary imagination through spiritism, metempsychosis, and other similar phenomena, which of course recall the work of Leopoldo Lugones as in the stories "Nuestros esqueletos" (Our skeletons, in *Crónicas de amor, de belleza y de sangre*) and "Mi compañero Race" (My buddy Race, in *No leas este libro*).

If we were to attempt an understanding of Juan José de Soiza Reilly through the codes of his own sensibility and poetics, we might arrive at the conclusion that reading and writing are simultaneously mortal (deadly) and acts of love. They are acts of tension and concentration and definitive gestures. The metaphor of the pen as weapon, which has been used to the point of exhaustion, enjoys a long tradition within Argentine culture, but Soiza's words do not join that tradition. He may brandish his pen like a desired weapon, but for him it is used to define man's state of mind and a writer's style.

María Gabriela Mizraje

Works

El alma de los perros, prólogo de Manuel Ugarte. Valencia: Sempere y Cía, n.d. (c. 1907). 2nd ed., 1909. Also: Buenos Aires: Matera, 1922; Montevideo Ferrari, 1928, with prologue by Manuel Ugarte and critical study by Enrique Rodó. Buenos Aires: EUDEBA, 1950. (This is only a selection of the many editions of the volume.)

El amor, la mujer y otros venenos. La novela semanal (Buenos Aires) 4.243 (10 July 1922): n.p. (Later included in No leas este libro.)

Carne de muñecas (novelas de amor). Buenos Aires: Tor, n.d.

La ciudad de los locos: aventuras de Tartarín Moreira. Barcelona: Maucci, 1914. (A novel followed by 17 short stories and five critical studies, with illustrations by José Friedrich.)

La ciudad, los locos y los sueños, compilación, estudio preliminar y notas de María Gabriela Mizraje. Buenos Aires: Hidalgo Editora, 2003.

Criminales. Almas sucias de mujeres y hombres limpios. Buenos Aires: Sopena, 1926. Reprint, Buenos Aires: Angulo, n.d. (1930s).

Crónicas de amor, de belleza y de sangre. Barcelona: Maucci, 1911.

El dolor de un niño. La novela semanal (Buenos Aires) 4.229 (3 April 1922): n.p. (Later included in No leas este libro.)

La escuela de los pillos, carta-prólogo de Jorge Eduardo Coll, apuntes biográficos del autor por Alejandro Andrade Coello, poema a Juan José de Soiza Reilly por Evaristo Carriego. Buenos Aires: Vicente Matera, 1920. Reprint, Buenos Aires: Tor, 1939.

Un hombre desnudo. La novela semanal (Buenos Aires) 4.162 (20 December 1910): n.p.

La muerte blanca. Amor y cocaína. Buenos Ai-res: Sopena, 1926. Reprint, Buenos Aires:

Agencia General de Librería y Publicaciones, 1927; Buenos Aires: Tor, 1943. Reprinted as *La Muerte Blanca*. Buenos Aires: Editorial Caymi, 1947.

La mujer de fuego. Novela de la juventud (Buenos Aires) 2.32 (16 June 1921): n.p.

Mujeres de amor. Buenos Aires: Sopena, 1926. Reprinted, Buenos Aires: Angulo, n.d. (1930s).

Mujeres de carne y hueso. La mejor novela (Buenos Aires) 1.2 (10 January 1928): n.p.

No leas este libro. El amor, las mujeres y otros venenos, prólogo de Alberto Lesplace. Buenos Aires: Sopena, 1925; Edición corregida y aumentada, 1927.

Pecadoras. Buenos Aires: Sopena, n.d. (1924 or 1925). Reprint, Buenos Aires: Tor, n.d. (c.1926); Buenos Aires: Ediciones de la Flor, 1974.

Las timberas. Buenos Aires: Sopena, 1927–28. Reprints, Buenos Aires: Angulo, n.d. (1930s); Buenos Aires: Tor, 1939.

Criticism

Arce, José de. "Investigando alrededor de Juan José de Soiza Reilly." *La semana universal* (Buenos Aires) 15 (11 April 1912): n.p.

Arlt, Roberto. "Este es Soiza Reilly." *El Mundo* (Buenos Aires) (31 May 1930): n.p.

Cammarota, Atilio. *Juan José de Soiza Reilly. Guerrero de la pluma y de la verba. Una síntesis biográfica*. Buenos Aires: N.p., 1963.

Paco Ignacio Taibo II (b. 1949)

MEXICO

Often known simply as "PIT II," Paco Ignacio Taibo II was born in 1949 in Gijón, Spain, the son of a famous Spanish writer of the same name. From 1958 to the present he has lived in Mexico City, dedicating himself to a life of political activism ranging from participation in the student movement of 1968, the organization of workers' unions during the 1970s, writing and teaching history as a specialist in the anarchist movements in 1920s Mexico and Spain as well as radicalism throughout the twentieth century, working as a journalist uncovering the corruption of the Mexican political system, and, finally, exploring the crisis of Mexican society as a detective fiction writer. Taibo has penned over 50 books, including 19 novels, three short-story collections, and a variety of nonfiction reports, history books, and biographies. In addition to the classic North American hard-boiled writers, his professed influences include the mixture of historical and fictional characters in John Dos Passos's novels *Manhattan Transfer* (1925) and *U.S.A. Trilogy* (1937), the exploration of Mexican politics and reality in Carlos Fuentes's *La región más transparente* (*Where the Air Is Clear,* 1958), the historical atmosphere of Victor Hugo, and the brutal realism of Émile Zola.

Taibo has earned many awards for his detective fiction. He received the International Dashiell Hammett award three times: in 1989 for *La vida misma* (*Life Itself,* 1987), in 1991 for *Cuatro manos* (*Four Hands,* 1990) and *La bicicleta de Leonardo* (*Leonard's Bicycle,* 1993) in 1994. He also received the 1992 Planeta/Joaquín Mortiz Prize as well as the 1994 Award for the Best Police Novel in France. With the majority of his books translated into English, Taibo has been nominated four times for the best book of the year by the *New York Times* and twice by the *Los Angeles Times.* In July 1998, he received the Italian Bancarella Award for his biography of Che Guevara, *Ernesto Guevara también conocido como el Che* (*Guevara, Also Known as Che,* 1996). Taibo's dedication to the revitalization of the hard-boiled detective genre has been noted worldwide by his pioneering of the International Association of Crime Writers as well has his founding of the *Semana Negra,* an enormous celebration of detective fiction, film noir, and popular culture held in Gijón, Spain every July.

Since the birth of hard-boiled detective fiction by Dashiell Hammett and Raymond Chandler, the sleuth has been a moral guide for a changing society plagued by a lack of faith in justice and an absence of law. From North American hard-boiled detective fiction Paco Ignacio Taibo II appropriates the ideology of disaffection and disorder to analyze the crisis of a post-1968 Mexico that seeks to reconcile a history of repression with the democratic ideals of a changing modern world. Combining characteristics of the detective fiction of Dashiell Hammett, Raymond Chandler, and Ross Macdonald with the violence and terror of crime novelists such as Chester Himes, Jim Thompson, and Horace McCoy, Taibo has forged a new genre that he has dubbed the "*neo-policíaco* novel" (new detective novel). The *neo-policíaco* novel consists of a simultaneous assimilation and violation of the hard-boiled and noir genres in order to create a text that possesses the essential anecdotal, linear storytelling of a mystery novel with technical experimentation within the text in order to address questions of truth, knowledge, and investigation in contemporary post-1968 Mexico City—a society of shadows, doubt, and half-truths that the author often refers to as the "Kafkaesque." In this way, Taibo explores and reveals a society of disorder and chaos victimized by the hypocrisy of the rich, the self-interest of corrupt government officials, the violence of the police, and the influence of drug traffickers. Essential themes that arise throughout Taibo's novels revolve around the legacy of the Tlatelolco Massacre in 1968 and the struggle of Mexico's citizens against a corrupt political system that co-opts history to its own ends, victimizing the weak in the process. Mexico City, as the backdrop, emerges as a monster whose urban violence and victimization of the weak threatens its inhabitants not only ecologically but politically, economically, and socially as well.

In Taibo's first hard-boiled detective novel, *Días de combate* (Days of combat, 1976), he establishes the *neo-policíaco* novel with his detective Héctor Belascoarán Shayne, a cultural hybrid who is the son of an Irish mother and Basque father but who considers himself pure Mexican. In this novel, the first of nine in the Belascoarán series, the detective renounces his role as part of the bourgeois order by quitting his job as an engineer and becoming a detective through correspondence school in order to pursue the strangler known as "El Cerevro" (The brain). Belascoarán Shayne, always motivated by a sense of stubbornness and curiosity, uncovers a tacit truth about Mexican society that becomes the central theme permeating Taibo's novelistic production. At the climax of the novel when he corners and confronts the killer, Belascoarán Shayne realizes that the strangler he pursues represents a mere projection of the true villain in Mexico. El Cerevro challenges the detective to identify the true killer in Mexico: the state, responsible for the death of countless ordinary citizens. Belascoarán Shayne's response establishes the fundamental vision of Mexico portrayed in Taibo's novels, "El Gran Estrangulador es el sistema" (The Great Strangler is the system). In this way, the grand irony that pervades Taibo's novels refers to the fact that the crime, chaos, and disorder of Mexico is ultimately created by those authorities and forces in charge of maintaining the peace: the police, the government, and the judicial system.

In the second installment of the Belascoarán Shayne series, *Cosa fácil* (*An Easy Thing*, 1977), Taibo's detective simultaneously investigates the death of two engineers while battling wealthy corporate tycoons connected to corrupt government officials, protects the daughter of a Mexican film starlet, and searches for Emiliano Zapata. Developing a three-tiered plot, Taibo plays with the structures common to Ross Macdonald's Lew Archer series in which the detective is confronted with several mysteries that intertwine in the end, fabricating a complex web of collective culpability in society. Nevertheless, in *Cosa fácil*—although Taibo's detective awaits the moment in which these plots will intersect, ironically self-aware of his own

Lew Archer–like status—Belascoarán Shayne realizes that such a structure requires an order and logic that Mexican society's violent rhythms resist.

Of Belascoarán Shayne's three office-mates, he is most connected with "El Gallo" (The rooster) Virreal, the sewer expert who implicitly addresses the hidden presence of the state in Mexico through the metaphor of the cloaca, or sewer, in *Cosa fácil*. El Gallo and Belascoarán share the responsibility of keeping vigil over the unseen operations of the monstrous city, protecting its citizens from the hidden elements that seek to destroy them.

The title of the third novel of the series, *No habrá final feliz* (*No Happy Ending*, 1989), ironically mocks the notion of a happy ending while at the same time forewarns the reader of the immanent danger awaiting Belascoarán Shayne. Investigating the death of several people connected with a covert paramilitary group known as "Los Halcones" (The falcons), the detective confronts the most malevolent force that inhabits Mexico: the government itself. Los Halcones, who were historically responsible for a massacre of protestors on June 10, 1971, pursue Belascoarán Shayne mistakenly assuming that one of the victims, before his death, had hired the detective to investigate the group and the massacre of 1971. Characteristic of what would come in later novels outside the Belascoarán Shayne series, Taibo mixes history with detection in order to expose the ironic reality of a system that victimizes rather than protects its people. The end of the novel, however, reveals that, despite his stubbornness and curiosity, Belascoarán Shayne is not strong enough to defend himself against the invisible enemies whose infinite strength lies in the fact that they masquerade as officials of peace and order.

Nevertheless, despite being gunned down in the final scene of *No habrá final feliz*, Belascoarán Shayne returns to reinforce the view of Mexico City as an illusion of democracy poisoned by the rich and powerful in *Regreso a la misma ciudad y bajo la lluvia* (*Return to the Same City*, 1989). Rejecting the idea of Mexico City as a monster, Belascoarán Shayne prefers to think of it as "la cueva de mentiras, la caverna de los antropófagos" (the cave of lies, the cavern of cannibals), which ironically echoes Plato's cave reinforcing the overwhelming presence of shadows, doubts, and lies that prey upon the citizens hiding the "enemy" behind fabrications of truth and history.

Of the nine installments in the Belascoarán Shayne series, the first five (*Días de combate, Cosa fácil, No habrá final feliz, Algunas nubes* [*Some Clouds*, 1995] and *Regreso a la misma ciudad y bajo la lluvia*) establish the basic precepts of the *neo-policíaco*. Nevertheless, since the end of the 1980s, Taibo has abandoned his detective in order to develop other projects that combine aspects of the historical novel with essential traits of hard-boiled and noir fiction in order to expand the realm of the *neo-policíaco* novel. Novels such as *Sombra de la sombra* (*The Shadow of a Shadow*, 1986), *La vida misma*, *La bicicleta de Leonardo*, and *Cuatro manos* exhibit classic technical experimentation such as the juxtaposition of time and space, disjunction of point-of-view, ironic self-awareness, and the incorporation of texts (such as letters, official documents, historical accounts, political pamphlets, and novels) within the text, emphasizing more than ever the problematic nature of knowledge and truth in a world of illusions and governmental duplicity. Taibo replaces the figure of the private detective with other types of investigators such as a group of friends who stumble into extraordinary circumstances in *Sombra de la sombra*, journalists seeking "the truth" in *Cuatro manos*, and, ironically, an author of detective fiction in *La vida misma* and *La bicicleta de Leonardo*.

In *Sombra de la sombra*, Taibo posits the novel's action in Mexico City during the 1920s, a period whose chaos and uncertainty implicitly reflect the crisis of post-1968 Mexico. In an atmosphere of anarchist movements and workers' strikes, four friends, through the investigation of the mysterious death of a trombone player in a military band, uncover a plot connecting high-ranking Mexican politicians and military officials with influential American businessmen whose plan is to incite another revolution in order to gain control of northern Mexico's oil supply. This text addresses the nature of official versions of written history that communicate little of the facts of a historical period by suppressing certain aspects in favor of the prejudices of the powerful. The novel concludes with a government representative demanding the silence of the journalist Manterola, an idealist and populist who works for the newspaper *El Demócrata* (The democrat).

With *La vida misma*, Taibo opens the possibilites of the *neo-policíaco* novel to not only analyze its own constructions through the figure of a writer of detective fiction, but also to examine politics in Mexico by exposing the incompatibility of Mexican reality with the literary logic of detective novels. Hired because of his fame, familiarity with Mexican politics, and understanding of investigative procedures, José Daniel Fierro becomes the chief of police in a small fictional town in north-central Mexico named Santa Ana whose municipal government is controlled by the Communist party. Fierro utilizes the models established by fictional detectives such as Marlowe, Spade, and Archer to investigate a series of murders within the context of growing tension between the local leftist government and the PRI-dominated state government. In letters he writes to his wife, Fierro describes the plot of his next novel, which mirrors the events of Santa Ana and whose central theme the author Fierro describes as "el mexicanísimo oficio mexicano de matar por órdenes" (the most Mexican of Mexican duties, killing on order [144]). Realizing the incompatibility between the logic of the linear narration common to detective fiction and the unreality of Santa Ana, which he compares to the mythical town of Comala from Juan Rulfo's classic novel *Pedro Páramo* (1955). Fierro views the new novel as a triumph because the sheriff discovers nothing and things simply happen without a closed ending, much like life itself.

Taibo continues the theme of government plots and cover-ups in *Cuatro manos* and *La bicicleta de Leonardo*, combining with it an experimental attitude in the construction of the text by dispersing the action temporally and spatially and rupturing the point-of-view in the narration. *Cuatro manos*, which Taibo feels is his best novel, essentially focuses on two journalists, one American and one Mexican, who face-off against the disinformation industry of an unknown branch of the CIA. Nevertheless, the plot of this novel rejects the linear nature of traditional mystery and espionage novels by incorporating such disparate historical figures as Stan Laurel, Pancho Villa, Leon Trotsky, and Harry Houdini as well as exploring events in history such as the Iran-Contra affair and the Spanish Civil War. *La bicicleta de Leonardo* recounts the investigation of José Daniel Fierro, the writer of detective novels that first appeared in *La vida misma*, into the disappearance of the star player for the University of Texas women's basketball team. Similar to *Cuatro manos*, this text also fragments the narration by placing the action in various time periods, including the American evacuation of Vietnam, the anarchist movements in Barcelona during the 1920s, and the life of Leonardo da Vinci. Both texts contain an "investigator" yet reject the unifying point-of-view that such a character brings to detective fiction, thereby forcing the reader to confront a complex text by placing the onus of investigation on the reader and underscoring the problem of knowledge and truth.

From a basic belief in the social purpose of detective fiction, Paco Ignacio Taibo II has integrated and assimilated the North American hard-boiled genre to the crisis and chaos of post-1968 Mexico. By means of metafictional irony, these texts represent the height of the *neo-policíaco* novel to simultaneously violate the rules of a genre as well as to confront the reader with issues of knowledge and truth in a corrupt political system. Taibo successfully combines the literary and political to create a genre that denounces elitism and upholds true democratic ideals both in the realm of the aesthetic as well as the social.

William J. Nichols

Works

The Hector Belascoarán Shayne Series

Adiós, Madrid. Mexico City: Promexa, 1993.

Algunas nubes. Mexico City: Alfaguara, 1995. English version as *Some Clouds*, trans. William I. Neuman. New York: Penguin Books, 1992.

Amorosos fantasmas. Mexico City: Promexa Misterio, 1990.

Cosa fácil. Mexico City: Grijalbo, 1977. English version as *An Easy Thing*, trans. William I. Neuman. New York: Viking Penguin, 1990.

Desvanecidos difuntos. Mexico City: Promexa Misterio, 1991.

Días de combate. Mexico City: Grijalbo, 1976.

No habrá final feliz. Mexico City: Planeta, 1989. English version as *No Happy Ending*, trans. William I. Neuman. New York: Mysterious Press, 1993.

Regreso a la misma ciudad y bajo la lluvia. Mexico City: Planeta, 1989. English version as *Return to the Same City*, trans. Laura Dail. New York: Mysterious Press, 1996.

Sueños de frontera. Mexico City: Promexa Misterio, 1990.

Outside the Belascoarán Series

La bicicleta de Leonardo. Mexico City: Joaquín Mortiz, 1993. Reprint, Barcelona: Editorial Thassàlia, S.A., 1996. English version as *Leonardo's Bicycle*, trans. Martin Michael Roberts. New York: Mysterious Press, 1995.

El caso Molinet. Mexico City: Colección Documento, 1993.

Cuatro manos. Mexico City: Ediciones B, 1990. English version as *Four Hands*, trans. Laura C. Dail. New York: St. Martin's Press, 1990.

Cuentos policíacos mexicanos, edited with Víctor Ronquillo. Mexico City: Selector, 1997. (Anthology of detective fiction stories by Mexican writers.)

De paso. Barcelona: Ediciones La Letra SCCL, 1986.

Ernesto Guevara, también conocido como el Che. Mexico City: Planeta/Joaquín Mortiz, 1996. Reprint, Barcelona: Planeta, 1997. English version as *Guevara, Also Known as Che*, trans. Martin Michael Roberts. New York: St. Martin's Press, 1997.

Héroes convocados: manual para la toma del poder. Mexico City: Grijalbo, 1982.

Máscara azteca y el doctor Niebla (después del golpe). Mexico City: Alfaguara, 1996.

"Los maravillosos olores de la vida," in *Cuentos policiacos mexicanos*, 57–70. Also in *Variaciones en negro: relatos policiales iberoamericanos*, ed. Lucía López Coll and Leonardo Padura. Havana: Editorial Arte y Literatura, 2001, 85–95; and, *Variaciones en negro: relatos policiales hispanoamericanos*, ed. Lucía López Coll. Bogotá: Norma, 2003, 125–38.

Nomás los muertos están bien contentos. Mexico City: Joaquín Mortiz, 1994.

Que todo es imposible. Mexico City: Roca, 1995.

Sintiendo que el campo de batalla. Mexico City: El Juglar Editores, 1989.

Sombra de la sombra. Mexico City: Planeta, 1986. Reprint, Bilbao: Txalaparta, 1996. English version as *The Shadow of a Shadow*, trans. William I. Neuman. New York: Viking, 1991.

La vida misma. Mexico City: Planeta, 1987. Reprint, Madrid: Ediciones Júcar, 1988. English version as *Life Itself*, trans. Beth Henson. New York: Mysterious Press, 1995.

Criticism

Balibrea-Enríquez, María Paz. "Paco Ignacio Taibo II y la reconstrucción del espacio cultural mexicano." *Confluencia: revista hispánica de cultura y literatura* 12.1 (1996): 38–55.

Braham, Persephone. "Violence and Patriotism: *La novela negra* from Chester Himes to Paco Ignacio Taibo II." *Journal of American Culture* 20.2 (1997): 159–69.

Hernández Martín, Jorge. "On the case." *Américas* 47.2 (1995): 16–21.

———. "Paco Ignacio Taibo II: Post-Colonialism and the Detective Story in Mexico," in *The Postcolonial Detective*, edited with introduction by Ed Christian. Houndmills, UK: Palgrave, 2001, 159–75.

Nichols, William J. "A quemarropa con Manuel Vázquez Montalbán y Paco Ignacio Taibo II." *Arizona Journal of Hispanic Cultural Studies* 2 (1998): 197–231. (Interview.)

———. "Social Crisis, Economic Development and the Emergence of the 'novela negra' in Mexico and Spain: The case of Paco Ignacio Taibo II and Manuel Vázquez Montalbán." Doctoral dissertation, University of Arizona, 2000.

Peras, Delphine. "Latin America's New Grit." *World Press Review* 43.9 (1996): 41.

Ramírez, Juan C. "Paco Ignacio Taibo II: La lógica de la terquedad, la variante mexicana de una locura." *Mester* 21.1 (1992): 41–50.

Segura, Gerardo. "Mis personajes tienen reglas: interrogatorio a Paco Ignacio Taibo II," in *Todos somos culpables: entrevistas con escritores policiacos mexicanos*. Saltillo, Coahuila: Instituto Coahuilense de Cultura, 1996. 91–103.

Sherman, Scott. "Democratic Detective." *Boston Review* 21.2 (1996): 30–35.

Sklodowska, Elzbieta. "Transgresión paródica de la fórmula policial," in *La parodia en la nueva novela hispanoamericana (1960–1985)*. Purdue University Monographs in Romance Languages. Amsterdam/Philadelphia: John Benjamins Publishing, 1991, 111–39.

Stavans, Ilán. "An Appointment with Hector Belascoarán Shayne: A Profile of Paco Ignacio Taibo II." *Review: Latin American Literature and Arts* 42 (1990): 5–9.

———. "Paco Ignacio Taibo II," in *Antiheroes: Mexico and Its Detective Novel*, trans. Jesse Lytle and Jennifer A. Mattson. Madison, NJ: Fairleigh Dickinson University Press, 1997, 108–15.

———. "Sam Spade, otra vez," in *The Riddle of Cantinflas: Essays on Hispanic Popular Culture*. Albuquerque: University of New Mexico Press, 1998, 25–29.

Stavans, Ilán, and Carrie Van Doren. "A Brief (Happy) Talk with Paco Ignacio Taibo II." *Literary Review: An International Journal of Contemporary Writing* 38.1 (1994): 34–37.

Torres, Vicente Francisco. *Esta narrativa mexicana: ensayos y entrevistas*. Mexico City: Leega, S.A., 1991.

Trujillo Muñoz, Gabriel. *Testigos de cargo: la narrativa policiaca mexicana y sus autores*. Tijuana, Mexico: CONACULTA/CECUT, 2000, 71–74.

Gabriel Trujillo Muñoz (b. 1958)

MEXICO

Gabriel Trujillo was born on July 21, 1958 in Mexicali, Baja California. While he is a trained physician and surgeon, since 1981 he has dedicated himself to literature and cultural production as a teacher, researcher, journalist and, author. His research focuses primarily on regional history and artistic manifestations along the U.S.–Mexican border. He is the author of several dozen books and in addition to his fiction—he writes mostly detective and science fiction—has penned texts that describe the history, people, and social and cultural movements of northern Mexico.

Trujillo's first examples of detective fiction are to be found with the publication of his short stories "Lucky Strike" and "De sueños y nostalgia" (Of dreams and nostalgia) that were published in the anthology *Tierra natal* (Native land, 1987), edited by Sergio Gómez Montero. In 1990, "Lucky Strike" and the story "Hotel frontera" (Border hotel) were selected for an anthology dedicated to the detective genre, *En la línea de fuego* (*Line of Fire*), edited by Leobardo Saravia Quiroz, that showcased young writers from the border region, the first anthology of its type in Mexico. As a whole, the volume speaks to the reality of the border area, which is vastly different from that of the interior of the country. The common denominators of violence, drug trafficking, immigrant flux, corruption, and tension with the United States bring to the fore the precarious existence of those who live in this zone between two worlds. The book caused quite a stir among literary critics from the capital. Federico Patán, writing in *Unomásuno*, stated that one of the virtues of *En la línea de fuego* is its role in alerting readers to some truly interesting writers who will be worth following as their careers develop. Patán singles out Trujillo, saying that he is "el más interesante de los cuentistas elegidos" (the most interesting of the selected authors). Likewise, Federico Campbell, in his book *Máscara negra* (Black mask, 1995), offers exuberant praise for Trujillo's stories included in *En la línea de fuego*. The volume sold out in Mexico in very short time. It was picked up by the San Diego State University Press, which published a revised version titled *Line of Fire: Detective Stories from the Mexican Border* (1996) as part of their "Baja California Literature in Translation" series. This new edition contains Trujillo's stories "Lucky Strike" and "A Personal Matter," a story of black-market contraband and espionage dealing with the Chinese mafia and the Mexican authorities in Baja California during the 1930s. "Lucky Strike" takes place somewhere between Calexico, California and Mexicali, Mexico at around 1936. A hit man from the U.S. side is paid by the Colorado River Land Company to carry-out an assassination that will benefit the company and enable it to successfully expropriate a significant portion of land in the Mexicali valley. "Hotel frontera" is a rather clever story in which a number of characters—including a down-on-his-luck Rudolph Valentino, Phillip Marlowe, and José Revueltas—find themselves stranded at the border hotel.

In 1992 and 1994, Trujillo Muñoz participated in round-table discussions organized by Paco Ignacio Taibo II on the topic of Latin American detective fiction and the international book fair in Guadalajara. In 1995, he published his first detective novel, *Mezquite Road*, in which the character Miguel Ángel Morgado appears for the first time. Morgado is a lawyer who was born in Mexicali and resides in Mexico City, where he works on behalf of human rights. For reason of friendship, he finds it necessary to return to his hometown to investigate a murder. Morgado is, by sorts, the alter ego of Trujillo himself, a green private investigator who bursts onto the scene of national detective fiction with a decentralized view from the periphery. *Mezquite Road* forms part of the boom in detective fiction that emerged in force in Mexico during the 1990s. Together with authors such as Juan Hernández Luna, Hugo Valdés, and José Amparán, Trujillo Muñoz breaks with centralist (Mexico City) hegemony and causes the genre to expand into the entire national territory as the staging ground for its representation of corruption, social criticism, and its fears, desires, and pain. Therefore, the northern border—and especially Baja California—is presented as the ideal place for fiction that holds violence as its center of attention and reflection, the narrative space where power reveals its fissures, low blows, and plots.

The critic Ignacio Trejo Fuentes stated in the journal *Siempre* that in the work of Gabriel Trujillo "se percibe con nitidez la vida fronteriza, aunque esta vez desde uno de sus ángulos más sombríos, el gangsterismo desatado, la violencia incontenible" (one perceives border life with clarity, although this time from one of its darkest angles, unbridled gangsterism, uncontrolled violence). Gerardo Segura describes *Mezquite Road* as a passionate portrayal of Mexicali and admires Trujillo for his direct style of narration, while Sergio Rommel Alfonzo declares that the novel is more than a detective story, it is "la descripción apasionada y cómplice de una manera de vivir y ver el mundo desde la frontera. Critica a una sociedad violenta en la que todos estamos inmersos y en la que todos tenemos la culpa" (the impassioned description and accomplice of a way of life and viewing the world from the border. It criticizes a violent society in which we are all immersed and for which we are all to blame).

In 1997, Gabriel Trujillo's Tijuana-based story "La energía de los esclavos" was included in the anthology *Cuentos policiacos mexicanos*, edited by Paco Ignacio Taibo II and Víctor Ronquillo, along with stories by fellow-writers Agustín Sánchez González, Miriam Laurini, Mauricio-José Schwarz, Rafael Ramírez Heredia, and the editors themselves. It was the only anthology of its type published in the 1990s and it is characterized—as Trujillo's story demonstrates—by new ways of approaching criminality, corruption, and the abuse of power while at the same time using nontraditional places to do so.

In 1998, Trujillo Muñoz won the Abigael Bohórquez national prize awarded by the Centro Cultural Tijuana (Tijuana cultural center) and the Consejo Nacional para la Cultura y las Artes (National council for culture and the arts—a government agency) for his book *Testigos de cargo* (Witnesses for the prosecution), a study of Mexican detective fiction from the nineteenth century to the present. The book contains 16 essays on individual authors and a final essay on the Mexican–U.S. border as the site for detective fiction written by U.S. authors.

Conjurados (Conspirators, 1999), though not strictly speaking a detective novel, merits mention as a well-crafted political thriller set during the final stages of the dictatorship of Porfirio Díaz. It takes place in the port of Ensenada in 1904 with two journalists who are struggling to balance their love for adventure with the challenges placed before them by the revolutionaries and the agents of the dictatorship alike (cf. Juan Pablo Villalobos).

In 2000, Gabriel Trujillo published *Tijuana city blues*, a book comprised of three novellas in which the main character, once again, is Miguel Angel Morgado. In the novellas—*Tijuana city blues*, *Turbulencias* (Turbulence), and *Descuartizamientos* (Slayings)—Morgado becomes involved in police investigations related to human organ contraband along the border, the solving of a missing-persons case from half-a-century ago and a single-engine airplane lost in the desert. That same year the author wrote a play, *Carne cruda* (Raw meat), about a serial killer along the border, which was based on a criminal case from the 1960s. It was staged by the group "Mexicali a secas" and directed by Angel Norzagaray.

In 2002, the prestigious Latin American publishing group Editorial Norma published Trujillo's *El festín de los cuervos* (The crows' feast). The volume brings together the now-complete border saga featuring Miguel Angel Morgado. The last novel of the series is *Laguna salada* (Saltwater lagoon), which is joined by *Mezquite Road*, *Tijuana city blues*, *Loverboy* (formerly *Turbulencias*), and *Puesta en escena* (On stage, formerly *Descuartizamientos*). As a compilation, *El festín de los cuervos* offers one of the most complete, telling, and significant visions of border life available. Trujillo is a gifted narrator, an astute social critic, and one of the most important figures in contemporary Mexican detective fiction, both as an author of fiction and critic.

Gabriel Trujillo Muñoz
Darrell B. Lockhart

Works

Conjurados. Mexico City: Sansores y Aljure, 1999.

"La energía de los esclavos," in *Cuentos policiacos mexicanos*, ed. Paco Ignacio Taibo II and Víctor Ronquillo. Mexico City: Selector, 1997, 79–106.

El festín de los cuervos: la saga fronteriza de Miguel Ángel Morgado. Bogotá: Norma, 2002.

"Lucky Strike," and "De sueños y nostalgia," in *Tierra natal*, ed. Sergio Gómez Montero. Mexico City: INBA-UNAM, 1987.

"Lucky Strike," and "Hotel frontera," in *En la línea de fuego: relatos policiacos de frontera*, ed. Leobardo Saravia Quiroz. Mexico City: Tierra Adentro, 1990.

"Lucky Strike," and "A Personal Matter," trans. Monica Valenzuela et al, in *Line of Fire: Detective Stories from the Mexican Border*. San Diego: San Diego State University Press, 1996, 1–6, 7–17.

Mezquite Road. Mexico City: Planeta, 1995.

Testigos de cargo: la narrativa policiaca mexicana y sus autores. Tijuana, Mexico: CONAC-
ULTA; CECUT, 2000.
Tijuana city blues: tres novelas cortas. Mexico City: Sansores y Fernández Editores, 1999.

Criticism

Alfonzo, Sergio Rommel. "Mezquite Road." *Yubai* (Mexicali) (January–March 1996): n.p.
———. "Tijuana City Blues." *Bitácora* (Tijuana) (7 July 2000): n.p.
Berumen, Humberto Félix. "Tijuana City Blues." *El mexicano* (Tijuana) (25 February
2001): n.p.
———. "Testigos de cargo." *El mexicano* (Tijuana) (20 May 2001): n.p.
Campbell, Federico. *Máscara negra.* Mexico City: Planeta, 1995.
Foz, Claire. "Fan Letters to the Cultural Industries: Border Literature about Mass Media."
Studies in Twentieth-Century Literature 25.1 (2001): 15–45.
Irby, Patricia L. "*Mezquite Road.* A Border Detective Mystery." Master's thesis, San Diego
State University, 1996.
Leñero, Isabel. "*Mezquite Road*: el mundo oscuro de la justicia contemporánea." *La crónica*
(Mexicali) (29 September 1995): n.p.
Patán, Federico. "Leobardo Saravia: en la línea de fuego." *Unomásuno* (6 April 1991): n.p.
Segura, Gerardo. "Tres negros de la frontera norte." *Hojas de utopía* (Mexico City) (Janu-
ary–February 1997): n.p.
Trejo Fuentes, Ignacio. "Gabriel Trujillo M. Noticias de Mexicali." *Siempre* (Mexico City)
(12 October 1995): n.p.
Villalobos, Juan Pablo. "Conjurados." *Bitácora* (Tijuana) (19 November 1995): n.p.

Pablo Urbanyi (b. 1939)

ARGENTINA

Pablo Urbanyi was born in Hungary in 1939 and at the age of seven immigrated with his family to Argentina, where he became a citizen. His first book, the short-story collection *Noche de revolucionarios* (Night of revolutionaries), was published in 1972. Two years later, his novel *Un revólver para Mack* (A revolver for Mack)—a parody of the detective novel—met with rave reviews from critics and readers alike. In 1975, he began work for the Buenos Aires newspaper *La Opinión* (Opinion), where he remained until 1977, when he was forced to leave the country due to the political situation following the military coup d'etat of 1976. He has since lived in Canada, where he wrote his second novel, *En ninguna parte* (No place, 1981), which was published in Buenos Aires. The collection of essays *De todo un poco, de nada mucho* (A little of everything, not much of anything) appeared in 1988. In 1992, he published a second book of short stories, *Nacer de nuevo* (To be born again) and two more novels followed: *Silver* (1994) and *Puesta de sol* (Sunset, 1997).

Un revólver para Mack was published in 1974. The early part of the 1970s is a significant moment in the history of detective fiction in Argentina, when the hard-boiled novel affirms its dominance and supplants the classic puzzle-novel. In 1969, Ricardo Piglia initiated the "Serie negra" (Hard-boiled detective series) collection published by Tiempo Contemporáneo. This collection of works has been compared in importance and impact with the series "La brújula y la muerte" (Death and the compass) initiated by Jorge Luis Borges and Adolfo Bioy Casares during the 1940s. For the new generation of writers emerging during the 1970s, the hard-boiled novel was the genre and style of choice to begin their careers. *Un revólver para Mack* belongs to the first stage of this trend that resulted in a boom of hard-boiled detective novels that reclaimed the tradition of Dashiell Hammett, Raymond Chandler, and Horace McCoy. Authors and texts of this generation include *Los tigres de la memoria* (The tigers of memory, 1973) by Juan Carlos Martelli, *Triste, solitario y final* (Sad, lonely, and final, 1973) by Osvaldo Soriano, *The Buenos Aires Affair* (1973) by Manuel Puig, *El agua en los pulmones* (Water in the lungs, 1973) by Juan Martini, *Noches sin lunas ni soles* (Nights without moons or suns, 1975) by Rubén Tizziani, *Ni un dólar partido por la mitad* (Not even a dollar ripped in half, 1975) by Sergio Sinay, and *Su turno para morir* (His turn to die, 1976) by Alberto Laiseca.

The elements of humor, satire, and parody—traits that on the whole define Urbanyi's literature—are central to *Un revólver para Mack*. In this sense, the novel, while in line with its hard-boiled contemporaries listed above, is also inscribed in the tradition initiated by Borges and Bioy Casares in their collaborative work *Seis problemas para don Isidro Parodi* (*Six Problems for Don Isidro Parodi*, 1942), the first book of detective stories written in Argentina. Urbanyi himself indicates as much in his published lecture "El espacio que dejaron Borges y Bioy Casares para una novela paródica en Argentina" (The space that Borges and Bioy Casares left for a parodic novel in Argentina).

The importance of the place *Un revólver para Mack* occupies in Argentine detective fiction of the 1970s can be attributed to the memorable detective who is both the novel's main character and narrator. Of bodily corpulence that is inversely proportionate to his intelligence, Mack Hopkins belongs to the class of detective who is dull-witted, bumbling, and fatally destined to menial jobs that require only a sense of intimidation and obedience. He is the complete opposite of the intellectual detective, but he is also a complex character in whom violence and innocent cruelty are combined with honesty and a quixotic desire to protect weak women and fix the world. Mack, who is capable of gunning down in cold blood a group of inoffensive stoned hippies, has the favorite pastime of feeding the pigeons in the Plaza de Mayo (the central square in downtown Buenos Aires). Mack Hopkins's real name is Gerardo Romero. If Mack has decided to use a made-up professional name, its because while reading a "historia de drogas norteamericana" (North American drug story) he discovered that his true sur-name was the same as a Mexican killer. The novel thus mockingly fictionalizes a problem that writers of the genre in Argentina have had to deal with: that of adapting the detective novel to Argentine reality. This problem is resolved in Urbanyi's novel through parody by following the classic model of the *Quijote*. *Un revólver para Mack* narrates the misfortunes of an ex-policeman—and fan of detective novels—who gave up his badge to try his luck as a private detective.

The novel is narrated by Mack, through his voice and perspective. As a result, while reading this story as seen through the ingenuous and partially blind eyes of the protagonist, the reader knows more than the detective-narrator. The story in *Un revólver para Mack* that in the beginning is presented as confusing, alarming, and implausible, is only so from Mack's perspective. Mack, contracted by a pow-erful businessman, must complete his mission of tracking down a man about whom he has conflicting clues and find an undisclosed number of compromising photos of a naked couple about which he has no information in order to identify them. The novel tests the logic of hard-boiled narrative to an extreme, where a investigation that began with a trivial matter or false information soon balloons into a case with cadavers and dark secrets. The secret in *Un revólver para Mack* is a drug ring—similar to the drug stories that the character reads in his abundant spare time—in whose operation he unwittingly interferes. In the end, Mack gets himself out of the pickle, solves the case, and drops his ridiculous pseudonym.

The character of Mack reappears in two of Urbanyi's subsequent stories: "El caso de cosas" (The case of things, 1977) and "Concurso" (Contest, 1981). In the stories, Mack has gone back to using his real name, Romero; he has abandoned his profession of detective and works in a small town for the local lottery. In 1992, *Un revólver para Mack* was translated into French after the author made signifi-cant revisions. This new version tells essentially the same story and includes as an epilogue "El caso de cosas" in which Romero remembers one of his past adventures as a detective.

Sergio Pastormerlo

Works

"El caso de cosas." *Hispamérica* 17 (1977): 79–91.
"Concurso." *Cuadernos hispanoamericanos* 367–368 (1981): 120–41.
"El espacio que dejaron Borges y Bioy Casares para una novela paródica en Argentina," in
    Kriminalromania, ed. Hubert Poppel. Tübingen: Stuffenburg Verlag, 1988.
Un revólver para Mack. Buenos Aires: Corregidor, 1974.

René Vergara (1921–1983)

CHILE

Absent from the majority of Chilean literature encyclopedias, René Vergara is virtually unknown, not only in his country but also internationally. He is one of the most representative authors of detective fiction in Chile and a fervent cultivator of this genre, putting in the reader's hands all of his knowledge and experience as a professional detective and police officer for more than four decades. For many years Vergara worked for the Chilean Homicide Brigade. His job allowed him to participate in many international investigations, such as the assassination of the former Venezuelan president Rómulo Betancourt (1958–1963). He was also a criminologist and criminology professor in Chile and Venezuela and worked for many international organizations in Chile such as England's Royal Police and the Federal Bureau of Investigation in Chile.

Vergara was on many occasions inspector for the OAS (Organization of American States), and he founded the *Scientific Police Magazine* in Venezuela. His job gave him the opportunity to work in different countries in Latin America, the United States, and Europe. This fact lends a decidedly international flavor to his writing: knowledge of regional geography and crime organizations in other countries. One of Vergara's most important characters was inspector Carlos Cortés—a sort of Chilean antihero. This detective stands in direct contrast to the English detective prototype such as the renowned Agatha Christie hero, inspector Hercule Poirot. This opposition is evident in the fact that the author claims to be a natural-born investigator who believes that crime is a response to certain social circumstances, contrary to the cerebral idea that crime is nothing more than the aberrant behavior of social misfits. In other words, Vergara—from a Latin American detective's perspective—views crime as a response to the fate deciding one's lot in life and that the individual's social environment determines reality. He believes that fate plays a significant role in people's lives and actions, which can result in radical change. He does not need to invent stories, since he gleans them from the everyday reality of Latin American people, their lives, and the miserable environment that surrounds them.

Vergara has a special sensibility toward the unseemly elements of society, which convey an authentic image and personal take on crime according to the writer's own experiences. In his personal experiences, the author finds that Latin American reality is often defined by inexplicable occurrences that lead to doubt and unanswered questions, ambiguities, and mysteries about death. Therefore, this is the reason that Vergara narrates themes and events based on popular beliefs and customs; for instance, meetings with death, fatal premonitions, and popular myths about death and the dead. He always writes about crimes and criminals as common elements that he incorporates into everyday life, since they are universal recurrences in any society. He perceives the individual environment, destiny, and circumstances as determinist elements (social markers) in the conduct of individuals. Hence, one must perceive his detective fiction as a social chronicle performed by many actors going about their daily lives.

Vergara is an outspoken social critic who views capitalism in Latin America and other countries as a competitive system that transforms individuals into desensitized beings who lack basic human emotion—the price of survival in such a system. Furthermore, the writer achieves universality by tackling crimes and criminals as inevitable and inescapable problems associated with the poor as a direct result of social inequities and the absence of opportunity. These terrible conditions condemn many to a life of total misery. Vergara inserts these conditions as a constant theme into the Chilean scenario in many of his works. By so doing, the reader obtains a sense of universality, while at the same time known Chilean locales afford him credibility with his readers who come to identify with these settings and their familiarity. The author converts Santiago de Chile's microcosms into a mysterious world with his stories of crime and death. Many familiar sites in the city such as El Mapocho, La Quinta Normal, Yungay, Matadero, La Dehesa, Chillán, or Avenida La Paz are easily recognizable to the local reader, but may also be representative of many similar places in urban environments throughout the world.

Personally and professionally, Vergara's broad experience as an astute and capable crime investigator is evident in his first compilation of short stories, *El pasajero de la muerte* (Death's passenger, 1969). Here, the writer showcases one of the most common crimes in big cities: the murder of cabdrivers. Vergara's analysis of the crime identifies not only what the investigator is thinking, but also what are the criminal's thoughts. These two contrasting points-of-view guide the reader to discover the real motivation of crime and the effect it has on society. The characters in this collection of crime stories are common workers who become the victims of criminals who grew up in the marginal and poor zones of the city.

In 1971, two additional volumes of short stories appear: *¡Qué sombra más larga tiene ese gato!* (What a long shadow that cat has), and *Taxi para el insomnio* (Taxi for insomnia). In the first, Vergara presents other sectors of society. In this case, he shows the upper class as falling victim to crime, the product of the social system they themselves have created. The cat may be considered as a metaphor of justice, which inexorably reaches the criminals. One of the most significant stories narrates the murder of the aristocrat Rebeca Levi de Bryner. This case presents not only an attack on the upper class, but also illustrates how the criminal conscience contributes to the creation of its own trap, which the criminal falls into. The criminal's own mistakes help to reveal the essential clues necessary to solve the crime. In the second volume of short stories, the writer presents three different aspects of crime. The first part describes the murder of a woman at the hands of her nephew, and how then the killer goes after a child who witnessed the murder. Obviously, these events show how the weak in society are abused by the strong, and in this case, the abuse of women and children at the hands of men. The second part contains two horrific stories that depict raw violence in cases such as a man beaten to death with a hammer and the murder of a gay man decapitated by his lover as proof of societal homophobia. The third part is a philosophic-existentialist analysis elaborated by inspector Cortés. Vergara uses this kind of philosophical thinking as an important element in the plot, which shows not only the inspector's investigative psychology, but also criticizes those investigators who plant false evidence or pressure and torture criminals into confessing.

Another important Vergara collection is *De las memorias del inspector Cortés* (From the memoirs of inspector Cortes, 1976). In this book, Vergara proposes a new ethic in relation to detective fiction, because his stories occur in places common to the reader such as poor urban neighborhoods where misery, passion, and weakness converge to create a monstrous protagonist. These images are so real that the reader perceives them as part of everyday life. Vergara, as noted, invents his own Chilean hero, trying to give him many of the characteristics he considers every Chilean or Latin American man to possess such as sincerity, security, and even malice, as well as the knowledge of the reality of his country and its people. For this reason, he creates a native protagonist as a model for the Latin American detective: inspector Cortés, better known as "El Mono" (The monkey). He is as human as anyone: skinny, hairy, and homely with long, dangling arms, enjoys drinking cold beer, and is an imposing figure at six feet tall and 170 pounds. He is more intuitive than analytic, more inclined toward the collective than the individual; in other words, he represents the Chilean type.

In addition, *De las memorias del inspector Cortés* contains elements of the fantastic such as inexplicable occurrences that are part-and-parcel of everyday life but which no one can explain. For example, visions and otherworldly apparitions, the testimony of a dead thief, or premonitions of death all appear in the stories. In the face of such inexplicable events, a police investigation seems useless. Other aspects illustrated by Vergara in this work are social deviations such as homosexual pedophilia, spousal abuse, rape, necrophilia, and the proliferation of venereal diseases. However, in the last part of the book, the author approaches existentialist thought about human nature and the reasons behind criminal conduct. Vergara concludes that heredity, environment, and destiny are significant and determinant elements in human behavior.

Más allá del crimen (Beyond crime, 1978) is a series of stories in which the omniscient narrator crosses the line between life and death and presents an undeniable reality. The narration presents a polyphony of narrative voices that emerge to give representation to an unconscious collectivity. The book is divided in two parts, the first of which consists of an autobiography by the author: his childhood, his life, and the image of his family, especially his mother. The second part narrates a series of stories occurring in Chile, memories of his childhood neighborhood, and other poor neighborhoods of Santiago. There are dialogues among dead people who mock the detective's hypotheses and question the police's explanations of strange occurrences. In other words, Vergara develops a game of crime and inquiry, showing in many cases the police abuse of criminals to solve crimes and to obtain a reasonable explanation for their actions. It is significant that Vergara underscores the fact that not only the criminals are guilty of reprehensible behavior, but also some police officers are guilty of bad conduct and abusive authority.

Indeed, as one might perceive, Vergara's detective fiction is based on social reality, because the author views this reality as a source of inspiration. For this reason, the author must be considered one of the most important observers and critics of Latin American society and a major contributor to the Latin American detective genre.

Oscar A. Díaz-Ortiz

Works

Crímenes inolvidables, 1923–1954. Santiago: Wordtheque, 2000.
De las memorias del inspector Cortés. Santiago: Nascimento, 1976.
Más allá del crimen. Santiago: Nascimento, 1978.
La otra cara del crimen: el caso de Alicia Bon. Buenos Aires: Francisco de Aguirre, 1970.
El pasajero de la muerte: cuentos y relatos policiales. Santiago: Teele, 1969.
¡Qué sombra más larga tiene ese gato! Buenos Aires: Francisco de Aguirre, 1971.
Taxi para el insomnio. Buenos Aires: Francisco de Aguirre, 1971.
"Tríptico policial," in *Crímenes criollos: antología del cuento policial chileno*, ed. Ramón Díaz Eterovic. Santiago: Mosquito Editores, 1994, 205–35.

Criticism

Agrupación amigos del libro. *¿Quién soy?* Santiago: Editorial Nascimento, 1979.

Raúl Waleis (pseudonym of Luis V. Varela) (1845–1911)

ARGENTINA

Raúl Waleis (the anagrammatic pen name of Luis V. Varela), the founder of the detective novel in Spanish, was born in Montevideo, Uruguay. His parents, Florencio Varela and Justa Cané (both of Argentine patrician families) had fled to Uruguay as exiles. At age 17, after the fall of the dictator Juan Manuel de Rosas and consequent national unification, Luis Varela returned to the land of his ancestors where he later earned a degree in law at the University of Córdoba. He soon began work for *La Tribuna* (The tribune), one of the principal newspapers in Buenos Aires, which was operated by his brothers. The name of one of them, Mariano, appears as a member of the founding commission of the influential Club del Progreso (Club for progress). Meanwhile, Luis began a political career that took him to the positions of vice-secretary of the Ministry of the Interior in 1868, representative of the Buenos Aires legislature in 1874 and 1877, and president of the Supreme Court in 1877 and 1889. He died on November 12, 1911 in Buenos Aires at his house on Lavalle Street. Literature had aroused his interest very early on in his life. In 1862, he published the poems of *Hijas del alma* (Daughters of the soul) in Santa Fe; in 1867, *La Tribuna* published *Amor filial* (A son's love), a one-act play in verse, followed by *El ciego* (The blind man, 1871) a play in three acts.

These brief biographical notes clearly place Varela/Waleis as a prime exponent of the generation of 1880. He was at the center of the controversies of his time, and given the course of his career, was one of the most eminent thinkers and defenders of the new social model for the country. Far from the concerns and achievements of the popular literature that surrounded him (especially the Gauchesque), and in contrast to the phenomena of mass distribution associated with Anglo and French detective fiction, the birth of the Argentine detective novel was rooted in the ideological corpus of the elite. Waleis's first novel, the 319-page *La huella del crimen* (The trail of the crime) of 1877 (not 1878 as was believed until recently) was followed by a second novel that same year, the 350-page *Clemencia* (Clemencia). The author announced that a third novel, *Herencia fatal* (Fatal inheritance) was to be published soon after so as to complete the trilogy. Waleis acknowledged his debt to Emile Gaboriau and considers himself his pupil. Likewise, he cites the influence of Balzac, Poe, and Xavier de Montespin (Ponce 1997). This serves as reliable proof of his profound knowledge of the *folletín* (novel serialized in a newspaper or magazine) and the nascent detective genre. Faithful to the ideology of the generation of 1880, Waleis outlined a didactic literary project whose objective was to educate and correct without forgetting the very pleasure of reading, for which he relied on the principles of Miguel de Cervantes: to "instruir deleitando" (to instruct while delighting) and "corregir instruyendo" (to correct while instructing). The pedagogical scope of his literature is twofold: on the one hand, he intends to "educar a la mujer" (educate women), and on the other, to "popularizar el derecho" (place the law within popular reach). The prefaces to the novels written by Juan Carlos Gómez and Aditardo Heredia place the texts within the social context of the period, and each make some rather interesting and insightful observations about the detective novel and the usefulness of popular forms of literature (Ponce 1997).

For all his grand intentions, Raúl Waleis's ambitious project failed. This failure is evident in the silence and oversight of his work for more than a century. One could argue that the social conditions of nineteenth-century Argentina did not lend themselves to the emergence of widespread interest in detective fiction that would have led to the creation of a body of writers and readers. However, the success of other forms of emergent lowbrow or popular artistic expression—for example, the *folletines gauchescos* (serialized gaucho narratives) by Eduardo Gutiér-rez, in particular *Hormiga negra* (Black ant), and the abundant use of *cocoliche* (a hybrid Italian-Spanish dialect) in the theater of the famous Podestá brothers, and the highly successful sainete (short comedic theatrical pieces)—would seem to indicate that the reasons for Waleis's failure are to be found in his works themselves.

His detective fiction can be read as one of the forms of exoticism in vogue at the time, justified by the simple fact that the plot takes place in Paris and that almost all the characters are French. Waleis's failure stems from the fact that his narrative is at too much a remove from local environment and reality. Rather than taking an interest in the adventures of his detective André L'Archiduc, alias "el Lince" (The linx), the popular reader Waleis intends to educate prefers the gauchesque epics or melodramatic tales of immigration. The didactic dogma of Waleis can't hold a candle to Fray Mocho's (pseudonym of José Sixto Alvarez) anecdotally rich collection *La vida de los ladrones célebres de Buenos Aires y su manera de robar* (The life of famous Buenos Aires thieves and their style of robbery, 1887) or *Memorias de un vigilante* (Memoirs of a cop, 1897).

Like Gaboriau, Leroux, or Doyle, Waleis's point of departure in his novels is that of social discord, the loss of balance that the proper authorities must restore. So-called legal or law novels operate on this basis of re-establishing social harmony that has gone awry, which implies a reconstruction of the past to discover where things went wrong. The disruption must be exemplary, spectacular even, and arouse the greatest possible popular interest. "Es un caso que va a ser célebre" (This case in going to be famous) we read at the beginning of *La huella del crimen*. The conflict between good and evil is the foundation of this structure, and it is initiated through its most violent manifestation—crime. This is the case in *La huella del crimen*, where a body is discovered in a wooded area, a mystery that the investigators must unravel. In contrast, in *Clemencia*, the reader must reach the second half of the novel before confronting a murder, which then sets the investigation into motion.

In fact, this difference in the construction of the plot is a consequence, in part, of the influence of the *folletín*, in which structure does not faithfully follow the linear progress of the investigation and splits into narrative tangents of love and passion that dominate the text. We find the same thing happening in works such as Gaston Leroux's *El misterio del cuarto amarillo* (The mystery of the yellow room) or in Arthur Conan Doyle's *A Study in Scarlet*, before this practice was condemned by English novelists. On the other hand, the social disorder that Waleis's characters seek to change is not necessarily of a criminal nature. Waleis addresses what could be called "social crimes" that threaten to disrupt order and decency. For example, in *Clemencia*, he dedicates a significant number of pages to criticizing the institution of marriage as it was perceived at the end of the nineteenth century, which led, according to him, to female infidelity. One of his characters, Rafael Meris, speaks of crimes that are different from the violent, bloody ones: crimes "que no pueden encontrar solución en el marco de las leyes escritas por el hombre" (that cannot find a solution within the framework of man's written law [66]). This aspect returns us to the didactic nature of Raúl Waleis's literature—to his project of educating the masses that defines his work. The many components of his narrative all work toward this common goal. In this sense, the detective and agent of good, L'Archiduc, is little more than a narrative detail, although he appears in both novels.

The fact that L'Archiduc is a member of the police force deserves a brief commentary by way of comparison with other well-known characters of early detective fiction such as Auguste Dupin, the famous gentleman-detective who directly competed with inept policemen. This tendency that expressed distrust in the institutions created by the state to provide public safety will reach its peak in the 1950s with the hard-boiled fiction of the United States. Waleis's choice, which distinguishes him from European writers, is nevertheless in line with the attitude adopted by subsequent Argentine writers. For example, the protagonist of the short story "La pesquisa" (The investigation) by Paul Groussac is a detective who works in Buenos Aires. How does one explain this unique trend? It is, perhaps, due to historical circumstances. By 1870, Argentina declared itself a modern state after more than a century of social anarchy. Argentina's positivist ruling class had taken the country under its wing and decided to integrate Argentina into the modern world following the European model, specifically that of France. Recognizing the police figures of authority, then, can be interpreted as a declaration of trust in the state and its institutions.

However, nothing is perfect and the state and justice can commit countless legal mistakes. In real life, in his speech in defense of a defendant, the attorney Luis V. Varela, upon carefully analyzing and examining the circumstances of the crime (which allowed him to prove the innocence of his client), affirms: "La justicia humana ha buscado regir la sociedad, dañándola lo menos posible. Ella no mira, en nuestros tiempos, en la pena otra cosa que la espiación [*sic*] de un delito y la prevención de otros por medio del ejemplo" (Human justice has sought to govern society by doing as little damage as possible. In these times, it does not see in the punishment anything but the expiation of one crime and the prevention of another through example [*Defensa en tercera instancia del reo Pedro Luro, por el abogado Luis V. Varela*]).

In the novel, the detective created by Waleis constitutes the best example given that he spent two years in prison after an unfair trial. His excellent behavior, his knowledge of prison life and the criminals, his intelligence, and also his friends allow him to join the police force and climb the career ladder. In the first novel, L'Archiduc is in his fifties and knows all the ins-and-outs of the profession. In *Clemencia*, however, we experience, in the second half of the novel, a return to the character's first investigation, which happened in 1853, about a quarter-century before. This curious flash to the past—not very common in the genre—"humanizes" the character by endowing him with a history and placing him within a temporal scheme.

L'Archiduc represents the archetype of the positivist hero. In order to carry-out his investigation, he proceeds with meticulous and logical methods, comparable to those of Dupin, Rouletabille, or Holmes, which are based on observation and analysis. Each crime is, in his view, a mathematical problem. His behavior at the crime scene surprises judges and policemen: he sees what others cannot and does not hesitate to lie or kneel down (as Rouletabille or Holmes would) to better study all the details. Nor does he hesitate to disguise himself as a police officer or a civilian in order to blend in with the crowd and eavesdrop on indiscreet conversation. His powers of logic are so surprising that some journalists compare him to Mephistopheles and ask in awe if he is the devil. The detective purposely cultivates this image as well as the theatrical resources available to him in order to impress his audience and the reader (from a technical standpoint, the narrator resorts to traditional ellipsis) despite the absence of a partner (Holmes/Watson, Poirot/Hastings) who traditionally is used to underscore the intelligence of the protagonist.

His status as a police officer allows him, during his investigations, to benefit from the help that the legal apparatus provides. Thus, the precious aid of doctors and the detailed descriptions and dialogues—always didactic in nature—all serve to illustrate the benefits of scientific progress. The same occurs with the process of justice and its mechanical aspects such as reports, inquiries, and interrogations. Confessions by guilty criminals occupy an important place even though the mystery has already been solved. His status exposes him to the inherent risks of the profession, contrary to what happens with Dupin or Holmes. Furthermore, another personality trait likens him more to the bureaucratic French detectives than to the English ones: his capacity to place himself in the shoes of the other, to understand him, and to grasp the mechanisms of his thought-process are all significant traits that will later appear in the famous French detective character Jules Maigret.

Evil, embodied in a villain, always arises to confront detective L'Archiduc. In *La huella del crimen*, it is Baron Campumil, and in *Clemencia*, Enrique Latouret. Both are nemesis figures—perpetrators of crimes and protagonists in the plot. In the background, one finds the social problems that led them to commit a murder in order to defend their honor against female infidelity (false in one case, real in the other). The author's misogyny is scarcely overshadowed by his message: in the Western *fin-de-siécle* world of the late nineteeth century, women are considered inferior beings; they do not control their own destiny; arranged marriages are the source of failed unions and the main cause of betrayal. Against such "crimes," man (the masculine sex) is not protected under law and has no other option than to take justice into his own hands. After killing his wife, Latouret states: "Yo sabía que Elena me engañaba y que Comin era su amante. . . . ¿Qué hacer? Sólo había una solución. . . . Vengarme de los dos, salvar a mis hijos y no perderme . . . yo, que era la víctima y que era inocente" (I knew Elena was cheating on me and that Comin was her lover. . . . What to do? There was only a solution. . . . Take revenge on both of them, save my children and not lose myself . . . I was the victim, I was the innocent one).

In both novels, conflict between good and evil is portrayed through the presentation of two opposing perspectives: that of the detective, and that of the criminal. The latter, of course, has erased his tracks and secured a good alibi, which makes the detective's job harder. In *La huella del crimen*, the detective proves the innocence of Juan Picot, a nobleman fallen into disgrace (recall that love and wealth are two inseparable topics of the *folletín*). In *Clemencia*, he proves the innocence of Emilio Comin, the young lover who made some bad choices after being disillusioned by his girlfriend Sofía's arranged marriage to an older man. In fact, the presence of suspects, of whom Clemencia (a mysterious character of the first novel who appears also in the second) is one, is a pretext to divert the plot into a discussion of what Waleis calls "other crimes." Such "other crimes" include crimes of love (Clemencia is the fruit of an incestuous relationship) and social crimes (the legal blunders suffered by Juan Picot and André L'Archiduc). The story thus takes the form of a mosaic of the social disruptions of which men are conscious but cannot be changed due to the weight of conventions that oblige them to keep a hypocritical silence. The literary device of the mask enters this world of appearances with all its might: the characters disguise themselves and hide their faces so that they can better betray.

Such a world is a stage and men are actors who play a role that imprisons them. The setting chosen by Waleis underlines this theatrical feature. Although his goal is to educate the Argentine masses, he does not hesitate to situate the majority of the action in Paris instead of Buenos Aires. The French capital represents the model for society: "La Francia es París, y París no es una ciudad. París es un mundo." (France is Paris and Paris is not a city. Paris is a world) (*Clemencia* 3). Nevertheless, Waleis's choice reveals an impotency with regard to locating his stories in his own country (as a literary space, the Buenos Aires of the time didn't offer a clear view). However, Paris, at least in his eyes, was a window on the world. After all, didn't Edgar Allan Poe also situate his Dupin series in Paris?

In Waleis's schematic universe, the conflict between good and evil is resolved, although not in an ideal way, since it suffers the restraints of the limits that the law imposes and so is unable to respond to the difficulties emerging from a changing world. Varela/Waleis's goal is still understood as essentially didactic, but we shouldn't dismiss his intentions of social prophylaxis. In the construction of his narrative, the Argentine writer must also address the questions posed by the difficulties of adapting a codified genre. His answers are not necessarily original, but they are coherent and systematic. For his significant and early contribution, Waleis must be considered to be the indisputable father of detective fiction in Spanish.

Néstor Ponce

Works

Clemencia. Buenos Aires: Imprenta y Librerías de Mayo, 1877.
Defensa en tercera instancia del reo Pedro Luro, por el abogado Luis V. Varela. Buenos Aires: La Tribuna, 1872.
La huella del crimen. Buenos Aires: Imprenta y Librerías de Mayo, 1877.

Criticism

Ponce, Néstor. "Una poética pedagógica: Raúl Waleis, fundador de la novela policial en castellano," in *Literatura policial en la Argentina: Waleis, Borges, Saer,* ed. Néstor Ponce, Sergio Pastormerlo, and Dardo Scavino. *Serie Estudios e Investigaciones,* 32. La Plata: Facultad de Humanidades y Ciencias de la Educación, Universidad Nacional de La Plata, 1997, 7–15.
———. *Diagonales del género: estudios sobre el policial argentino.* Paris: Editions du Temp, 2001.

Rodolfo Walsh (1927–1977)

ARGENTINA

Rodolfo Jorge Walsh was born on 9 January 1927 in Choele-Choel, a small town surrounded by farms in the southern Argentine province of Río Negro. He was the descendant of Irish immigrants who arrived in Argentina in the mid-nineteenth century, fleeing the famine in Ireland. Rodolfo, one of five children, was five years old when the family moved to Juárez in the province of Buenos Aires, where his father intended to start his own *chacra* or small farm. Tough economic times, bad seasons, and his father's gambling problem led to disaster. In 1937, the family lost everything and was forced to split up. Two of his brothers went to live with a grandmother in Buenos Aires, Rodolfo and his brother Héctor were sent to a boarding school run by nuns, and Katie, the only girl, stayed with her parents.

Walsh's childhood and much of his early life were marked by poverty and struggle. He began working at a young age for the Hachette publishing house as a proofreader, translator, and then eventually was able to put together an anthology of stories, his *Diez cuentos policiales argentinos* (Ten Argentine detective stories, 1953). This was the first anthology of detective fiction ever published in the country and it has become a classic, although it is virtually impossible to find. From there, Walsh went on to publish his own detective stories in the popular magazines *Vea y Lea* (See and read) and *Leoplán* (Reading plan). In 1950, he won second place in the First Detective Story Contest sponsored by *Vea y Lea* for his story "Las tres noches de Isaías Bloom" (The three nights of Isaías Bloom). Also in 1950, Walsh married Elina Tejerina and they had two daughters, María Victoria and Patricia. Motivated by political reasons and a sense of justice, Walsh became increasingly involved in the militant movements of the left. Almost exactly one year after the military coup d'état that ushered in the infamous "Proceso de Reorganización Nacional" (Process of national reorganization), Rodolfo Walsh was killed in a hail of bullets by a paramilitary death squad on 25 March 1977. Before he was killed, one of his daughters was also murdered by the military government. The tragic, politically charged circumstances of his death as well as his never-tiring efforts, both in his personal life and his literature, of fighting injustice and exposing corruption have resulted in a surge of critical and biographical works that have elevated him to the status of one Argentina's most beloved writers. Likewise, there have been many reprintings of his books, which continue to sell out. One of the most recent as well as one of the most complete and informative books on Walsh is Michael McCaughan's biography *True Crimes. Rodolfo Walsh: The Life and Times of a Radical Intellectual* (2002). It contains a great deal of information about Walsh's life and his works, including an exhaustive bibliography on the author.

In 1953, Walsh published his collection of stories *Variaciones en rojo* (Variations in red), which received the Buenos Aires municipal fiction prize. He claimed that he wrote the book in one month. The stories introduced two of the most memorable characters in Argentine detective fiction, Daniel Hernández and Inspector Laurenzi. Both, in different ways, represent reformulations of classic detective figures such as Sherlock Holmes and Dupin. In one of Walsh's most famous stories, and one that is long enough to be considered a novella, "La aventura de las pruebas de imprenta" (The adventure of the print proofs), Daniel Hernández must use his characteristic intelligence to solve a locked-room case. The stories in the volume typically follow the same type of puzzle-narrative model. The stories involving Laurenzi are considered to be some of Walsh's best from the collection, due in part to the character himself. Another of his most famous stories is "Cuento para tahúres" ("Gambler's Tale"), which has been widely anthologized and translated into English by Donald A. Yates. Walsh maintained a long friendship with the American academic, who is one of the pioneering critics of Latin American detective fiction. The Walsh–Yates relationship is detailed in McCaughan's book. One last story that is worth mentioning by way of survey is his "Esa mujer" (That Woman). The woman alluded to but never mentioned in the story is Eva Perón. The story is among the author's best and also contains many detective elements while providing a strong statement against Peronism. There has been much written about the stories, so it doesn't bear repeating here aside from reaffirming Walsh's status as a cornerstone of Argentine detective fiction.

Many of his other texts have been considered to belong to the genre, not in the classic sense of his early stories but more in line with narratives of (true) crime. This is particularly the case with his documentary-like book *Operación masacre* (Operation massacre, 1957), which exposes the case of illegal executions carried out in a garbage dump in 1956. This has been Walsh's most studied text to date. His books *Caso Satanowsky* (The Satanowsky case, 1958) and *¿Quién mató a Rosendo?* (Who killed Rosendo?, 1969) are similar in that they are journalistic-type reports on famous, real murder cases that Walsh investigated thoroughly. *Caso Satanowsky* deals with the murder of the lawyer Marcos Satanowsky, who was assassinated by agents of the secret service. Walsh's reports were originally published in the periodical *Mayoría* (Majority) between June 1958 and January 1959. His investigation and reports were responsible for identifying the guilty parties.

As stated previously, Walsh's works as well as his life story have garnered a great deal of critical attention. Likewise, there are many new editions of his works and collections of previously unpublished material such as his letters and assorted documents that are collected in *Ese hombre y otros escritos personales* (That man and other personal writings, 1996), edited by Daniel Link. It is worth identifying some of the most significant contributions that have lead to a better understanding and appreciation of Walsh's diverse body of works: *Textos de y sobre Rodolfo Walsh* (Texts by and about Rodolfo Walsh, 2000) edited by Jorge Lafforgue; and *Rodolfo Walsh, vivo* (Rodolfo Walsh, alive, 1994) edited by Roberto Baschetti, are both excellent collections that contain many insightful essays and also excellent bibliographies. Of course, aside from special collections such as these, there are many quality essays that approach Walsh's work from a variety of critical angles—many specifically in relation to detective fiction. Recent anthologies of his detective stories include *La máquina del bien y del mal* (The machine of good and evil, 1992)—the second volume in the *La muerte y la brújula* (Death and the compass) detective fiction series edited by Jorge Lafforque—and *Cuento para tahúres y otros relatos policiales* (Gambler's tale and other detective stories, 1999).

Darrell B. Lockhart

Works

"Los asesinos," in *Breve antología de cuentos policiales*. Buenos Aires: Sudamericana, 1996.

"La aventura de las pruebas de imprenta," in *El relato policial en la Argentina: antología crítica*, ed. Jorge B. Rivera. Buenos Aires: Eudeba, 1986, 45–118.

Caso Satanowsky. Buenos Aires: Ediciones de la Flor, 1973.

"Cuento para tahúres," in *Cuentos policiales argentinos*, ed. Jorge Lafforgue. Buenos Aires: Alfaguara, 1997, 193–98. English version as "Gambler's Tale," in *Latin Blood: The Best Crime and Detective Stories of South America*, ed. and trans. Donald A. Yates. New York: Herder & Herder, 1972, 43–50.

Cuento para tahúres y otros relatos policiales. Buenos Aires: Punto Sur, 1987. Reprint, Buenos Aires: Ediciones de la Flor, 1999.

Diez cuentos policiales argentinos, ed. Rodolfo Walsh. Buenos Aires: Hachette, 1953.

"En defensa propia," in *Tiempo de puñales*. Buenos Aires: Seijas y Goyanarte, 1964, 45–52.

Ese hombre y otros escritos personales, ed. Daniel Link. Buenos Aires: Seix Barral, 1996. (Personal letters and previously unpublished papers.)

Un kilo de oro. Buenos Aires: Jorge Alvarez, 1967.

La máquina del bien y del mal. Buenos Aires: Clarín/Aguilar, 1992.

Obra literaria completa. Mexico City: Siglo XXI Editores, 1981.

Los oficios terrestres. Buenos Aires: Jorge Alvarez, 1965.

Operación masacre. Buenos Aires: Sigla, 1957. Reprints, Jorge Alvarez, 1969; Ediciones de la Flor, 1972.

¿Quién mató a Rosendo? Buenos Aires: Tiempo Contemporáneo, 1969. Reprint, Ediciones de la Flor, 1985.

"Shadow of a Bird," in *Latin Blood: The Best Crime and Detective Stories of South America*, ed. and trans. Donald A. Yates. New York: Herder & Herder, 1972, 183–200.

"Simbiosis," in *El cuento policial argentino: una propuesta de lectura productiva para la escuela secundaria*, ed. Elena Braceras, Cristina Leytour, and Susana Pittella. Buenos Aires: Plus Ultra, 1986, 151–61.

"Las tres noches de Isaías Bloom," in *Tiempo de puñales*. Buenos Aires: Seijas y Goyanarte, 1964, 53–61. Also in *Breve antología de cuentos policiales,* ed. María Inés González and Marcela Grosso. Buenos Aires: Sudamericana, 1995, 117–28.

Variaciones en rojo. Buenos Aires: Hachette, 1953.

Criticism

Amar Sánchez, Ana María. "El sueño eterno de justicia: género policial y no ficción en Walsh," in *El relato de los hechos. Rodolfo Walsh: testimonio y escritura*. Rosario: Beatriz Viterbo, 1992, 125–56.

Baschetti, Roberto, ed. *Rodolfo Walsh, vivo*. Buenos Aires: Ediciones de la Flor, 1994.

Bechara, Marcelo Alejandro. *Periodismo y literatura: lo fantástico y lo policial en Walsh*. Entre Ríos, Argentina: Facultad de Ciencias de la Educación, Universidad Nacional de Entre Ríos, 1998.

Braceras, Elena, Cristina Leytour, and Susana Pittella. "Walsh y el género policial," in *Textos de y sobre Rodolfo Walsh*, ed. Jorge Lafforgue. Buenos Aires-Madrid: Alianza, 2000, 99–104.

Cohen Imach, Victoria. "Las máscaras o el pintor de paredes: asunción de la periferia en *Variaciones en rojo* de Rodolfo Walsh." *Hispamérica* 58 (1991): 3–15.

Crespo, Bárbara. "*Operación masacre*: el relato que sigue." *Filología* 27.1–2 (1994): 221–31.

D'Anna, Eduardo. "Rodolfo Walsh: novela policial, sistema policial." *El lagrimal trifurca* (Rosario, Argentina) 12 (1975): 40–44.

Fernández Vega, José. "De la teología a la política: el problema del mal en la literatura policial de Rodolfo Walsh." *Hispamérica* 83 (1999): 5–15.

Lafforgue, Jorge. "Walsh en y desde el género policial." *El gato negro: revista de narrativa policial y de misterio* (Argentina) 5 (1994): 27–30.

Lafforgue, Jorge, ed. *Textos de y sobre Rodolfo Walsh*. Buenos Aires-Madrid: Alianza, 2000.

Lafforgue, Jorge, and Jorge B. Rivera. *Asesinos de papel: ensayos sobre narrativa policial*. Buenos Aires: Colihue, 1996.

Lago, Sylvia. "Rodolfo Walsh: el violento oficio de escritor." *Casa de las Américas* 32.184 (1991): 56–69.

McCaughan, Michael. *True Crimes. Rodolfo Walsh: The Life and Times of a Radical Intellectual*. London: Latin American Bureau, 2002.

Pesce, Víctor. "Rodolfo Jorge Walsh, el problemático ejercicio del relato," in *Los héroes "difíciles": la literatura policial en la Argentina y en Italia*, ed. Giuseppe Petronio, Jorge B. Rivera, and Luigi Volta. Buenos Aires: Corregidor, 1991, 95–110.

Ponce, Néstor. *Diagonales del género: estudios sobre el policial argentino*. Paris: Editions du Temp, 2001.

Rama, Ángel. "Las novelas policiales del pobre," in Baschetti, 79-86.

Simpson, Amelia S. *Detective Fiction from Latin America*. Rutherford, NJ: Fairleigh Dickinson University Press, 1990.

～

Bibliography of
Literary Anthologies and Criticism

LATIN AMERICA

Anthologies

Breve antología de cuentos policiales. Buenos Aires: Sudamericana, 1995.

León, Olver Gilberto de, ed. *Selección de cuentos policiales de grandes escritores latinoamericanos*. Montevideo: Signos, 1991.

López Coll, Lucía, ed. *Variaciones en negro: relatos policiales hispanoamericanos*, introduction Leonardo Padura Fuentes. Bogotá: Norma, 2003.

López Coll, Lucía, and Leonardo Padura, eds. *Variaciones en negro: relatos policiales iberoamericanos*. Havana: Editorial Arte y Literatura, 2001.

Simpson, Amelia S., ed. and trans. *New Tales of Mystery and Crime from Latin America*. Rutherford, NJ: Fairleigh Dickinson University Press, 1992.

Truque, Zonia Nadhezda, and Mauricio Contreras Hernández, eds. *Cuentos policiacos*. Bogotá: Magisterio, 1996.

Yates, Donald A., ed. *El cuento policial latinoamericano*. Mexico City: Ediciones de Andrea, 1964.

———. *Latin Blood: The Best Crime and Detective Stories of South America*. New York: Herder & Herder, 1972.

Criticism

Giardinelli, Mempo. *El género negro*, 2 vols. Mexico City: Universidad Autónoma Metropolitana, 1984. Reprint, 1996.

———. *El género negro: ensayos sobre literatura policial*. Córdoba, Argentina. Op Oloop Ediciones, 1997.

Lafforgue, Jorge. "Narrativa policial entre dos orillas," in *Atípicos en la literatura latinoamericana*, ed. Noé Jitrik. Buenos Aires: Universidad de Buenos Aires, 1997, 351–62.

Monsiváis, Carlos. "Ustedes que nunca han sido asesinados." *Revista de la Universidad de México* (March 1973): n.p.

Padura Fuentes, Leonardo. "Modernidad y postmodernidad: la novela policial en Ibero-américa." *Hispamérica* 84 (1999): 37–50.

———. "Miedo y violencia: la literatura policial en Hispanoamérica," in *Variaciones en negro: relatos policiales hispanoamericanos*, ed. Lucía López Coll. Bogotá: Norma, 2003, 9–26.

Planells, Antonio. "El detective literario: panorámica del género policiaco de Poe a Borges." *Escritura: teoría y crítica literaria* (Caracas) 10.19–20 (1985): 71–101.

———. "El género detectivesco en Hispanoamérica." *Revista interamericana de bibliografía/Inter-American Review of Bibliography* 36.4 (1986): 460–72.

———. "El género policiaco en Hispanoamérica." *Monographic Review/Revista monográfica* 3.1–2 (1987): 148–62.

Ponce, Néstor. *Literatura y paraliteratura: la narrativa policial en Argentina y en Hispanoamérica*. Palaiseau: École Polytechnique, 1996.

Simpson, Amelia S. *Detective Fiction from Latin America*. Rutherford, NJ: Fairleigh Dickinson University Press, 1990.

———. "Detective Fiction," in *Encyclopedia of Latin American Literature*, ed. Verity Smith. London: Fitzroy Dearborn, 1997, 256–58.

Sklodowska, Elzbieta. "Transgresión paródica de la fórmula policial," in *La parodia en la nueva novela hispanoamericana (1960–1985)*. Purdue University Monographs in Romance Languages. Philadelphia: John Benjamins Publishing, 1991, 111–39.

Stavans, Ilán "Detectives en Latinoamérica." *Revista de la Universidad de Mexico* 42.446 (March 1988): 9–11.

Yates, Donald A. "The Spanish American Detective Story." *Modern Language Journal* 22 (1956): 52–58.

———. "La novela policial en las Américas." *Temas culturales*. Buenos Aires: Servicio Cultural e Informativo de los Estados Unidos (1963): 3–13.

ARGENTINA

Anthologies

Bajarlía, Juan Jacobo, ed. *Cuentos de crimen y misterio*. Buenos Aires: Jorge Alvarez Editor, 1964.

Braceras, Elena, and Cristina Leytour, eds. *Cuentos con detectives y comisarios*. Buenos Aires: Colihue, 1995.

Braceras, Elena, Cristina Leytour, and Susana Pittella. *El cuento policial argentino*. Buenos Aires: Plus Ultra, 1986.

Carrasco, Félix, et al. *20 cuentos policiales argentinos*. Buenos Aires: Plus Ultra, 1976.

———. *24 cuentos policiales argentinos*. 1977. Reprint, Buenos Aires: Plus Ultra, 1980.

Colautti, Sergio, et al. *El revés del crimen: 9 cuentos policiales de autores cordobeses*. Córdoba: Copiar, 1995.

Ferro, Roberto, ed. *Policiales: el asesino tiene quien le escriba*. Buenos Aires: IMFC (Ediciones Instituto Movilizador de Fondos Cooperativos), 1991.

Fèvre, Fermín, ed. *Cuentos policiales argentinos*. Buenos Aires: Kapelusz, 1974. Reprint, Buenos Aires: Kapelusz, 1995.

Figueroa, Adriana, et al. *Cuentos policiales*. Buenos Aires: Editorial "dg," 1987.

Lafforgue, Jorge, ed. *Cuentos policiales argentinos*. Buenos Aires: Alfaguara, 1997.

Lafforgue, Jorge, and Jorge B. Rivera, eds. *Asesinos de papel: historia, testimonios y antología de la narrativa policial en la Argentina*. Buenos Aires: Calicanto, 1977.
———. *El cuento policial*. Buenos Aires: Centro Editor de América Latina, 1981.
López, E. Liliana, ed. *Cuentos policiales clásicos*. Buenos Aires: Setiembre, 2000.
Manguel, Alberto, ed. *Variaciones sobre un tema policial*. Buenos Aires: Galerna, 1968.
Olguín, Sergio S., ed. *Escritos con sangre: cuentos argentinos sobre casos policiales*. Buenos Aires: Norma, 2003.
Pellicer, Rosa. "Libros y detectives en la narrativa policial argentina." *Hispamérica* 93 (2002): 3–18.
Pérez Zelaschi, Adolfo, et al. *Tiempo de puñales*, introduction by Donald A. Yates. Buenos Aires: Seijas y Goyanarte, 1964.
Piglia, Ricardo, ed. *Las fieras*. Buenos Aires: Clarín/Aguilar, 1993.
———. *Las fieras: antología del género policial en la Argentina*. Buenos Aires: Alfaguara, 1999. (Expanded version of previous item.)
Rivera, Jorge B., ed. *El relato policial en la Argentina: antología crítica*. Buenos Aires: Eudeba, 1986.
Ruiz Ibarlucea, Alicia, ed. *Cuentos policiales argentinos*. Buenos Aires: Abril, 1990.
Varela, Sergio, ed. *Pasacalles: cuentos policiales argentinos contemporáneos*. Buenos Aires: Distal, 2000.
Walsh, Rodolfo J., ed. *Diez cuentos policiales argentinos*. Buenos Aires: Hachette, 1953.

Criticism

Braceras, Elena, Cristina Leytour, and Susana Pittella. "Introducción. La literatura policial y su inserción en el campo de la literatura popular," in *El cuento policial argentino: una propuesta de lectura productiva par la escuela secundaria*. Buenos Aires: Plus Ultra, 1986, 9–88.
Feinmann, José Pablo. "Estado policial y novela negra argentina," in *Los héroes "difíciles": la literatura policial en la Argentina y en Italia*, ed. Giuseppe Petronio, Jorge B. Rivera, and Luigi Volta (pp. 143–53). Buenos Aires: Corregidor, 1991.
Fèvre, Fermín. "Estudio preliminar," in *Cuentos policiales*. Buenos Aires: Kapelusz, 1974, 7–32.
Gandolfo, Elvio E. "Policial negra y argentina: perdonalos Marlowe, porque no saben lo que hacen." *Fierro* (Buenos Aires) 23 (July 1986): n.p.
Lafforgue, Jorge. "Prólogo," in *Cuentos policiales argentinos*. Buenos Aires: Alfaguara, 1997, 9–22.
Lafforgue, Jorge, and Jorge B. Rivera. "La morgue está de fiesta . . . Literatura policial en la Argentina." *Crisis* 33 (1976): 16–25.
———. "La narrativa policial en la Argentina," in *Historia de la literatura argentina*, ed. Susana Zanetti. Buenos Aires: Centro Editor de América Latina, 1982.
———. *Asesinos de papel: ensayos sobre narrativa policial*. Buenos Aires: Ediciones Colihue, 1996.
Martínez, Victoria. "El acto de investigar: el rol de la mujer en la literatura policial de la Argentina y los Estados Unidos," in *Primeras jornadas internacionales de literatura argentina/comparística. Actas*, ed. Teresita Frugoni de Fritzsche. Buenos Aires: Facultad de Filosofía y Letras, Universidad de Buenos Aires, 1996, 425–30.
Petronio, Giuseppe, Jorge B. Rivera, and Luigi Volta, eds. *Los héroes "difíciles": la literatura policial en la Argentina y en Italia*. Buenos Aires: Corregidor, 1991.

Ponce, Néstor. "Un justiciero en busca de piedad: avatares del detective en el policial argentino." *Río de la Plata* (Paris) 17–18 (1997): 497–507.
———. *Diagonales del género: estudios sobre el policial argentino*. Paris: Editions du Temp, 2001.
Ponce, Néstor, Sergio Pastormerlo, and Dardo Scavino. *Literatura policial en la Argentina: Waleis, Borges, Saer*. La Plata: Facultad de Humanidades y Ciencias de la Educación, Universidad Nacional de La Plata, 1997.
Rivera, Jorge B. "Introducción," in *El relato policial en la Argentina: antología critica*. Buenos Aires: Eudeba, 1986, 7–41. Also as "El relato policial en la Argentina," in *Los héroes "difíciles": la literatura policial en la Argentina y en Italia*, ed. Giuseppe Petronio, Jorge B. Rivera, and Luigi Volta (pp. 59–83). Buenos Aires: Corregidor, 1991.
Sablich, José. "Contextos reales y ficcionales en la novela negra argentina de la década del '70," in *Calibar sin rastros: aportes para una historia social de la literatura argentina*, ed. Jorge Torres Roggero and María Elena Legaz. Córdoba, Argentina: CONICET/CIFF-yH, 1996, 157–85.

BRAZIL

Anthologies

Amâncio, Moacir, ed. *Chame o ladrão: contos policiais brasileiros*. São Paulo: Edições Populares, 1978.
Brandão, Adelino, et al. *Contos de mistério e suspense*, introduction by Fausto Cunha. Rio de Janeiro: Livraria Francisco Alves Editôra, 1986.
Cavalheiro, Edgard, and Raimundo de Menezes, eds. *Histórias de crimes y criminosos (uma antologia de contos brasileiros)*. São Paulo: Campanhia Distribuidora de Livros, 1956.
Martins, Luís, ed. *Obras-Primas do conto policial*. São Paulo: Livraria Martins Editôra, 1960.

Criticism

Medeiros e Albuquerque, Paulo de. "O romance policial brasileiro," in *O mundo emocionante do romance policial*. Rio de Janeiro: Francisco Alves, 1979, 205–20.
Reimão, Sandra Lúcia. *O que é romance policial*. São Paulo: Brasiliense, 1983.
Simpson, Amelia S. "Detective Fiction in Brazil." *Studies in Latin American Popular Culture* 7 (1988): 17–32.

CHILE

Anthologies

Díaz Eterovic, Ramón, ed. *Crímenes criollos: antología del cuento policial chileno*. Santiago: Mosquito Editores, 1994.

CUBA

Anthologies

Alvarez, Imeldo, ed. *Narraciones policiales: antología*. Havana: Capitán San Luis, 1993.

Fernández, Juan Carlos, et al. *El secreto de Plácido y otras narraciones*. Havana: Editorial Letras Cubanas, 1979.

Heras León, Eduardo, et al. *Cuentos policíacos cubanos*. Montevideo: ASESUR/Signos/ Amauta, 1989.

Martí, Agenor, ed. *Varios cuentos policíacos cubanos*. Havana: Editorial Letras Cubanas, 1980.

———. *Cuentos policiales cubanos*. Havana: Editorial Letras Cubanas, 1983.

Criticism

Céspedes, Francisco Garzón. "Cuba: el papel del género policiaco en la lucha ideológica." *Casa de las Américas* 89 (1975): 159–62.

Fernández Pequeño, José M. "Teoría y práctica de la novela policial revolucionaria." *La palabra y el hombre: revista de la Universidad Veracruzana* 66 (1988): 93–101.

———. "La novela policial cubana ante sí misma (1979–1986)." *La palabra y el hombre: revista de la Universidad Veracruzana* 70 (1989): 205–16.

Jiménez, Onilda. "Un nuevo fenómeno de la literatura cubana: la novela policial." *Círculo: revista de cultura* (Verona, NJ) 9 (1980): 93–100.

Malinowsky, Heike. "Un ejemplo de la literatura popular moderna: la novela policial cubana," in *La literatura en la sociedad de América Latina*, ed. José Morales Saravia. Lima: Latinoamericana, 1986, 255–70.

Martí, Agenor. *Sobre acusados y testigos*. Havana: Editorial Letras Cubanas, 1980.

Revueltas, Eugenia. "La novela policiaca en México y en Cuba." *Cuadernos americanos* (Nueva época) 1.1 (1987): 102–20.

Sandoval, Alejandro. "Narrativa policial cubana." *Plural: revista cultural de Excélsior* (Mexico) 11.8 (1982): 57–64.

Simpson, Amelia S. "From Private to Public Eye: Detective Fiction in Cuba." *Studies in Latin American Popular Culture* 8 (1989): 107–28.

MEXICO

Anthologies

Bermúdez, María Elvira, ed. *Los mejores cuentos policiacos mexicanos*. Mexico City: Libro-Mex, 1955.

———. *Cuento policiaco mexicano: breve antología*. Mexico City: Universidad Nacional Autónoma de México/Premiá, 1987.

Saravia Quiroz, Leobardo, ed. *En la línea de fuego: relatos policiacos de frontera*. Mexico City: Tierra Adentro, 1990.

———. *Line of Fire: Detective Stories from the Mexican Border*. San Diego: San Diego State University Press, 1996.

Taibo, Paco Ignacio, II, and Víctor Ronquillo, eds. *Cuentos policiacos mexicanos: lo mejor del género en nuestro país*. Mexico City: Selector, 1997.

Torres, Vicente Francisco, ed. *El cuento policial mexicano*. Mexico City: Diógenes, 1982.

Criticism

Revueltas, Eugenia. "La novela policiaca en México y en Cuba." *Cuadernos americanos* (Nueva época) 1.1 (1987): 102–20.

Segura, Gerardo. *Todos somos culpables: entrevistas con escritores policíacos mexicanos.* Saltillo, Coahuila: Instituto Coahuilense de Cultura, 1996.

Stavans, Ilán. *Antihéroes: México y su novela policial.* Mexico City: Joaquín Mortiz, 1993.

———. *Antiheroes: Mexico and Its Detective Novel,* trans. by Jesse H. Lytle and Jennifer A. Mattson, foreword by Donald A. Yates, epilogue by Hiber Conteris. Cranbury, NJ: Associated University Presses, 1997.

Trujillo Muñoz, Gabriel. *Testigos de cargo: la narrativa policiaca mexicana y sus autores.* Tijuana, Mexico: CONACULTA/CECUT, 2000.

Yates, Donald A. "The Mexican Detective Story." *Kentucky Foreign Language Quarterly* 8.1 (1961): 42–47.

URUGUAY

Anthologies

Delgado Aparaín, Mario, ed. *Cuentos bajo sospecha.* Montevideo: Ediciones Trilce, 1989.

Index

(Boldface indicates the author entry)

About the Editor and Contributors

Daniel Altamiranda is a professor at the University of Bologna in Buenos Aires and Chair of Spanish at the Instituto de Enseñanza Superior No. 2. He has published on literary theory, contemporary Latin American writing, and Golden Age drama. His most recent books are *Teorías literarias I* and *Teorías literarias II* (2001).

José Alberto Bravo de Rueda was born in Lima, Perú. He received his Ph.D. from the University of Maryland, College Park in 1997. He has taught at North Carolina Agricultural and Technical State University since 1995. He is also a creative writer whose works include the novel *Hacia el sur* (1992), the short-story collection *El hombre de la máscara* (1994), and a short story in *Nuevas voces hispanas* (2000).

Hiber Conteris teaches Latin American Studies at the University of Arizona. A native of Uruguay, Conteris received his Ph.D. from the École Practique des Hautes Etudes, Sorbonne, Paris. A playwright and prose-fiction writer, he is the author of some 20 books that include *La cifra anónima*, which won the Casa de las Américas Prize (1988), a detective novel, *El diez por ciento de tu vida* (1986), translated into English as *Ten Percent of Life*, and his most recent novel, *Oscura memoria del sur* (2002).

Juan José Delaney, born in Buenos Aires in 1954, is currently professor of Argentine literature at the Universidad del Salvador. In 1993, he participated in the International Writing Program at the University of Iowa. He is the author of the short-story collections *Papeles del desierto* (1991) and *Tréboles del sur* (1994) and the novel *Moira Sullivan* (1999). He also founded and directed the detective fiction magazine *El gato negro*. In 2002, he received a grant from the Fondo Nacional de las Artes to write the book *Marco Denevi y la sacra ceremonia de la escritura. Una biografía literaria* (2003).

Oscar A. Díaz-Ortiz is an associate professor of language, culture, and Spanish American literature at Middle Tennessee State University in Murfreesboro, where he is the director of Latin American Studies. He has published a book on the nineteenth-century Spanish American essay and various articles on Colombian, Mexican, and Chilean literature. He currently is working on studies of violence in Colombian film.

J. Patrick Duffey is associate professor of Spanish and co-director of the Center for Southwestern and Mexican Studies at Austin College, Sherman, Texas. A graduate of the University of Texas at Austin, Duffey is the author of *De la pantalla al texto. La influencia del cine en la narrativa mexicana del siglo XX* (1996). He is also the author of several articles on the influence of film on both Spanish and Latin American vanguard prose.

Mempo Giardinelli, born in Resistencia, Chaco in 1947, is one of the most prolific voices in Argentine literature. He lived in exile in Mexico between 1976 and 1985, and now resides in Argentina. His vast narrative production (both novels and short stories) has been translated into 15 languages and his works have earned him some of the most prestigious literary awards in Latin America, including the Premio Rómulo Gallegos in 1993 for his novel *Santo oficio de la memoria*. His detective fiction includes the novels *Luna caliente* (1983), *Qué solos se quedan los muertos* (1985), and *El décimo infierno* (1999). He is also the author of a collection of essays on detective fiction, titled *El género negro* (1984; 1998).

José Eduardo González is an assistant professor of Latin American literature and ethnic studies at the University of Nebraska–Lincoln. He is the author of *Borges and the Politics of Form* and co-editor of *Primitivism and Identity in Latin America*. He has also published several articles on literary theory, literary history, and Latin American narrative.

Cristina Guzzo received her Ph.D. from Arizona State University in 1997. In Argentina, where she was born, she was a professor at the Universidad de Buenos Aires and the Universidad Nacional de Salta. She is currently an assistant professor of Spanish at Ball State University. She has published numerous articles on Latin American literature and culture and the book *Las anarquistas rioplatenses: 1890–1990* (2003).

Claudia S. Hojman Conde is a professor at the Universidad de Buenos Aires where she teaches literary analysis and writing. She has coordinated poetry workshops at the Centro Cultural Ricardo Rojas (UBA), and writing workshops through the Universidad de Belgrano and the Biblioteca del Congreso de la Nación. She is the editor of the book *Borges* (1997), a collection of essays on the Argentine writer Jorge Luis Borges.

Darrell B. Lockhart is an assistant professor of Spanish at the University of Nevada, Reno where he teaches Latin American literature (narrative and theater), popular culture, and film. He received his Ph.D. in 1995 from Arizona State University. Aside from his interest in detective and science fiction from Latin America, he is a specialist in Latin American Jewish literature and cultural production and has written numerous articles on this topic that have been published in the United States, Argentina, and Chile. In addition, he is the editor of the book *Latin American Jewish Writers: A Dictionary* (1997), and the co-author of *Culture and Customs of Argentina* (1998).

María Gabriela Mizraje, a native of Buenos Aires, is a prolific scholar who has taught at a number of universities in Argentina, and given many lectures at universities in the United States. She currently works for the Secretaría de Cultura in Argentina. Her extensive publications include articles in academic journals, several critical editions of literary works, as well as books that include *Argentinas de Rosas a Perón* (1999) and *Norah Lange: infancia y sueños de walkiria* (1995).

William J. Nichols is an assistant professor of Spanish at Texas A&M International University in Laredo. He works on contemporary Spanish literature and popular culture with a specialization in detective fiction. His doctoral dissertation, titled *Social Crisis, Economic Development and the Emergence on the "Novela Negra" in Mexico and Spain: The Case of Paco Ignacio Taibo II and Manuel Vázquez Montalbán*, analyzes the political, social, and aesthetic underpinnings of detective fiction through a transatlantic approach to the genre. He is currently preparing his dissertation for publication as a book while exploring other areas of Hispanic popular culture such as film and comics.

Sergio Pastormerlo holds a doctorate degree in literature from the Universidad de la Plata, Argentina, where he teaches literary theory and criticism. He also teaches Argentine literature at the Universidad del Sur (Bahía Blanca). In collaboration with Néstor Ponce and Dardo Scavino, he published *Literatura policial en la Argentina: Waleis, Borges, Saer* (1997). He also edited the collection of essays, *Literatura argentina. Perspectivas de fin de siglo* (2001).

Néstor Ponce is a professor at the Université de Rennes 2 (France). He is a specialist in Latin American literature, with particular emphasis on detective fiction. He is the author of *Argentine, crises et utopie* (2001) and *Diagonales del género: estudios sobre el policial argentino* (2001). He has been a visiting professor at the UNAM in Mexico and at the Universidad Nacional de La Plata in Argentina. He is also the author of two works of fiction, *El intérprete* (1998), which won the Premio Fondo Nacional de las Artes (Argentina), and *La bestia de las diagonales* (1999), a finalist for the Premio Planeta.

Alicia Rolón teaches Latin American literature at Gettysburg College. She has published critical essays on the works of Carmen Naranjo, Osvaldo Soriano, Mempo Giardinelli, and Matilde Sánchez in major American, Argentinean, and Spanish literary journals. Her book *Historia, oralidad y ficción: la narrativa de Mempo Giardinelli entre 1980 y 1991* is forthcoming by Ediciones Foridablanca (Buenos Aires).

María Alejandra Rosarossa holds a teaching position in English literature at the Universidad Católica Argentina, from where she will earn a doctoral degree upon completion of her dissertation. She is a specialist in comparative studies (Anglo-Latin American literatures and cultures) and a researcher on this topic at the Universidad de Buenos Aires, where she has taught American literature. She currently teaches Spanish at Arizona State Univeristy. Rosarossa is the co-editor of *Los Estados Unidos y América Latina: Modernism/Posmodernismo* (1999), and *Los Estados Unidos y América Latina: Problemática del fin del milenio* (2000).

Silvia Saítta was born in Buenos Aires. She holds a doctorate degree in literature and teaches at the Universidad de Buenos Aires, in addition to being a researcher at Conicet. She is the author of the books *Regueros de tinta. El diario "Crítica" en la década de 1920* (1998), which received the first prize for best Argentine history book from the Fundación El Libro, and *El escritor en el bosque de ladrillos. Una biografía de Roberto Arlt* (2000). She has compiled several anthologies of Arlt's work, including *Aguasfuertes porteñas: Buenos Aires, vida cotidiana* (1993) and *Aguasfuertes gallegas y asturianas* (1999). Together with Luis Alberto Romero, she compiled and wrote the prologue to *Grandes entrevistas de la historia argentina* (1998).

Flora H. Schiminovich was born in Argentina and is now a citizen of the United States. A professor at Barnard College in New York City, she is the author of *Macedonio Fernández: una lectura surrealista* (1986) and *La pluma mágica* (1994). She has written numerous articles about women writers and poets, politics, and fantastic and detective fiction in Latin America. Her contributions include chapters in *Gender and Genre: Redefining Women's Autobioigraphies* (1991), *Tradition and Innovation: Reflections on Latin American Jewish Writing* (1993), *España en América y América en España* (1994), *Jewish Writers of Latin America: A Dictionary* (1997), *Antología del teatro breve hispanoamericano* (1997), *Les Nouveaux Realismes in America* (2000), and *Handbook for Latin American Studies* (HLAS) volume 60 (Library of Congress). She is at present working on volume 62 of the same series.

Juan Antonio Serna is a native of Monterrey, Nuevo León, Mexico. He holds several degrees from universities in Mexico, a Masters degree from the University of Houston, and a Ph.D. degree from Arizona State University. He has taught at the elementary through university levels in both countries. In 1989, he was a Fulbright Scholar at New College of the University of South Florida. He is currently an assistant professor at Georgia Southern University. Serna is the author of several articles and encyclopedia entries that have been published in Mexico, the United States., England, and Australia. He is the author of *El subalterno en la escritura masculina de los noventa: la novela de Nuevo León* (1999), and is currently working on a book on contemporary Mexican culture.

Gabriel Trujillo Muñoz was born in Mexicali, Baja California, Mexico in 1958. He is a physician, surgeon, poet, narrator, and essayist, and a professor at the Universidad Autónoma de Baja California. He has published nearly a hundred books: the novels *Mezquite Road* (1995), *Laberinto (as time goes by)* (1995), *Espantapájaros* (1999), *Orescu* (2000), *El festín de los cuervos* (a collection of five novellas; 2002); the short-story collections *Miríada* (1991), *Trebejos* (2001), and *Mercaderes* (2001); and the essays *Los confines. Crónica de la ciencia ficción mexicana* (1999), *Biografías del futuro* (2000), and *Lengua franca* (2001). He has received numerous national and international awards for his fiction and essays.

Horacio Xaubet was born in Montevideo, Uruguay in 1948. At age 19 he migrated to the United States where he has lived since. He lived in the San Francisco Bay area for 20 years and obtained his B.A. and M.A. from San Francisco State University, and earned his Ph.D. degree in Romance languages and literatures from the University of California, Berkeley. He is the author of *Desde el fondo de un espejo: autobiografía y (meta)ficción en tres relatos de Felisberto Hernández* and several articles, interviews, and reviews on contemporary Latin American narrative.

Richard Young teaches literature, film, and popular music in Spanish and Latin American studies programs at the University of Alberta. He has written several books, including *Octaedro en cuatro tiempos: texto y tiempo en un libro de Cortázar* (1993). He has edited *Latin American Postmodernisms* (1997) and *Music, Popular Culture, Identities* (2002), and has been editor of *Revista canadiense de estudios hispánicos* since 1996. His current research is on representations of urban life in contemporary Argentinean fiction.

Linda S. Zee is an associate professor of Spanish at Utica College. She is a specialist in contemporary Latin American literature, especially female writers. Her current research involves detective fiction, popular culture, and film in Latin America.